To Mary & Howard—

Advance praise for Michael Meeropol's SURRENDER

"*Surrender* is a fine history of the bleak continuity between Reagan and Clinton, two presidents whose expansions devalued the public sector and for that reason will not be sustained. Meeropol warns of the dangers now ahead, and reminds us all that surrender to an economics of inequity and stagnation is neither compulsory nor wise."

> —James K. Galbraith, Lyndon B. Johnson
>   School of Public Affairs, University of Texas at Austin

"A readable and very compelling demonstration that Bill Clinton's 'New Democrat' economic policy is really the fraternal twin of 'Reaganism.' And that neither has any chance of solving the economic problems of most Americans."

> —Thomas Ferguson, University of Massachusetts, Boston

"*Surrender* shows how antipeople, antiworker policy begun in the Reagan era continues to make the rich richer and ordinary Americans poorer and less secure. This is an important book."

> —Bernard Sanders, United States Representative, Vermont

All the best for many past and future discussions

Michael Meeropol

SURRENDER

SURRENDER

How the Clinton Administration
Completed the Reagan Revolution

Michael Meeropol

Ann Arbor

THE UNIVERSITY OF MICHIGAN PRESS

A CIP catalog record for this book is available from the British Library.

Library of Congress Cataloging-in-Publication Data

Meeropol, Michael.
  Surrender : how the Clinton administration completed the Reagan
revolution / Michael Meeropol.
    p.   cm.
  Includes bibliographical references and index.
  ISBN 0-472-10952-9 (cloth : acid-free paper)
    1. United States—Economic policy—1993–   2. United
States—Economic policy—1981–1993.   3. Government spending
policy—United States.   4. Budget—United States.   I. Title.
HC106.82 .M43   1998
338.973'009'049—dc21   98-25387
                                                           CIP

Grateful acknowledgment is made to the following authors, publishers, and journals for permission to reprint previously published materials.

M. E. Sharpe for excerpts from *Beyond the Twin Deficits, A Trade Strategy for the 1990s* by Robert Blecker. Copyright © 1992.
  Random House for excerpts from *Day of Reckoning* by Benjamin R. Friedman. Reprinted by permission of Random House, Inc. Copyright © 1988 by Benjamin R. Friedman.
  Simon & Schuster and George Borchardt for excerpts from *The Seven Fat Years: And How to Do It Again* by Robert L. Bartley. Copyright © 1992 by Robert L. Bartley. Reprinted with the permission of The Free Press, a Division of Simon & Schuster.
  St. Martin's Press for excerpts from "Budget Deficits and the US Economy: Considerations in a Heilbroner Mode," by Robert Pollin, in *Economics as Worldly Philosophy, Essays in Political and Historical Economics in Honour of Robert L. Heilbroner,* ed. Chatha and Nell Blackwell. Copyright © 1993.
  Timothy Smeeding for table from "W(h)ither the Middle Class?" by T. Smeeding, G. Duncan, and W. Rodgers, in *Income Security Policy Series,* Syracuse University (February 1992): 13.
  Times Books for table from *Restoring the Dream,* ed. Stephen Moore. Copyright © 1995.
  Urban Institute Press for excerpts and tables from *The Reagan Record* by John L. Palmer and Isabel Sawhill, copyright © 1984; for excerpt and tables from "Is U.S. Income Inequality Really Growing? Sorting Out the Fairness Question," in *Policy Bites* by Isabel Sawhill and Mark Condon, copyright © 1992; and for excerpts and table from *The Tax Decade, How Taxes Came to Dominate the Public Agenda* by Eugene Steurele, copyright © 1992.

To my wife, Ann
and to our children, Greg and Ivy

Contents

Acknowledgments

In a very real sense, everyone who has taught me economics and history has had a hand in the creation of this book. At Swarthmore College I benefited from the instruction of Joseph W. Conard, Frank Pierson, and William Brown in the Department of Economics and Jean Herskovits and Robert Bannister in the Department of History. At Cambridge University I was supervised by Robin L. Marris, Joan Robinson, and Bob Rowthorn of the Faculty of Economics. At the University of Wisconsin I had the pleasure of studying with economists Jeffrey G. Williamson, John Conlisk, William P. Glade, Peter Lindert, Rondo Cameron, and John Bowman, historians William A. Williams and Morton Rothstein, and Latin Americanist Maurice Zeitlin.

This book results from the research and writing I accomplished during a sabbatical in the 1994–95 academic year. However, my interest dates back to my first sabbatical, in 1980. For both sabbaticals, I want to acknowledge the institutional support of Western New England College, where I have taught for over two decades. Part of my 1980 sabbatical was spent at Cambridge University. This gave me the opportunity to reflect about the gathering storm of conservative economic criticism of the United States government policies from the early 1960s through the end of the 1970s. When I resumed teaching, I was able to create a course on Reaganomics, which I taught from 1982 to 1989.

There are many people at Western New England College whom I want to thank. Student assistants Michelle Hinojosa and Andrea Higgins have been a tremendous help. Michelle has worked for three years tracking down materials, duplicating and inputting data, and Andrea has assisted this past year. The college duplicating-center staff, especially Sandy Mackin and Jim Garrison, have been efficient and cooperative throughout, even in the last-minute rushes to meet the publisher's deadlines.

The staff in the Academic Computing Department, Russ Birchall,

Janet Condon, Kevin Gorman, Mike Hathaway and Steve Narmontas, have worked on my equipment, patiently taught me new word-processing skills, run old disks through their machines to produce usable files, and in general been there for me whenever I had a question or problem. Western New England College is fortunate to have such hard-working professionals in these crucial positions.

Donna Utter, faculty secretary in the School of Arts and Sciences, has been tireless in her efforts to produce a manuscript to the publisher's specifications. I never would have made my deadlines without her help. Avril McGougan, Arts and Sciences secretary, also helped with printing when Donna was not available.

Suzanne Garber and Dan Eckert, the interlibrary loan staff of the D'Amour Library of Western New England College, have been vigorous in their pursuit of both books and journal articles unavailable at the college library. Nancy Contois and Sarah Schweer have been very helpful in ordering books that were of use for my research. I thank Valerie Bolden-Marshall for her good-humored forbearance with my habit of hoarding library books, and May Stack for the support she gives to the academic community. Special thanks are due to Iris Bradley-Lovekin of the periodicals department for some last-minute research assistance.

Finally, I wish to thank Greg Michael, director of Career and Human Resources at the college for discussions of the impact of the Americans with Disabilities Act on his work and the college in general. Greg also shared with me materials prepared by the College and University Personnel Association about the ADA as well as an ADA Compliance Manual.

For archival research, I have asked much of many government workers who have cheerfully assisted me in finding important materials. At the Bureau of Economic Analysis of the Department of Commerce I have been helped by Virginia Mannering, Michael Webb, and Phyllis Barnes. At the Bureau of the Census, Jean Tash sent me much-needed household and family income data. At the Bureau of Labor Statistics, I was helped by Anne Foster, John Glaser, Thomas Nardone, and Brian Sliker. At the Bureau of the Public Debt, Department of the Treasury, Lori DeRose sent to me a full series of the National Debt of the United States. I want to thank Carolyn Cunningham, Adrienne Scott, Shirley Tabb, and Shelia Wade at the Freedom of Information Section of the Federal Reserve Board, as well as Frank Russek at the Congressional Budget Office and Linda Schimmel of the

CBO's Publication Services department. All of these public servants do important work in helping citizens learn about the economic realities of the times in which we live. Ironically, these workers were defined as "nonessential" when the two partial government shutdowns occurred in 1995 and 1996. They, as well as the citizens who depend on the information they collect, analyze, and distribute, were hostages to partisan politics of the worst kind.

I have also been assisted by people at various nongovernmental organizations. At the Urban Institute, C. Eugene Steuerle has been a source of good advice about the many materials available there. At the Center for the Study of American Business, Melinda Warren shared various reports on the slowdown and then speedup in the growth of federal regulatory intrusion into the private sector since the early Reagan years. At the Economic Policy Institute, John Schmitt and Edie Rasell called my attention to various policy issue briefs. At the Employee Benefit Research Institute, I was assisted by Bill Pierron. My daughter Ivy helped me find material in the *Congressional Record* and the Library of Congress, and also helped me get the 1993 *Green Book,* the best source for research materials about government entitlement programs. In this regard, I want to acknowledge the positive role of the office of Congressman Richard Neal of Massachusetts. The library at Western New England College received copies of the *Economic Report of the President* as soon as they were off the presses in February of each year thanks to his efforts. Full understanding of the American economy and the role of government begins with the statistics in the annual reports of the president's Council of Economic Advisers and the annual or biannual publication of the House Ways and Means Committee (the *Green Book*).

Several years before beginning work on this book, I presented some of my findings at a workshop for Western New England College faculty. I thank John Andrulis, Herbert Eskot, and Richard Skillman for important feedback on that very early effort. My interpretation of the first few years of the post-1983 recovery was published in *Challenge* in 1987, and I want to thank the then editor, Richard Bartal, for his encouragement and support as I developed my ideas. In addition, discussions with colleagues at the Center for Popular Economics were extremely valuable for me. In the early phases of my writing, I benefited from the encouragement and support of historian Gerald Markowitz, a good friend and colleague for the past thirty-five years. My wife, Ann, an accomplished writer, helped me with the earliest versions of the manuscript. Thomas Weisskopf, C. Eugene Steuerle, Alain Jehlen, Emmett Barcalow, and John Andrulis read some sections and made a number of valuable suggestions. In two separate courses, a number of students read the manuscript in its early drafts. I thank Tara Bishop, David Cayer, Paul Dias, Michael Flaherty, Amy Gardner, Ting Giang, Melissa Hiltz, Robert Kusiac, Edward Lavoie, Heather Lebiedz, Susan Moredock, David Rollend, Christal Russo, K. Jonas Svallin, and Christopher Wsolek for their feedback.

When it came time to submit the manuscript, I benefited from the detailed criticisms of Ellen McCarthy of the University of Michigan Press and Gerald Epstein and Robert Pollin, the readers for the press. Noam Chomsky read the entire manuscript and offered many trenchant criticisms. My colleague and good friend of twenty-seven years at Western New England College, John Anzalotti, also read the manuscript with a keen historian's eye. I know for certain that both the manuscript and my own thinking have benefited from all of their criticisms, even the ones I disagreed with.

Gerald Markowitz read the entire manuscript just before its final submission. His encouragement and suggestions are very important to me, not just in writing this book. Jerry and I have shared a lifelong love of the study and writing of history. It goes without saying, however, that neither Jerry nor any of the other readers should be held responsible for errors and limitations in the book. As the manuscript leaves my hands in a malleable form for the final time I want to thank Melissa Holcombe and Richard Isomaki of the University of Michigan Press for their help in improving the final version at the copyediting stage.

Just as she had three years ago, my wife, Ann, helped with the writing of a number of recently written chapters. Given the incredible demands of her schedule, I greatly appreciate the time and effort she has given to help improve the manuscript in a number of key places. During the years I have worked on this project, in fact for the past thirty-two years, Ann has been a loving companion, soul mate, and intellectual support. For her constant faith in the value of the project and in my ability to see it through to completion, I cannot thank her enough.

Our children Ivy and Greg also share in whatever success I have achieved. As they have grown to adulthood and entered the uncertain economy of the 1990s, their hard work, aspirations, and accomplishments have reminded me why we always strive to leave the world a little better than we found it. I thank them for the lives they are leading, which continue to make Ann and me proud to be their parents.

Preface

Nineteen ninety-eight marks seven years since the beginning of the recovery from the last recession. The recovery began so slowly that in 1992 an angry public swept the incumbent president from the White House. In 1994, the anger still palpable, the Democratic Party lost control of Congress in a massive repudiation of William J. Clinton, the new president. By 1996 voters had enough "good feeling" to give President Clinton almost 50 percent of the popular vote in a three-way race. In 1997 growth in the economy was even faster than predicted. When the president and Congress agreed on a budget-balancing plan, the amount of net cuts in government spending necessary to achieve balance had fallen from a 1995 projection of $200 billion to $24 billion. By early 1998, even these optimistic projections had been rendered moot by the strength of the economy. Nineteen ninety-seven had surprised all prognosticators with faster growth and lower inflation than they had predicted. The president's Council of Economic Advisers correctly celebrated a year when the economy turned in its best performance in a generation. President Clinton proposed a balanced budget for fiscal 1999, three years earlier than projected just six months before.

So the "great pain" and "tough choices" anticipated by all commentators while Congress and the president wrestled with the budget in 1995 and early 1996 had by the end of 1997 evaporated into a euphoric reaction to a "successful" economy. Two years of economic growth at a rate of more than 2.5 percent a year had caused this feeling, but how long will this euphoria last? The answer is, until the next recession, when growth will be negative, even if for a short time. Then, all positive projections will evaporate, and, once again, the "pain" of cutting spending and/or raising taxes to achieve budget balance will return.

The speed with which fear over the "painful choices" of budget balance had given way to the euphoria of 1997 should remind us that even though we live in the short-term present, a long-run perspective is essential in understanding which public-policy choices are appropriate.

Accordingly, this book takes a long-term approach. It traces what has come to be known as the "Reagan Revolution" in economic policy.

In 1980, while on sabbatical leave, I returned to Cambridge, England, where I had studied economics in the mid-1960s. In one year Prime Minister Margaret Thatcher had revolutionized economic policy, and strong protests were voiced by many Cambridge economists. I had read some of the conservative writings on economics in American public-policy journals published during the late 1970s, and I brought some of this work to the attention of colleagues in Cambridge. These discussions led to the organization of a conference sponsored by the *Cambridge Journal of Economics*. In the summer of 1981, "New Orthodoxy in Economics" drew participants from the United States, Great Britain, the European continent, Argentina, and Australia to discuss the theoretical underpinnings of the Thatcher government's plan for Britain and the Reagan administration's projections for the United States.

After that conference, I began to teach about the economic policy changes that the Reagan White House and the Volcker-led Federal Reserve were instituting. At first I simply presented my students with alternative diagnoses of what ailed the economy before 1981 and what the Reagan administration proposed as cures. Beginning in 1984, with the recession of 1981–82 behind us and the economy in a strong recovery, I was able to give my students some evidence for the successes and failures of those policies. In 1987, challenged by students' questions, I resolved to study the accumulated evidence since the end of the recession. Had the changes introduced in 1981, combined with the strong anti-inflationary policies of the Federal Reserve, "fixed" the problems identified by conservative economists and public-policy people? I compared the recovery from the 1981–82 recession to the recovery from the 1974–75 recession. I have continued to utilize this comparative approach as information has accumulated.

When the data on President Reagan's eight-year tenure was complete, and the recession of 1990 had marked the end of the economic recovery, I decided to synthesize years of teaching and thinking about these issues into a coherent interpretation that would reach a larger audience. I planned a sabbatical for 1994–95, thinking that I would write a history. With the success of the Republicans in the 1994 elections, my historical project took on a sense of immediacy. In 1996, I extended the analysis to cover the 1994 victory and the Republican budget proposals for zero deficit by 2002.

While President Clinton and the Republicans were locked in a great battle of wills, with two government shutdowns and high-decibel partisanship flooding the media, I rewrote the first and last chapters to keep up with the changes. When President Clinton agreed to balance the budget by 2002, albeit with a tax and spending mix different from the Republicans', I knew that the Reagan Revolution had succeeded.

This project began as a history of the Volcker and Reagan policies with an analysis of their successes and failures from a long-term perspective. Our judgment about those years remains important as a prologue to our understanding of present decisions. Currently, there is real commitment to budget balance. The effects of the changes necessary to balance the budget are no longer merely theoretical possibilities; we will soon feel the impact of those changes. My desire is to make the issues related to the Reagan Revolution accessible to the general reader and student of public policy. I believe the reader will discover that the specialized language and competing theoretical perspectives about economics and public policy are readily understandable. It is my hope that readers will follow the story of the past eighteen years of policy and experience and become well positioned to exercise their roles as citizens. The next few years will put this book's analysis to the test. Just as we Americans participated in a major "experiment" in economic policy between 1979 and 1990, we are about to enter a new experimental phase through the year 2002. If the analysis of this book proves accurate, when the next recession begins, we will be faced with the "pain" and "tough choices" that the past two years of euphoria have postponed. This is not good news; however, if we take the lessons of history to heart, we will be able to shake off the dogmatic dictates of current policy and escape a repetition of the mistakes of the past.

A Note on Data Many of the tables in both the text and the endnotes are based on quarterly time series data. Rather than include all of the raw data, which would be rather voluminous, the publisher and author have decided to post them on the web site of the Department of Economics at Western New England College. The address for the page is <mars.wnec.edu/~econ/surrender>. Once there, readers can follow directions to the numbered tables that apply to the data being discussed in the text. Readers without access to the World Wide Web can request a hard copy by writing to the author at Western New England College, 1215 Wilbraham Road, Springfield, MA 01119.

A Revolution
in Economic Policy

On November 5, 1996, Bill Clinton was elected to a second term as president of the United States. That same night, in congressional races, Republican majorities were returned to both the House of Representatives and the Senate. Lost in the sound and fury of the election campaign was a striking fact. When President Clinton had submitted his budget proposal the previous February, he had effectively surrendered to the policies demanded by the Republican majority in Congress. Though there had been two shutdowns of the federal government and a raucous debate between the president and the majority of Congress, they were merely arguing over the method of achieving a policy on which they had already agreed.[1] The agreement was that by 2002 the federal budget deficit would be reduced to zero without raising taxes— In fact, there would be some tax cuts.[2] This was not the president's only surrender. He later "compromised" with the Republican majority in Congress by signing a welfare reform bill that ended a sixty-year federal guarantee of income to poor children in single-parent homes.[3]

Eight months after the election, on July 30, lopsided majorities in both houses passed a budget and tax agreement that had been crafted by the Clinton administration and the Republican majority in Congress. Due to the strong economic growth that had occurred in 1996 and 1997, the amount of spending reductions necessary to achieve budget balance by 2002 was significantly lower than when Congress had passed a bill with the same goal in 1995. The tax cuts were much less than the Republicans had proposed in 1995.[4] Nevertheless, the overall result of this agreement was to complete a revolution in economic policy making.[5]

To understand the significance of that agreement, compare the policies adopted by the United States government between 1975 and 1979 to the policies followed from 1991 to the present. The years have been chosen because these are the years following recessions, which, by law, the government of the United States must take action to counter.[6] After the recession of 1974, economic policy was designed to increase the rate of growth, reduce the level of unemployment, and soften the blow of unemployment and poverty for those unable to find work or earn a decent level of income. After 1990 the policymakers focused on cutting the budget deficit and slowing the economy in order to keep inflation from rearing its ugly head. Making sure the unemployed were receiving unemployment compensation and that the poor could take advantage of governmental assistance were not merely less important than achieving budget balance, they were considered counterproductive.[7]

The policies followed in response to the 1974 recession were consistent with a general expansion of the role of government in the economy from the Great Depression through 1979.[8] The election of Ronald Reagan to the presidency in 1980 signaled the beginning of a serious effort to alter that trend. Though the so-called Reagan Revolution was only partially successful in changing policy and though the effects it had on the economy have been the subject of hot dispute, with the hindsight of history it is clear that those initial efforts finally met success in the bipartisanship before and after the presidential election of 1996.

The Fruits of the Revolution

This book will follow the steps of this revolution. Here, we will merely outline the results. Government tax and spending policy will no longer be used to reduce unemployment. Instead, the Federal Reserve System, the U.S. Central Bank, has been conceded total authority to battle either inflation or unemployment. In practice, the Central Bank has focused more on preventing inflation, so that anytime the unemployment rate gets "too low" they feel it necessary to raise it in order to slow down the economy. The Congress and the president are silent in the face of such action. Thirty—and even twenty—years ago, such actions would routinely produce howls of protest from Congress and even the president.[9]

Redistribution of income to the nonelderly poor is no longer a federal responsibility. Even redistribution of income to the elderly is to be constrained so as to permit the federal budget to achieve balance. After an expansion of the role of the federal government in redistributing income between 1960 and 1980, the new priority for government, both at the federal and at the state and local levels, is to finance the Defense Department and a growing police and prison industry.

Between 1960 and 1979, the Social Security system went from representing 12.6 percent of the federal budget to 20.7 percent. In 1960, Medicare did not exist; by 1979 it covered 5.2 percent of the budget. Redistributing income to the poor (identified as income security) went from 8 percent of the federal budget to 13 percent.[10] The "Reagan Revolution" made a strenuous effort to cut this redistribution but mostly succeeded in cutting taxes. In terms of overall spending it was unsuccessful. In 1989, the proportion of the budget covered by Social Security and Income Security had fallen slightly to 32.2 percent (from just over one-third), but Medicare had risen to cover 7.4 percent of the federal budget.[11]

The 1997 law puts controls on the growth of Medicare spending.[12] Looking to the long term, there are proposals in the air to privatize some aspects of Social Security, to automatically reduce cost-of-living increases because the government's measuring rod for the cost of living has been judged faulty, and otherwise control what the pundits and policymakers have called "runaway entitlement spending."

Meanwhile, income distribution, which had trended toward more equality between 1945 and 1979, had become more unequal in the period between 1979 and 1993, and it was unclear whether the period after 1993 had merely interrupted a trend or actually reversed it.[13] Income distribution is a very important economic-policy issue from a political point of view. During the 1994 congressional election, Democrats had criticized the Republicans' campaign document, called the *Contract with America*,[14] on the basis of "fairness." The policies advocated by the Republicans would, in the words of Representative Carrie Meek (D.-FL), "produce another tax windfall for the wealthy while leaving the middle class and poor behind."[15]

The effect of proposed policy changes on income distribution is one of the major arguments between those who approved of and wanted to extend the Reagan economic legacy and those who wanted to reverse it. Both sides appealed to the principle of fairness. From Representative Meek's perspective, fairness involved less inequality in the distribution of income. For supporters of the Reagan Revolution, fairness involved avoiding undue burdens on individuals who work, produce, and invest, thereby creating more income for everyone.[16] The Republican majority in Congress and not a few Democrats claim that policies that might increase income inequality are acceptable if they have such a positive influence on the rate of growth of income that even the poorest individuals would benefit greatly. In other words, economic growth raising the absolute level of income for the poor would more than make up for increased inequality. This is the key idea behind the statement attributed to President Kennedy, "A rising tide lifts all boats." Those who agree with Representative Meek argue that the middle class and the poor were hurt by the Reagan economic program, that the economy's growth did not benefit them.

The linchpin of the revolution was the drive to balance the federal budget and cut taxes as a means toward shrinking the role of the federal government in the economy. The desire to do this was based on a general view of how the (economic) world functions: a belief that, left to their own devices, individuals pursuing their self-interest and constrained only by competition will interact in such a way as to produce the best of all possible (economic) results. On the theoretical level, this is an argument that government should stay out of the way as much as possible, though it has some clearly important roles, such as enforcing the law and providing for the defense of the nation against foreign enemies.[17]

On a more practical, political level, the requirement of a balanced budget provides significant support for policymakers who do not wish to expand government spending on programs that might be popular, such as guaranteeing all children equal educational opportunity, repairing every bridge and road that needs it, fixing every leaky roof in a public school, and wiring every public library for the Internet. It also makes it difficult to introduce new spending initiatives such as providing complete cradle-to-grave health coverage for all citizens. In response to felt needs, leaders can exclaim, as President George Bush did in his inaugural address, "We have more will than wallet," and that ends the argument in favor of such expensive items as guaranteed health care for all Americans.

Stages of the Revolution

President Reagan created the first installment of the revolution by pushing through a significant tax cut in 1981. However, he never was able to follow through with the spending cuts necessary to avoid big increases in government borrowing. In 1990, George Bush compromised with Congress on a combination of tax increases and spending cuts that some saw as a betrayal of the Reagan policies, but that in the long run reduced borrowing and constrained spending increases. In 1992, Bill Clinton was elected in part on a promise to reverse Reagan's policies. His package of tax increases and spending cuts in 1993 supposedly repudiated Reagan's policies, but except in very minor ways they were consistent with them. More importantly, over the years after 1993, the federal budget deficit declined significantly, and federal spending fell a bit in relation to total income.[18] The one effort made by the Clinton administration to move economic policy in a different direction, the full reform of the health care system, was soundly defeated by a coalition of Republicans and conservative Democrats.

In 1994, the Republicans gained control of the House and Senate after a campaign where they featured a series of promises in the Contract with America. The economic policies promised in that document included a balanced-budget amendment to the Constitution, a series of tax cuts, and a sweeping reform of the welfare system.[19] From the beginning of that congressional campaign, Democrats such as Representative Meek attacked the proposals as trickle-down economics, enriching a few and claiming that the rest of society would benefit from the crumbs. When the Republicans won the election and introduced their proposals as legislation, Democrats blasted them as "extremist." In 1995 and 1996 the battle was joined between the president and the Republican Congress over budget proposals that were vetoed by the president. As mentioned above, the government actually was shut down twice over these budget battles before Congress and the president reached a compromise in April 1996.[20]

Hidden in the noise from the "battlefield," the Clinton administration's surrender was barely noticed by the public, which was focusing instead on the lead-up to the presidential election campaign and then the campaign itself. But as the compromise emerged during the discussions over the 1998 fiscal year budget, the success of the revolution was no longer in doubt. First had been Reagan's election, then a decade of change and even more revolutionary proposals thwarted by a Democratic Congress. Then there was the alleged Bush betrayal in 1990. Some saw the election of Bill Clinton as a repudiation of Reaganomics, with the Republican Contract with America as its revival. Clinton's "tough stand" against Republican "extremism" allegedly blunted that revolution, but in fact when Bill Clinton submitted his budget in February 1996 and signed the welfare reform law in August 1996 he signaled surrender: the Reagan Revolution was going to achieve its major goals.

With the signing of the budget and tax bills in August 1997, the surrender was complete. Budget balance was an iron-clad pledge from both political parties and both branches of government. As a result of the constraint of budget balance and the (albeit modest) tax cut approved for the 1998–2002 budget years, the impact of government on the economy, which had grown from the Great Depression through the 1970s, was bound to shrink. The reduction of government activity was most obvious in the redistribution of income to the poor.

Appealing to the Lessons of History

It is often stated that history is the laboratory of the social sciences. Unlike most of the physical sciences, in which access to a laboratory permits one to conduct controlled experiments, the social sciences must look to human existence, which occurs once and then becomes history. Thus, disciplines in the social sciences must take history as evidence in the search to discover regularities of human existence beyond the biological ones.

To accurately evaluate the recently concluded revolution in economic policy, one must study recent economic history. Economic history involves the use of economic analysis to answer certain historical questions. It also employs the systematic study of historical experience to "test" certain economic propositions. For example, one of the crucial conflicts about economic behavior during the 1980s concerns the incentive effects of reducing the *marginal* tax rate on individuals and businesses. Lawrence Lindsey devoted his doctoral dissertation to an analysis of taxpayer responses to marginal tax-cuts.[21] He argued that the historical experience of the 1980s showed that powerful incentive effects led businesses and individuals to work harder and take more risks as a result of the Reagan tax cuts in 1981. But those who criticize the tax cuts as trickle-down economics (because they gave no tax relief to low-income people, with the lion's share of reductions going to very high-income people) argue that the negative impact on income distribution actually slowed economic growth.[22] Both of these arguments use the historical record in an attempt to validate a particular theoretical conception of "how the world works."[23]

This is a good example of how economic history serves both history and economics. Economic theories may be tested against historical experience. Historical interpretation can be revised through economic analysis of the information available. Such a study can help the student, scholar, and citizen learn more about how the world functions, how to live in it and, perhaps, alter the world to suit our ends. This has been the hope of philosophers, scientists, and anyone who has believed in the value of education.

Here are the bare-bones "facts" of recent economic history. In 1979, the Board of Governors of the Federal Reserve System, under the leadership of Paul Volcker, launched a stringent anti-inflation policy. The following year, Ronald Reagan was elected to the presidency; his tax cut and general budget proposals in 1981 precipitating the Reagan Revolution in economic policy. For the decade of the 1980s, the United States economy would be dominated by the impact of both sets of policies—the Volcker-Reagan policies, if you will. In 1990, a recession ended a long economic expansion. A debate about the actual impact of these policies was a major theme of the election campaign of 1992. The presidential election of 1996 continued the debates from 1992 and 1994 in the same contentious vein.[24] As Congress and the president collaborate on keeping the federal budget on track to balance by 2002, we will continue to be treated to every politician's, policymaker's, and opinion-leader's interpretation of the meaning of the Volcker-Reagan period.

This study will use the historical experience of the 1979–90 period in order to referee between competing economic interpretations. It will also use economic analysis in an attempt to understand what actually happened to the United States economy and its people during that period and since. Our goal is to not only answer questions about the successes or failures of the Reagan-Volcker changes but to show the essential continuity of policy since 1990 in order to suggest predictions about the future course of the U.S. economy based on what we have learned about the 1979–90 period.

Learning from this information is difficult. The public is inundated with information in our modern age. The citizen, student, or scholar must be a critical analyst in order to make sense of this information. So much information is collected and stored that it is impossible for any one person to be cognizant of it all.

One also has to determine the significance of certain facts. Since we cannot "run" history twice as a controlled experiment, social scientists engage in the process of abstraction. The pieces of economic reality or the "facts" that the investigator considers important are emphasized so as to focus attention on the important causal factor(s). Of course different investigators consider different elements of reality worthy of attention.

We recognize the truth in this when we analyze the various arguments made by scholars, politicians, and journalists about the economic impact of the Reagan Revolution. Some emphasize the decline in the rate of inflation; others emphasize the rise in the national debt and the budget deficit. Some emphasize the length of the recovery from the 1981–82 recession; still others focus on the depth and severity of that recession. Some emphasize the continued strength in manufacturing-productivity growth; others focus on the minimally impressive increases in overall productivity. Some analysts believe that the distribution of income has become more unequal and perceive this as dangerous for the long-run growth and stability of the nation. Others believe that when we seek to measure well-being, the absolute rise in income for the vast majority of the population is more significant than the distribution of income.[25]

In an attempt to assess the success or failure of a set of economic policies, we must have a clear view of what constitutes success. To study economic policies and their impact on the economy in the 1980s and since, we need to set up standards of comparison for the "facts" presented by analysts. This work will elucidate the analyses that have defined as successes or failures the economic policies of the 1980s and since. We will subject the competing theories to the relevant data and make every effort to enable the reader to readily see where the arguments and supporting evidence conflict. It is this writer's task to attempt to convince the reader that the facts and the comparisons I have chosen are appropriate to answer the economic questions that will inevitably arise as Americans live with the results of their leaders' taxation and spending decisions designed to achieve a balanced budget by the year 2002.

The reason the arguments about the Volcker-Reagan economic program currently resonate is not merely because of the sound and fury generated by the budget battles between President Clinton and Congress in 1995 and the presidential campaign of 1996, and certainly not because of the bipartisan self-congratulations of the budget and tax bill signings in August 1997. In fact, those battles merely obscure the most important reason why an investigation of the successes and failures of that program is essential today. No matter what happens in the congressional election of 1998, the president and Congress are on a bipartisan mission to complete the economic-policy revolution. What the Volcker–Reagan program delivered to the American people between 1981 and 1989, and that program's *non*-reversal between 1990 and now, are essential background for all citizens, policymakers, and students of economic policy making as we attempt to cope with economic realities between 1998 and 2002 (when the budget is supposed to be in balance).

Our judgment as to how successful the Volcker-Reagan period was and how significant the large budget deficits were for that alleged success or failure will inform our views on whether the governmental consensus in favor of eliminating the federal budget deficit is rational. The stakes are extremely high. If Congress and the president stick to their agreed-upon timetable, the next recession will confront the people and policymakers with an extremely stark choice. We can either continue on the path toward budget balance and hope the recession will cure itself (with help only from the Federal Reserve), as was done in 1990–95, or we can take steps to cure the recession that require abandoning our goal of budget balance, as was done when Congress cut taxes in 1975 to combat the recession. How we confront that choice will depend on which conclusions about the Reagan era and the period since 1990 are accepted by the opinion-leaders and public officials.

Plan of the Book

Chapter 2 will introduce the important principles and vocabulary of economic analysis that will be necessary for understanding the arguments and evidence presented in the rest of the book. The next two chapters will first flesh out what I have called the conservative economic diagnosis of the unacceptable performance of the American economy through most of the 1970s and then present alternatives from other schools of economic analysis. The following two chapters will present a detailed description of the actual Reagan and Volcker policies between 1979 and 1989. Chapter 7 will introduce a variety of judgments about the impact of those policies, and chapter 8 will attempt to assess the record created by those policies. Chapter 9 will discuss a variety of alleged problems identified by scholars, policymakers, and politicians as stemming from the Reagan-Volcker policies.

Chapter 10 presents an analysis of the Bush administration and the first two years of the Clinton administration with an eye toward determining whether or not there was a reversal of the "Reagan" part of the economic-policy revolution in those years and why the recession of 1990 was followed by such an anemic recovery. Chapter 11 fully develops the argument merely asserted above, namely that after the 1994 congressional elections, the Clinton administration surrendered, completing the policy revolution started by Volcker and Reagan fifteen years previously. Though it may seem churlish in the face of virtually unanimous euphoria about the agreement to balance the budget and about the good economic news of 1996 and 1997, the chapter closes with a strong warning that all the good trends will last only until the next recession, and then we will be faced with the true costs of the recent decisions. The book closes with a short coda that identifies a series of policies alternative to the ones agreed upon by the president and Congress.

2

Understanding the Economy

Human beings depend on the economy for sustenance. People require food, clothing, shelter, education, health, and nurturing. Additionally, people desire improvements and variety in these necessities, as well as products and activities beyond the essentials. The economy is the totality of the actions that produce goods and services to satisfy human needs and desires. *Economics* derives from the Greek *oeconomicus*, literally "estate management."[1] A nation's economy is, in effect, one gigantic estate, "managing" the production of the goods and services people need and desire. In judging economic policy we want to measure the success of an economy. That has proven extremely difficult.

How do we characterize the satisfaction level of a society where scarce medical resources are used to provide prenatal care for all pregnant women instead of long-term care for all stroke victims? Is the satisfaction of the family with a healthy newborn comparable to the satisfaction of the family that benefits from long-term care for a stroke victim? How can we compare the degree of the satisfaction?

How do we characterize the satisfaction level of a society where land is used to grow food instead of being developed into a shopping mall? How do we measure the satisfaction of a person eating in a soup kitchen? Or a middle-class family eating a Thanksgiving dinner? Or another family eating dehydrated food in an overseas refugee camp? How does that compare to the pleasure of numerous shoppers at the mall, and the benefits of their convenience because they can find many products at affordable prices with one trip as opposed to many separate trips? And what difference would it make if this were the only mall, or one of five in a twenty-mile radius?

Finally, how do we measure the satisfaction level of a community using scarce resources to refurbish a local public school, compared to the satisfaction level that would exist if this community were to save the money and provide a tax incentive for a business to locate a plant in the same town? How do we measure the satisfaction of children in a freshly painted school that has intact windows and an adequate heating and cooling system as compared to the satisfaction of a family whose breadwinner has found a job at the new plant?

Each one of these alternatives produces different kinds of satisfaction and for different people. If we could reduce the measure to the same units, say, income measured in dollars, conceivably such comparisons would become easier. On the issue of medical resources, one could ask how much the two choices cost in dollars and then attempt to make a rough measure of the benefits to society from them. In the farmland-versus-shopping-mall question, one might say the answer is quite easy. If a farmer believes he/she can make out better by selling the land to the developer than by continuing to farm, the shopping mall becomes economically superior. The well-maintained school versus the abatement of business taxes is more complicated. While the benefit to the community from an increased number of jobs can be measured by the incomes of those hired, the benefits from the improvement in the school can only be estimated. Nevertheless, in principle, if we are willing to construct the measure of the satisfaction of needs and desires in units of dollar value, then we can approximate the successes and failures of economies.

Gross Domestic Product

The simplest and most widely used measure of the economic well-being of a society is the gross domestic product (GDP), the dollar value of all goods and services produced in a nation in a given year. GDP makes no distinction between the intensity of the wants or needs of individuals beyond what is indicated by the quantities and prices of items produced. The GDP as a measure of the well-being of society involves no judgment about how the goods and services ought to be distributed. In principle, a six-trillion-dollar GDP claimed by one individual is the same as a six-trillion-dollar GDP divided equally among all individuals. In reality, both extremes would create serious consequences for the future. In the first instance, the starving millions would precipitate drastic reductions in production, assuming they didn't simply take everything from the one individual. In the second instance, most economists believe that an equal sharing of total production regardless of the contributions people make to that production would significantly damage incentives, leading to reduced output. Between these extremes lies a wide range of income distributions that would not produce such dire consequences. Thus, when we measure success by the level of GDP, we usually ignore the role of income distribution as an independent element in measuring the well-being of the population.[2]

It is also true that when using GDP to measure the economic well-being of society, we make no distinction between a GDP that rises because more people are getting sick and spending money on hospital stays and a GDP that rises because more houses are being built and people are moving into them. In other words a rising GDP is assumed to improve the quantity of "economic well-being," but it is possible that some specific goods and services produced are not improving well-being; in fact, increasing the production of such goods or services may be symptoms of declining well-being.

If we take GDP and divide it by the population we get GDP per person (per capita). This measure tells us what is potentially available to everybody in the economy to satisfy their wants and needs. Note the word *potentially*. It is possible for some growth in per capita GDP to involve absolute declines in the standard of living for a percentage of the population. However, with growing GDP per person, in principle it is possible for some people to improve their standard of living without reducing the goods and services available to anyone else.

When we speak of a growing GDP per person, we of course want to measure the actual availability of goods and services. Since we measure the GDP as the dollar value of those goods and services, when analyzing growth over time we speak in terms of *real* GDP, that is, GDP corrected for inflation. Otherwise, we would greatly overestimate any improvement in society's ability to satisfy human needs and desires whenever prices in general rise.

In addition to the rate of growth of real per capita GDP, another important way to analyze the success or failure of an economy is to see how much of society's potential GDP is actually produced. The potential GDP is the level of production that would occur if all resources were utilized fully, in other words, all capable people working, all factories functioning, and all potentially cultivatable land is utilized. Economists have come to realize that full utilization cannot involve every worker, every factory, and every acre of land, so conventions are usually established to identify the highest practicable level of production. In the 1960s, the Council of Economic Advisers identified the potential GDP as that which would be produced if only 4 percent of the labor force were unemployed. The council estimated that such unemployment would result from one of two reasons. The first was because the worker was between jobs or was looking for a first job. The second was because some unemployed are, in fact, unemployable— their skills or geographic location do not match the requirements of the jobs available. This group is known as the structurally unemployed. In the early 1960s, the council believed that the 4 percent rate would constitute a minimally acceptable unemployment level comprising the structurally unemployed and the temporarily unemployed. Any unemployment over and above that 4 percent would be considered wasted human resources.

Another way of measuring the failure of the economy to achieve its potential production is to look at the capacity utilization rate. In principle, this involves measuring how much output could be produced by the existing buildings and machines owned by American businesses, and comparing this potential to the actual output. Periods of low unemployment should produce high capacity utilization. The gap between the output that would have been produced at the minimal level of unemployment with high levels of capacity utilization and the output that actually was produced represents a permanent loss of output to society. Thus, in addition to the rate of growth of the GDP per capita, the success of an economy is generally measured by how closely actual GDP approximates potential GDP, as indicated by the unemployment rate and the capacity utilization rate.

Economic Growth

What determines GDP and GDP growth? Human beings work with tools to transform natural resources into finished products. They also work to deliver services to one another. Economists divide the physical inputs used in producing goods and services into three factors of production: land (natural resources), labor (human effort, mental and physical), and capital (produced means of further production). The coordination of these efforts requires leadership, or entrepreneurship, often presented as a separate factor of production. In our society leadership is exercised either by owners of businesses or by individuals hired by owners.

Coordinating the work of human beings is not a simple process.

Even in the most tightly organized work process, human effort is to some extent voluntary. Consider a situation in which people are hired to work in a fast-food restaurant for a certain number of hours a day. The specific tasks of those employees (grilling hamburgers, taking orders at the register, cleaning the machines, etc.) may have been defined when they were hired, but the employees have control over how carefully and quickly they work, as well as how cooperatively they interact with others. Now these employees are not completely free to make these decisions. If someone consistently undercooks hamburgers and behaves in an unfriendly and unhelpful manner toward customers so that they complain, he or she will soon be out of work. However, a moment's reflection will indicate that between messing up so completely that one will be fired and devoting oneself single-mindedly to perfection in cooking, serving, cleaning, and interacting there is a wide range of possible behaviors over which each employee has control.

Thus, even when owners or managers exercise leadership, work involves a significant voluntary element. This voluntary element helps us focus on the fact that labor, the human factor of production, often makes its contribution through cooperation. The fast-food worker who does a "good job" is cooperating with her or his fellow workers and with the manager or boss. An exception to this generalization is the individual who is totally self-employed. In the more usual process of production, human beings cooperate under the direction of leaders who are either hired by owners or are the owners themselves.[3] The ability of owners and leaders to induce cooperation from workers is one of the keys to economic growth in a society such as the United States, where leadership is granted its power to direct by owners.

Economists in the radical tradition beginning with Marx divide the human element in production between owners and those who work for them. Owners must expend a tremendous amount of energy inducing enough cooperation from their workforce to achieve a sufficient level of production.[4] The growth of the modern profession of management is the result of proliferating theories and analyses of how to induce more diligent, intense cooperation among the various members of working "teams" in the real world of business. Marxists believe that owners have historically induced hard work through the exercise of power over their employees, predictably producing resistance by workers. Thus, Marxists argue that conflict inevitably arises between owners and workers over the pace and difficulty of work and the remuneration for it. Modern management theory, on the other hand, begins with the premise that all members of an organization have a stake in its success and that the job of a good manager is to create the right atmosphere to instill a cooperative spirit. Both approaches agree, however, that an emphasis on cooperation, much of which ends up being voluntary, is essential in the delivery of the services of the factor of production labor.[5]

Economic growth takes place whenever any or all of the factors of production increase in either quantity or capability. A capability increase occurs when a factor of production achieves a higher productivity. If an acre of land is planted more closely, weeded more thoroughly, and defended more successfully from blight, pests, and foraging animals, then the amount of food grown on that acre will increase. Similarly, if one hundred workers in a field are given better tools to work with, then the amount of food grown per worker will increase.

Even without better tools, individuals with more training or a better diet so that they are healthier and stronger can accomplish more work in the same period of time. Economists usually include such increased production as examples of a productivity increase by that individual, believing that training and education are among the most crucial causes of a society's successful economic growth. Further increase in output might occur if a group of workers develop greater esprit de corps, leading them to increase their effort so that their "team" can produce more. This is an example of a *voluntary* increase of effort. These workers might rest less, work faster, and work more diligently, might help each other in their tasks, and might rotate their tasks to alleviate boredom. There are many ways one might imagine this happening, but the end result would be more output from the same number of people.

Such increased efforts could also result from less benign causes. These workers might be captives of war put to work under duress. The intensity with which they work would be regulated by how hard their overseers drive them and how closely they are supervised. Whether from voluntary enthusiasm or coercion, both examples of increased intensity of work effort are counted as improvements in productivity, though we might just as accurately identify these changes as increases in the *quantity* of human effort expended. Economists, unable to agree on how to measure such a quantity, continue to identify quantitative increases in the factor of production labor as hours worked and numbers of people working. All other output increases are lumped together as increases in productivity.

In addition to improvements in the productivity of particular factors of production that increase output per acre or output per person (or even output per machine) advances in knowledge can raise the productivity of all factors of production. These advances in knowledge are often called technological progress or new technology. The substitution of word processing and storage of information on microchips for typing and storage of paper increases the productivity of a building (using space more efficiently), of people (no retyping, no layering of sheets with carbon paper to make copies), and of equipment (keys are struck much less frequently to create the same final written product). Examples abound: contour plowing in agriculture, the development of electricity, the frontiers of bioengineering. Technological progress involves discovery, development, and ultimately application to the process of production. The impact on economic growth occurs with the application, but it could never occur without the prior discoveries. The systematic search for knowledge is considered an important cause of the economic successes of the modern era. Before the Industrial Revolution, economic growth occurred in waves. Great civilizations arose, reached great heights, and then declined, leaving no permanent change in the standard of living of the vast majority of people on the planet. With the systematic search for and application of new knowledge, the post–Industrial Revolution economy has embarked on a trajectory of continuous (if very uneven) economic growth.[6]

Beginning with Adam Smith's *An Inquiry into the Nature and Causes of the Wealth of Nations*, economists have focused on analyzing economic growth. It is not possible or necessary to summarize the various analyses of the causes of economic growth. The important thing to note is that most approaches to economics agree that the crucial dynamic of both long- and short-term economic growth is the amount of productive investment that occurs in society. In the simplest formulation, productive investment involves the creation of a tool, but it can be as complicated as building a high-speed computer, a laser microscope, or a numerically controlled machine tool. Such investment has for the most part been engaged in by private investors seeking to make a profit by producing and selling goods and/or services at a cost lower than the price.

Along with productive investment in physical capital, long-term improvement in the quality of the labor force as a result of widespread education and training has been crucial in making the new investments possible. Productive investment also can involve training a doctor, engineer, systems analyst, teacher, or sales clerk. In other words, without the constant increase in the capability of the labor force, the new physical capital investments cannot be successfully utilized. In the course of the introduction of these new investments, newly discovered knowledge gets applied. The discoveries and inventions are added to the process of production, sometimes creating entirely new products. New technology spreads through the system of production. Finally, new forms of organization, some of which have reduced the leeway workers have to determine the amount of effort they expend on the job, have been extremely important. The assembly line introduced by the Ford Motor Company in 1913 increased the intensity with which workers had to work. They were no longer in control of their time. Initially workers resisted, and turnover at the plant was high. Ford responded by doubling the traditional pay to five dollars a day. This had the effect of solidifying the commitment of the workers to the job, and turnover virtually disappeared. For the next sixty years, the assembly line, with ever-increasing intensity of work coupled with rising productivity from improvements in the machinery, was the centerpiece of American manufacturing success.

So increased production occurs through growth in the size of the labor force, growth in the availability of natural resources (clearing of land, discovery of raw-material reserves), and the increase in the physical capital stock of the nation via new investment. All of these involve quantitative increases in the factors of production. Growth also occurs as a result of increased productivity of the land, labor (including increased effort), and/or capital in society. Private investment decisions have been and continue to be the major method by which more factors of production are utilized and productivity is increased. Investment actually creates more capital. When private investment grows dramatically, economies have demonstrated explosive, at times erratic, growth. It is also true, however, that some elements supporting economic growth, for example, education and basic scientific research, have been appropriately provided by governments. Thus, from the earliest days of the Industrial Revolution, governments have played a crucial role in helping the process along. However, even in the twentieth century, when the role of government in industrial economies has expanded dramatically, it is still true that the main instrument for expansion has remained private investment.[7]

The proper role of government appears to have been a major source of controversy between the Clinton administration and the

Republican congressional majority. Both groups agree that there are important roles for government. They differ on where to draw the line. The Clinton administration has proposed careful consideration of how best to make government more efficient in its delivery of necessary services—education, basic scientific research, a physical infrastructure of roads and bridges and so on. The Republicans may agree in principle that this is essential, but they also argue that Congress has historically been incapable of restricting government activity to its appropriate roles and constantly overspends in response to "special interests." Their solution to this wasteful spending was to try and impose a constitutionally mandated balanced budget on congressional decision-making.

Deficits and the National Debt

This is a very important point to make, all the more so because it is rarely admitted. We often read and hear rhetoric such as the following.

> Just as every American sits at the kitchen table and balances his or her budget, just as every small business must balance its budget, Congress must begin balancing our nation's budget—now.[8]

This statement is from the Republican *Contract with America,* but nowhere in that document do the authors bother to explain why it is necessary for government to balance its budget.[9]

They don't explain why because there is no serious economic argument—aside from an argument that government borrowing will reduce private investment by crowding out private borrowers, an argument we will explore in depth in future chapters—to support the assertions of politicians and journalists that government deficit spending is always bad for the economy.[10] However, there is no question that many economists and business leaders believe that government spends too much money on unnecessary projects and/or undeserving people.[11] Seen in this light, balancing the government budget is a *means to an end.* The end is not to stop running deficits, but to reduce government spending.[12] The economist Milton Friedman, who is a strong critic of government intervention in the economy,[13] stated this point explicitly.

> I would rather have a federal government expenditure of $400 billion with a $100 billion deficit than a federal government expenditure of $700 billion completely balanced.[14]

However, he is a strong supporter of a balanced-budget amendment to the Constitution because he believes that is the only way to control government spending.[15]

Every year that a governmental entity spends more money than it receives in revenues, it must borrow the difference.[16] That borrowing is called a deficit. Each year that the federal government borrows to finance a deficit, the amount borrowed becomes part of the national debt. Each year's deficit is added to the sum of all previous deficits to increase the national debt. The only way that national debt can be reduced is to actually run a surplus, to spend less than the revenue coming in.[17]

What damage do deficits and debt do? Let us go back to the rhetoric of the *Contract with America.* "Just as every American . . . balances his or her budget . . ."[18] When people try to contemplate the issue of budget deficits there is an immediate parallel drawn with a family going into debt or a business going into debt. But let's really examine that parallel. First of all, lots of families and businesses go into debt. The important issue is what one buys when one goes into debt. Borrowing to attend college is considered completely responsible. Borrowing to buy a house is considered completely responsible. When the federal government borrows money and uses it to build or repair a highway, or build a post office, or dredge a river, those actions are an investment for the benefit of the people of the United States, just as the family who borrows to finance a college education or a new home is making an investment in its future. In all those cases the borrowing is completely appropriate, yet you would never guess from most of the political rhetoric that government ever borrows money for such a purpose.

The same thing holds true for a business. Businesses routinely borrow to make investments. Unfortunately, when the federal government spends money, there is no distinction drawn between investment in the future (such as education, construction, research) and spending for current services, like the salaries and expenses of members of Congress or spending that merely redistributes income, such as Social Security payments. Economist Robert Eisner puts it this way:

> If United Airlines buys a new plane, that is investment. If Chicago builds a new runway for that plane to land on, that outlay is considered "government expenditure" and is counted, implicitly if not explicitly, as consumption. Similarly, a new truck purchased by business is investment. The highway that is constructed for it to ride on—

unless a rare private toll road—is not. If the Internal Revenue Service spends $100,000,000 for new computers to process tax returns, that is not investment. . . . If business firms buy new computers . . . that is investment.[19]

Since Eisner wrote, the Department of Commerce's Bureau of Economic Analysis has begun dividing government expenditures into "current" and "investment" categories. If this distinction becomes part of the public's consciousness about the causes of government borrowing, that would go a long way toward bringing rationality to future discussions. It is important that we recognize that much of the federal deficit is matched by the creation of valuable assets, just as individual households experience "deficits" when they take out a mortgage on a home, and businesses experience "deficits" when they borrow to make investments. We will explore the actual economic impacts of deficits, as opposed to the imagined disasters that routinely echo in the halls of Congress, when we examine various interpretations of the Reagan era and revisit the historical experience of the United States economy during that period. At this point, it is important to note that the true rationale behind the urge to balance the budget has nothing to do with the alleged damage done by budget deficits and everything to do with the alleged damage done by government spending per se. And even this emphasis on spending per se in only part of a more general concern with government intrusiveness in the economy in general [20]

The Business Cycle

While we recognize that government has a role to play in fostering economic growth, we must reiterate that most creation of new assets and introduction of new technology occurs through the medium of private investment. When potential investors lose confidence that they will achieve an acceptable income, they will refrain from investing. Because private investment is so important a part of the economy, their restraint causes a serious interruption in economic growth. These periodic interruptions became part of the regular pattern of economic activity as early as the eighteenth century in Britain and have been part of the U.S. economic experience since independence. Interruptions in economic growth, first called panics, then depressions, and now recessions, represent periods during which the potential GDP is not realized. In fact, the actual GDP declines.[21] Even without an identified recession, the growth of GDP can be insufficiently rapid with the gap between actual and potential GDP increasing.[22]

Since the publication of John Maynard Keynes's *The General Theory of Employment, Interest, and Money* in 1935, the economics profession has come to blame the failure of GDP to reach its potential on insufficient aggregate demand. For the purpose of analysis, the measurement of aggregate demand is divided into private consumption, private investment, government purchases of goods and services, and net foreign purchases of domestic products. The reason for this division is that the four parts of aggregate demand are engaged in by different individuals and institutions with differing motivations. Private consumption involves the gratification of a want. Private investment involves the creation of a new asset with the purpose of productive usage in the future.[23] All human beings engage in private consumption, though some consume without making market purchases. However, only some make private investment purchases, often as leaders of organizations—using the organization's income. Governments purchase goods and services to deliver what citizens desire (though there is a great deal of debate as to whether citizens can adequately communicate their desires to government and whether government officials are responsive to citizens' desires).[24] In government the decision makers are clearly using the organization's income, though government income mostly comes from taxes on individuals and businesses. Finally, the level of net foreign purchases of products depends on decisions of foreigners.

Note that in the analysis of both economic growth and aggregate demand, investment occurs. This is why most economists identify investment as the main cause of economic growth and prosperity in our society. Investment must be high and rising to achieve a close approximation of potential GDP. It also plays a major role in increasing potential GDP itself because it is the vehicle for discovering and applying new technologies, thereby increasing productivity. Though private consumption is a much larger percentage of GDP than investment, it usually *responds* to changes in income rather than causing such change. Investment plays a much more dynamic role. Since private individuals and corporations invest according to their incentives, the institutional framework of society in which those incentives are formed is crucial to the success of the economy.

Thus, when the economy performed unacceptably in the 1970s, some interpretations focused on the incentive structure of the society, though analysts disagreed about how those incentives affected the economy. The Reagan-Bush economic policies of the 1980s were an experiment in applying a particular method of stimulating incentives in the hope of reversing the unacceptable trends from the 1970s. The debate about the Clinton administration's brief, halting efforts to reverse some of the policies of the 1980s and the continuing debate about what combination of taxes and spending is desirable in the context of achieving a balanced budget hinge on what incentive structure is deemed most appropriate for our economic well-being.

The Reagan revolutionaries and the Republican majority in Congress after 1994 both focused on cutting taxes and reducing regulation. The Clinton administration sought to focus the tax cuts narrowly to subsidize certain kinds of activity, spending on higher education, for example, while streamlining regulation with their so-called reinventing government program.[25] It is interesting to compare this "debate" to the strong arguments during the 1970s and 1980s, when the impetus to regulatory relief coming from the Reagan administration was significantly resisted by the Democratic majority in Congress.

How Does One Use the Evidence?

In delving into the effect of regulation and taxation on incentives to invest, we need to know how to measure successful stimulation of, or damage to, investment activity. If investment (corrected for inflation) rises from $831.6 billion in 1984 to $861.9 billion in 1989,[26] is that success or failure?

If we are concerned about the impact of the federal deficit or the national debt, how do we measure that impact? If the federal deficit rises from $207.8 billion in 1983 to $221.2 billion in 1986, or if the national debt increases from $290.5 billion in 1960 to $365.8 billion in 1969,[27] are these successes or failures?

Without more information, it is impossible to answer these questions. Why? Imagine running a business that at the end of the year clears a profit of $60,000. Would this be a success? Every owner of a business knows that more information is needed to decide. How much was invested? If the investment totaled $240,000, then the $60,000 profit reveals a rate of return of 25 percent. If taxes took 40 percent of that, the net return would be 15 percent, marking a reasonably successful venture. What else might one have done with the $240,000? Less risky investments like government bonds or even corporate bonds would have yielded rates of return far below 15 percent. Thus, compared to any viable alternative this $60,000 of profit is a success. But suppose the $60,000 profit was on an investment of $600,000. The result then would be a 10 percent rate of return. With taxes taking 40 percent, the after-tax rate of return would be 6 percent. Would tax-free municipal bonds have yielded more? If so, a $60,000 profit on a $600,000 investment is a failure.

Investment levels and the absolute size of both the federal budget deficit and the national debt are misleading by themselves. We need to know the level of investment as a percentage of total output because we need to account for the contribution that investment makes to the economy. If investment rises more slowly than total output, its impact on the economy is declining, and that increased output is disappointingly low. The federal budget deficit can increase in total dollars but still shrink as a percentage of output. The same is true of the national debt. In the historical examples of increased investment, federal deficit, and national debt presented above, in each case absolute increases occurred while the relative sizes were shrinking.[28]

Thus, when we turn to the unacceptable economic performance of the pre-Reagan period and analyze the Reagan Revolution, we have to carefully identify our standards of success or failure and constantly keep in mind the way we measure the impact of policies.

3

Explaining Unacceptable
Economic Performance

After taking control in 1994, the Republican majority in Congress presented an economic analysis that is remarkably similar to the one developed in the late 1970s that led to the "Reagan Revolution." Taxes were too high. Government regulated the economy too much. The welfare system rewarded dependency and punished work. Government spending was out of control. Correcting these problems would set the economy back on course, the course initially charted by Ronald Reagan. In 1996, when Bill Clinton was running for reelection, he argued that the economy was in good shape in part *because* he had rationalized government regulation with his vice president's "reinventing government" program and had constrained government spending while raising taxes in order to cut the budget deficit. He also noted that he had signed the bill that ended welfare "as we know it," fulfilling a campaign promise. He promised that during his second term, he would work for tax cuts, and in 1997 he and the Republican majority in Congress agreed on a tax cut that would reduce federal revenues by $94 billion over the following four years.

In order to show how these promises and compromises relate to what Reagan attempted, we need to revisit the original diagnosis that was propounded in the late 1970s.

For much of that decade, from the point of view of political leaders and economic analysts, the United States economy behaved unacceptably. Table 1 should indicate the superiority of the period before 1969 to the period between 1969 and 1980.

In terms of economic growth, productivity growth, average rates of unemployment, and capacity utilization, the period before 1969 was significantly better than the next decade. The rate of growth was significantly faster between 1960 and 1969 than in the following ten years.[1] In the first of these two periods productivity growth was higher,

TABLE 1.   Success (1960–69) versus Failure (1970–79)

Year	Rate of Growth of Real GDP	Rate of Growth of Productivity	Unemployment Rate	Capacity Utilization Rate[a]
1960	2.2	1.1	5.5	80.1
1961	2.1	3.1	6.7	77.3
1962	6.0	4.7	5.5	81.4
1963	4.3	3.4	5.7	83.5
1964	5.8	4.4	5.2	85.6
1965	6.4	3.1	4.5	89.5
1966	6.4	3.5	3.8	91.1
1967	2.6	1.8	3.8	86.4
1968	4.7	3.5	3.6	86.8
1969	3.0	0.1	3.5	86.9
1970	0.0	1.4	4.9	80.8
1971	3.3	4.0	5.9	79.2
1972	5.4	3.5	5.6	84.3
1973	5.7	3.2	4.9	88.4
1974	−0.4	−1.6	5.6	84.2
1975	−0.6	2.7	8.5	74.6
1976	5.6	3.7	7.7	79.3
1977	4.9	1.5	7.1	83.3
1978	5.0	1.3	6.1	85.5
1979	2.9	−0.7	5.8	86.2

Source: ERP 1996, 283, 333, 325, 337.
[a]Manufacturing capacity utilization, 1960–66; total industry capacity utilization, 1967–79.

unemployment rates were lower, and the capacity utilization rate was higher.[2] Since investment is so crucial to the success of an economy, it is also useful to observe the profit rate in order to judge the incentives to investment during these two decades. Here again, the economy's performance clearly deteriorated. Over the period of 1959 to 1968, profit rates in the nonfinancial corporate sector averaged 10.8 percent before taxes and 6.6 percent after taxes. Between 1969 and 1979 there were two business cycles, during which profits averaged 8.3 percent and 6.8 percent before taxes, and 5.2 percent and 4.3 percent after taxes. Not only were profit rates lower in 1970s as a whole, they continued to decline over the course of the decade.[3]

Table 2 looks at the impact of the economy on individual and family incomes over the same period.

As mentioned in chapter 2, the per capita GDP tells us what is potentially available to raise the standard of living of all Americans. Between 1959 and 1969, the real per capita GDP rose 33.8 percent. Between 1969 and 1979, that growth slowed to 24.3 percent. This was because there were three years of decline in per capita GDP during

TABLE 2.   How Individuals and Families Fared, 1960–79

Year	Rate of Growth of Real GDP per Capita (%)	Rate of Growth of Median Real Income of Families (%)	Rate of Growth of Median Real Income of Year-round Full Time Workers (%)	
			Male	Female
1960	0.2	1.8	NA	NA
1961	0.5	0.9	3.3	0.8
1962	4.4	3.1	1.9	2.0
1963	2.8	3.3	2.4	1.7
1964	4.4	3.9	2.4	2.9
1965	5.0	4.4	1.5	2.8
1966	5.2	5.2	4.3	0.2
1967	1.5	2.1	1.6	0.2
1968	3.7	4.8	2.7	3.4
1969	2.0	4.6	5.6	6.8
1970	−1.2	−0.2	1.2	2.0
1971	2.0	−0.1	0.5	0.7
1972	4.3	4.9	5.4	2.5
1973	4.7	2.0	3.1	1.0
1974	−1.3	−2.6	−3.6	0.8
1975	−1.6	−1.8	−0.7	−1.3
1976	4.6	3.2	−0.2	2.1
1977	3.8	0.6	2.2	0.0
1978	3.9	3.2	0.7	1.6
1979	1.9	1.3	−1.3	−1.0

Sources: Column 1: *ERP* 1997, 333; column 2: Bureau of the Census, Current Population Reports, Series P 60, table F-5; columns 3 and 4: Bureau of the Census, Current Population Reports, Series P 60, table P-15.

the recessions in 1970 and 1974–75. This combines with the information in table 1 to demonstrate that the *economy* was failing to operate in a successful manner. How the average citizen fares in this economy is best captured by observing the median income, that is, the income received by the person or family right in the middle of the income distribution—half the people (or families) in the country receive more, half receive less. Unless income is distributed equally, the median is always below the average (per capita) GDP. Consider our extreme example of a six-trillion-dollar economy concentrated in the hands of one person. In that case, since everyone but the single individual at the top has nothing, the median income is *zero*. Now a slowdown in the growth of median income can result from a slower-growing GDP per capita *or* a significant increase in inequality (or some combination of both).

In addition to these two measures, the median income of year-round full-time workers is particularly revealing. Their rising incomes after World War II created the great American middle class. These were the workers who bought houses, automobiles, televisions, and home appliances and settled the suburbs in the 1950s and 1960s. They flocked to sporting events, movie theaters, and other cultural centers and took vacation trips by car, eating in restaurants and staying in motels. Finally, they sent their children to college, passing on the optimistic prediction that they would live with a higher standard of living than their parents. The very success of this postwar working generation in developing a middle-class lifestyle validated the American dream that if you work hard and play by the rules you can climb the ladder of success and increased affluence.

Table 2 makes it very clear that the median income of all families and of year-round, full-time workers grew much more slowly after 1969 than before. Even if we ignore the years of negative growth, assuming them to be associated with recessions, the 1959–69 period saw an average rate of growth of 3.4 percent in median family income, while the six years of positive growth in the 1969–79 period saw median family income grow an average of 2.5 percent. Year-round full-time workers, male and female, also experienced a slowdown. Men in this group had a 28 percent increase in median income between 1960 and 1969, while women experienced a 25 percent rise. Between 1969 and 1978, those percentages were just 9 and 10 percent respectively.[4] The experience of the average family and the average year-round full-time worker in the 1970s helps explain the rising popular discontent with the economy and with economic policy during that decade. And we must remember that when the median income growth slows, half the population's income growth is even lower. It was in that context that the debates about economic policy were joined.

The Misery Index

Despite this broad array of deteriorating economic indicators, most of the focus during the late 1970s was on a new concept, the "misery index." The misery index was created by adding the unemployment rate to the inflation rate.[5]

The misery index averaged 7.1 between 1960 and 1969 and 13.1 between 1970 and 1979 (see table 3). Now in fact unemployment and inflation are not the same kinds of problems. Unemployment is unam-

TABLE 3. The Misery Index, 1960–80

Year	Unemployment Rate (civilian) (%)	Inflation Rate (%)[a]	Misery Index[b]
1960	5.5	1.7	7.2
1961	6.7	1.0	7.7
1962	5.5	1.0	6.5
1963	5.7	1.3	7.0
1964	5.2	1.3	6.5
1965	4.5	1.6	6.1
1966	3.8	2.9	6.7
1967	3.8	3.1	6.9
1968	3.6	4.2	7.8
1969	3.5	5.5	9.0
1970	4.9	5.7	10.6
1971	5.9	4.4	10.3
1972	5.6	3.2	8.8
1973	4.9	6.2	11.1
1974	5.6	11.0	16.6
1975	8.5	9.1	17.6
1976	7.7	5.8	13.5
1977	7.1	6.5	13.6
1978	6.1	7.6	13.7
1979	5.8	11.3	17.1
1980	7.1	13.5	20.1

Source: ERP 1997, 346, 369.
[a]Consumer price index.
[b]Unemployment rate plus inflation rate.

biguously a waste of resources. The existence of unemployed resources means that we as a nation could have more output than we have. To do this, we would merely have to find a way to utilize the human beings who are willing and able to work. Worse, this unused potential cannot be recouped. Since human beings have finite lives, the potential to work represented by the weeks or months or years that they are unemployed is forever lost to the economy. This loss, as mentioned in chapter 2, affects people other than the unemployed and their immediate families. The fallout from unemployment potentially affects the future prosperity of every member of an economy. When potential GDP is not produced, it translates into reduced income for the entire society. My company's sales may not rise as much as in previous years, and I may not get a raise or a promotion. My town's revenue may not rise, and the town may not be able to hire more police officers. My children's school may not get a new roof.

Inflation is an entirely different thing. It does not unambiguously harm everyone in the economy. Inflation, because it is a general rise in the price level, hurts only those who find the "price" of what they sell (their income) rising less than this general rise. If all incomes rose the same rate as the general price level, then inflation would inflict no pain on anyone. The problem is that this does not happen. There are winners and losers in an inflationary economy. The most obvious losers are creditors; the most obvious winners are debtors. This occurs because interest payments on loans most often are fixed. Suppose I pay an 8 percent interest rate on my eighty-thousand-dollar mortgage. Neither the 8 percent interest nor the amount of the mortgage changes when the rate of inflation increases (except in a variable-rate mortgage). The real benefit of those interest payments is felt by the lender after inflation has been taken into account. While the lender waits for repayment, his or her ability to buy goods and services with the money loaned is decreasing at the rate of inflation. The borrower, meanwhile, is benefiting from this same process.

Since lenders and borrowers are generally aware of this effect of inflation, all actual interest rates contain some kind of "inflation premium," an addition to the interest rate in order to protect the lender from anticipated inflation (an addition that borrowers are willing to accept because they anticipate the benefit from inflation during the time of the loan). Unfortunately, the ability of lenders and borrowers to predict inflation is quite limited. When inflation accelerates, we can be pretty confident that much of the actual inflation did not find its way into interest rates contracted before the acceleration. Similarly, when inflation decelerates, interest rates will have overcorrected for inflation, placing a serious burden on the debtors, who do not benefit from the inflation they predicted.[6] On the other hand, inflation that has remained fairly steady for an extended period of time probably surprises very few lenders and borrowers with either windfall losses or gains.

Generally, those who have control over the prices they charge for their goods or services, whether it be workers with strong labor unions or businesses who can set their prices,[7] can keep up with or even stay ahead of inflation. Those who receive pensions denominated in dollars rather than purchasing power or who receive government benefits that need to be increased by stingy state legislatures to keep up with inflation usually fare much worse.

Most important, changing rates of inflation create uncertainties for businesses. When business is confronted by unpredictable inflation, its uncertainty usually translates into a reduction in investment, leading to both a reduction in aggregate demand and a slowdown in the rate of growth of real GDP. Uncertainty occurs in part because the tax system measures the tax base in dollar amounts, not in terms of purchasing power. In the case of the taxation of business income, this can have a significant effect. Part of the cost of doing business is the depreciation of equipment and structures utilized in the business. Depreciating equipment and structures for tax purposes permits a business to reserve from taxable income sufficient sums of money to replace the equipment at the end of its useful life. So if one bought a $100,000 machine and assumed it would depreciate over a useful life of ten years, taking the simplest method (equal amounts per year) would leave you with a depreciation cost of $10,000 per year. With no inflation over the life of the machine, the cost of replacing that machine will be $100,000 ten years from now, and that $100,000 will have been accumulated tax free over the life of the structure. But if inflation were to average 1 percent over that ten-year period, the replacement cost of that building would be $110,000, while the tax system would permit depreciation of only $100,000. Thus, $10,000 of income necessary to cover replacement costs becomes subject to taxation. This example should demonstrate that the real burden of a tax system changes, sometimes dramatically, as the rate of inflation changes. Unanticipated inflation indirectly affects the economy by punishing certain investment decisions. This has led many to believe that inflation inevitably produces a recession, but in fact it is only volatile *changes* in inflation that increase uncertainty. Inflation that has been more or less predicted does not have that impact and probably does no harm to the economy.

The Special Impact of Inflation on Income from Capital

Savings are often invested in interest bearing assets or in real estate or stock ownership. Income in the form of interest is taxed for its full dollar value, even though some of that interest is merely the inflation premium. Thus if I have saved $100,000 for retirement and have bought bonds with a 10 percent rate of interest, the $10,000 income is subject to tax. With a rate of inflation of 5 percent, only half of that $10,000 is a real income, that is, involves an increase in purchasing power. The other 5 percent merely covers the rise in prices, yet I pay the same tax on it. If my tax rate were 36 percent, I would pay $3,600 in tax on my

$10,000 interest income. With the 5 percent inflation rate, only $5,000 of that interest income represents an increase in purchasing power, yet I pay the same $3,600 in taxes.[8] Clearly inflation can play havoc with the taxation of interest income.[9] By the way, the same havoc occurs when businesses that borrow heavily deduct all their interest payments from taxable income. Even if inflation has eroded the real cost of paying interest on loans,[10] as a taxpayer I get the full $10,000 deduction. At the 36 percent tax rate, that saves me $3,600 in tax payments.[11]

Another major form of savings is to purchase real estate or stock. Though both of these assets produce streams of taxable income (rent and dividends), they also produce another very important potential income, capital gains. A capital gain is achieved when one holds an asset and then sells it for a higher price than one paid for it. Thus, one buys some stock for $1,000 and sells it a year later for $1,200. The $200 difference is a capital gain. Individuals and institutions with significant asset ownership get most of the benefits from capital gains. Inflation can seriously interfere with the proper taxation of capital gains.

In principle, every year that one holds an asset that increases in value, one ought to calculate that increased value as part of one's economic income. The total economic income accruing to an individual in a given year includes the net increased value of all assets owned and/or acquired. For the purposes of taxation, however, the law does not recognize income that stems from the increased value of an owned asset (house, stocks, etc.) unless one realizes that value by selling the asset. So let us consider stock bought five years ago with a value of $100,000 and sold this year for $200,000. The difference between the two is the capital gain, and the entire $100,000 is subject to taxes. With no inflation, the entire gain is real income and the tax applies to the real gain. Inflation reduces the real gain represented by that $100,000. Yet the tax rate is applied to the entire $100,000 no matter how much of that gain merely compensated for inflation.[12] To deal with this problem, until 1978, 50 percent of all capital gains were excluded from taxable income. In that situation, the tax rate would be applied to $50,000. If the inflation had been 50 percent over the five years, such an exclusion would have exactly balanced it. However, any lower inflation rate (or shorter period of time) would have created a situation where the exclusion of 50 percent of capital gains *overcorrected* for inflation.[13]

Because accelerations in the rate of inflation have the potential for significantly reducing wealth that is held in the form of interest-earning assets, it is not surprising that inflation would be considered as serious a problem as unemployment by citizens who hold such wealth. Perhaps more surprising is that ordinary citizens, most of whom own no financial assets and many of whom are actually net debtors because they have not yet paid off their home mortgages, should have similar fears about inflation. For whatever reasons, governments have been charged by their citizens with the responsibility of curbing both inflation and unemployment, of minimizing the misery index.

Aggregate-Demand Management

The uncertainties of inflation, its assumed impact as a disincentive to save and invest, and fear that inflation will feed on itself have led policymakers to try to curb it. In addition, the experience of the Great Depression of the 1930s caused government officials in the market economies of the world to accept the fact that their responsibilities include efforts to battle unemployment.[14] Just as Keynes and his followers believed that GDP often fell below its potential because of insufficient aggregate demand, they also believed inflation was caused by too much aggregate demand (until the early 1970s, it was thought these were problems that alternated, that you could not have both at once). Government efforts to alter aggregate demand to counter either inflation or unemployment are called *aggregate-demand management*.

The traditional tools for fighting inflation involve restrictive fiscal (taxing and spending) policy and restrictive monetary (interest rate) policy. Such restrictions, by reducing aggregate demand, may well ease inflation but often at the cost of increasing unemployment. Or consider the traditional tools for reducing unemployment, expansionary fiscal and monetary policy to increase aggregate demand.[15] This may ignite or accelerate inflation as it reduces unemployment. This is where the misery index comes in. The 1970s had been plagued by what had come to be called *stagflation*, the combination of unacceptably high inflation with unacceptably high unemployment. In this situation the traditional tools for fighting inflation only made unemployment worse, and vice versa. Stagflation, because both problems are on the increase, leads to a higher misery index than if the problem were confined to either inflation or unemployment. The stagflation of the 1970s with its high misery index paved the way for new approaches to economic policy.

Back in 1961, it was a different story. The Council of Economic Advisers convinced President Kennedy to support vigorous attempts to use aggregate-demand management to accelerate the recovery from the 1960–61 recession. In 1962, a tax credit rewarded businesses that invested in equipment with a reduction in their taxes equal to 7 percent of the cost of the equipment. Then, for the first time, in 1964, a general tax cut was passed by Congress not in response to a recession but in an attempt to prolong a recovery. By the end of the decade of the 1960s, the period of expansion had gone on so long that some economists were bragging that "fine tuning" the economy with appropriate fiscal and monetary policies had ushered in the age where the business cycle could be controlled and virtually abolished.

The stagflation of the 1970s threw that approach to economics into disrepute. Critics of using monetary and fiscal policies for aggregate-demand management were listened to more respectfully and new, so-called supply side approaches to economic policy presented themselves, particularly in the form of a 1978 recommendation for three consecutive years of 10 percent income tax cuts.[16]

Reaganomics

Because Ronald Reagan came to the presidency promising a revolution in economic policy and because he was able to deliver on a number of crucial campaign promises, such as lowering taxes and shifting spending priorities, the focus for students of the Reagan Revolution is usually on his program, beginning in 1980. However, economic policy began to change as early as 1978, when the portion of capital gains excluded from taxation increased from 50 to 60 percent; in the fall of 1979 the Federal Reserve System under then-chairman Paul Volcker adopted a new approach to monetary policy. The general shift in policy, which was paralleled by new economic policies pursued by the British government under Prime Minister Margaret Thatcher, can be labeled conservative economics, right-wing economics, or a return to orthodoxy in economics.[17] Whatever one wants to call it, it has dominated U.S. economic policymaking ever since. In order to adopt the most neutral language, we will label it conservative economics.

Ronald Reagan behaved as have very few politicians in American history. In the fall of 1980, as he campaigned for the presidency against Jimmy Carter, he told the electorate that he was going to cut taxes and reduce government spending on social programs while raising spending on defense. He also promised that he could do so and still achieve a balanced budget, which turned out to be a hollow claim. What was remarkable, however, was not that failure but his ability to deliver on his promises on taxes and spending. He specified that he was going to ask Congress for a three-year, across-the-board income tax cut so as to rekindle the incentives necessary for a private-enterprise economy to function well. He delivered the tax cut, some domestic spending cuts, and increased defense spending.

Meanwhile, the fall of 1979 marked the beginning of the Federal Reserve System's strong anti-inflation policies. Thus, the Reagan tax cuts and spending changes of 1981, though dramatic in themselves, are even more significant in combination with the actions of the Federal Reserve System, which continued on its anti-inflationary course until late 1982.

The Conservative Diagnosis

If we were to summarize the Reagan administration's analysis of what was ailing the United States economy in the 1970s, the key would be to "blame government" for interfering with the market.[18] In February 1981, less than a month after Reagan took office, his Council of Economic Advisers issued a Program for Economic Recovery.

> The most important cause of our economic problems has been the government itself. The Federal Government, through tax, spending, regulatory, and monetary policies, has sacrificed long term growth and price stability for ephemeral short-term goals. In particular excessive government spending and overly accommodative monetary policies have combined to give us a climate of continuing inflation. That inflation itself has helped to sap our prospects for growth. In addition, the growing weight of haphazard and inefficient regulation has weakened our productivity growth. High marginal tax rates on business and individuals discourage work, innovation, and the investment necessary to improve productivity and long-run growth. Finally, the resulting stagnant growth contributes further to inflation in a vicious cycle that can only be broken with a plan that attacks broadly on all fronts.[19]

Let us examine these points and connect them to the general thrust of the theory of conservative economics. The major starting point is the view that government as such produces nothing: labor and entrepreneurship, the human factors of production, do all the producing, aided by the nonhuman factors, land and capital. Since government produces nothing, it interferes with the private decision-making of laborers and entrepreneurs whenever it raises taxes to finance its activities. Thus, even something as necessary as national defense has a negative impact on the private sector, according to conservative economists. Thus, national-defense spending is a necessary evil, just as the taxes to finance a national-defense establishment are a necessary evil. The general presumption is that government activities interfering with private decision-making in the economy should be minimized because, except in some clearly defined cases, they do more harm than good.

The Proper Role for Government

The role of government in a market economy such as the United States is usually divided into six major areas of activity. I will list them in increasing order of controversy.

1. Provide a legal framework appropriate for the successful operation of the market system.
2. Maintain competition.
3. Provide social goods and services.
4. Adjust the composition of output to take account of social costs and benefits.
5. Supplement or curb private aggregate demand so as to permit only minimal unemployment while at the same time maintaining price stability.
6. Redistribute income.

In principle, all of these roles for government have been accepted by the majority of the population in the United States as appropriate. We might note that in western Europe and Japan it has been explicitly acceptable for government to do more. Those governments operate a number of industries (airlines, railroads, even at times profitable manufacturing businesses) that are judged important enough that the political leadership of the country does not trust them to private hands. Those countries also use loan guarantees, subsidies, and special tax advantages to determine not merely the level of investment but the composition of investment, something United States policymakers have been opposed to in theory.[20]

However, we should note that in reality, many of our major industries have developed as a result of government activity. To take the most dramatic present development, the Internet is a result of a Defense Department program to link all the nation's defense apparatus into one unbreakable web of connectivity. Meanwhile, our tax system actually has played a major role in determining the direction of investment. Both results have allegedly been inadvertent and not the result of a positive policy decisions. Government activity here plays the role of giving private business special incentives and reduced risk. This aspect of government activity is usually downplayed by policymakers and economists.

In Europe, there are also many more restrictions on the freedom of capital in labor-management relations and in closing plants to relocate investment activity. Yet although the western Europeans and Japanese go much further than does the United States, the view of conservative economists was that by 1981, the United States economy was burdened by too extensive a role for government.

1. In the first *Economic Report of the President* issued by Reagan's Council of Economic Advisers, there is a detailed description of the acceptable and limited role for government activities in a free-market economy. Enforcing contracts, maintaining the legal protection to the rights of private property, managing the currency, and maintaining competition are in theory absolutely essential activities for even the most conservative of economists.[21] In this context it is important to emphasize the role of government as an enforcer of contracts and protector of private property rights. Without strong police powers exercised by a governmental body, individuals will be loathe to enter into contracts because they will only have their own personal strength and power to enforce them. If you and I make an agreement that you will do some work for me, when the work is done, if there are no police, how can you "force" me to pay you? On the other hand, if I pay you first, how can I "force" you to finish the work?

If such difficulties would occur in agreements where personal knowledge may create trust, how much more difficult would agreements be if the individuals involved were total strangers? If I am buying raw materials from you to produce something to sell, how do you know that when I finish the product and sell it I will pay you what I promised? If I pay you in advance, how can I guarantee you will deliver as promised? Without some police power to appeal to, individuals will be loathe to enter into any contracts.

Without such contracts, a "market economy"—that is an economy where most production and distribution occurs through voluntary exchange of goods and services, including the services of factors of production—is impossible. Market activity, such as might exist, will be quite limited. An interesting sidelight in the development of economic analysis is that Adam Smith's major work *The Wealth of Nations* was originally part of a series of lectures on jurisprudence and police. The section on police included a subsection giving Smith's analysis of the workings of economic markets. This shows that for Smith, the absolutely essential precondition for widespread market activity is the existence of a government with strong enough police powers to create the legal framework necessary for the operation of the market system.[22]

2. When we turn to the second role for government, there is a question as to how far to go in maintaining competition. Since the enactment of the Sherman Antitrust Act of 1890, government activities to maintain competition have involved attempting to "break up" large business firms that appeared by their relative size in a particular industry to be restraining competition, or to stop mergers that might decrease competition from taking place. Many conservative economists believe that antitrust activity had been overdone in the 1970s. They argue that the government was insufficiently aware of the fact that competition can work even with only a few firms in an industry. A theory of "contestable markets" was developed that suggested that even a single producer of a product might be constrained in pricing decisions as if there were competition providing there was no legal barrier to the entry of new firms. That is because if the market *might* be contested, firms will behave as if it already were contested.[23] In such a situation, an attempt to break up a large, successful business would do nothing to increase competitive behavior, which would already be taking place.

3. Providing social goods and services such as police forces and defense establishments is considered a necessary government activity by all but the most extreme libertarians. In general, conservative economists believe government provision of social goods and services should not interfere with potential private provision. Thus, increasing government spending on national defense was acceptable to the Reagan budget makers, but spending on rail passenger service, aid to local governments' mass-transit systems, and other activities that could be done by the private sector were considered wastes of the taxpayers' money.[24] When the Conrail corporation was formed to operate a number of bankrupt northeastern railroads, it was understood that this was

an emergency measure to provide a needed service. From the point of view of conservative economics, once the emergency had passed, it would be important to put these resources back in private hands.[25]

Taking Account of Social Costs and Benefits

4. Adjusting the output of the private sector to take account of social costs and benefits is based on the idea that when individual decision makers consider producing a product, they focus only on what it costs them to produce it. Thus, an electric utility considers the cost of buying coal, but not the health and other costs imposed on other people when the coal is burned. Meanwhile, the individuals deciding whether to buy a product at a particular price, consider only the benefits they expect to gain from it. Thus, the benefits to an individual of pursuing an education would be the only basis on which people would buy such a service (even if we are willing to assume that person could accurately predict those benefits). However, what society at large gains from the contributions made by the existence of an educated citizenry does not enter into individual calculations. These extra costs and/or benefits are said to "spill over" to uninvolved third parties. Economists call them *externalities.*

President Reagan's Council of Economic Advisers acknowledged this point in a section on externalities.

> Because some of the benefits of living in a nation of people with a common language and culture are external, individuals considering only their own benefit from education will most likely buy too little. . . . Government intervention may therefore be justified where either marginal costs or benefits are external.[26]

Thus, it is clear that conservative economic theorists accept this role for government. The problem arises, they argue, with the method of achieving these refinements in the operation of the economy and with the overregulation that is caused by the activities of political pressure groups. The first step in the argument is the assertion that the private market system is competitive enough so that with each individual and business attempting to pursue their own self-interest, maximizing profits (business) or income (individuals), the competitive structure of all markets will guarantee that goods and services will be produced and offered for sale up to the point where the price of the item equals its marginal costs, the cost of producing the last unit. That cost represents the sacrifice made by society to produce that product. When all goods and services are produced up to the point where price equals marginal cost, the benefits to the consumer measured by price exactly balances society's sacrifice.[27]

Consider the earlier example of the choice between using land to grow food or building a shopping center. Focusing only on the decision making by owners or potential buyers of the land and consumers who might purchase food grown on the land or items available in the stores in the mall, we can illustrate the point of matching costs to satisfaction. The farmer's costs depend on the fertility of the soil and the productivity of the farm. The consumers' actions will depend on the prevailing prices being paid for the type of food produced on that farm. The interaction of the farmer's costs and the consumers' behavior leads to the profit the farmer can expect should he/she sell all that could be produced on the farm at the going market price.

Then we have to compare that to the income that could be derived by a contractor who put up a shopping mall and rented out stores that would sell various items to consumers. Again, the prevailing market prices for the items available in the stores would send a signal to the various businesses as to how much they could afford to pay the developer to lease space in the mall. This signal would then tell the developer how much he/she would be willing to bid to purchase the land from the farmer and still make a profit from building and leasing space in the mall. The *farmer* is then left with the choice of whether to accept the developer's price or stick with farming. If the developer's price exceeds the long-term value to the farmer of remaining in farming,[28] then society's signaling device, the price system, will encourage the farmer to transfer the factors of production he/she controls out of farming and into mall development. This transfer of resources from lower-value to higher-value activity shows them being stretched as efficiently as possible to satisfy as much of society's unlimited wants as possible, given the state of technology. This ongoing process creates, according to most economists, "the best of all possible worlds."

However, when social costs and benefits diverge from private costs and benefits, even conservative economists believe that actions by government are justified to correct for this failure by the market. Thus, for example, the mall developer may be required to file an "environmental impact statement" to demonstrate that groundwater, wetlands, wildlife habitats, and local air quality will not be damaged by the building and operation of the new mall. If any of these are harmed by the construction, the market decision makers (the farmer who will have taken the money and departed, the developer who may have done the same, the shoppers who may not hunt or fish and who may not notice declines in air and water quality) will be very unlikely to add those costs to their own calculations. Thus, there is no question that, in theory, government regulation has a legitimate role to play in dealing with externalities.

However, conservative economists, particularly the first chairman of President Reagan's Council of Economic Advisers, Murray Weidenbaum, have argued that in practice the efforts to correct for such malfunctioning have involved such a heavy hand of government regulation as to impose astronomical costs on the private sector. Weidenbaum's Center for the Study of American Business had estimated in 1979 that all costs of operating regulatory agencies and the compliance costs of their regulations added up to approximately $100 billion.[29] The implication was that no benefits could possibly justify such high costs, though Weidenbaum himself didn't say this. He actually stated that such high costs made it essential that benefits be very carefully calculated. Any costs imposed on business in excess of the actual benefits to society would produce reductions in business investment with insufficient compensating increases in well-being. In other words, reduced output and employment in a business that, without government regulation, would produce only a small amount of air pollution will be too great to justify the slightly cleaner air that people will breathe because of government regulation.

Discretionary Monetary and Fiscal Policy

5. When it comes to engaging in aggregate-demand management, the Reagan Council of Economic Advisers criticized previous policymakers for using these tools of stability in such a way as to promote *instability*. In an effort to combat first unemployment and then inflation, policies swung back and forth between stimulation and contraction. The result was that business found it harder and harder to plan their investments. Another criticism was that there were lags between the recognition of a problem, the enactment of a new policy (a tax change or a change in monetary policy), and the impact of the policy change on the economy. Because of this, there was no guarantee that the policy actually affecting the economy at any given time was working against the business cycle. It would be next to impossible, according to

this view, to exactly calculate the right time to apply fiscal or monetary stimulation or contraction. Policy reversals might occur too late to do any good and might even make things worse.

This brings us to the Keynesian-monetarist controversy. Monetarists believe that policymakers should keep the rate of growth of the money supply steady and let the market self-correct. Their reasoning is that the rate of growth of the money supply has a powerful influence on the rate of growth of the economy as a whole. The problem is that when the rate of growth of the money supply changes, the powerful impact it makes on the rest of the economy occurs after an unpredictable delay. Thus, if the Federal Reserve were to regularly change the rate of growth of money, the result would be *instability* because it would be impossible to predict when the impact of each shift would be felt.[30]

In addition, monetarists believe that fiscal policy is incapable of stimulating aggregate demand. This argument denies the importance of one of the major contributions of Keynesian economics, the multiplier effect. According to one of Keynes's students, writing in 1931, an increase in government spending, say building roads, would increase the incomes of the people and businesses engaged in actually doing the work. These people would take that increased income and spend some (probably high) percentage of that increase. Economists call that percentage increase the *marginal propensity to consume* (MPC). The increase in spending would become income to other people who would then spend some percentage (MPC) of it and so on. The increase in spending would increase employment. The sum total all of the employment increases would end up being a multiple of the initial increase.[31] The sum total of all income increases would, likewise, be a multiple of the initial one. That initial rise in spending from any source acts like a rock thrown into the middle of a pond. Just as the splash causes ripples to spread outward from the point of impact, the initial rise in spending similarly ripples through the economy.

The monetarists have always argued strongly against this view. They believe that the multiplier process is quite weak or even nonexistent. Instead of actually raising aggregate demand, rising government spending would be offset by falling private investment. Suppose government spends money on libraries, state universities, government-operated public utilities, and so forth. The existence of these government-provided services precludes private investors from providing the same services. Thus, the existence of public libraries means that no would-be investor will accumulate books and create private libraries, although the potential for doing this is quite obvious. (Virtually every private educational institution has a "private library" for the use of its fee-paying students.) Or take the existence of a large public sector in higher education. Clearly this has reduced opportunities for the private sector in education and has undoubtedly restricted investment in that area.

As another example, consider the Tennessee Valley Authority. TVA is a utility owned by the federal government. Because of its existence, no private utility is making investments to create generating capacity to service those potential customers. When Milton Friedman, the most prominent monetarist, argued this point in his 1962 book *Capitalism and Freedom,* he noted that the only way to truly guarantee that rising government spending will raise total aggregate demand would be if government were to spend on activities that were totally worthless, because only then would there be no reduction in private sector opportunities.[32] This is clearly an exaggeration since Friedman would certainly agree that public-sector activity for national defense has no private-sector equivalent to preempt.

Government Borrowing Crowds Out
Private-Sector Borrowing

There is another step to the argument, however: financing government spending by borrowing money, that is, by deficit spending, will "crowd out" private borrowers from the market for these capital funds. If the private sector's savings remain the same and the government increases its borrowing, then the borrowing of private investors and the public sector will compete for the same amount of private savings, pushing the interest rate up. The government can pay any interest rate, but some private borrowers will refrain from investing in the face of higher borrowing costs. The only way to avoid the rise in interest rates is for the Federal Reserve to create enough new money to finance the government deficit so as to avoid government dipping into that private pool of savings. But, then, according to Friedman, we really have monetary policy, not fiscal policy. If the Federal Reserve did not create new money, the increased government borrowing will crowd out much of the private-sector borrowing that had existed. How *much* private-sector borrowing is crowded out will depend on how much (if any) extra private savings are generated by the rise in interest rates.[33] We should note again that despite all the rhetoric one hears in Congress and elsewhere, this supposed impact of public-sector borrowing on interest rates and private investment is the only economic consequence of deficit spending by government. All other implications are either variations on this theme or complete nonsense.[34]

Proposals for Alternative Approaches to
Aggregate-Demand Management

The monetarists believe monetary policy is quite powerful, but because its impact occurs after an uncertain period of time, changing it can be destabilizing. Thus, they proposed that discretionary changes in monetary policy be forbidden by an act of Congress and that the Fed be ordered to keep the rate of growth of the money supply within a narrow band of 3–5 percent per year.

This would be a major change, because throughout the postwar period, the Fed had concentrated on manipulating interest rates in order to either expand or contract the amount of credit creation that goes on in the economy. The monetarists argued that the Fed ought to ignore what happens to interest rates or unemployment in the short run. The stagflation in the 1970s was blamed on the Fed's changing monetary policy to first expand and then contract the rate of growth of money. These policy gyrations created an inflationary trend and helped increase uncertainty and business pessimism.

One of the strongest efforts of both monetarists and conservative economists in general was to utilize the experience of the 1970s to demonstrate that it was impossible for policymakers to select a target of unemployment, such as the 4 percent proposed by the 1962 *Economic Report of the President.* This target rate of unemployment was actually enacted into law as an amendment to the Employment Act in 1978 (The Humphrey-Hawkins Full Employment and Balanced Growth Act). In the late 1950s, A. W. Phillips had discovered a striking regularity in the relationship between unemployment and the rate of growth of money wages (the *Phillips Curve*) in the United Kingdom between 1861 and 1957.[35] The relationship he discovered was an inverse one. At very low rates of unemployment, the tiniest reduction in unemployment would be associated with explosive wage increases. At very high rates of unemployment, no or little reduction in wages would result from large increases in unemployment. In the 1960s, economists noted similar inverse relations between unemployment and the rate of inflation. In the United States, the 1950s and 1960s seemed to demonstrate a fairly stable relationship,[36] leading policymakers to believe that they could select a "menu" of alternative pairs of inflation and unemployment, and that, therefore, a "target" such as the 4 percent proposed by the 1962 *Economic Report* could be one of the "selections."

The 1982 *Economic Report of the President* argued strongly that there was no long-run inverse relationship, that the Phillips Curve was a short-run phenomenon and that in the long run, any effort to trade off lower unemployment for higher inflation would lead to a situation of higher inflation without permanently lowering unemployment. The evidence was presented in a diagram showing that the relatively stable-looking trade-off of the Phillips Curve in the 1950s and 1960s had disappeared in the 1970s.[37] The council argued,

> The irony of the 1970s was that the attempt to trade inflation for employment resulted in more inflation and rising unemployment. . . . the lesson to be learned from the experience of the United States since World War II is that high rates of unemployment can coexist with either high or low inflation. There is no reason to expect a systematic association between the average unemployment rate and the average rate of price-level change, and none is found in the data when one considers periods of several years or longer.[38]

One of the major theoretical arguments used to support the conservative economic-policy agenda was the idea that the economy will tend toward some "natural" rate of unemployment and that any effort to permanently push the unemployment rate below this level will only succeed in increasing inflation. This view that there is such a rate of unemployment—called the nonaccelerating inflation rate of unemployment, or NAIRU—was widely accepted within the economics profession by the end of the 1970s.

This is in sharp contrast to Keynesian economics. The argument of Keynes and his followers was that aggregate demand could become stabilized, and often did, at a level of output that left an unacceptably high percentage of the workforce unemployed and of the nation's industrial capacity unused. They further argued that government stimulation of aggregate demand could improve that situation. The NAIRU analysis denied the final point. There just was a long-run unemployment rate to which the economy naturally tended, and any effort to "go against nature" by pushing unemployment below it would end up doing more harm than good.

It is also true that economists who argued for the existence of such a rate agreed that it was not some fixed number but instead varied depending on institutional factors. For example, some economists stressed that unemployment compensation, as a cause of "voluntary" unemployment, might determine it. In Europe many focused on the ability of unions and business and government to agree on a national incomes policy that might significantly lower the NAIRU. Interestingly enough, the attempt to identify that rate became an important political issue in the 1970s, especially in the United States during the debate over amending the Employment Act. As mentioned above, the amendment, passed in 1978, actually identified as the target level of unemployment the old 1961 rate of 4 percent, despite widespread opposition from economists. Clearly, the message of those who believe a NAIRU exists and that it is significantly higher than 4 percent is to absolve Congress, the president, and the Federal Reserve Board of having to meet their obligations under that law. In fact, by constantly defining the rate upward during the decade of the 1970s, economists entered the 1980s with the idea that any government policy designed to lower unemployment below 6 percent was self-defeating.[39]

Another crucial point for the conservative economists was the problem of high levels of taxation. This analysis produced the part of the Reagan economic program known as supply-side economics. Though the percentage of U.S. GDP taxed in 1980 was no higher than the percentage taxed in 1960, the inflation of the 1970s had moved more and more taxpayers into higher *marginal* rates of taxation.[40] This occurred because the individual income tax is a progressive tax. This means that as your income rises, the rate at which you pay taxes on the next dollar earned (the marginal tax rate) rises also. The theory behind progressive income taxation is that as your income rises, the percentage that you have to spend on necessities falls, and your discretionary income rises. Thus, raising the percentage of total income taxed does not impose a higher burden because less of that income is required for necessities. Progressive income taxes are organized into brackets, with rates progressing from zero to some maximum. In 1981, there were sixteen such brackets (see table 4).[41]

These brackets were fixed in dollar terms, and thus as inflation occurred, people whose income merely kept up with the rate of inflation found themselves pushed into higher tax brackets—a problem known as bracket creep. These higher tax brackets meant rising marginal tax rates on larger percentages of people. One analysis presented by the Council of Economic Advisers in 1982 noted that despite Congress's seven specific tax cuts between 1960 and 1980, the marginal tax

TABLE 4. The Progressive Federal Income Tax before 1981

Taxable-Income Bracket ($)	Tax Rate (%)
0–3,400	0
3,400–5,500	14
5,500–7,600	16
7,600–11,900	18
11,900–16,000	21
16,000–20,200	24
20,200–24,600	28
24,600–29,900	32
29,900–35,200	37
35,200–45,800	43
45,800–60,000	49
60,000–85,000	54
85,000–109,400	59
109,400–162,400	64
162,400–215,400	68
215,400 and over	70

Source: Joint Committee on Taxation, *General Explanation of the Economic Recovery Tax Act of 1981* (Washington, DC: Government Printing Office, 1981), 405, cited in Lawrence B. Lindsey, *The Growth Experiment: How the New Tax Policy Is Transforming the U.S. Economy* (New York: Basic Books, 1990), 51.

rates faced by families earning the median income went from 17 percent in 1965 to 24 percent in 1980.[42]

The key to the supply-side argument is that as the marginal tax rate rises, the incentive for individuals to earn income declines, because each additional dollar's worth of effort to earn more (either by working or saving) is rewarded with a smaller amount of after-tax income. Thus, the effect of rising marginal tax rates is a decline in both the supply of labor and the supply of savings. Unlike Keynesians who stressed that the investment decision was independent of the supply of savings, supply-siders assert that whatever income is saved will be automatically invested. Keynesian economic theory argued that balanced increases in government spending and taxation would have a net positive impact on aggregate demand. The increased government spending would all go toward raising GDP. The increased tax revenue, however, would not reduce consumer spending the same amount. Some of the taxes would be paid by reduced savings. This is the so-called balanced-budget multiplier concept.[43] Supply-siders argued that such a balanced increase would produce the negative side-effect of decreasing the supply of labor and the level of savings and therefore would reduce investment. The way to stop this ongoing damage to incentives would be to dramatically lower marginal tax rates.

According to the supply-side view, the unacceptable performance of the economy in the 1970s was related to the disastrous impact on incentives of high and rising marginal tax rates. This was particularly emphasized in the case of income from capital. As inflation raised the replacement costs of equipment, the use of historical cost covered a smaller percentage of what really needed to be set aside for replacement investment. This translated into a higher marginal tax rate on new investments. An alternative way of viewing this is that it means that businesses will only make investment decisions if a much higher pretax rate of return is predicted. To estimate this return accurately required a correct prediction of inflation over the life of the investment. With long-lived equipment, it is not surprising that uncertainty about inflation would translate into uncertainty about prospective rates of return.

Redistribution of Income

6.   This problem of incentives becomes more acute according to conservatives when we introduce the issue of redistributing income. The Council of Economic Advisers in 1982 acknowledged the legitimate role of government in redistributing income.[44] However, it went on to note that

> there is still an efficiency cost. Transfers reduce the incentive of recipients to work, and the taxes imposed on the rest of society to finance these transfers also cause losses in efficiency.[45]

There was a great deal of work done by economists in the 1970s to demonstrate that the existence of unemployment compensation led to increased voluntary unemployment. This led the Reagan administration to say that redistribution of income should be carefully targeted only at the "truly needy." All transfer payments received by the middle class and those with incomes close to but above the poverty line should be carefully scrutinized with hope that they will be significantly reduced. As part of a generalized complaint about overspending by government, redistribution programs that cost "too much" and give money to people who "don't need it" were emphasized. Thus in the first year of the Reagan administration the Omnibus Budget and Reconciliation Act of 1981 (OBRA) cut programs that gave, in the view of the budget planners, unnecessary subsidies to people.

The Social Security system itself is a redistribution program that seriously violates conservative economists' theories. It is a universal program whose beneficiaries include millions of people who "don't need" the cash transfers to which they are entitled. Long before Ronald Reagan's election, conservatives had charged that the system was *(a)* inefficient as a method of preparing for one's retirement, *(b)* too generous, too expensive, an unnecessary redistribution of income, and *(c)* bankrupt and unable to deliver on its promises to the current working generations.[46] As long ago as 1964, candidate for president Barry Goldwater had suggested making Social Security a voluntary system.

Reducing the amount of income redistributed to those who don't need it is a centerpiece in any serious conservative economic agenda. To understand why, it is necessary to distinguish between contributory entitlements and means-tested entitlements. An entitlement means exactly what the word says. If you qualify for a program, you are automatically paid. Congress does not need to appropriate a sum of money that includes your payment. Instead, Congress establishes the rules of eligibility, and the amount of money actually spent is determined by how many eligible people present themselves.

But the term entitlement masks a significant difference among entitlement programs. If by virtue of previous employment history (which usually involves paying a payroll tax or working in a certain type of employment for a certain period of time) you qualify for payments, such as Social Security or unemployment compensation, then you will receive the payment or service the entitlement program provides, whether you need it or not.[47] Another major contributory system is Medicare. Here one does not receive a retirement check, as in Social Security, but one's medical expenses are provided for—again, whether you have the income to pay or not. Millionaires can get Medicare and Social Security. Even unemployment compensation would be available to the rare millionaire who was laid off from a job that had been covered under the law.[48]

Means-tested entitlements, by contrast, require that potential recipients not have income (and assets) above a certain amount. Those who have the "means" to support themselves are not entitled to benefits such as Supplemental Security Income (SSI), food stamps, Medicaid, and housing and energy assistance. Clearly, from the point of view of conservative economics, only means-tested entitlements are legitimate roles for government in the redistribution of income. The solution for Social Security, according to this view, would be to break it into three: a private pension plan, a private disability and survivors' insurance plan, and a means-tested redistribution program targeted only to the elderly who *needed* the transfers because they did not have sufficient retirement income of their own.[49]

The Conservative Diagnosis: A Summary

To summarize the conservative diagnosis: the U.S. economy by the end of the 1970s suffered from inefficient, excessively expensive regulation; incentive-debilitating tax levels, marginal tax rates in particular; unnecessary redistribution of income; inappropriate, destabilizing demand management; and excessive expansion of the money supply. All had combined over the course of the decade to create stagflation, that is, persistent inflation combined with sluggish investment and productivity growth. The cure was to be found in lowering marginal tax rates, reducing spending, steadying and slowing rates of growth in the money supply, with the consequent end of discretionary aggregate-demand management, reducing regulation, and celebrating the ability of the private sector to do things that were good for the country unencumbered by government intervention.

4

Alternative Analyses

The Carter administration, the Democratic majority in Congress, and the mainstream majority in the economics profession differed with conservative economists in a fundamental way. They did not believe that the unemployment rate would be reduced merely by improving the incentives of individual workers. They did not believe that letting investors keep a higher percentage of their profits would by itself increase investment. In other words, though incentives were clearly important, by themselves they would not solve the problem of unemployment. More important was increasing the opportunity of people to work by increasing the *ability* of business to hire people. Incentives existed already. The way to increase the opportunity to work was to raise aggregate demand.

The role of incentives for investors was a bit more complicated. It was mainstream economists, for example, who devised the investment tax credit in 1962. However, investment incentives were just as likely to be stimulated by rising consumption on the part of average citizens as by cuts in the rate of taxation on profits. In fact, most mainstream economists would argue that lower taxes on profits coupled with slower-growing demand would reduce the incentive to invest, while higher taxation of profits coupled with more rapidly growing demand would increase the incentive to invest. Imagine a business contemplating a project to increase its capacity to produce, either by adopting some new technology or by expanding the building space and the number of machines used. If the business expects consumer demand to rise significantly by the time the new investments have increased production, even if the rate of business taxation were to rise, the investment would still be worthwhile if gross profits due to higher volume and/or lower production costs were to rise more. Similarly, if a business expects consumer demand to barely increase, such an investment is unlikely to be undertaken, even if there is a cut in the tax bite on profits.

Because mainstream economists did not emphasize the incentive effects of taxation to the exclusion of other factors, they did not think the stagflation of the 1970s was merely the symptom of a structural crisis. Nor did they think the solutions proposed by supply-siders and monetarists were going to succeed. However, until the late 1970s, and then particularly after Ronald Reagan was elected, they did not systematically examine and respond to the conservative critique.[1]

The Carter Administration Analyzes the 1970s

After Mr. Reagan's election, the outgoing Carter administration had to prepare one final *Economic Report of the President*. The Council of Economic Advisers was in a position to present a document unfettered by the political need to sell a program to the Congress and the public. Thus, we can be pretty certain that the 1981 report represents the true feelings of the council, perhaps limited only by a desire to put as good a face as possible on the difficult year of 1980. How did the Carter administration analyze the difficulties the United States economy had faced in the 1970s?

The first thing to be noted is that the council did not accept the conservatives' characterization of the 1970s as a economic disaster for the nation. The apocalyptic language of the Reagan analysis was absent from the Carter report. Instead, it soberly admitted that inflation was high and growth in productivity low, and it recognized that the anti-inflation policies adopted in March 1980 had resulted in a short but significant recession.

In explaining the general problem of stagflation, the Carter administration and economists from the Brookings Institution like Barry Bosworth focused on the rapid increases in oil prices in 1973–74 and 1979 and on increases in food prices in the early 1970s.[2] Far from abandoning the Phillips curve analysis, as conservative economists had done, these economists stated that there had been a worsening of the trade-off between inflation and unemployment because inflation had occurred as a result of supply shocks.

Supply shocks differ from sustained inflation caused by excess aggregate demand. The latter occurs when the sum total of the desires of business, consumers, governments, and foreigners to purchase goods and services exceeds the economy's ability to produce sufficient quantities to satisfy those desires. Temporary surges in inflation may occur when shortages in strategically placed goods, such as food or oil, occur. They may also occur when whole categories of goods, such as imports, experience significant changes in prices. But that was only part of the story. Barry Bosworth of the Brookings Institution stated,

> Given the magnitude of the disruptions in world commodity markets during the 1970s, a worsening of inflation was not a surprise; but the persistence of high inflation rates long after the reversal of the initiating factors and in the face of recession and high unemployment was.[3]

In theory, the rise in particular prices should not even create temporary inflation. Instead, goods and services subject to greater-than-average increases in demand will have price rises, while those goods and services that experience falls in demand will suffer price declines. The problem for the U.S. economy was that prices and wages had become sufficiently rigid in the downward direction that compensating price falls were unlikely, or at least quite slow to develop. Instead of resources automatically flowing out of areas where demand declined into the areas of higher prices and higher rates of return, thereby moderating the price increase, the process of adjustment was slow. Areas of the economy that experienced falls in demand felt the pain of unemployment and business losses, while the incomes of the majority fell as a result of the price shocks in key products such as oil and food. The government was then faced with the unpleasant dilemma of permitting money incomes of the population to rise to compensate for the increased prices of oil and food—in other words, to use expansionary fiscal and monetary policy to defend the real income of the population against the increase in oil and food prices —or accept a long period of high unemployment to keep the price increase confined to oil and food and force other prices and wages down. Generally, the government did a little of both, fighting whichever of the two problems was considered most politically damaging. President Gerald Ford provided a perfect example of that dilemma by reversing himself between October 1974 and January 1975. In October he went on national television asking the country to support him in requesting a tax increase from Congress to fight inflation. In January, he was back on television asking for a tax cut complete with cash rebates to fight the recession.[4]

The policies adopted in 1975 played a major role both in the continued expansion of the role of government and in successfully combatting the recession. Emergency extensions of unemployment compensation together with the tax cut caused a significant rise in the federal budget deficit.[5] Meanwhile, the Federal Reserve cooperated by pursuing an expansionary monetary policy.[6] In general, the role of the government in the economy continued to grow.

However, President Carter spent his entire presidency obsessed with what his policymakers called a "soft landing" recovery from the recession of 1974–75. He wanted the unemployment rate to fall gradually enough to avoid rekindling the inflation of 1973–74. Unfortunately for his reelection efforts, from 1976 until he left office, the inflation rate rose.[7] Because he was so anxious to restrain this inflation, he did not respond to the 1980 recession as President Ford had responded to the 1975 recession, arguing that

> twice in the last decade the tendency for government to stimulate the economy somewhat too freely during the recovery from recession probably played a role in retarding the decline of inflation or renewing its acceleration. That is why I was so insistent that a tax cut designed for quick economic stimulus not be enacted last year.[8]

Because of the vigorous antirecession policies of the Ford administration, the federal budget deficit rose to 3.4 percent of GDP in 1975. In 1980, on the other hand, it was only 2.7 percent of GDP, in part because of President Carter's refusal to recommend a tax cut during 1980, even when a recession occurred in the second quarter.[9]

Though not emphasized at the time or since, that nonresponse marked the first time since 1960 that an administration had not responded to a recession with a move toward fiscal stimulus.[10] This represented a major break with the policy that had been followed since the passage of the Employment Act of 1946, and especially since the 1960s. Before 1980, politicians and economists had always assumed that there were significant political limitations on anti-inflation policies. It had always been clear that if the government and the population were willing to accept prolonged periods of high levels of unemployment, any rate of inflation could be reduced, even eliminated altogether. The years of relatively low levels of unemployment and short-lived recessions had created an expectation on the part of the citizenry that the government ought not and would not permit "high" unemployment to last "too long."

Notice that these terms are imprecise. Congress did respond dramatically to President Ford's request for a tax cut in 1975, so clearly the recession of 1975 produced unacceptably high levels of unemployment. We have already noted that Congress passed, and President Carter signed, the Full Employment and Balanced Growth Act of 1978, which specifically identified the old 4 percent rate as the only acceptable level of unemployment. This law was strenuously opposed by many economic and business leaders because they feared serious efforts to implement it would produce inflation.

By 1980, however, the concern about inflation was so great that President Carter felt politically safe in refusing to recommend an emergency tax cut because in his view it was more important to prevent a reacceleration of inflation than to reduce unemployment quickly. In effect, he ignored his own law as the unemployment rate jumped from 5.8 percent in 1979 to 7.1 percent in 1980.[11] This ended up being an important first step toward demonstrating the willingness on the part of policymakers to risk the political consequences of permitting unemployment to rise *and stay high* in order to fight inflation.

General Conclusions from the Mainstream

The general view of the 1970s from the Carter economists was that the economy was in basically good shape. A record number of jobs had been created.[12] Real income rose as fast as it did in the 1950s, though not as fast as in the 1960s. Investment as a percentage of GDP remained quite high. They disagreed with the view that the problems of the 1970s proved that aggregate-demand management and government intervention in general had failed.[13]

But the electorate disagreed. They responded to the promise of candidate Ronald Reagan that he would cut taxes in such a way that would fight unemployment and inflation at the same time. They also responded to the short, sharp recession of 1980, caused by both the Federal Reserve's shift to tight money and the Carter administration's single-minded pursuit of an anti-inflation budget. The recession, though short, created great resonance for the rhetorical question asked by candidate Reagan on national television, "Are you better off now than you were four years ago?" Given the recession and the "perceived misery" of inflation, enough people answered in the negative that both Reagan and many conservative Republican senators were elected. This gave him outright control of the Senate and an ideological majority in the House with which to put his program into effect.

What is particularly interesting about this occurrence is that the tight monetary policy imposed by the Federal Reserve in late 1979 under the leadership of its new chairman, Paul Volcker, and the absence of expansionary fiscal policy by the Carter administration were in large part responsible for the affirmative answer candidate Reagan received. The success of the Volcker-Reagan program in reducing inflation and producing a recovery of the economy after the 1982 recession would have been impossible without the electorate's reaction to the 1980 recession, which itself had been caused by Volcker's change in policy. The negative reaction to the recession in 1980 proved that the public still expected (and even demanded) that the government do something about high unemployment. Because Carter was perceived as having done nothing, he was voted out of office. When the congressional elections came in 1982, the economy was once again in recession, an even deeper one. The voters took out their frustrations on Republican members of Congress despite strenuous campaigning by President Reagan. Only with the recovery of 1983–84 did the public begin to give President Reagan very high approval ratings and then reelect him in a landslide in 1984.

Radical Explanations

If we were to simplify the conservative analysis described in chapter 3, we would locate all economic difficulties in government actions that damage incentives. The mainstream response, by contrast, sees problems in the absence of government intervention, particularly the failure to achieve the economy's potential because of unemployment and low capacity utilization and periodic interruptions in economic growth. However, a nagging problem is associated with this argument. Mainstream economists have no explanation for the decline in the rate of growth of productivity that is evident from table 1. If the damaged incentives do not explain it, what does? All explanations suggested by mainstream economists appeared, by the end of the 1970s, to have accounted for at best one-third of the slower growth of productivity.[14] To provide an alternative to the conservatives, we need to turn to a group of economists whose focus on conflict attempts to explain the slowdown in economic growth and stagflation.

These economists opposed the Volcker-Reagan program from a radical point of view, a tradition in economics that begins with the work of Karl Marx. While mainstream opponents of the Reagan program stressed that the economy was not in a crisis that required the solutions proposed by supply-side economists and monetarists, radicals generally agreed that the economy showed serious structural difficulties and that reformist "business as usual" would not correct them. Clearly, they did not support the conservatives' economic policies or the analysis on which they were built. However, they did accept the premise that the economy was in deep trouble.

Whereas the conservatives identified unacceptable economic performance, especially the slowdown in productivity growth, as stemming from damaged incentives of individuals, particularly investors, radicals began with the entire structure of the economy. That structure can either facilitate rapid improvements in productivity and translate those improvements into economic growth, or it can retard growth in productivity and interfere with growth in the economy as a whole. Which of these results occur depends on the dynamics of the structure of the economy.

From the radical perspective, a powerful element of human solidarity comes out in concepts of "fairness" that are instinctively understood by participants. We noted in chapter 2 that human activity in producing goods and services depends in some measure or other on the voluntary participation of individuals in a group effort. This voluntary participation is influenced by those individuals' belief in how fairly they were being treated. This treatment certainly includes pay, but it does not relate only to pay. Other issues involved are autonomy, respect, and participation in decision making. Without a sense on the part of people that their participatory activity has some meaning behind it and that they are valued participants, their efforts will fall far short of their capabilities. If this happens to a sizable proportion of the population, the economy's ability to grow will be harmed, and desires for a rising standard of living will remain unsatisfied.

Two Aspects of the Growth in Productivity

To analyze whether the structure of an economy is helping or hindering economic growth requires an important distinction. There are two ways output per unit of labor can be increased. The first, which is a real increase in productivity, is to enhance the ability of workers to produce *using the same effort*. An example is providing workers with better machines, say substituting a scanner for a cash register at the supermarket checkout counter. Another example is using the same machines in a less wasteful way—such as substituting contour plowing for straight-line plowing, which cuts down soil erosion. Another example is providing workers with a better understanding of what their tasks so they are in a better position to anticipate problems in production and reduce downtime. Consider someone who runs a copy machine but knows nothing about how it works. This person runs the copier until it stops—because it has run out of paper, or because it has broken down—and then calls for help. Now compare someone who understands the working of the machine—not enough to repair it, but enough to open the machine and clear paper jams. Perhaps the knowledgeable operator can call for routine maintenance *before* the machine breaks, avoiding any downtime whatsoever.

All three of these examples are true increases in the productivity of labor. However, as mentioned in chapter 2, there is another way to increase productivity, one that looks the same in government statistics even though it is very different: increasing the *intensity* with which people work. This can occur by increasing the speed with which they work. Our copy machine operator, for example, can feed the machine the instant it is ready or wait several minutes before inserting the next item to be copied. As mentioned above, there is a tremendous gap between the maximum amount of work that can actually be done in the time one is on the job and the minimum (which would involve doing nothing the whole time!). Those who work in the radical tradition have always stressed the conflict between owners of businesses, who would like the physical maximum out of their employees, and the workers, who would like to finish the workday with enough physical and psychological energy to enjoy their leisure hours.

The Significance of Conflict

The conflict over the intensity with which work is done is one part of a general conflict between labor and capital that is at the heart of the radical tradition in economics. These groups (called *classes* by classical political economists and Marx) represent a division of the human factor of production in the economy. The division is based on the difference between those who own sufficient wealth-producing property (*means of production,* in Marx's language) to survive on the income from that property alone, and those who do not own sufficient property and thus must work for someone else. The "someone else" who owns sufficient property is known as the capitalist; the property is referred to as capital. Those who do not own enough capital to be independent must work for some capitalist or starve. In its most abstract form this is the simple model of a market economy that is the starting point of radical economic analysis.

Note that unlike mainstream economists, for whom the distribution of income and wealth is unimportant in explaining how the economy functions, the distribution of wealth and power is crucial to the radicals' explanation. Because wealth is distributed more unequally than income, the size of the class of capitalists is quite small, at least relative to the size of the class of workers. The difference in wealth leads to a significant imbalance of power between capitalists and workers when they meet in the workplace. Instead of workers selling their labor in a competitive market, with thousands of workers competing for jobs while hundreds of businesses compete to hire them, the radical tradition sees a rigged market with a chronic surplus of labor and a relatively small group of capitalists.

Capital makes profit only by utilizing the labor of others and paying that labor less than the total that is produced. (In Marx's language, capital exploits labor by paying labor less than the value of the product it produces.) Every rise in wages means a reduction in profit unless productivity rises faster. Sometimes, the rate of profit can be reduced even if wages do not rise. The rate of profit is the ratio of profits to capital invested, and if the amount of capital invested rises but total profits don't rise as much, then the *rate* of profit is lower. If I make $30,000 one year with a $100,000 investment, my 30 percent rate of return is excellent. If next year, I expand my investment to $500,000 and make $40,000, my rate of return is less than 10 percent, and the expanded investment will have been a failure.

According to this tradition in economic analysis, the continuous danger of falling profitability is a source of the chief successes of market economies, internally generated economic growth. The threat of reduced profitability leads owners of capital to constantly search for newer and cheaper ways of producing goods and services. Though this pattern seems commonplace today, the appearance of this behavior during the industrial revolution was an unprecedented change for humanity. Previous to the industrial revolution, human economic existence had been subject to rises and falls. Technological change was usually of the nature of a once-and-for-all adjustment, such as the development of irrigation systems. The economic systems that existed prior to the rise of capitalism did not generate pressure for constant discovery and introduction of new technology. Thus, the pace of technological change was quite slow until the rise of capitalism, the rise of market economies.

But let us recall what we have mentioned above, that growth in productivity can occur as a result of increased intensity of effort, as well as from improvements in technology. Much increased intensity is the result of a structure in which cooperation among workers and capitalists occurs. One of the key arguments of economists working in the radical tradition is that what appeared to be an unexplainable decline in productivity growth in the 1970s resulted in part from reductions in intensity of effort. To understand this process, one needs to focus on the distribution of income, wealth, and power and whether that distribution meets a popularly perceived standard of justice.

The Unequal Distribution of Income, Wealth, and Power

Assessing the impact of the distribution of income, wealth and power on the well-being of society as a whole has been controversial. First we should distinguish income from wealth. Income measures the flow of purchasing power to an individual or an institution in a given period of time, usually a year. Differences in the yearly flow of income play a major role in the ability to satisfy basic needs and discretionary wants or to accumulate assets. Many believe that differences in income flows play an important role in rewarding hard work, unique contributions, risk-taking investment—in sum, success. These rewards, coupled with the punishment of low income for slackers or for poorly skilled, unintelligent, or risk-averse individuals, are said to be the incentives necessary to make a market economy grow and prosper.

On the other hand, there are many who believe on purely ethical grounds that a more equal distribution of income is fairer than an unequal one. Alan Blinder summarized the position this way:

> That all men and women are not created equally equipped to play the economic game is clear. . . . [My] attitude holds that we ought to soften the blows for those who play the economic game and lose, or who cannot play it at all.[15]

He goes on to argue that most transfers of income from the relatively well off to the relatively bad off raise the total level of satisfaction in society because the intensity of the gain felt by the relatively poor individual is greater than the intensity of the loss felt by the well-off individual. Blinder acknowledges that these transfers cannot be pushed so far that incentives are damaged. What he does not consider is whether a distribution perceived as unjust will also damage incentives.

One of the effects of inequality in the distribution of income is that only those whose incomes are large can afford to save large amounts of current income to acquire assets. These assets—a house, jewelry, stocks, bonds, life insurance policies, a business, and so on—constitute wealth. Wealth has the potential to produce its own future income. Wealth, again, is more unequally distributed than income. Such inequality, usually based on previous inequality of income, is often seen as the reward for success.

Power is a very difficult concept to introduce into this analysis. On an elementary level, power consists of the ability of an individual or institution to compel behavior on the part of another individual or institution. For most economists, the institution that exercises power in an economy is the government. If government were relegated to a somewhat minimal role, power would be disbursed so widely as not to be a factor interfering with the functioning of the market system. The majority of economists believe that there is no significant market-determined distribution of power.

The radical response is that the power identified by mainstream economists as emanating from the government is exercised on behalf of those with sufficient wealth to influence government decisions. Those with the most economic clout are in a position to make sure that when government exercises its power to alter the economy, it almost always does so in order to enhance the profitability of certain crucial businesses or to enhance the long-run viability of a business-dominated system. Thus, the Republican desire to shrink government as expressed in the *Contract with America* does not extend to the defense establishment. From aerospace to high-speed computers to the Internet to the automobile industry, it was government production, government research and development—in short, government money—that made these industries the profit centers they are today.[16] True, sometimes the "business community" is forced to accept some limitations on its "freedom," as with the passage of the National Labor Relations Act during the depression or the development of environmental regulation in the

1970s. But by and large, the richest, most powerful individuals and institutions, far from being victimized and limited by government intervention in the economy, are for the most part subsidized and aided by such intervention. This point of view is rarely heard when policy is debated either in the media or in Congress, but scores of historical case studies support it, going all the way back to the development of numerically controlled machine tools in the early years of this century. We will have occasion to mention departures from the theoretical idea of free-market economics during the Reagan years to remind ourselves that this point of view should not be dismissed out of hand.

The Significance of Income Distribution for Economic Growth

In addition to believing that power is exercised only by government, not by private concerns based on an imbalance of wealth, the mainstream of the economics profession generally ignores the distribution of income when analyzing growth. It was not always so. Beginning with the classical political economy of David Ricardo, the distribution of income among landlords (rent), capitalists (profit), and workers (wages) was considered the key to understanding economic growth. Marx rejected the three-class model of society presented by Ricardo in favor of a two-class model, capitalists (who receive profits) and workers (who receive wages).

The significance of income distribution between wages and profits remains an important element in the radical tradition descended from Marx as well as in the post-Keynesian economic tradition. Much of the analysis emphasizes the share of profit in society as a crucial determinant of the level of investment activity. In this respect, a trend in the distribution of income that favors profits will have a positive impact on investment. Similarly, a trend favoring wages will have a negative impact.

However, the opposite effect is also possible. If income becomes too unequally distributed, the size of the market for goods and services may not grow sufficiently to justify more investment. In other words, a trend in the distribution of income that favors profits *too much* may actually have a *negative* impact on investment. In this situation, increasing wages relative to profits has a positive impact. Which of these alternative tendencies prevails will depend on many factors and cannot be simplistically captured by some notion of incentives as developed by supply-side economists.

Since radicals agree with conservatives that the economy was in deep trouble by the late 1970s, it is important to understand why they reject the mainstream view that better application of aggregate-demand management combined with policies to keep inflation from ratcheting upward was all that was necessary.

They don't accept the view of the anti-Keynesians (the new classicals, the monetarists, the supply-siders) that getting government out of the way of private sector incentives will permit the self-correcting mechanism in the system to cure business cycle downturns before they become disasters. However, they do not believe that Keynesian style aggregate-demand management is sufficient. They deny the possibility of permanent counteraction to the business cycle, but they do acknowledge that between World War II and the early 1970s, aggregate-demand management combined with a number of other factors to create a structure within which productivity growth was rapid and sustained and recessions were short and shallow.

Explaining Post–World War II Prosperity

There are two major radical schools of thought on this period of success, one we will call the stagnation school, the other the long-swing school. The differences between the two schools need not concern us here.[17] They both agree that the period from 1945 to approximately 1973 was one of extraordinary and unsustainably high growth. Among the elements that contributed to this extended period of prosperity were the following: (1) a capital-labor truce, (2) a social safety net, (3) U.S. military and economic hegemony in the world economy, (4) cheap raw materials, and (5) a government committed to preventing depressions.[18]

1. Conflict between workers and management had become quite serious during the depression and immediately following World War II. Business interests had fought bitterly against the National Labor Relations Act, which had created a legal framework under which the government could force businesses to officially recognize the union chosen by a majority of their workers. Previous to the passage of that act, businesses could recognize and bargain with unions or attempt to ignore them. If workers wanted a union to represent them and the

business did not wish to bargain, then workers would have to strike *just to be recognized*. In fact, the necessity of striking merely for recognition was held up by some members of Congress as a reason the National Labor Relations Act was necessary to *reduce* the amount of strike activity.

After a big increase in strike activity and wages right after World War II, Congress amended the National Labor Relations Act so the law would not tilt so clearly in favor of organized labor. The amendments also led to the purging of Communists from the union movement, which, while welcomed by most union leaders, reduced the potential for radical demands. By the early 1950s, many businesses had determined that they could get along with labor unions. In collective bargaining, wages and working conditions could be negotiated, but unions would explicitly ignore pricing policy and recognize "management prerogatives" that might alter the work process in order to raise productivity. Business realized that union-driven wage increases need not cause reductions in profit if productivity increased at least as much as wages. Under this accord, wages rose, the number of strikes declined, and productivity grew faster than wages for the entire period from 1945 to 1966.[19]

2. The key piece of legislation in the construction of the social safety net was the Social Security Act. Social legislation like this came late to the United States, but it was a crucial element in maintaining aggregate demand during the brief business-cycle downturns that occurred after World War II. Not only did this law create the pensions that have come to be called Social Security, but it also enacted unemployment compensation, which whenever the economy slips into a recession automatically increases the ability of laid-off workers to continue consuming at close to their previous level. If the recession is short enough, the short-term subsidies to the consumption spending of unemployed workers will keep the recession from spiraling downward as a result of rising bankruptcies by businesses dependent on workers' consumption for their survival.

In addition to cushioning the fall in aggregate demand that occurs when the economy slips into a recession, the existence of programs like Social Security creates political legitimacy for the system. In other words, those who might be losing out will be steered away from support for drastic radical proposals to restructure society if they feel that despite their personal difficulties, in general the society is dealing fairly with them and seeing to their needs. Given that capitalist societies were severely shaken by the events of the 1930s, with many countries succumbing to fascism, while in others the left-wing minority became quite strong, such political legitimacy is not to be taken lightly.

3.   With the end of World War II, the United States enjoyed a twenty-five-year period of economic and military hegemony. One aspect involved the role of the U.S. dollar as the crucial international currency. All other nations defined the value of their currency in terms of dollars. Since the United States emerged from World War II with a very large percentage of the world's monetary gold as well as owning the debt instruments of its allies, all nations wishing to engage in international economic activity needed dollars. This meant that United States businesses wishing to invest abroad merely had to use dollars to acquire these assets. Thus, the government found many willing borrowers for government assistance loans. The government also found willing sellers in countries where military facilities were deemed necessary. The role of the United States dollar as the only truly acceptable international currency meant that businesses could acquire assets abroad and the government could pursue military and political objectives abroad with United States dollars. If the rest of the world had not been not so starved for these dollars, the only way the United States economy could have pursued these goals would have been to sacrifice some domestic consumption by sending goods overseas to earn the foreign currency that would finance these activities.

However, quite early in the postwar period, dollars flowing overseas began to exceed foreign currencies flowing to the United States. Foreigners were using those dollars to build up their own international reserves and to stabilize their own currencies. The stability of this system depended on the security of the dollar's value in terms of gold and the ability of the United States military to keep the world safe for free flows of capital. This role should not be underestimated. The military hegemony of the United States helped define the "rules" for international economic behavior, especially in the world of newly independent or "Third World" nations.[20]

With the dollar underpinning international trade and the military enforcing the "rules of the game," trade barriers were reduced significantly beginning in 1949, international capital flows expanded dramatically, and the international economy as a whole experienced continuous and rapid growth.

4.   The availability of cheap petroleum is particularly important in the light of the role played by oil prices in the 1970s and 1980s. The

discovery of cheap oil in the Middle East in the late 1930s coupled with the lesson taught would-be nationalists by the overthrow of the Iranian government in 1953 guaranteed that oil prices would remain low throughout the immediate postwar period. This availability contributed to the spread of the automobile culture not only in the United States but in Europe and Japan as well. In addition to automobiles, the use of oil to heat homes and as an input into the petrochemical industry played a major role in supporting economic growth. Cheap raw materials in general help raise productivity and profits while permitting wages to rise as well.

In addition to cheap oil, the qualitatively significant surge in consumption and investment represented by the spread of the automobile culture was induced by government spending on roads and the subsidizing of mortgages. Creating and maintaining a giant "peacetime" military and using it to fight two wars (Korea and Vietnam) was the other major governmental prop to aggregate demand, providing significant jolts in the early 1950s, early 1960s, and post-1965 period.

5. Finally, the commitment by governments in all of the capitalist countries to refuse to permit a rerun of the 1930s led to the use of aggregate-demand management. Contrary to the Reagan administration critiques, radicals believe that for over twenty-five years aggregate-demand management was quite successful. The most important part of that success was the increase in the absolute and relative size of government spending as a percentage of GDP. Both schools in the radical tradition agree on the crucial role of military spending in the success of the U.S. economy after 1945.

Explaining the Slowdown of the 1970s

To explain the difficulties of the United States economy in the 1970s, those who believe that the structure described above had been the basis of the 1945–73 prosperity argue that the *very nature of the success* had within it the seeds of failure.[21] In other words, granted that this institutional structure sustained the economy in very dramatic, if uneven, growth, it was still capitalism. Capitalism has a dynamic that is constantly in danger of interruption as profitability is eroded. Every one of the successes of the 1945–72 period set in motion certain tendencies that by the late 1960s and early 1970s had produced extraordinary difficulties that ultimately led to the end of this phase of capitalism. In the United States that breakdown led to the ascendancy of conservative economics.

The capital-labor accord produced a wage-bargaining process that some economists believe contributed to the persistence of inflation even during short-term business-cycle downturns.[22] The accord also produced resentment on the part of minorities and women left out of the capital-labor truce. These groups demanded similar increases in income and status and access to the advantages of the organized labor movement. This increased the demands on capital, since business was a major source of taxes to pay for such programs. To the extent that taxes on wages were used, that increased the pressure of organized labor on business to come up with higher wages to help pay these higher taxes.

By the mid-1960s, organized labor began to feel it had sacrificed too much for the accord. Productivity increases permitted business to raise profits dramatically, while wages increased only modestly. Thus, when the late 1960s ushered in an era of very low rates of unemployment, labor was anxious to play catch-up. This conflict was not solely played out over the issue of wages. One particularly dramatic episode in the conflict over the intensity with which people work was illustrated in the struggle at the General Motors Vega plant in Lordstown, Ohio in 1972. This was a fully automated, brand-new plant, and the General Motors Assembly Division attempted to speed up the line. The workers balked, and there was a strike. The president of the local union told journalist Studs Terkel,

> In some parts of the plant, cars pass a guy at 120 un hour. The mainline goes at 101.6. They got the most modern dip system in paint. They got all the technological improvements. They got unimates. But one thing went wrong . . . They didn't have the human factor. We've been telling them since we've been here: we have a say in how hard we're going to work. They didn't believe us. Young people didn't vocalize themselves before. We're putting human before property value and profits,
> We're still making 101 cars an hour, but now we have the people back GMAD laid off. They tried to create a speed-up by using less people. We stopped 'em.[23]

The unwillingness of workers to accept the continuous increase in the intensity with which they work and more aggressive efforts to raise wages combined to create a squeeze on profits. When business began to find its profits squeezed, labor was unwilling to moderate wage demands until forced by recessions in the mid-1970s and especially by the recessions of 1980 and 1981–82. The capital-labor accord proved unsustainable in the wake of the squeeze on profits. By the end of the 1970s, there was no more capital-labor truce, and the best evidence of this is the dramatic rise in the rate of inflation coupled with the decline in real wages.

The social safety net was initially quite modest. It did not apply to all workers, and initially the ratio of workers to beneficiaries was quite high. In the 1960s, the social safety net expanded dramatically, and the reason for that spread is not hard to understand. Once the link between work for a capitalist and income is broken in principle, there is no reason why every citizen should not be entitled to access to such programs. If securing the political legitimacy of the system requires a "citizen wage" to supplement the private-sector wage that is paid for contributing to a capitalist's profit, then all groups in society with a potential complaint about the system (discriminated-against minorities and women, the poor in general) need to be co-opted according to the already existing formulas. This is what happened in the 1960s with the spread of the safety net.

For much of the 1960s and 1970s, the spread of the safety net actually succeeded in significantly reducing poverty. Unfortunately, this also reduced the leverage of capital on the working class. In effect, it reduced the *power* of capital to get workers to work harder even though there was less promise of increased income. This showed up in the statistics as a decline in productivity growth, but even before that, there was a decline in the rate of profit. With the fall in productivity growth in the 1970s, the safety net became too expensive, and capital began to fight back. By the end of the 1970s, the means-tested entitlement programs had ceased growing (in fact, inflation was reducing some real benefit levels). However, Social Security had been made inflation-proof and rose quite rapidly through the end of the decade. From the perspective of this analysis, the system that had been so successful between 1945 and 1972 was now too expensive. The ascendancy of conservative economics marks a very strong effort to escape from that difficulty by changing the rules. The push to balance the budget can here be seen as a way of making sure those rules are permanently changed. Budget balance, especially by constitutional amendment, would make it virtually impossible for the majority of the population to push through spending programs because it would require tax increases to fund them.

Note that the radical interpretation has a lot in common with the conservative analysis. Both groups agreed that there were fundamental problems with the economy as it existed at the end of the 1970s. In this they were united against the more sanguine views of the mainstream group of economists, who saw problems but didn't believe such radical solutions were necessary. On the other hand, the radicals disagreed with both the conservative and the mainstream economists because the latter two groups focused on altering the role of government in a basically private-enterprise economy. The radicals believed that the nature of hierarchy and power and inequality in a private-enterprise economy was at the root of America's problems. They believed further that neither the liberal reformism of the mainstream economists nor the radical conservatism of the Reagan administration would solve the economy's problems. Today, with the debate focusing on how to balance the budget and shrink government, we see the same dichotomy in the responses of liberals and radicals to those proposals. The liberals say the Republican proposals go too far, while the radicals assert that the proposals have nothing to do with solutions to our economic problems but everything to do with diverting the attention of the population from what is really wrong.

5

The "Revolutionary Offensive," 1979–84

In 1979 the Federal Reserve announced that it was no longer going to "target" interest rates but would instead concentrate on controlling the growth of the money supply. With this decision, the Central Bank was announcing its conversion to monetarism. Henceforth, monetary policy would consist of controlling the rate of growth of money and letting the market determine interest rates.

This was the year of the second surge in oil prices (the first had occurred in 1973–74). The Iranian revolution had occurred in the beginning of the year, and the initial disruption of oil flows led to a big increase in prices. Just as in 1973–74, that produced an upward surge of inflation in the United States.[1]

Meanwhile, the international value of the dollar fell from 1976 through 1979,[2] and by the end of 1979, central bankers from the other advanced countries of the world were insisting that the United States government do something to stop its persistent inflation and the declining dollar. The reasons are instructive. The declining dollar was reducing the real value (purchasing power) of the dollar reserves held by foreign central banks. Recall that the entire international payments system since World War II had been dependent on the dollar as the major international currency. Even when the major economies of the world had gotten onto their feet in the 1950s, the dollar remained the most important international currency because it was rigidly tied to gold at the price of thirty-five dollars an ounce. The stability of the dollar price of gold meant that central banks could build up dollar deposits for future international purchases and have confidence that they would be accepted elsewhere in the world years into the future.

Even after the dollar price of gold began to rise in the early 1970s, the United States as the largest single economy in the world still remained the logical source of international currency reserves. If the rate of inflation in the United States were not high relative to rates elsewhere in the world, then the dollar would remain a good reserve currency. Thus, the Organization of Petroleum Exporting Countries continued to price oil in dollars, even after the significant U.S. inflation of 1974–75.

Money plays three roles. It is a medium of exchange, a standard of value, and a store of value. We use money for the convenience of buying milk, gasoline, clothing, theater tickets, and automobiles and for making investments. Without a universally accepted medium of exchange, each time we wanted milk or gasoline, we would need to find a dairy farmer or oil refiner who needed something we could supply (in my case, economics lessons!). We also use money for the convenience of getting paid in something universally accepted. Otherwise, I would have to peddle this book *only* to dairy farmers, oil refiners, and others who had what I wanted.

Money's role as a store of value is also quite important. When I put my month's salary in the bank, I am confident that I can leave it there for the entire month and maybe more before I need it to pay the next bill. I do not need to worry that by the time I am ready to use it to buy something, the price of that something will have doubled or tripled or worse.

In international economic relations, the dollar was both the principle medium of exchange and the principle store of value, even after the dollar price of gold began to rise. People from, say, Austria could purchase something produced in France even if they didn't have any French francs as long as they had dollars. The United States experienced less inflation than other advanced countries between 1973 and 1976, and that helped the dollar retain its role as an international store of value.[3]

However, during 1978 and 1979, foreign central bankers began to suspect that the Fed was letting the dollar slide in value. There even was a term for this policy, "malign neglect." The problem was that for American policymakers there was a contradiction involved in the desire to keep the dollar an important international currency (which required stability in its role as a store of value) and the desire to maintain the international competitiveness of American export goods (and the domestic competitiveness of goods that had significant competition from imports). A declining dollar produced declining prices for American exports and rising prices for imports into the United States. However, the declining dollar and worry about *future* declines led some to begin to question the long-run stability of the entire international-payments system.

In 1973, the international community had abandoned all pretense of maintaining a system of fixed exchange rates among currencies with the dollar anchored to gold. In 1974 and 1975, the price of gold averaged just over $160 per ounce, ranging from a low of $117 to a high of $194.[4] The average price fell in 1976 and rose in 1978. The next year saw the largest percentage increase in the average price since 1974, the year of the previous oil price shock. The average for all of 1979 was $307, but it was well above that by the end of the year. The highest recorded price for the year was $517 in December. This price rise was a sign that skittish international investors were beginning to hedge against problems with *all* currencies, not just weak ones. By January 1980, the price had peaked at $850, and some were beginning to seriously consider whether to stem worldwide inflation it would be necessary to reestablish an anchor whereby the dollar would be permanently worth some amount of some commodity, most likely gold.[5]

However, despite such skittishness, there was a positive side for the U.S. economy. Lowering the prices of American exports while raising the dollar price of American imports could play a role in reducing the trade deficit. A trade deficit occurs when Americans purchase more abroad than foreigners purchase in the United States, resulting in a net outflow of dollars. This outflow reduces aggregate demand, because the dollars spent overseas do not employ Americans and do not (for the most part) increase the income of Americans. In 1977, the trade deficit was 1.2 percent of GDP. The previous high had occurred in 1972, when it was .6 percent. By 1980, the decline in the value of the dollar had reduced the trade deficit to near .5 percent of GDP.[6]

On balance the reduced trade deficit did not outweigh the dangers to the international payments system that persistent U.S. inflation was creating. Thus, the newly appointed chairman of the Federal Reserve Board, Paul Volcker, decided to abandon incremental interest rate increases in favor of something dramatic that would shock the financial markets out of their inflationary expectations.[7] On September 28, 1979, he persuaded his colleagues on the Federal Reserve Board to target the money supply instead of interest rates. After a few days at a major international conference, he returned to the United States, where the full Federal Open Market Committee agreed to the policy change.[8]

The long-run impact of this change was that interest rate increases could henceforth be identified as "market driven," not caused by Fed policy. The willingness to hold the line on monetary growth and do nothing no matter how high interest rates went signaled full commitment to the goals of crushing inflation and preserving the international-reserve status of the dollar. In a statement before the Joint Economic Committee of the Congress, eleven days after the announcement, Volcker spelled out the goal of what he called "the new measures": "Above all, [they] should make abundantly clear our unwillingness to finance a continuing inflationary process."[9]

The "Monetarist Experiment"

Tracking the immediate impact of Federal Reserve monetary policy requires observing a crucial interest rate, the Federal Funds rate. Every day, at the close of business, commercial banks in the Federal Reserve System must have a certain percentage of their outstanding deposits either on hand as reserves or on deposit at a local Federal Reserve Bank. These reserves cannot be invested by the bank either in government securities or in loans to the private sector. They just have to sit there. Since these reserves produce no income for the bank, banks want to minimize them. On the other hand, they violate the law if they do not have the required level of reserves at the close of business every day.

The Federal Funds market is one in which banks whose reserves exceed the legal requirement make overnight loans to banks whose reserves are below the legal requirement. The interest charged on those loans is called the Federal Funds rate. When the Fed engages in monetary manipulations to alter the availability of reserves to banks, it changes the availability of these overnight monies, thereby altering the interest rate.

It is not surprising, therefore, to see the Federal Funds rate jump from an average of 10–11 percent during the first three quarters of 1979 to an average of 13.58 percent in the last quarter of 1979.[10] Meanwhile, the rate of growth of money (M1, the narrowest measure), which had been rising since 1974, peaked at 8.2 percent per year in 1978 before falling to 6.8 percent in 1979. Then, the Fed was able to hold the line on M1 growth for two more years.[11] Perhaps just as important as what the Fed did was what the Fed said. The next "Monetary Report to Congress" stated,

> Monetary policy clearly has a major role to play in the restoration of price stability. . . . inflation can be sustained over the long run only if the resulting higher level of dollar expenditures is accommodated through monetary expansion. The Federal Reserve is determined not to provide that sustenance, but will adhere instead to a course, in 1980 and beyond, aimed at wringing the inflation out of the economy over time. . . . If recessionary tendencies should develop during 1980 . . . the steady anti-inflationary policy stance represented by continuing restraint on growth in the supply of money and credit would be consistent with an easing of conditions in financial markets, as demands for money and credit weaken.[12]

In addition to promising to adhere to this policy until inflation was defeated, the Fed also promised that declines in interest rates would only occur if the *demand* for credit slackened. There would be no greater increases in the supply of money and credit, even in the case of a recession.

Interestingly enough, both M2 and M3 (broader measures of the money supply) did not respond to this policy change. From 1979 through 1981, the rate of growth of both measures of the money supply increased.[13] Meanwhile, the Federal Funds rate fluctuated wildly.[14] It reached its peak in June 1981 at 19.1 percent. The recession began in August 1981, causing the rate to fall to 12.37 percent by year's end. In the face of a worsening recession, for the first seven months of 1982 the Fed stuck to its restrictive policy, and the rate never fell below 12.5 percent. Finally, in August 1982, the rate began to fall, reaching a nadir of 8.51 percent in February 1983.[15]

By the middle of 1982, the Fed had abandoned its "monetarist experiment" and let M1 rise faster than its initial target for that year. At the end of that year, the Fed was talking about maintaining a concentration on "monetary aggregates," but in fact the stringent adherence to monetary targets was honored in the breach. M1 growth rose to 8.7 percent in 1982, to 9.8 percent in 1983, fell back to 5.9 percent in 1984, and rose dramatically to 12.3 and 16.9 percent in 1985 and 1986.[16] The Federal Funds rate rose to another peak in August 1984 (11.64 percent) before beginning a long decline to 7.53 percent in 1985 and 5.89 percent in 1986.

Now it is important to understand that these numbers for M1 growth and for the Federal Funds rate are introduced merely to show the direction of Fed policy. How did the economy respond? The rate of inflation peaked in 1980 and then began to fall.[17] The Fed's control over the money supply led to a sharp rise in all interest rates in 1981. As mentioned above, the Federal Funds rate peaked at 19.1 percent in June. An important interest rate for the business sector, the prime rate peaked at 12.5 percent in January, and mortgage rates peaked at 16.38 percent in November.[18] Real interest rates also took a dramatic jump upward in 1981.[19] By any measure, therefore, the Fed succeeded in making monetary policy very restrictive up to the end of 1982. At that point, fears of a worldwide default on loans by Third World countries unable to service debts to U.S. and other international banks at the sky-high interest rates then prevailing, coupled with fears that the recession might lead to a major depression, temporarily overcame the Fed's desire to fight inflation at any cost.

Freeing Interest Rates from Controls

Another very important change occurred in 1980 that would have tremendous implications for the impact of monetary policy over the next decade. In March 1980 Congress passed the Depository Institutions Deregulation and Monetary Control Act. The principal elements of the bill gave the Fed a lever of control over banks that were not members of the Federal Reserve System. The bill imposed reserve requirements on all banks. It also removed all interest rate ceilings and repealed Regulation Q, a rule with which the Fed had controlled the interest rates of commercial banks and savings and loan institutions, preserving a differential that gave savings and loans an advantage in attracting small savers' deposits. Though no one realized it at the time, this law was the first step toward the complete deregulation of the savings and loan sector of the economy, with consequences that we are still living with today.[20]

Regulation Q in effect kept free markets from determining certain crucial prices—that is, interest rates. Economists usually are opposed to any form of price control. Economics textbooks attempt to show that minimum-wage laws, rent control, price controls on gasoline, "usury" laws (which put caps on interest rates), and so forth result in an artificial shortage of, and an inefficient distribution of, the good or service with the controlled price.

The argument is based on supply and demand. The price and quantity sold of any item depend on the number of people who want to buy it (and how many each wants) at various alternative prices, matched up against the different quantities of the item that producers are willing and able to offer for sale at alternative prices. People willing to pay a higher price for a product are viewed as gaining a greater satisfaction from it than those willing to pay only a lower price. Meanwhile, the willingness of producers to offer quantities of an item is constrained by the scarcity of the resources used in producing it. Thus, higher prices are necessary to cover the higher costs of increasing production. At only one price, the equilibrium, will the total quantity offered for sale by the producers be exactly balanced by the total quantity purchased by consumers. At a lower price, a shortage will develop, showing that both producers and consumers would be happier if a higher quantity were offered for sale at the higher price. If that lower price cannot rise toward the equilibrium (say with price controls on gasoline), that shortage will persist. The clear conclusion is that the artificial shortage interferes with the efficiency of the market. The purpose of the market is to stretch our limited resources to satisfy as much of our unlimited wants as possible. The existence of such artificial shortages clearly interferes with our efforts to make our limited resources satisfy us as much as possible.[21]

Before returning to Regulation Q, let us examine other examples of price controls to see how economists have argued against them. Rent control typically limits what can be charged to tenants in certain apartment buildings. The existence of these limits allegedly signals to builders and owners of buildings that they will not be able to receive high-enough incomes to justify increasing supply. This leads to a slower growth in housing than would exist without the controls. Rent control is often blamed for the deterioration of existing housing stock, as owners feel the rate of return is too low to justify ongoing maintenance.

An artificially high price, such as a minimum wage, according to this approach, reduces the willingness of employers to hire low-skilled workers and raises the unemployment rate of such workers. That is, there will be a surplus of workers willing and able to work at the artificially high wage. Employers would be willing and able to hire more workers if the wage would fall, and some of the currently surplus workers would be willing and able to work if the wage would fall. Thus, the artificially high wage reduces employment.[22] Price controls on gasoline in both 1974 and 1979 produced shortages similar to those caused by rent control, according to this argument. There were long lines at the gasoline pumps. People were willing and able to buy more gasoline than they in fact could get.

When we apply this reasoning to financial markets, the conclusion is that state-imposed (and Federal Reserve–imposed) limits on the interest rates that banks can charge and pay reduce the flow of savings to those institutions and then from those institutions to borrowers. Regulation Q, for example, meant that commercial banks and savings and loan institutions could not attract deposits in competition with other lending institutions whose ability to offer interest to depositors was unconstrained. Interest ceilings on, for example, home mortgage rates had produced periods of disintermediation (periods when new lending ceases) whenever the Fed tightened up on monetary policy. Higher interest rates would push up against legal ceilings. Instead of efficiently rationing the credit among borrowers most intensely desiring the funds and therefore willing and able to pay the higher interest rates, all supply of the particular kind of credit would cease. In the case of mortgages,

> It was not that borrowers such as home buyers or contractors were necessarily unwilling to pay higher interest rates—the shutdown came from investors, who refused to provide the money when they knew their returns were artificially depressed by the government ceilings. An investor who held funds in a regulated account at a savings and loan, drawing 5 percent or so, would withdraw his money and move it to another storage place, one that was unregulated and promised a much higher return.[23]

From the point of view of supply and demand these regulations were grossly inefficient. From the point of view of Federal Reserve control over the economy, however, this situation meant that with slight increases in interest rates, the Fed could shut off credit creation and slow, even stop, the economy. Thus Regulation Q had an upside. The downside was apparent during periods of inflation such as were experienced in the 1970s. Unregulated money market funds offered interest rates well in excess of those limited by Regulation Q. Assets in such funds tripled in 1978 to a total of $9.5 billion, growing to $42.9 billion in 1979 and to $236.3 billion by 1982.[24]

In repealing the Regulation Q ceilings, the 1980 law also raised the limit of insured deposits to a maximum of one hundred thousand dollars, thereby permitting savings and loans to attract large deposits with very high interest rates. In order to cover those high interest rates, S&L's were further permitted to diversify their portfolios beyond home mortgages. Up to 20 percent of their assets could now be in consumer loans, commercial paper, or corporate debt. With insurance on the deposits they took, these banks were now primed to seek out the riskiest, and therefore highest-paying, loans available. If they succeeded, they made money. If not, the depositors would be insured anyway.

An Important Implication of Financial Deregulation

Another impact of deregulation was that the Fed could no longer stop the economy quickly by driving interest rates up to the legal ceiling, thereby inducing disintermediation. From 1980 forward, the Fed would have to drive interest rates much higher in order to achieve the kind of monetary slowdown they had promised. Note how this need for higher interest rates than in the past when attempting to fight inflation was satisfied by the ostensible change of policy focus from interest rates to money growth. While higher interest rates helped restrain inflation by restraining aggregate demand, particularly in 1984, a bubble of debt kept expanding throughout the decade until the savings and loan debacle in 1989 revealed that the taxpayers had just been stuck with a $180-billion-dollar loss.

As the Federal Reserve drove interest rates higher and higher in 1981, the Reagan administration not only failed to argue against that policy, they actually supported it. In the first report by the Reagan Council of Economic Advisers the members asserted that one of the pillars of the administration's policy was "in cooperation with the Federal Reserve, making a new commitment to a monetary policy that will restore a stable currency and healthy financial markets."[25] This was in marked contrast to the responses of previous administrations when confronted by tight money policies. In previous situations of anti-inflation policy, members of Congress and members of administrations would regularly complain about the Fed's unfair high-interest policies and blame the "independent" Fed for thwarting a recovery or not doing enough to fight a recession. A few members of Congress would usually use this occasion to recommend "taking a look" at the independence of the Fed. This complaining did not occur in 1981 and in fact in did not happen until quite late in 1982. The Reagan administration made it very clear by what they said and by what they did not say that the Fed's anti-inflation policy was acceptable, even though it was causing a recession. For example, in February 1982, with the recession deepening, President Reagan went out of his way to support the Fed.

> I want to make clear today that neither this administration nor the Federal Reserve will allow a return to the fiscal and monetary policies of the past that have created the current conditions. . . . I have confidence in the announced policies of the Federal Reserve Board. The Administration and the Federal Reserve can help bring inflation and interest rates down faster by working together than by working at cross-purposes. This administration will always support the political independence of the Federal Reserve Board.[26]

Unfortunately, the fiscal policy that was the ultimate result of the Reagan administration tax and spending policies did produce some "working at cross-purposes." We turn now to the policies introduced by the Reagan administration as part of the turnaround in economic policy.

Reaganomics: The Economic Recovery Tax Act

In its first year in office, the Reagan administration made significant strides in implementing its new approach to fiscal policy and other government interventions into the economy. The two fiscal policy elements in the Reagan program are summarized by the Council of Economic Advisers as "cutting the rate of growth in Federal spending" and "reducing personal income tax rates and creating jobs by accelerating depreciation for business investment in plant and equipment."[27] Table 5 summarizes the changes in the personal income tax (for married couples filing jointly).

The change in tax policy had been promised in the campaign and had been on the legislative agenda at least since 1978, when Representative Jack Kemp and Senator William Roth had proposed a three-year, 30 percent across-the-board reduction in personal income tax rates. That supply-side proposal was combined with a major overhaul of depreciation guidelines, and the result was the Economic Recovery Tax Act of 1981. The council described its main impact as "shifting the burden of taxation away from capital income, thereby providing substantially greater incentives for capital investments and personal saving."[28] Note that this is not quite what supply-side economic theory had called for. Supply-siders had argued that all income should be subjected to lower marginal tax rates and that this would increase the incentives not only to save and invest but encourage workers to enter

TABLE 5. Changes in the Federal Income Tax Resulting from ERTA (married couples filing jointly)

Taxable-Income Bracket ($)	Tax Rate before ERTA (%)	ERTA Tax Rates		
		1982	1983	1984
0–3,400	0	0	0	0
3,400–5,500	14	12	11	11
5,500–7,600	16	14	13	12
7,600–11,900	18	16	15	14
11,900–16,000	21	19	17	16
16,000–20,200	24	22	19	18
20,200–24,600	28	25	23	22
24,600–29,900	32	29	26	25
29,900–35,200	37	33	30	28
35,200–45,800	43	39	35	33
45,800–60,000	49	44	40	38
60,000–85,000	54	49	44	42
85,000–109,400	59	50	48	45
109,400–162,400	64	50	50	50
162,400–215,400	68	50	50	50
215,400 and over	70	50	50	50

Source: Joint Committee on Taxation, *General Explanation of the Economic Recovery Tax Act of 1981* (Washington, DC: Government Printing Office, 1981), 405; cited in Lawrence B. Lindsey, *The Growth Experiment: How tthe New Tax Policy Is Transforming the U.S. Economy* (New York: Basic Books, 1990), 51.

the labor force. In other words, the supply of savings and entrepreneurship would rise, but also the supply of labor.

In fact, because of rises in Social Security payroll taxes already scheduled, between 1980 and 1985 the actual ratio of federal taxes paid on income rose for the bottom 40 percent of the population and fell for the top 60 percent of the population. For the top 5 percent of the population that fall was from an average rate of 29.7 percent in 1980 to 24.4 percent in 1985, while for the top 1 percent the fall was from 31.9 percent to 24.5 percent.[29] Since ownership of capital is concentrated in these high-income groups, it is clear that the rate of taxation on capital income did fall quite dramatically. In 1980, while the top 20 percent of the population received 43.5 percent of the wage income, that same top 20 percent received 70 percent of the rents, interest, and dividends and 89 percent of the capital gains. By 1985, the top 20 percent had increased its share of wages (46 percent) and capital gains (94.5 percent) while suffering a negligible percentage decline in rents, interest, and dividends (to 69.5 percent).[30]

One other important aspect of the Economic Recovery Tax Act should be mentioned. In order to avoid any future problem of bracket creep, the act included a provision that after the three years of rate cutting, all tax brackets would henceforth be *indexed* to the rate of inflation. That meant that each year's previous increase in the consumer price index would be applied to the endpoints of each tax bracket. So, if the rate of inflation were 4.3 percent in 1984, each of the income levels defining the brackets in table 5 would be raised by that amount. This would guarantee that a rise in money wages to keep up with inflation would not subject a taxpayer to a higher marginal tax rate. According to tax expert C. Eugene Steuerle, this feature of ERTA provided over time the most significant level of tax relief by far. He estimated that the indexing provision saved taxpayers $57 billion between 1984 and 1990. That was half of the reduction that resulted from the combination of ERTA tax cuts and the many subsequent changes in the individual and corporate income taxes and the Social Security payroll tax for the rest of the decade.[31]

Regulatory Relief

Though the tax changes were the major focus of the supply-side wing of the Reagan economic policymaking team, they were not the only elements in the Reagan administration's program. Murray Weidenbaum had been appointed as head of the Council of Economic Advisers, and it was obvious that this strong critic of expensive government regulation would make every effort to reduce what he believed to be a heavy burden on the private sector. Very early in the Reagan administration, Executive Order 12291 directed federal agencies "to use benefit-cost analysis when promulgating new regulations, reviewing existing regulations or developing legislative proposals concerning regulation."[32] One of the elements of this order was to force all newly proposed regulations to be approved by the Office of Management and Budget before being published in the *Federal Register*.

In addition, a Task Force on Regulatory Relief chaired by then vice president George Bush was set up to assess already existing regulations. Within the first year of operations, they looked at one hundred existing regulations and targeted over a third for elimination or revision.[33] Even more important than these specific activities, the Reagan administration signaled by key cabinet appointments that it would be much more circumspect in using of existing regulations. James Watt, appointed secretary of the interior, and Anne Gorsuch (later Burford), appointed to head the Environmental Protection Agency, were the most dramatic examples of individuals who by virtue of their attitudes toward regulations on private-sector activity would be disinclined to use the powers of their agencies to interfere with business, even if those businesses were engaging in technical violations of existing rules or statutes. In fact, over the next few years, many supporters of stronger environmental regulations called the activities of these departments "repeal by nonenforcement." What this meant was that since the statutes governing protection of the environment, the Clean Air Act, the Clean Water Act, the new Superfund Act were not going to be repealed by Congress, the only way to reduce the burdens of regulation imposed by these acts on business was not to enforce them. This cynical view was re-enforced when one of Gorsuch-Burford's appointees, Rita Lavelle, was found to have perjured herself before Congress on her contacts with businesses that were under investigation for pollution violations. In the ensuing controversy, Burford herself resigned.[34]

In the area of civil-rights enforcement, the Reagan administration pursued similar policies. The two major regulatory bodies were the Office of Federal Contract Compliance Programs (OFCCP) in the Department of Labor and the Equal Employment Opportunities Commission (EEOC). The latter was charged with processing complaints of discrimination in employment, while the former actually issued affirmative action guidelines to government contractors on the hiring of racial minorities and women. By the 1970s it had become clear to most people in the civil-rights community that it was not sufficient to outlaw overt discrimination. Subtle, hard-to-detect instances of discrimination could have the same impact as outright prohibitions against hiring, say, a woman electrician or a black firefighter. This is where affirmative action comes in.

The concept of affirmative action has been so distorted by arguments about "reverse discrimination" and "quotas" that it is useful to recall what the term actually means. It means that when a historical pattern of discrimination has left a business, an institution, or an occupation disproportionately white and/or male, the entity in question must try to remedy the imbalance. Sometimes this effort might involve vigorous advertising among groups that had previously not been hired. Sometimes it might involve serious reconsideration of the credentials required for the job. For example, clerks in stores may not need a high school education in order to do their work, and in certain localities, requiring a high school diploma would exclude many ethnic minorities.

During the 1970s, the roles of both the EEOC and the OFCCP were expanded. The EEOC was given the power to sue businesses over alleged discriminatory practices. The OFCCP began to review government contractors' affirmative action programs before contracts were awarded. Though quotas were never imposed by these organizations, an effort was made to encourage businesses to set "goals" and "timetables" for increasing minority and/or female employment.

No matter how justified these activities might have been, even good-faith efforts to comply with the letter and spirit of the various civil-rights acts and to satisfy the EEOC and/or the OFCCP would clearly increase the costs to business. Thus, the increasing role of the government in civil-rights enforcement also fits into the Weidenbaum analysis. On top of this, as affirmative action programs became more and more intrusive, the opposition to the substance of affirmative action became stronger. Whenever a group of people are vying for a job, affirmative action involves some form of favoritism to members of a group that had been subjected to discrimination in the past.[35] The Reagan administration, by their appointments and actions, came down strongly on the side of those who see most affirmative action as involving unfair "reverse discrimination."

This approach neatly dovetailed with the more general view, following Weidenbaum, that government intervention into the hiring and promotion processes of private-sector firms imposed substantial costs on businesses. The rising costs of regulation had been blamed by many economists for at least part of the unacceptable slowdown in productivity growth in the period before Reagan's election. When one couples the cost of compliance with civil-rights-dictated policies with the view that the impact of affirmative action is negative (because of "reverse discrimination"), the result is a requirement that the benefits of regulation be carefully justified.

President Reagan appointed William Bradford Reynolds to head the Civil Rights Division of the Justice Department. He opposed the use of goals, timetables, and, of course, quotas as responses to past discrimination. Reynolds told Congress,

> We no longer will insist upon or in any respect support the use of quotas or any other numerical or statistical formulae designed to provide non-victims of discrimination preferential treatment based on race, sex, national origin or religion.[36]

Nonvictims were here identified as racial minorities and/or women attempting to find jobs or achieve promotions in companies or other institutions that had practiced discrimination in the past. The Reagan administration made it clear that individuals who had not themselves been subjected to discrimination had no right to compensation.

The Reagan Justice Department attempted to get the courts to declare unconstitutional affirmative action agreements that involved fixed-percentage hiring to police and fire departments. In addition, it intervened to attempt to overturn fifty-one affirmative action plans in other governmental bodies that had fairly strict goals and timetables. At first, the courts did not support these actions, but by the end of the decade, enough Reagan appointees had been appointed to the Supreme Court to shift the burden of proof in many cases of alleged discrimination.[37]

In the early Reagan budgets, all areas of civil-rights enforcement suffered budget and personnel cuts. The Civil Rights Division was held to level funding (which reduced its real funding because of inflation), so that staff declined by 13 percent between the 1981 and 1983 fiscal years. The OFCCP budget fell 24 percent in real terms, and staff was cut 34 percent, while at the EEOC the (real) budget fell 10 percent and staff fell 12 percent. Note this was at a time that the population was rising, the size of the labor force was rising, and the number of complaints received was going up.

Sanctions against companies found to have wrongfully discriminated also fell dramatically. Because of the administration's argument "that only identifiable victims should be compensated,"[38] awards for back pay fell from $9 million in 1980 to less than $4 million in 1983.[39] This sent a powerful message to business that the cost of engaging in discriminatory behavior (or of failing to vigorously pursue affirmative action policies) would be much lower than during the Carter years.

Clarence Pendleton, a member of the small but very prominent group of black conservatives (whose prominence was enhanced at a conference held right after the 1980 election in Fairmont, California) was appointed head of the Civil Rights Commission. Clarence Thomas, another attendee at the conference, was named head of the Equal Employment Opportunities Commission. Both organizations backed away from vigorous pursuit of affirmative action programs. Indeed, Mssrs. Thomas and Pendleton were widely quoted as opposing most forms of affirmative action, such as "set asides," "goals and timetables," and so forth, because they were, in their view, impossible to enforce without violating the "color-blindness" of the civil-rights statutes and the Fourteenth Amendment to the Constitution.[40]

It is safe to say, in summary, that the Reagan administration represented an entirely new climate for the regulation of business. Not only was the increase in regulations slowed, but major efforts were made to extend the deregulation that had already begun under Jimmy Carter. In 1978, airlines had been deregulated.[41] In 1980, steps toward reduced regulation in interstate trucking and railroads were taken. In 1981 began the deregulation of intercity bus transportation. Following up on the 1980 banking law, new regulations were issued permitting mortgage-lending institutions to offer variable-rate mortgages as a way of protecting lending institutions from unexpected surges in inflation. In 1982, Congress passed and President Reagan signed the Garn-St. Germaine Act, which effectively decontrolled savings and loan institutions. This completed the process begun in 1980 and permitted them to compete for loans with higher interest rates and money market accounts and to diversify their assets beyond low-yield mortgages.

In the area of broadcasting, the Federal Communications Commission deregulated most commercial radio broadcasting and simplified the license-renewal application. As part of the Omnibus Budget Reconciliation Act of 1981, Congress extended the period between license renewals for television and radio stations. The rationale for these changes and for the settlement of the AT&T antitrust suit was that competition from new directions was vitiating the original rationales for regulation. In the area of television, cable TV provided new areas of competition that reduced the necessity for government regulation. In the area of telecommunications, AT&T was subject to new competition in setting long-distance rates and selling/leasing equipment and that meant the subsidy from one part of AT&T to another was not as great a concern as previously. The settlement of the suit cut AT&T loose from its monopolies of local telephone service to sink or swim in the competitive markets for long-distance service and equipment. Meanwhile, each local system would continue to be regulated at the local level.[42]

According to research done by the Center for the Study of American Business, between 1981 and 1984 real dollars spent on regulation fell slightly. If we assume that the indirect costs of compliance remained in the same ratio to the budgets of regulatory agencies, this represented a real reduction in the regulatory burden on business. Even more important, this provided a significant brake in the trend that had seen regulatory budgets more than double between 1970 and 1981.[43]

Redistribution of Income

When it came to redistribution of income, the Reagan administration's first set of proposals contained in the Omnibus Budget Reconciliation Act (OBRA) of 1981 attempted to reduce benefits and eligibility for a number of means-tested programs. The major means-tested program that comes to mind when people think of "welfare" is Aid to Families with Dependent Children. Before it was abolished in 1996, this program was administered by the states, and thus benefits and eligibility rules varied. However, since the federal government provided a significant amount of the revenue necessary to finance the program,[44] it was able to force the states to change their rules, by the device of making certain rules necessary for the receipt in federal revenues.

Since AFDC was a means-tested program, rules had to be set up to "test the means" of the potential recipients. One approach would be to restrict AFDC to people with no income, but that would create the perverse effect of encouraging people with minimal income to refrain from earning any (or hiding what they do earn) in order to qualify. Another simple procedure would be to permit people to earn income but reduce the AFDC grant one dollar for each dollar earned. This would, however, create the same disincentive to earn—at least up to the AFDC grant itself—because the recipient would be subjected to a 100 percent marginal tax rate.

So states are required to disregard some income in determining eligibility and benefits. A numerical example provided by the House Ways and Means Committee *Green Book* showed that before 1981, AFDC recipients with low levels of outside earnings would find their benefits reduced approximately 34 cents for every dollar of outside earnings. As a result of the passage of OBRA in 1981, the benefits were reduced on average 47 cents for every dollar of outside earnings in the first four months on welfare, and that reduction increased to 75 cents per dollar after four months.[45] The administration attempted to get Congress to go further, asking that when families shared housing, the part counted as "need" for the purposes of determining eligibility and benefit level would be prorated as a percentage of the cost of that housing. They also requested that any energy assistance received by families be counted as income against the AFDC grant. Congress rejected these aspects of the administration proposal.

According to the Urban Institute, the changes that Congress did accept meant the AFDC program cost 14 percent less in 1985 than it would have had the changes not occurred. An administration official testified that "408,000 families lost eligibility and 299,000 lost benefits as a result of the OBRA changes. The changes saved the Federal and State governments about $1.1 billion in 1983."[46] These results are even more significant if we recall that 1981–82 was a period of quite substantial recession. The number of individuals in poverty increased from 29.27 million in 1980 (13 percent of the population) to 35.3 million (15.2 percent of the population) in 1983 before beginning to fall (though the percentage did not go below 13 percent until 1989).[47] In 1980, the number of individuals receiving AFDC in an average month was 10.6 million, or 36 percent of those in poverty. By 1985, the number of AFDC recipients had risen to 10.8, million representing only 32 percent of those in poverty. Note that this was in the third year of the recovery from the recession of 1981–82.[48] There is no question that the administration's cuts succeeded in decreasing the availability of this means-tested program.

Another important means-tested entitlement is the food stamp program. This program is completely funded by the federal government, and the rules of eligibility are set at the federal level. The first and second Reagan budgets, as well as the Agriculture and Food Act of 1981, reduced the cost of the program, by tightening eligibility among other things. According to the Congressional Budget Office, these changes saved $7 billion for the fiscal years 1982 through 1985. The immediate impact was that in 1982, when the recession was most severe, the number of people participating in the program actually fell, while the percentage of people in poverty receiving food stamps fell from 64.7 percent in 1981 to 59.3 percent the next year.[49] The total spending on food stamps (in inflation-adjusted dollars) also fell between 1981 and 1982.[50] Then in 1983, the number of participants and the percentage of the poor receiving benefits increased. In 1984, the percentage of the poor receiving food stamps rose and then began a decline that continued until 1988. Meanwhile, the absolute number of participants declined from 1983 through 1988. Thus, despite the fact that the recession increased the number of people eligible for food stamps, the changes enacted in 1981 and 1982 significantly slowed participation over the next three years.[51]

Medicaid is another important means-tested entitlement and by far the most expensive. It involves payments directly to health care providers to cover the treatment of enrollees. Anyone on AFDC was automatically eligible. In the early 1980s, approximately 70 percent of the people served by Medicaid were "AFDC-related eligibles."[52] By increasing the difficulty of applying for and receiving AFDC, the initial changes in 1981 reduced the real-dollar expenditures on adults and children on Medicaid for the next three years.[53] In addition,

> the Reagan Administration initially proposed to limit federal spending in FY 1982 to a 5 percent increase over FY 1981, with future rates of increase tied to growth in the gross national product (GNP). . . . Congress rejected the cap but passed an alternative that retained the open-ended federal match at slightly reduced rates.[54]

With a decreased percentage of the poor receiving AFDC and food stamps, it would appear that more of them would join the labor force. However, research in the early 1980s showed no significant increase. The supporters of the conservative economic agenda believed that the initial cuts that occurred with OBRA was only a first step toward seriously reducing the welfare state. They constantly argued that they were taking a "long-term" approach. Reducing the attractiveness of the welfare state, except for those really cut off from the labor market, would go hand in glove with rapid economic growth and job creation.

One of the important elements in the reform of means-tested programs not adopted by Congress was a work requirement for all able-bodied adults receiving AFDC (often referred to as "workfare"). Congress settled instead for permitting states to create such programs. Such requirements, combined with benefit reductions and tightened eligibility rules, were designed to increase the incentives of welfare recipients to enter the labor force. Note that the method of instituting the benefit reductions and eligibility changes actually decreased the amount of income that could be disregarded before AFDC payments had to be reduced. By economic theory, this should reduce the incentive for people to get off public assistance and into the labor force. In the 1968 presidential campaign candidate Richard Nixon proposed a goal of "getting people off of welfare rolls and onto payrolls." However, policymakers recognize that high rates of benefit reduction as a result of earning income discourage people from trying to earn their way off the welfare rolls. This is where the workfare requirements come in.

Concentrating benefits only on the "truly needy" (defined by two White House aides as "unfortunate persons who, through no fault of their own, have nothing but public funds to turn to"[55]) reduces the amount available to those who earn themselves part of the way out of dependency on public funds. The only way to counteract these negative incentive on the willingness to work would be to force recipients to work. When Congress permitted states to experiment, it opened the door to such programs.

By contrast, the one means-tested entitlement that is totally appropriate from the point of view of the above definition of "truly needy" is the Supplemental Security Income (SSI) program. This program applies to the elderly poor, blind, or disabled who are ordinarily not expected to have any connection to the labor market. Thus, by the analysis advanced in chapter 3, it would be inappropriate to reduce benefits in order to induce these recipients to go to work. However, the Reagan administration made two proposals to cut this program, requests that were rejected by Congress. Congress instead enacted a significant increase in benefits over and above the automatic cost-of-living adjustment. Thus, SSI expenditures in real terms rose from 1981 to 1984,[56] while benefits as a percent of the poverty level of income for both individuals and couples rose between 1980 and 1984 (for couples it rose to 101.8 percent of the poverty level).[57]

The Reagan administration's approach to the welfare state targeted some programs for total elimination. One of these was public-service employment, which would have cost $4.8 billion in 1985 had the administration and Congress made no changes in it. Community Services block grants and the Work Incentive (WIN) program would have, together, cost $1.2 billion in 1985. The Urban Institute collected the proposals as well as congressional enactments and created table 6.

In discussing the economic rationale behind focusing redistribution programs onto the "truly needy" D. Lee Bawden and John L. Palmer of the Urban Institute commented that one

> might have . . . expected [the administration] to emphasize human capital investment programs—programs primarily intended to increase future productivity in the workforce. . . . Instead, the administration proposed to reduce expenditures for these programs (education and training; public service employment, nutrition programs, Medicaid, and social services) by nearly 40 percent. Some of these programs were of questionable value and were ripe for pruning. However, in its proposals the administration appeared to distinguish

TABLE 6. Estimated Outlay Changes in Means-Tested Entitlements Resulting from Reagan Administration Proposals and Congressional Actions through Fiscal Year 1984

Program	Projected Outlays under pre-Reagan Baseline[a]	Proposed Changes (% of baseline)	Enacted Changes (% of baseline)
Veterans' compensation	10.7	−8.4	−0.9
Veterans' pensions	3.8	−2.6	−2.6
Supplemental Security Income	8.1	−2.5	+8.6
Aid to Families with Dependent Children	9.8	−28.6	−14.3
Food stamps	14.5	−51.7	−13.8
Child nutrition	5.0	−46.0	−28.0
Women, Infants, and Children	1.1	−63.6	+9.1
Housing assistance	12.3	−19.5	−11.3
Low-income energy assistance	2.4	−37.5	−8.3
Medicaid	24.9	−15.7	−2.8
Other health services	1.8	−44.4	−33.3
Compensatory education	4.1	−61.0	−19.5
Head Start	1.0	n[b]	n[b]
Vocational education	0.8	−37.5	−12.5
Guaranteed Student Loans	4.1	−22.0	−39.0
Other student financial assistance	4.5	−68.9	−15.6
Veterans' Readjustment Benefits	1.1	−9.1	−9.1
Social services block grant	3.4	−41.2	−23.5
Community services block grant	0.7	−100.0	−37.1
General employment and training	5.7	−43.9	−38.6
Public-service employment	4.8	−100.0	−100.0
Job Corps	0.7	−42.9	−7.7
Work Incentives program	0.5	−17.2	−35.1
Total	125.80	−37.57	−18.93

Source: D. Lee Bawden and John L. Palmer, "Social Policy: Challenging the Welfare State," in *The Reagan Record,* ed. John L. Palmer and Isabel V. Sawhill (Cambridge, MA: Ballinger, 1984), 186–87.
[a]In billions of dollars.
[b]The dollar amount is less than $50 million.

little among more or less effective programs, even though evaluation research has demonstrated significant differences in effectiveness.[58]

In other words, there did not seem to be any consistent application of the theory of the appropriate role for government in these areas when it came time for the Reagan administration to wield the budget ax. Of the programs other than public service employment slated for major reduction—Job Corps, compensatory education, and the Women,

Infants, and Children (nutrition) program—Congress resisted the administration's proposals while letting public-service employment disappear.

Entitlements without Means Tests

When it came to what we have referred to as contributory entitlements, the Reagan administration attempted to reduce access for those who could work. They introduced stringent procedures for screening those applying for Social Security Disability Insurance (DI). Between 1980 and 1982, investigations and benefit terminations increased dramatically, and costs actually fell 10 percent. The number of disabled workers fell from 2,861,253 in 1980 to 2,468,966 in 1983 before beginning to rise.[59] This produced a furious response in litigation from many of those denied benefits. In some cases, local U.S. attorneys stated publicly that they would refuse to defend the government in suits filed by individuals seeking to have the courts put them back on disability. In 1987 the General Accounting Office did a study of those recipients of DI who had been terminated between 1981 and 1984.

> As of 1987, 63 percent of the beneficiaries who were determined ineligible for benefits . . . had been reinstated to the disability benefit rolls.
> . . . only about 26 percent of those found ineligible remained terminated; 58 percent of these terminated individuals (or 15 percent of those earlier found ineligible) had returned to work.[60]

Another major reduction in entitlement payments involved unemployment compensation. According to conservative economic theory, one of the major determinants of the rate of unemployment is the generosity of unemployment compensation. The longer unemployment benefits last, the longer a laid-off worker is willing to sit around waiting for his or her old job or an equally good job in the same area. The economist would like such a worker to willingly accept a lower-paying new job, perhaps in a different industry, perhaps move to where new jobs are available. This flexibility, which is crucial, according to these economists, for the efficient functioning of the labor market, is undermined by generous and long-lasting unemployment benefits. Thus, the Reagan administration made efforts to limit the ability of states to extend the availability of unemployment compensation during the 1981–82 recession. Before 1981, a state could extend the number of weeks a person received unemployment compensation from the basic twenty-six-week period to thirty-nine weeks under one of two circumstances: (1) 4 percent of its labor force was out of work and collecting benefits and this represented a 20 percent increase over the state rate for the previous two years, or (2) 5 percent of its labor force was out of work and collecting benefits. As part of OBRA 1981, both of these threshold percentages were raised by 1 percent. Thus, in the 1974–75 recession, the percentage of unemployed workers receiving unemployment compensation rose from a low of 40 percent in June 1974 to a high of 80 percent in December 1975.[61] By contrast, though the percentage of unemployed covered in 1980 averaged 50 percent, in the depths of the recession, 1982, the percentage was only 45 percent.[62] Again, this is consistent with an economic argument that for the labor market to function well, unemployed workers must not hold out foolish hopes that a job just as good as the one lost due to plant closure or business transformation will miraculously appear. It is also consistent with a political view that sees much unemployment as voluntary, subsidized by unemployment compensation.[63]

When we introduced the discussion of redistribution of income in chapter 3, we noted that the Social Security retirement system was perhaps the most significant violator of the conservative economic view on income redistribution. To the extent that Social Security is a pension, it is inefficient, some economists contend, to force all workers to "buy" one specific retirement plan. To the extent that Social Security redistributes income from the working (payroll-tax-paying) generation to the retired generation without a means test, it is a serious violation of the economic principles that should govern redistribution of income.[64] Martin Feldstein, later to be President Reagan's second chair of the Council of Economic Advisers, made a very significant impact on the public-policy debate with a study that claimed that the existence of Social Security had harmed our national savings rate.[65] The idea is that people assume Social Security will provide some or all of their retirement income, and thus they save less than they would have if there had been no Social Security. Meanwhile, the government, unlike a private pension plan, does not invest the savings from each individual's contributions so that the nest egg will grow till that person withdraws it. Instead, the government takes the taxes paid by the current workers and pays it out to retired people. Thus, there is no national saving taking place within the Social Security system.

As mentioned in chapter 3, many conservative economists believe that the Social Security system ought to become means-tested for the part that redistributes income and ought to be open to competition from other life insurance, disability insurance, and retirement plans. Currently, with one payroll tax, the worker receives one required disability, life, and employment insurance plan and is involved in significant redistribution of income, sometimes to people who don't need it. The first stage in attempting to reduce the redistribution involved in Social Security (and reduce the budget impact of the system as well) was a proposal made in 1982 to cut back by 40 percent the Social Security benefits for those opting for early retirement (between ages sixty-two and sixty-five). There was a great outcry, and the United States Senate went on record to the tune of ninety-two to zero with a nonbinding resolution in opposition.[66]

After that, the Reagan administration convened a bipartisan commission chaired by economist Alan Greenspan (later to replace Paul Volcker as chairman of the Federal Reserve Board) that came up with the Social Security rescue plan of 1983. This plan "fixed" Social Security so as to balance tax revenue inflows against projected payments through the year 2030. To raise revenue, they accelerated the projected increases in payroll taxes, forced all federal employees into the Social Security system, and provided for taxation of 50 percent of benefits for single taxpayers making more than twenty-five thousand dollars a year and couples making more than thirty-two thousand dollars a year. To reduce expenditures, they provided for increases in the retirement age and delayed the cost-of-living adjustment from July 1983 to January 1984.[67]

Congress did agree with the administration that certain subsidies to those who didn't "need it" should be cut back. Congress

> initiated or supported the reinstitution of a means test for guaranteed student loans (which were heavily subsidizing the college education of high income students) partial taxation of social security benefits for those with high incomes, and greater taxation of UI [unemployment insurance] benefits for the middle class.[68]

Interestingly enough, the major budgetary reduction in benefits occurred in the Medicare program, and this was a congressional initiative. Medicare is a non-means-tested entitlement available to the same population that qualifies for Social Security retirement or disability. It comes in two parts, part A, which pays for hospital and other institutional stays and is financed as part of the same payroll tax that finances

Social Security, and part B, known as Supplementary Medical Insurance, which is paid for by the premiums of participants and general revenues. SMI covers physician reimbursement among other payments. Because it is not means-tested, Medicare is subject to the same objection from the conservative-economics perspective as Social Security. In addition, Medicare is what C. Eugene Steuerle and Jon Bakija call an "open-ended" expenditure, unlike Social Security.

> Analysts often apply the term open-ended to financial guarantees and subsidies, where beneficiaries of government assistance largely determine the amount and size of taxpayer subsidies. . . . In the case of Medicare, the open-ended nature of the system derives from the absence of effective limits either on total payments that will be made or on what demand will be met. . . . Social Security cash benefits are not open-ended. . . . the determination of how much is to be spent is known and determined by a fixed formula.[69]

The problem with such open-ended programs is that consumers tend to overconsume products for which they do not have to pay the full cost out of pocket. People enrolled in the SMI part of Medicare may pay premiums and make partial payments for the services they consume (called copayments), but since they are not charged the full cost of the services, they consume with less attention to cost and hence consume more than if they were responsible for paying the full costs.

The same problem occurs with all subsidized consumption. In some cases, such as with education services, such overconsumption is justified because people who had to pay the full cost would consume less than society wants them to. This is because, as mentioned in chapter 3, the rest of society receives important benefits when an individual consumes education services—benefits the individual cannot always capture in higher income. In the area of health, an example is widespread inoculation to prevent the spread of infectious diseases. The benefit to the individual who has her or his child inoculated is less than the total benefit to society if most or all children are inoculated. Thus, it is an appropriate role of government to subsidize the overconsumption of inoculations by people who might not purchase such a service if forced to pay out of pocket.

When it comes to personal health expenditures on doctors and hospitals, especially by the elderly, overconsumption allegedly brings few benefits to the rest of society. If there were no Medicare, individuals faced with the need to purchase medical services would be very careful what they spent their money on. Physicians and hospitals, knowing that consumers were stretching their medical dollars as far as possible, would be careful not to price themselves out of the market. Meanwhile, those who cannot afford to purchase hospitals' and physicians' services in the marketplace would still have recourse to Medicaid.

From the point of view of conservative economics, the very existence of a non-means-tested, open-ended entitlement like Medicare makes no sense. Subsidizing the consumption of hospital and physician services leads to both a rapid expansion in the demand for such services and a rapid escalation of costs. Add to that the subsidy to employer-provided health insurance built into the tax system. An employee does not pay income tax on the contribution her or his employer makes to purchase health insurance, but would have to pay both Social Security and income tax on the same amount if it were paid as a wage. To give the employee the same after-tax income in dollars as the employer delivers in health insurance premium payments would cost the business the premium payment plus the Social Security and income tax rate payment applicable to that worker. Clearly, it is in the interest of both employer and employee to maximize the income of employees received in tax-exempt fringe benefits such as health insurance. In addition, there is Medicaid, which subsidizes the consumption of medical services by the poor. According to the economic conservatives, these processes whereby medical expenditures are made by third parties (that is, neither the health care provider nor the patient) inevitably lead to escalating costs and big increases in the actual production and consumption of physicians' and hospitals' services.

In 1968, Medicare accounted for 2.6 percent of federal expenditures. In 1981, the year before Reagan's first budget impacted the economy, Medicare spending had risen to 5.8 percent of federal spending. By contrast, Social Security payments for pensions, survivors, and the disabled rose from 13.4 percent of federal expenditures to 20.6 percent, a rate of growth that was only half as fast.[70] Though it was clearly important for the Reagan planners to trim Social Security, since it represented such a large part of the budget, Medicare's rate of increase also had to be addressed. As part of the 1983 Social Security rescue plan, Congress changed the formula for the reimbursement of hospitals. According to the Urban Institute, this change "amounted to the largest reduction in social program spending resulting from a single action since the [Reagan] administration took office" (see table 7).[71]

TABLE 7. **Estimated Outlay Changes in Entitlements without Means Tests Resulting from Reagan Administration Proposals and Congressional Actions through Fiscal Year 1984**

Program	Projected Outlays under pre-Reagan Baseline[a]	Proposed Changes (% of Baseline)	Enacted Changes (% of Baseline)
Social Security	200.6	−10.4	−4.6
Unemployment Insurance	29.8	−19.1	−17.4
Medicare	80.4	−11.2	−6.8
Total	310.8	−14.57	−9.6

Source: D. Lee Bawden and John L. Palmer, "Social Policy: Challenging the Welfare State," in *The Reagan Record,* ed. John L. Palmer and Isabel V. Sawhill (Cambridge, MA: Ballinger, 1984), 186–87.
[a]In billions of dollars.

However, nothing was done with either the Medicare or the Medicaid program to change the open-ended nature of these entitlements.

Shrinking the Size of the Federal Government

One area where the Reagan administration made strong efforts to cut the absolute cost of government was in federal aid to state and local governments. For fiscal year 1982, the absolute level of federal inter-governmental grants fell from $90.1 to $83.4 billion. The Reagan administration actually succeeded in rescinding some of the fiscal 1981 budget, so that if we use calendar years, both 1981 and 1982 registered falls in absolute spending.[72] In his 1982 State of the Union address, President Reagan proposed a readjustment in federal and state responsibilities. He proposed that AFDC and Food Stamps become the responsibility of the states; in return, the federal government would assume full responsibility for Medicaid.[73] Though he found little support for this proposal (called "The New Federalism"), it represented an important element in the view that the appropriate level of government to collect taxes and spend them is that level which is closest to the people. If the benefits of the provision of social goods and services, such as police departments, fire departments, schools, regional transportation systems, and so forth are accruing to people living in close proximity to each other in localities, counties, or, in some case, states, it makes no sense for taxpayers in faraway states to be subsidizing some of that expenditure through federal grants.

In addition, the administration suspected that federal grants had created "artificial inducements . . . forc[ing] upon the public more spending than it wants to support."[74] In this view, with a cutback in federal aid, states and localities would tax their citizens only for expenditures their citizens really desired. The argument against such an approach is based on the different income levels in the states. Some states with relatively low tax effort (measured as the percentage of state income paid in state and local taxes) could finance quite high levels of spending, while other states with quite high, burdensome tax effort might, because of low incomes, produce inadequate levels of spending. Why should the per pupil expenditure on education in, say, West Virginia be lower than the amount spent in, say, Massachusetts, even though the percentage of income paid in taxes to West Virginia localities is *higher* than to Massachusetts localities? Because of concerns such as these, state and local officials rejected the Reagan administration's proposals, and the "New Federalism" got nowhere in Congress.

Interestingly enough, over a decade later, the Contract with America called for transfer of many federal programs to the states. In the 1990s, many state governors became anxious to be freed from federal red tape and controls in the administration of such programs as AFDC. The proposals that were developed in Congress in 1995 were to replace detailed federal controls with block grants. In return for giving the states more freedom to set rules, the federal government would reduce the amount of money they send to the states and freeze that spending over time. Early controversy in 1995 centered around the food stamps program (which the Contract with America promised to return to the states but which Congress chose to keep under federal control) and the Federal School Lunch Program. It is important to note that the crucial issue in determining whether the state or the federal government ought to finance and/or control this or that program is whether its benefits are national in scope. A local sewage treatment facility benefits people in the immediate region. But can an antipoverty program be considered of only local concern?

To return to the effort to shrink the federal government, such a contraction did not occur because the increase in defense spending that had begun under Carter was accelerated by the Reagan administration (see table 8). Defense purchases had actually declined in real terms until 1976. After that decline was reversed, defense purchases continued to decline as a percentage of GDP through 1979. However, the last two Carter budgets, 1980 and 1981, provided for increases in defense spending above the growth in GDP. The first two Reagan budgets con-

TABLE 8. The Changing Role of Defense Spending in the Economy, 1975–88

Year	Defense Spending (billions of dollars)	Defense Spending (% of GDP)
1975	86.5	5.6
1976	89.6	5.2
1977	97.2	4.9
1978	104.5	4.9
1979	116.3	4.7
1980	134.0	4.9
1981	157.5	5.2
1982	185.3	5.8
1983	209.9	6.1
1984	227.4	6.0
1985	252.7	6.2
1986	273.4	6.2
1987	282.0	6.1
1988	290.4	5.9

Source: ERP 1997, 390–91.

Note: Data is for fiscal years. Fiscal 1975 and 1976 ran from July 1 to June 30. After a transitional third quarter in 1977, fiscal 1977 and subsequent fiscal years have run from October 1 to September 30.

tinued that trend. In 1984, because GDP grew so rapidly, the percentage spent on national defense fell (from 6.1 to 6.0 percent), but then it resumed its upward trend until it peaked in 1986 at 6.2 percent of GDP.

This increase in defense spending made it impossible to shrink the size of government, despite initial success with domestic spending in the first Reagan budget. Thus, in the end the tax cuts were never matched by spending reductions. This has produced a long political as well as analytical battle between those who blame the high deficits and resulting expansion of the national debt on the tax cuts and those who emphasize the failure of Congress to get spending under control. Whatever the cause, there is no dispute that even after the recovery from the 1981–82 recession the federal budget ran in the red to an unprecedented extent, except for periods of major wars.

Reagan's Successes: A Summary

The period from 1981 to 1984 was the high-water mark of the Reagan Revolution. By supporting the stringent anti-inflationary policy of the Volcker Federal Reserve Board, Reagan had in effect acquiesced in whatever recession would be necessary to cut inflation. The Economic Recovery Tax Act significantly curtailed the level and growth of the federal government's income tax revenue.[75] There was a significant reduction in the nondefense, nonentitlement part of the budget, masked by rises in defense spending. Reagan's more dramatic actions included various regulatory reforms, the attempts as well as the achievements. There is no question that the climate in Washington relating to the role of the federal government in our nation's economy had begun to change. From the point of view of those who adhered to the conservative diagnosis of what had ailed the economy, it truly was, in the words of the 1984 Reagan campaign slogan, "Morning in America."

6

"Morning in America"

Because the Reagan administration was unable to push all of its spending cuts through Congress, the passage of the Economic Recovery Tax Act of 1981 signaled that fiscal policy would be highly stimulative. To measure the stimulation of fiscal policy, economists break down the budget deficit into that part created by policy and that part created by the economy. Between fiscal 1980 and 1983, the budget deficit of the federal government went from 2.7 percent of gross domestic product to 6.1 percent.[1] However, much of that increase was due to the 1981–82 recession. When a recession occurs, tax revenues fall because people lose their jobs and businesses don't earn as much profit. Because our tax system is progressive, tax revenues take a smaller percentage of personal income when incomes decline. Meanwhile, unemployment compensation payments increase as more and more people are unemployed. These changes, which occur without any explicit action by Congress or the administration, are called automatic stabilizers because they automatically raise the deficit in recession, thus increasing the government stimulus to aggregate demand, and lower the deficit in periods of prosperity, thus moderating the increase in aggregate demand by decreasing the government stimulus.

In order to measure the direction of *policy,* we need to identify what the budget deficit *would have been* if there had been no recession and therefore no automatic decline in tax revenues or automatic increase in government payments for programs like unemployment compensation. This measure is called the high-employment budget. This tells us what the budget deficit would have been at some fixed level of unemployment. By fixing the level of unemployment, we in effect screen out the impact of the business cycle on the deficit and are left with only the impact of policy decisions.

When this is done for the years 1980–83, we can see that the policy changes instituted by the Reagan administration—the tax cuts, the attempts to cut civilian government spending, the rise in military spending—added up to a significant increase in the high-employment deficit. The Bureau of Economic Analysis of the Department of Commerce calculated the deficit that would have existed if the economy had been at 6 percent unemployment. As a percentage of the gross national product[2] that would have existed if unemployment were at that level, the high-employment or structural deficit went from a low of 0.53 percent in the second quarter of 1981 to a high of 2.93 percent in the fourth quarter of 1983.[3] Thus, if we ignore for a moment incentive effects predicted by the supply-siders, there definitely was a strong aggregate-demand stimulation to production as a result of the Reagan fiscal policy. However, the timing of the tax cuts and spending increases were such that in 1981, the fiscal stimulus actually was lower than in the previous year. It is true the Economic Recovery Tax Act mandated three across-the-board income tax cuts, but the first one of 5 percent only took effect in October, meaning it cut taxation as a percentage of 1981 income only 1.25 percent. On top of that, bracket creep was still going strong, as 1981 inflation measured 10 percent. With people moved into higher tax brackets, the ratio of income tax paid to real income increased. If we then add in the previously scheduled increases in the Social Security tax rates, it is clear that the policy regime provided a net fiscal drag rather than stimulus in that first year. Even adding in the automatic stabilizers, the total (actual) deficit as a percentage of gross domestic product was a bit lower in 1981 than it had been in 1980.[4]

Meanwhile, the Federal Reserve was attempting to adhere to its monetary targets. From the fourth quarter of 1980 to the first quarter of 1981, the rate of growth of M1 was 4.6 percent. From the first to the second quarter it rose to 9.6 percent. From the second to the third quarter of 1981, the rate fell to 2.0 percent. Then the rate rose back to 5.1 percent for the fourth quarter.[5] In short, a contractionary monetary policy combined with a not-yet-expansionary fiscal policy. Thus, after a very short recovery from the 1980 recession, the economy fell into recession in the third quarter of 1981.[6]

The Volcker Recession: Alternative Explanations

That recession lasted until the fourth quarter of 1982 and proved to be the deepest one of the post–World War II period. Since the purpose of our investigation is to discuss the impact of the Reagan-Volcker policy on the economy over the long run, it is not particularly important to dwell on what happened during the recession.[7] If the economy had come out of the recession and experienced a higher rate of growth, higher rate of productivity growth, more productive investment, and a more rapid expansion in the standard of living than in the previous period, one would have to concede that the pain and suffering of the recession had been worth it in some sense. Similarly, if the recession had not occurred but the economy had continued to perform at an unacceptable level, this would be an indictment of the economic policies adopted despite the fact that the economy would have been spared the recession.

It is instructive, however, to note the ways the three alternative points of view explain the recession of 1981–82. For those who supported the Reagan administration policies, the recession was an unavoidable consequence of the Carter administration's mismanagement of the economy and the Federal Reserve's acquiescence in inflation before 1979. For the mainstream critics of Reaganomics, the recession was the result of the Federal Reserve's rigid commitment to monetarism. Throughout 1981 and 82, the rate of growth of money remained positive, but the higher interest rates killed the economy. According to this perspective, a slower approach to the battle against inflation would have reduced inflation without such a serious decline in output as occurred in the recession.[8]

Finally, the radical approach emphasizes that as painful as recessions are, they are the only way the United States economy can reestablish patterns of profitability high enough to encourage the private-sector investment that is the key to economic growth. The 1974 recession, despite its severity, did not reestablish profitability at a sufficiently high level. The costs of labor and imported raw materials as well as the tax burden on business (in part exacerbated by inflation) were having a bad effect on the business climate. Only a dramatic shifting of the balance of power in the struggle for income shares would reestablish profitability at a level high enough and predictable enough so that new investment would be forthcoming.[9]

Thus, in a strange way, the radicals were agreeing with the conservatives—business had been burdened by taxation, regulation, and other high costs. However, whereas conservatives see this situation as one that damages incentives, producing inevitable consequences, radicals see the behavior of business as more purposeful. Business has the power to hold the rest of the economy hostage. In the face of a bad business climate, they can engage in a "capital strike."[10]

The radicals saw this situation of stalemate as reason to consider alternative kinds of economic organization where the power of capitalists to hold the economy hostage would be gone.[11] According to this point of view, the vast majority of citizens who are not wealthy and have very little chance of becoming wealthy are doomed to experience disruptions in their lives and a shrinking share of the economic pie because the only way to preserve prosperity is to bribe the tiny minority of wealthy people to invest some of their wealth productively. Conservatives, on the other hand, saw the burdens on business as obstacles to prosperity. Remove those burdens and business incentives would flourish, benefiting that vast majority of the population. Conservatives also denied that periodic recessions were always necessary for the long-term health of a capitalist market economy. Instead, they felt virtually all recessions, especially severe ones, were the result of mistaken government activities that destabilized the market.[12] Absent these governmental mistakes the business cycle would self-correct quickly.

Interestingly, in this part of the argument, it is the conservatives and the mainstream economists who are in agreement. Both groups believe that periodic recessions, especially severe ones, are not inevitable. Mainstream economists, however, disagree with conservatives because they believe that judicious application of the correct policies can smooth the business cycle and promote more rapid growth. Left alone, some recessions, they fear, might fail to self-correct, leading to long depressions. They also feel it is unconscionable to let the economy suffer through the slow process of self-correction when the right kind of policies applied at the right time can speed up the process.

No matter which position one takes about the cause of the recession of 1981–82, the success or failure of the Reagan-Volcker program needs to be analyzed in reference to the business cycle upswing that began in the fourth quarter of 1982 and did not end until the third quarter of 1990. This makes it the second longest expansion of the postwar period, the longest running from the first quarter of 1961 to the third quarter of 1969. It is essential to identify the elements of success and the elements of failure in the 1983–90 expansion. To do this, we will need to examine the various claims made by both supporters and detractors of the Reagan program. However, first we need to follow the course of policy up through 1989.

Beginning in 1984, it became apparent to all observers that the usual reduction in the structural deficit that accompanied previous recoveries from recessions was not occurring in the post-1982 recovery. Instead, the structural deficit rose after 1984 to 3.58 percent of GDP in 1985 and 4.31 of GDP in 1986 before declining slowly to 3.22 percent of GDP in 1989. This 1989 figure, coming at the end of a very long recovery, was much higher than in previous recoveries.[13] Even the recession year of 1975 with its major tax cut had produced an average deficit of only 2.54 percent of GDP. This structural deficit drove the total government deficit.[14] Thus, we conclude that fiscal policy remained quite expansive for the entire Reagan-Bush recovery.

Monetary policy was expansionary in a few periods, yet overall, as indicated by the real Federal Funds rate, the Fed was keeping a tight rein on the economy. Real interest rates were at unprecedented levels for the entire postrecovery period, despite the periods of expansionary monetary policy. That is because inflation came down almost as much as did the nominal Federal Funds rate. The same holds true for the prime rate. In the years before 1970, the highest average yearly rates in real terms were 3.3 percent in 1961 and 3.4 percent in 1963. In the period between 1970 and 1978, the highest rate was 2.51 percent, in 1978. After the imposition of the Volcker anti-inflationary program, the real prime rate jumped dramatically beginning in 1979. Even after the recession had squeezed most of the inflation out of the economy, the real prime rate never fell below 4.22 percent in any quarter between 1984 and 1989, and most of the time it was significantly higher.[15] The upshot of this was that in a very real sense monetary policy and fiscal policy worked at cross-purposes for most of the decade. Monetary policy was stamping on the brakes, trying to restrain inflation, while fiscal policy was revving the accelerator to increase aggregate demand.

These actions by the Federal Reserve were in part in reaction to the widespread view that deficit financing for the military buildup could have significant inflationary consequences if the economy grew rapidly enough to achieve "full employment," which, as we might recall, was defined in the 1980s at 6 percent of the labor force. In a major study of the proposed military buildup issued in February 1983, the Congressional Budget Office warned that

> if the Congress chose to continue increased defense spending as the economy approached full employment of resources, offsetting cuts in

nondefense spending or increases in taxes would become critical to avoid inflation. . . . If . . . the buildup was not compensated but instead was financed by larger deficits, . . . it could have increasingly inflationary effects in 1985 and 1986.[16]

With the economy growing very rapidly in 1984 and the deficit remaining very high, the Federal Reserve must have felt it had no choice but to step strongly on the brake. The decision was made at the March 1984 meeting of the Federal Open Market Committee. The economy was growing too fast, and the failure of the administration and Congress to agree on deficit-cutting actions heightened their awareness that only a tight monetary policy could prevent the recovery from exploding into another round of inflation, 1970s style.[17]

In the entire post–World War II period, this appears to be the first preemptive strike against inflation—in other words, a policy designed to combat an inflation that had not yet appeared. This 1984 action signaled the Fed's recognition that the "bond market," the institutions that buy and sell large volumes of interest-bearing notes and react strongly to fears of inflation by selling off a large volume of assets to protect their portfolios, had to be placated at all costs. Rather than wait for inflation to begin and then respond with restrictive monetary policy, the new Federal Reserve approach was to sacrifice economic growth whenever the economy appeared to be "too close" to "full employment." Such a situation means the economy might, sometime in the near future, be subject to inflationary pressures. As always, we must remind the reader that the terms in quotation marks are incredibly imprecise. Even if one could agree that "full employment" was 6 percent in the middle 1980s, what constitutes "too close?" The lowest monthly unemployment report for 1984 was 7.1 percent in June, before the effects of the tightening were felt. The rate rose to 7.4 percent in August before declining to 7.1 again in November and December.[18] The economy would not come close to "full employment" (6 percent) until the middle of 1987.

When it comes to tax policy, there is a mixed story. The Economic Recovery Tax Act had involved more than just supply-side-oriented reductions in individual income tax rates, reduced taxation of capital income, and indexing.

Congress . . . abandoned its cautious approach to President Reagan's proposals and went in the opposite direction. A bidding war started. Many new provisions were added to the original Reagan tax proposals, including extension of individual retirement accounts (IRAs) to higher income taxpayers who were already covered under employer-provided pension plans, a new deduction for some earnings when both spouses in a family worked . . . an exclusion from income subject to tax of interest earned on qualified tax-exempt savings certificates . . . a charitable contributions deduction for individuals who did not normally itemize expenses, a credit for increasing research activities within a business, the elimination of estate taxes for a large number of wealthy taxpayers, and an number of other special preferences.[19]

When the Treasury Department's Office of Tax Analysis projected the revenue loss associated with these provisions from the time of enactment up to 1990, they came up with a total figure of $323 billion, or 5.6 percent of GDP.[20] The fact that the tax reductions and defense-spending increases would make it impossible to keep the federal budget deficit from rising became apparent almost as soon as ERTA was passed. By early 1982, the president's budget message for fiscal year 1983 included significant tax increases, though the euphemism used was "revenue enhancements." Out of that message and the efforts of members of the Senate as well as people on the president's staff, most notably Budget Director David Stockman, came the Tax Equity and Fiscal Responsibility Act (TEFRA) of 1982. According to the analysis of the Treasury, that act "took back" $57.2 billion of the $323 billion in tax cuts contained in ERTA.[21]

As mentioned before, the effort to reform the Social Security system that began with an attempt to significantly cut back the payments to early retirees failed miserably.[22] From the point of view of conservative economics, the changes that ultimately passed in 1983 did nothing to rectify the real problem in the Social Security retirement system. Recall that in redistributing income, it is considered inefficient to redistribute money to people who don't really need it. But that is of course what Social Security does for all recipients who would not be in poverty without their retirement check. Nevertheless, all effort to achieve the comprehensive reform that conservative economic theory would require was abandoned. Instead, the 1983 law increased the retirement age by two years (phased in between 2000 and 2022), accelerated previously legislated payroll tax increases, forced new federal employees and employees of nonprofit organizations to join the system, and delayed for six months the next cost-of-living adjustment.[23]

There was one step taken in the direction of making the retirement check at least partially means-tested. As mentioned above, half of all

Social Security benefits became taxable for higher-income recipients. Twenty-two percent of all Social Security recipients paid income tax on their benefits. The income tax liability as a percentage of Social Security payments (exclusive of Medicare) never rose above 2 percent for the entire decade of the 1980s.[24] Nevertheless, the principle that Social Security payments were subject to taxation does reduce the amount of Social Security received by people who "don't need it."

In 1985, the Republican majority in the United States Senate offered a deficit reduction plan that involved limits on the growth of Social Security payments (in effect reducing the automatic cost-of-living increase for some recipients). President Reagan refused to support them, and the attempt was abandoned in the face of opposition from the Democratic majority in the House. According to Norman Ornstein and John Makin of the American Enterprise Institute,

> Had Reagan supported his own party in Congress in 1985, House Democrats would have been compelled to go along, and the growth of entitlements would have been curbed, budget deficits would have been far below those that actually occurred, and the great Reagan fiscal experiment of cutting taxes and still reducing the budget deficit might well have succeeded.[25]

These two authors argue that members of Congress felt pressured by the high deficits in the middle of the 1980s to revisit the growing spending on entitlements, particularly those without means tests, but that the political lessons learned in 1982 when the Reagan administration had floated the idea of cutting back on early retirement benefits for Social Security recipients had convinced the majority of Congress as well as the president that Social Security was, in the language of the day, the "third rail" of American politics. Touch it and you'll be zapped! It would be an entire decade before a deficit-cutting Congress would attack entitlements that mostly benefited the middle class, and even then the Republican-controlled Congress of 1995 explicitly ruled out changes in the Social Security system.

The impact of the actual changes made in Social Security between 1983 and 1989 still totaled $166.2 billion, according to the House of Representatives Committee on Ways and Means.[26] Of all the tax changes made after ERTA, the changes associated with the 1983 Social Security Act amendments are quantitatively the most significant. The rise in the Social Security payroll tax (but not the income taxation of half the benefits of high-income taxpayers), coupled with a decline in marginal individual income tax rates and the taxation of income from capital, fits very neatly into the conservative economic-policy basket. In fact, from a supply-side perspective, the most efficient tax is a regressive tax levied in a fixed amount on a person regardless of income. Such a tax has a marginal tax rate of zero and presumably has no negative incentive effects whatsoever. The payroll tax for Social Security has a marginal tax rate of zero once the maximum earnings level has been reached. Covered earnings are taxed at rates below 15 percent (combined employee and employer rates), and that, too, is considered low enough to have a negligible impact on behavior. Thus, we can conclude that the combined Social Security tax increases and the net effect of ERTA and TEFRA was to tilt the tax system in the direction of reducing the allegedly negative incentive effects of high marginal tax rates and specifically increasing the incentives of businesses to invest by decreasing the taxation of income from capital.

Toward Tax Reform

Beginning in 1984, and concluding with the enactment of the Tax Reform Act of 1986, the clear, positive (from a supply-side perspective) impact of tax legislation began to get muddied. The first steps were made in reforming the tax shelter problem. Tax shelters involve investing with borrowed funds, depreciating the asset bought, and deducting the interest on the loan against current income. As the value of the depreciation declines, the investor can sell the asset. When that happens, all the "losses" that had reduced taxable income due to depreciation and interest payments could be recouped. That income, which had been "sheltered" from taxation by the immediate deduction of interest and depreciation would now, however, be in the form of a capital gain, which up till 1986 was subject to a maximum tax rate of 20 percent. The incentives in place after 1981 were even greater than that, because the entire initial investment was subject to an immediate 10 percent investment tax credit. This produced the perverse effect of making some investments that actually lost money produce enough tax reductions to more than offset these losses.[27] To show how significant this became over time consider the following information:

> Between 1965 and 1982, the number of partnerships reporting net losses grew from 229,000 to 723,000. . . . Net "losses" reported in oil

and gas partnerships grew from $128 million to $13.2 billion, and in real estate from $619 million to $23 billion. Together, oil and gas and real estate partnerships accounted for about 60 percent of all losses reported on partnerships. . . . New public offerings of partnerships grew from $8 billion in 1979 to $64 billion by 1982.[28]

The Deficit Reduction Act of 1984 began the process of clamping down on the tax shelter market and did lead to an increase in revenue of $31 billion by 1990.[29] However, the most significant departure from the incentive effects of the Economic Recovery Tax Act occurred with the passage of the Tax Reform Act of 1986. Unlike ERTA, this was not a tax cut. President Reagan insisted that it be revenue neutral. Every cut had to be matched by increases in revenue somewhere else in the tax code. There were other broad themes required by the president. First, the poor should not have to pay income tax. Over the years, inflation had eroded the real value of the personal and dependent exemptions. The only way to reverse this would be to raise those exemptions dramatically. Second, the top rates had to be reduced and the number of brackets compressed to one or two above the zero bracket.

In practice, what happened was that lower published rates were "paid for" by abolishing a number of preferences, including those that could be used to shelter income. This had the effect of raising the marginal tax rate on a number of high-income taxpayers and actually increasing the effective rate of taxation on many businesses. As C. Eugene Steuerle, the assistant secretary of the Treasury who headed up the group that produced the first tax reform proposal in 1984 (called "Treasury One") noted, "Absent base-broadening, it is almost impossible in a revenue-neutral bill to reduce tax burdens for the poor without increasing average marginal tax rates in the economy."[30]

However, since the bill was also carefully crafted so as to be revenue neutral within income groups, the result was that average income tax rates for all income classes actually fell, though the most significant falls were for people with less than $20,000 in annual income.[31] This left only one source for the increase in revenue, the business sector. The change is dramatic.

It is apparent from the variations in effective tax rates under the pre-1986 law that the tax system was definitely treating investments differently depending on the type (see table 9).[32] Thus, on pure efficiency grounds, "leveling the playing field" among all kinds of businesses would definitely be a high priority. However, note also that on average

TABLE 9. Total Effective Tax Rates on Corporate Investment, by Broad Asset Type and by Industry

	Pre-1986 Law (%)	Tax Reform Act of 1986 (%)
Total	38	41
By asset type		
Equipment and structures	29	39
Equipment	11	38
Structures	38	39
Inventories	58	48
By specific equipment		
Automobiles	7	46
Office and computing equipment	8	42
Trucks, buses, trailers	8	41
Aircraft	7	41
Construction machinery	7	35
Mining, oilfield machinery	7	40
Service industry machinery	7	40
Tractors	7	38
Instruments	13	39
Other equipment	7	38
General industrial equipment	12	37
Metalworking machinery	7	35
Electric transmission equipment	25	44
Communications equipment	7	30
Other electrical equipment	7	35
Furniture and fixtures	7	34
Special industrial equipment	7	33
Agricultural equipment	6	40
Fabricated metal products	19	40
Engines and turbines	32	46
Ships and boats	6	42
Railroad equipment	27	29
Structures by industry		
Mining oil and gas	16	20
Other	48	46
Industrial structures	44	43
Public utility structures	28	37
Commercial structures	41	41
Farm structures	42	41

Source: C. Eugene Steuerle, *The Tax Decade: How Taxes Came to Dominate the Public Agenda* (Washington, DC: Urban Institute Press, 1992), 128-29.

Note: The effective rate of tax is calculated assuming a 4 percent rate of inflation.

the rates of corporate taxation were significantly higher after reform. This was in order to "pay for" the reductions on individuals. There was a fear that this would significantly harm investment incentives, but when one combines the effect of the new law on corporate and individual taxation, the rise in the cost of capital was quite small. Thus, the consensus among economists who looked at the impact of the Tax

Reform Act (at a 1990 conference) was that it had mostly a financial impact—reducing the use of tax shelters.

It was the issue of the full taxation of capital gains that became a tremendous sticking point. The original Treasury version had proposed full taxation of *real* capital gains. In other words, the exclusion of an arbitrary percentage of capital gains from taxable income would be ended, but the part of the capital gain that was only due to inflation would not be subject to tax. Recall our example from chapter 3. Holding stock for five years that was bought for $100,000 and sold for $200,000 produces a capital gain of $100,000. If inflation increased prices 25 percent over those five years, $25,000 of the $100,000 gain merely keeps up with inflation and is not an increase in purchasing power. The Treasury proposal would have "adjusted the basis" (the $100,000 purchase price of the asset is the "basis") for the inflation since purchase. Thus, upon selling the stock for $200,000, the capital gain would have been calculated from the "adjusted basis" of $125,000, the original purchase price plus the amount of inflation that had occurred since then. The tax rate would then be applied to $75,000.[33] The problem with this proposal was that it would not have increased revenue as much as abolishing the exclusion without the inflation adjustment. From the point of view of rational tax policy, it is not appropriate to tax nominal gains that exceed real gains. When this is built into the law, the rate of taxation of real increases in income will vary according to how much inflation has occurred while the asset is being held. On the other hand, abolishing the exclusion did dampen "the most common form of tax arbitrage—borrowing to purchase appreciating capital assets and profiting from the tax differential. Legal experts also argue that the capital gains exclusion has caused much of the complexity in taxation."[34] On this ground, we would have to consider it a plus.

However, the strong supply-siders (such as Robert Bartley and Lawrence Lindsey) believed that the end of the capital-gains exclusion was a serious blow to the positive incentive structure that had been put into place in 1981. Bartley argued that "capital gains were especially important to the young entrepreneurial company: this was the pot at the end of the rainbow that moves breakaway engineers to take out mortgages on their homes to start a company."[35] Lindsey argued that raising the capital-gains rate to a maximum of 33 percent (the top marginal rate in the 1986 reform)[36] probably would not increase revenue nearly as much as the tax writers believed, and thus he and other supply-siders believed that some capital-gains preference should be reintroduced into the tax system. Though Steuerle is among the tax experts who believe full taxation of real capital gains is the solution, not preferential treatment, he agrees with Lindsey that the revenue impact of full taxation of gains would not be very great. His reason is that capital gains can escape all taxation if the asset is held till death. Thus, people facing a high marginal tax rate should they sell assets and realize a capital gain will have an incentive to defer sales so as to realize gains when they have losses to offset them or when their other income is perhaps temporarily lower. Such a behavior pattern will tend to keep financial capital locked in to currently owned assets, reducing the flexibility of investors.

The dispute between those who wanted to reintroduce the preferential treatment of capital-gains income and those who decried such a move as a tax bonanza benefiting mostly the wealthy has raged ever since the passage of the Tax Reform Act. President George Bush asked for it repeatedly and was rebuffed by Congress. When President Clinton convinced Congress to raise income tax rates in 1993, they kept the top rate on capital gains at 28 percent, creating a small preference. As part of the bipartisan compromise in mid-1997, President Clinton and Congress agreed to a 20 percent maximum rate on capital gains realized after holding an asset for eighteen months.[37] In this context it is important to recall that most analysts of the 1986 tax change noted that the major impact of the rise in capital-gains taxation was the decline in the use of many tax shelters. It remains to be seen whether creating a new capital-gains exclusion will encourage the proliferation of tax shelters once again.

Regulation

After the initial efforts to curtail the growth of social regulation, the administration was stymied. Nevertheless, it is important to acknowledge the success emphasized by Murray Weidenbaum in a retrospective analysis.

> During the past eight years [1981–88], not a single major new regulatory law has been enacted (although several have been toughened). Nor has a new regulatory agency been established. This has been the first such extended period in the past half century.[38]

William Niskanen, his former colleague on the Council of Economic Advisers, emphasizes the missed opportunities and concludes about the areas of health, safety, and the environment that the "Reagan attempt to reform these regulations . . . was a near-complete failure."[39] If we observe the actual expenditures on regulatory agencies, we note that the decline in real spending between 1981 and 1984 was reversed briefly in 1985, fell again in 1986, but then rose dramatically in 1987. By 1989, the total expenditure on regulatory agencies was 17.2 percent higher than in 1981.[40]

These total-expenditure numbers mask mandates imposed on state and local government by Congress that end up increasing the regulatory burden on certain businesses. Perhaps one of the most significant examples is the nursing-home reform contained in the Omnibus Budget Reconciliation Act of 1987, which required that states enforce standards of care, including "nurse staffing, aide training, and patient assessment."[41] The costs of complying with these requirements either squeezed nursing-home profits or caused prices to rise, including the prices paid by Medicaid.

On balance, was the Reagan effort successful because it prevented much greater regulatory activity, or was it a failure because it didn't reduce regulation in absolute terms? To a certain extent this is the question of whether a glass of juice is half full or half empty. Slowing the growth of regulations, which Niskanen acknowledged did take place, changed the atmosphere under which business operated. Weidenbaum's emphasis on that should be sufficient for us to conclude that despite the inability to "reform" (critics would claim the effort was to gut them instead) regulations as Niskanen would have wished, the eight years of Reaganomics delivered on its promise to reduce the regulatory burden on business, particularly in the area of health, safety, and environmental protection. This is true even if not one regulation in existence in 1981 were rolled back. The reason is because when businesses are confronted with a new regulation, it takes time for them to find the least costly way of complying with it. Over time, there is a "learning curve," which simply translates into the idea that doing something over and over again gives one the experience to perfect one's ability to do it in the best possible way.

To take an example from everyday life, the first time a local town or city institutes a recycling requirement for citizens' trash collection, there will be difficulties experienced because people are not used to separating different types of rubbish, they do not have the various receptacles in which to store them, and they are not quite sure which items fit where. At first it will be a bothersome, time-consuming pain, and people will make mistakes or sometimes even willfully attempt to circumvent the new rules. As people experience compliance with the rules over the next weeks and months, the separation of trash becomes second nature and therefore less time-consuming. The organization of the various receptacles becomes more efficient and therefore less time-consuming. By the time six months have passed, citizens will probably be spending a negligible amount of extra time separating recyclables from the rest of their garbage. The initial costs to business of newly introduced regulations are akin to the initial bother and time caused by the beginning of a mandatory recycling program. Just as the costs decline for individual citizens, the costs to business decline, provided no new regulations are enacted in the meantime. That is the significance of the eight-year period in which new laws were not passed and new regulatory bodies were not created.

Even with the real increase in regulatory budgets, if we assume a learning-curve process at work, we should conclude that costs of compliance would have declined so that the overall burden of regulation would have declined. Interestingly, in detailing the actual deregulatory accomplishments of the eight-year Reagan effort, the 1989 *Economic Report of the President* identified only changes in economic regulation.[42] Even there, the report concluded on a pessimistic note.

> The potential for executive regulatory oversight to impose discipline on the regulatory process is limited. . . . regulatory reform is unlikely to be a high priority for any Administration in the near future because it is hard to convince the public of the need to streamline the regulatory process when specific regulations are at issue. . . . People recognize that in the aggregate many regulations may be burdensome, but almost always a vocal interest group will attempt to block the removal of any single regulation. A second reason is that program advocates in the Congress oppose the consequences of such oversight.[43]

Perhaps in response to this problem, the incoming Bush administration created the Council on Competitiveness, which for the next four years acted as an "appeal of last resort" for business interests whose "competitive position" might be harmed by new or existing regulations. In addition, during the 1990s, an effort was made to give owners of property the right to block government regulations that would reduce the economic value of that property without compensation. This "property rights" movement was endorsed in the Contract with America.

> The Job Creation and Wage Enhancement Act allows private property owners to receive compensation (up to 10 percent of fair market value) from the federal government for any reduction in the value of their property.[44]

We conclude, therefore, that the burden of regulation was eased somewhat during the 1980s, particularly in the early years of the Reagan administration. For the next decade, there was a major standoff, particularly in the area of social regulation. Neither the Bush administration nor the Clinton administration was able to break that stalemate. The issue of regulation remains quite important. The future course of regulation is unclear as the Clinton administration confronts the Republican majority in Congress once again.[45]

Redistribution of Income

The rule changes enacted in 1981 in the AFDC program were moderated somewhat in 1984 and then changed significantly in 1988. According to the numerical example referred to in the previous chapter, the Deficit Reduction Act of 1984 and the Family Support Act of 1988 reduced somewhat the rate of benefit reduction faced by a welfare recipient who has an opportunity to take a low-wage job.[46]

In 1988, the Family Support Act replaced the previously existing Work Incentive (WIN) program with the job opportunities and basic skills training program (known as JOBS). The purpose of this program was to help adults receiving welfare to avoid long-term dependency by providing education, training, and employment. States had to offer the following:

> (1) education activities, including high school or equivalent education, basic and remedial education to achieve a basic literacy level, and education for individuals with limited English proficiency; (2) job skills training; (3) job readiness activities; (4) job development and job placement; and (5) supportive services. . . . [They also had to offer] two of the following four activities: (1) group and individual job search; (2) on-the-job training; (3) work supplementation programs; and (4) community work experience (CWEP) programs. . . . States may also offer postsecondary education to JOBS participants.[47]

This program identified which adults must participate and requires states to achieve 11 percent participation rates of this identified group. By 1991, state reported information suggested that nationally about 15 percent of the nonexempt welfare population was participating in the JOBS program.[48] This amounted to 5.8 percent of the entire national AFDC caseload.

After falling in real terms from 1980 to 1985, the average monthly benefit per family and per person rose between 1985 and 1986 before falling through 1990.[49] Meanwhile, the number of families participating in the AFDC program fell from 1984 to 85, rose for two years, fell in 1988, and then rose again in 1989. With the beginning of the recession in 1990, AFDC caseloads rose dramatically for the next three years and continued rising through 1994.[50] The overall rise between 1984 and 1988 kept pace with the population, as the AFDC caseload remained in the area of 4.5 to 4.4 percent of the total. This dipped to 4.35 percent of the population in 1989, only to rise above 4.5 percent in the recession year.[51]

We can conclude that despite the moderation of the high benefit-reduction rate for working AFDC recipients, the combination of the OBRA 1981 changes and the continuing decline in real benefit levels constituted a strong disincentive to utilize the welfare system. So how are we to explain the fact that the AFDC caseload as a percentage of the population did not decline? How are we to explain the fact that the AFDC caseload as a percentage of the people in poverty actually rose from 1984 through 1988? How are we to explain the fact that the AFDC caseload of children as a percentage of the children living in poverty also rose?[52]

There are two possible answers. The attractiveness of AFDC was an "absolute" level of attractiveness. Even if it had been made less attractive than before, the fact that it existed at all made it a magnet because of the difficulties associated with earning a living at some low-wage job. The alternative answer is that the persistence of relatively high unemployment rates for most of the decade made the "choice" to work a harder and harder one. Interestingly, in the years when the unemployment rate finally fell below 6 percent (1988 and 1989), the percentage of the population living in poverty on AFDC stabilized at 34 percent (it actually fell by 0.2 percent between 1988 and 1989).

Regardless of which interpretation one would prefer to accept, it does appear that the initial steps toward making welfare so unattractive that people will voluntarily leave the rolls and find some other method of support was stymied beginning in 1984. This fact shows up in the research of Gary Burtless of the Brookings Institution. He created a trend rate of growth of labor supply that combined participation in the labor market with hours worked. For single women, which includes the majority of the adults receiving AFDC, the trend rate of increase in their supply of labor declined after 1981.

> The labor force participation rate of single mothers was 67 percent in March 1988. . . . the rate would have been 69 percent if participation growth had continued at the pace observed in the 1960s and 1970s.[53]

Recall that the supporters of the Reagan Revolution argued that they were beginning the process of weaning Americans away from the welfare state. Taking only the AFDC program as a case in point, we can conclude that the effort stalled for the rest of the decade. When the economy slipped into recession in 1990 and then experienced the slowest recovery of all the postwar recoveries, the resulting rise in the welfare rolls led the majority of Congress to abandon the approach taken by the Family Support Act.[54]

Instead of attempting to create incentives for people to voluntarily leave the rolls, the approach put forward by the congressional majority in 1995 was to end the entitlement status of AFDC and substitute fixed payments to the states. Thus, no matter how many people might qualify for welfare, there would be no more federal money. This points up a very serious problem with the desire to reform welfare. To really reform it so that it becomes a bridge to the labor market rather than a permanent fallback position for those unable (or unwilling) to connect productively with the labor market would cost more money than the existing system, not less. It is cheaper to give people money than to train them for a job, find them a job, and give them the child care and medical insurance necessary to have them keep that job.

There is one other very important point, that moving someone from some form of public assistance into the low-wage job market does not reduce poverty. For all of the 1980s, the federal minimum wage remained unchanged at $3.35 an hour. This translates into an income of $6,968 for a year-round, full-time worker. By 1981, this wage had become insufficient to raise a three-person family out of poverty, and while the poverty threshold rose throughout the 1980s, the minimum wage remained the same.[55] Though the evidence is clear that a very high percentage of recipients of AFDC left the rolls within two years, it is also true that a high percentage of those people returned to the rolls, in large part because of the inability of the low-wage job market to provide a bridge out of poverty. For many opponents of mean-tested entitlements like AFDC this is all the more reason not to permit people to rely on AFDC. Forcing people to "try harder" in the labor market will be the ultimately successful method of combating poverty.

For mainstream as well as radical critics of this approach, there is a serious omission of the historical context. Before the 1960s, there was a large and growing industrial sector that provided a ladder from low-wage, entry-level jobs requiring no skills up to high-wage, secure assembly line work and beyond. The low-wage market is nothing like that anymore, and to say that poverty results because the poor won't work in those jobs is nonsense. People do work in those jobs, but those jobs are no longer tickets out of poverty. The modern critics of the means-tested entitlements are in effect complaining that low-wage workers do not try hard enough. This is a prime example of what many social critics have called "blaming the victim."

In the case of food stamps, we have already noted that both cost in real terms and program participation fell from 1983 through 1987. In 1988, Congress

> increased food stamp benefits across the board, liberalized several eligibility and benefit rules, eased program access and administrative rules, and restructured the employment and training program and quality control system.[56]

The reason for the differing approach to food stamps and AFDC is to be found in a group of beneficiaries of the food stamps program that have not been mentioned in the previous discussion. In addition to helping recipients by increasing their ability to buy food, food stamps help farmers and retailers by increasing the consumer demand for their products. Of this group, farmers in particular are a well-organized, politically potent interest group. Thus, it is not surprising that food stamps were liberalized over the period of the two Reagan administrations, while AFDC continued to be restricted.

In the case of Medicaid, we note that after declining in real terms for AFDC-related recipients between 1981 and 1984, it rose modestly from 1984 to 1988 and then accelerated dramatically from that point onward. Meanwhile, though the other areas of coverage—the elderly, blind, and disabled—did not increase at the same rate, they too experienced accelerations, though for these groups the acceleration occurred after 1989.[57] Part of the reason for these increases was that after Congress made a token gesture in the direction of reduced expenditures, they spent most of the decade liberalizing access. In part this was a result of the increasing difficulty of qualifying for AFDC. Since AFDC was the major route to Medicaid, with the reduction in the ability to receive AFDC, Congress began increasing the ability of non-AFDC recipients to qualify.

> [T]hese legislative actions fundamentally changed Medicaid program eligibility, in that an individual no longer has to be receiving welfare to qualify for Medicaid. In 1992, about 60 percent of Medicaid recipients qualified for Medicaid by virtue of being on welfare, down from 80 percent in 1984.[58]

The general trend saw AFDC recipients and other low-income individuals with substantially reduced access to Medicaid, while other population groups increased their access. Between 1984 and 1990, Congress passed ten Medicaid amendments that liberalized access for pregnant women and children.[59] This led to an increase in the percentage of the general population covered by Medicaid and an increase in the percentage of the poverty population so covered. However, it should be noted that despite this, in 1990 only 42.2 percent of the poor were covered by Medicaid.[60] This created the worst of both worlds, a rising expenditure that was clearly unsustainable on the one hand, and a continuing failure to accomplish its original mission, which was to provide medical care to the poor.

In this context it is important to note that though Medicaid is supposed to be a means-tested program targeted at the poor, many of the elderly who enroll in Medicaid are "poor" only in a technical sense. In order to take advantage of the opportunity to have Medicaid finance long-term care in nursing facilities, many middle-class and even upper-middle-class families have retired elderly parents or grandparents transfer all assets to their children so that their incomes consist of nothing but Social Security and a private pension. They then become eligible for Medicaid assistance in payment of nursing-home fees, while their children or grandchildren get to spend the proceeds of their assets. For many families, this is the only way to protect a lifetime of assets from being dissipated on very expensive long-term care. Nevertheless, it is clear that such activity violates the spirit of the concept of Medicaid. While people might sympathize in general with the idea that a person who has worked hard to build up some assets would like to pass them on to the children and not lose them on astronomical expenditures for a nursing home, the Medicaid program was supposed to finance medical care for people who couldn't afford it, not for well-off people who wanted to make bequests to their children and therefore didn't *want* to pay for it.

Another version of this approach occurs when most assets are transferred years before the need to enter a nursing home, but the individual does begin the stay in the facility as a private purchaser without Medicaid. A process then occurs that is called a "spend-down." As soon as the cost of the nursing home has depleted assets down to some minimum (usually two thousand dollars exclusive of a home) and the income of the individual from private pensions and Social Security falls below the cost of care, this person qualifies for long-term care assistance under Medicaid, and the state begins to pay for the difference.[61]

Clearly the problem of middle-class families protecting the assets accumulated by an elderly relative while Medicaid pays for part of their nursing care is a dilemma. This dilemma is increased because Medicare, the non-means-tested medical entitlement, does not cover long-term care in a nursing home. Between 1984 and 1990, aged residents in nursing homes increased Medicaid expenditures on an average of 5 percent each year, and these were people who did not qualify for cash assistance.[62] In 1990, payments of nursing-home expenses accounted for approximately 35 percent of the Medicaid budget.[63] By the end of the decade the escalation in Medicaid expenditures was bound up in the general escalation in medical costs.

Medicare

Despite the changes in Medicare reimbursements for hospitals, Medicare spending rose from 7.0 percent to 8.8 percent of federal spending between 1983 and 1990. Though this is a significant reduction in the rate of increase, this needs to be compared with the fact that Social Security payments actually fell as a percentage of federal expenditures (from 21.1 percent to 19.8 percent).[64] As the percentage of the population over the age of sixty-five continued to rise, the average number of aged with Medicare part A rose from approximately 24.6 million in 1980 to 29.8 million in 1990. The average benefit per aged person enrolled rose 50 percent in real terms over that same decade. Average annual benefit per aged enrollee in Medicare part B rose much faster, 150 percent in real terms.[65]

Aside from the change in hospital reimbursements in 1983, there were no efforts to deal with the rise in health care expenditures elsewhere in the Medicare system or in general. The Reagan administration developed no policies to stem the tide of medical inflation and never even considered what by the end of the decade was a serious problem, namely the growing numbers of Americans without health insurance. Meanwhile, Americans' spending on health care rose quite rapidly during the 1980s. Health expenditures accounted for 5.92 percent of GDP in 1965, the year Medicare and Medicaid were enacted. By 1980, that spending had risen to 9.25 percent of GDP. When President Reagan left office that ratio had climbed to 11.51 percent of GDP, and it kept right on climbing through the years of the Bush administration.[66]

By 1991, this problem became a major issue in national politics. A relatively unknown former director of the Peace Corps, Harris Wofford, won a surprise victory in a special Senate election in Pennsylvania, defeating President Bush's attorney general, Richard Thornburgh, with the slogan, "If a criminal has a right to an attorney, a citizen has a right to a doctor." A number of Democratic candidates for president ran in the primaries with promises to introduce some form of national health insurance. Candidate Clinton promised it would be his number 2 priority (after deficit reduction and economic recovery, which he claimed were one and the same). President Bush, meanwhile, offered his own version of health insurance reform in 1992. Interestingly enough, with the defeat of President Clinton's efforts to get a health insurance bill through Congress, the Republicans in their Contract with America mentioned nothing about reforming the nation's health care system.[67] However, as part of the 1997 budget agreement, President Clinton and Congress agreed to increase spending $24 billion over five years to bring previously uninsured children into coverage.[68]

Unemployment Compensation

After the economy began to recover in 1983, the unemployment rate began to fall in 1984. However, the rate remained high by historical standards, only falling below 7 percent in 1987. Because the policy of not extending unemployment benefits continued, the percentage of the unemployed receiving compensation payments actually fell during the recovery. In 1983, an average of 44 percent of the unemployed received payments, but that percentage fell to 34 in 1984. For the next four years the average percentage of the unemployed receiving unemployment compensation was below 33 percent. This is in marked contrast to the previous recovery from recession (1976–79), in which the ratio of unemployed receiving payments averaged 52 percent.[69] Thus, we can safely say that the Reagan administration persisted in its policy position that unemployment compensation was more a hindrance to fighting unemployment than a help. The approach was to introduce and maintain flexibility in labor markets. Generous unemployment compensation would be particularly counterproductive, according to this perspective, during a recovery because with business beginning to expand output, individuals might be missing out on new career opportunities in rising industries and/or rising regions of the country if they were collecting unemployment checks and hoping for a recall to a job that was gone forever.

Cutting Government Spending

With the failure of the budget deficit to evaporate as the economy recovered from the 1982 recession, and with Congress balking at the specific program cuts proposed by the postrecession Reagan budgets, some members of Congress decided to attempt to *legislate* a balanced budget. The idea of a constitutional amendment to balance the federal budget had been kicked around before, and in fact it would come to the floor of the Senate in 1986. For a majority of members, this route represented too drastic a step. However, they were willing to try a *law* mandating a balanced budget (in some target year in the future), coupled with a mechanism to get there. The law, as finally passed, was the Gramm-Rudman-Hollings act, officially called the Balanced Budget and Emergency Deficit Control Act. The law charted reduced maximum targets for the federal deficit through 1991, when it was required to reach zero. The law cap was amended in 1987, and the target year for reaching a balanced budget was delayed until 1993.

To force Congress and the president to arrive at a five-year (then seven-year) program of targeted deficit reduction all the way down to zero, the law provided for automatic across-the-board budget cuts that would have to be divided half and half between the Pentagon and civilian federal spending (with Social Security, interest on the debt, and some programs that benefit the poor exempted). In a book written in 1987, Alan Blinder scornfully explained why a law whose sponsor, Senator Warren Rudman of New Hampshire, called a "bad idea whose time has come" passed with such large majorities:

> There were . . . arch-conservatives like Senator [Phil] Gramm [of Texas], who had long been dedicated to shrinking the government. . . . There were traditional Republicans, who were worried enough about fiscal rectitude to favor a tax increase. Exasperated by President Reagan's stubborn resistance to tax hikes, they hoped Gramm-Rudman would force his hand. Rather than risk gutting his precious defense budget, they hypothesized, the president would cave in on taxes. Let's call his bluff, they decided.
>
> Democrats, especially in the House, were willing, perhaps even eager, to give the president a Procrustean bed in which to sleep. Let him submit a budget that abides by Gramm-Rudman, they said, and then let him take the political heat. Others guessed, correctly as it turned out, that the Supreme Court would come to the rescue by declaring the law unconstitutional before it could do any harm. They could therefore show the folks back home that they supported balanced budgets without voting to cut a single spending program—a politically alluring prospect.[70]

As rational economic policy, deficit reduction across the board makes no distinction between extremely valuable government spending (such as on the Federal Aviation Administration, which is responsible for the safety of the flying public) and what might be easily recognized as pork barrel spending (such as dredging a harbor to benefit only the people in that area and indirectly a few transportation companies and customers). The law also required continued deficit reduction, even in the face of recession. It is true there was a weak "escape clause" in the bill, but that could only be invoked if a recession were predicted for the following year. For political as well as technical forecasting reasons, such predictions are almost never made. As Blinder pointed out, the law made no provision for increased deficit spending during the first years of a recovery, when reducing the deficit would work to slow and possibly end that recovery.[71]

Supporters of the law argued that the whole purpose of building in the automatic reductions was to force the president and Congress to agree on a budget that met the target without triggering those reductions. In the end, that did not happen. During the first budget go-round (1986), Congress passed a budget resolution hitting the Gramm-Rudman deficit target for fiscal year 1987 ($144 billion). However, President Reagan refused to accept that budget because it raised taxes and cut defense too much. Congress, in what was becoming known as budget gridlock, refused to permit defense spending to escape the budget-cutting ax and refused to continue cutting domestic programs as in the first Reagan budget. The impasse lasted until after the fiscal year had already begun. Then Congress came up with a budget that appeared to fit under the Gramm-Rudman deficit limit,[72] and it was passed as a continuing resolution in November 1986. When the deficit began to exceed the predictions, the time for automatic reductions had passed.[73]

In 1986, the Supreme Court had declared the automatic mechanism for cutting spending unconstitutional. Congress claimed they were going to "fix" the law by creating a new automatic mechanism. They did that in 1987 and stretched out the time for the achievement of a balanced budget. The automatic spending cuts or "sequester" were granted the president rather than the comptroller of the currency, as in the original law.[74] The act remained the law of the land up until the passage of the Deficit Reduction Act in 1990.[75]

The Thrust of Policy, 1981–89

After reviewing the evidence from both this and the previous chapter, it seems fair to say that on balance, the Reagan-Volcker program was able to move the policy regime in the directions outlined by the conservative critique of the pre-1979 economy detailed in chapter 3. The tax system became less progressive, and marginal tax rates, particularly at the high end, came down. Inflation was reduced dramatically and stayed low. Regulatory growth was stopped, and there was some reversal of the burden of regulation, if only as a result of the learning curve. Redistribution of income to the poor and unemployed was reduced compared to previous periods. There even was the first small step toward making Social Security means tested by the imposition of a tax on some benefits. Meanwhile, federal government spending on nondefense, noninterest, non–Social Security areas of the budget were cut, in some cases quite drastically.[76] This policy regime was the subject of extraordinary controversy during its operation, and that controversy continues to this day.

7

Seven Fat Years, or Illusion?

As promised at the beginning of this book, we will draw some conclusions about the success or failure of the conservative economic policies of 1979–90. To do this, we will first identify the various arguments that have been raised in support of the view that the Volcker-Reagan regime was successful. Then we will catalog the various arguments in opposition. Only after we have explained the arguments as coherently as possible will we be able to figure out which pieces of evidence are useful in refereeing among them.

The Conservatives Celebrate Reagan's Revolution

In 1992, with the election campaign being fought as a partial referendum on the economic policies of the 1980s, Robert Bartley of the *Wall Street Journal* and the magazine *National Review* both produced major efforts to restate the successes of the Reagan economic policy. Bartley's was a full-length book called *The Seven Fat Years and How to Do It Again*. The *National Review* produced a series of articles called "The Real Reagan Record."[1] In addition to these sources, the various reports of the Council of Economic Advisers throughout the Reagan and Bush administrations provide evidence and arguments for the successes of the Reagan economic policies.

Interestingly enough, the centerpiece of most of the analysis by the Council of Economic Advisers is the successful battle against inflation, while Bartley and the *National Review* focus on economic growth, productivity growth, and job creation. For starters, we note that inflation was significantly reduced and from 1983 on never exceeded 5 percent. The low rate did not stop the Federal Reserve from remaining extremely vigilant, even indicating in the late 1980s that zero inflation was a realistic goal. Once we recognize the success with inflation, we can turn our attention to the other macroeconomic impacts: investment, productivity growth, income growth, and job creation.

As mentioned in chapter 2, investment plays an important role because it is at the same time a stimulator of aggregate demand and the vehicle by which productivity increases find their way into the economy. Let us consider the most mundane of technological improvements, the substitution of the scanner at the supermarket checkout line for the eyesight, recognition, and digital dexterity of the clerk. It may not seem like much, but it takes a clerk perhaps three times as long to locate the price on an item and punch it into a cash register as it does to run the universal product code past the scanner. Thus, people wait shorter times at checkout counters and stores need fewer clerks to process the same number of people. Introducing scanners is clearly an example of an improvement in productivity.

But those scanners would not be at the checkout counter if some company had not invested in the equipment to make them and the supermarkets had not made investments to buy them. The actual fixing of new technology in new products and then integrating that new technology into an already existing production process requires investment.

If we then move to the world of information processing—clerical work and record-keeping—we note that the replacement of the typewriter and carbons by the computer and xerox machine that revolutionized the office in the 1970s and 1980s required massive investments. First the computer companies produced the hardware and software. Then the businesses bought them for their offices. Both of these demanded a great deal of thinking, figuring, learning, and adapting, but they also involved physical creation of new equipment.

So investment is a major indicator of the private sector's activity that does two positive things at once. On the one hand, it provides a kick of aggregate demand that, via the multiplier, induces consumption and raises GDP. On the other hand, it potentially increases society's productivity because investment involves adding new capacity *and* replacing old capacity. The best way to measure the impact of investment on an economy is to look at investment as a percentage of GDP. When investment rises faster than GDP (in other words, when investment as a percentage of GDP increases), it is playing a significantly stimulative role. Over a business cycle upswing, one can track the contribution of investment to increases in productivity by noting the average ratio of investment to GDP. Here, historical comparisons to other business cycle upswings are useful. Even though the relationship between investment and productivity is an uncertain one, the point is that investment at least provides a *potential* for improvement in productivity. Measuring investment as a percentage of GDP becomes a useful indicator of how well changes in the incentive structure (say, as a result of tax changes, regulatory relief, and the overall improvement of the business climate) have worked.

For Bartley and others, the level of investment in the 1983–90 period is not the only story. Equally important is the rise of the venture capital industry. The great computer-driven transformation of communications, information processing, home entertainment, retailing, and so on involved new products and new companies. Before these new companies are actually out soliciting investors, they are nothing but ideas in the minds of dreamers. Would-be entrepreneurs need start-up capital to transform their ideas into tangible assets so they can take the next step, product development. If they do not already possess this start-up capital, as is usually the case, they need to interest lenders who are willing to take risks for the sake of high potential payoffs. Bartley points out that

> the sale of shares, or IPO for initial public offering, is a latish stage in the capital investment process. . . . The most crucial seed money comes earlier. For this, US capitalism has developed an industry. . . . Venture capital firms raise money on the bet that their management can pick out the most promising new firms, provide the initial funding and produce extraordinary returns.[2]

Bartley explains the availability of venture capital that provided the initial money for the technological transformation of much of American industry and society during the 1980s as resulting from the capital-gains tax cut of 1978, followed by the successful retention of the capital-gains preference in the Economic Recovery Tax Act of 1981.

The availability of financial capital has been the subject of tremendous controversy. Many have criticized the focus on purely financial investment as opposed to real physical investment that actually improves the productivity of the economy and puts people to work. From the point of view of an individual deciding what to do with one hundred thousand dollars, it makes no difference whether she or he buys a life insurance policy, stock, or bonds or starts a business. The key decision will depend on the expected rate of return corrected for risk. However, the first three examples merely *move the savings* from control of the individual to control of the insurance company or from seller of the stock or the bond to the purchaser. No investment that affects GDP has occurred. Starting one's business, assuming it involves purchasing capital equipment and perhaps even some construction activity (retrofitting a building, for example), does physically increase the nation's capital stock. If the business starts up with the newest technology, the start-up investment is making a contribution to increasing society's productivity.

There was a significant acceleration in the amount of purely financial investment, specifically merger activity, during the 1980s.

> [M]ergers and acquisitions increased from 10,108 during 1979–83 (an average of 2,022 per year) to 18,389 during 1984–88 (an average of 3,678 per year). . . . the total value of mergers and acquisitions increased from $249.9 billion during the first five years of this period to $880.3 billion during the last five years.[3]

Such purely financial investment has the potential to increase society's productivity, but only indirectly. Getting the savings of millions of individuals into the hands of risk-taking entrepreneurs make new investments possible. Bartley and others have argued that even the financing of takeovers, often accompanied by struggles over the terms merging two giants, have created the fear of outside acquisition and have forced companies, in the words of *Fortune,* to "cut fat, restructure, and become more efficient."[4] And in fact, employment in *Fortune*'s top 500 corporations fell 3.5 million between 1980 and 1990. Nearly half the companies listed in 1980 were not listed in 1990: "Most of the missing had been merged with other companies."[5] The Council of Economic Advisers in their 1985 report devoted an entire chapter to the market for corporate securities and concluded that on balance the growth of purely financial investment, especially mergers and acquisition, had been good for the productivity of the businesses involved, because only the threat of an outside-takeover bid forced a management to be highly responsive to the needs of their shareholders.[6]

Another element in the argument that the Reagan years were a solution to the problems of the 1970s involves emphasizing the successes after 1982 and contrasting that with the period between 1973 and 1981. Thus, the 1989 report by the Council of Economic Advisers stated,

> Between 1973 and 1981, the rate of inflation was nearly three times as high as between 1948 and 1973, averaging more than 8 percent and

reaching 9.17 percent . . . at the business cycle peak in 1981. . . . Higher inflation was not buying lower unemployment, and the unemployment rate reached 7.4 percent at the business cycle peak in 1981. . . . Productivity growth plunged to a scant 0.6 percent per year between 1973 and 1981. . . . Growth in real GNP per capita was cut to one-half the 1948–73 rate, to a 1.1 percent annual rate between 1973 and 1981. Real median family income showed no growth, despite the growth in the proportion of two-earner families. . . . The poverty rate increased from 11.1 in 1973 to 14.0 in 1981.[7]

By comparison, the council emphasized the successes of the 1980s.

Since 1981, real GNP has risen at a 3.0 percent annual rate, a significant improvement over the 2.1 percent annual rate between 1973 and 1981. Real GNP per capita has risen at a 2.0 percent annual rate, compared with a 1.1 percent annual rate between 1973 and 1981. . . . Since 1981 private business sector productivity has grown at a 1.7 percent annual rate, more than double the 1973–81 rate. Manufacturing productivity has grown at a 4.1 percent rate since 1981, roughly one and one-half times the postwar average and more than three times the rate of 1973–81.[8]

Finally, the council argued that gross investment was above the postwar average as a percentage of total output, but that the net investment had been trending downward.[9] This is an important point. In the National Income and Product Accounts of the United States, gross investment includes a measure of the economic cost of replacing worn-out capital equipment.[10] That cost has been rising as a percentage of GDP for the last twenty years. From our point of view, gross investment is the appropriate measure, because even investment that replaces worn-out equipment incorporates the latest versions of that equipment, increasing productivity. Despite the low level of net investment, the productivity of the nation's capital stock was rising, contributing, according to the council, to the positive overall productivity performance of the economy.

The Mainstream Critique

Two elements usually surface in the mainstream critique of the 1983–90 period. The first and most dramatic is the so-called twin-deficits problem. The argument goes like this. When the recovery of 1983 began in earnest, the fiscal-policy changes had become so entrenched that the structural deficit was a very high percentage of GDP. Thus, as the economy began to show signs of a vigorous recovery in the second half of 1983 and all of 1984,[11] the federal deficit as a percentage of GDP rose. It was 4.9 percent in the fiscal 1984 and 5.2 percent in fiscal 1985.[12]

This led the Federal Reserve to tighten up on monetary policy. After falling steadily from April 1982 to February 1983 (from 14.94 percent to 8.51 percent) the Federal Funds rate climbed to 11.64 percent in August 1984 before falling back to 8.35 percent in January 1985. The entire average for 1984 was 10.23 percent. For 1985 it was 8.10 percent. This tight-money policy stopped the recovery of 1984 short of reducing the unemployment rate anywhere near the so-called natural rate of 6 percent. The unemployment rate fell to 7.3 percent in the fourth quarter of 1984 and stayed at 7 percent or higher until the fourth quarter of 1986, when it finally reached 6.8 percent. It didn't fall below 6 percent until the fourth quarter of 1987. Similarly, the capacity utilization rate rose from its nadir of 72.4 percent in the fourth quarter of 1982 to 81.8 percent in the third quarter of 1984. It fell to 78.7 percent in the third quarter of 1986 before rising to its maximum of 84.6 percent in the first quarter of 1989.[13]

The tight-money policy worked to counter the strong fiscal stimulus of the structural deficit during 1984 and 1985. As a result inflation was not rekindled by the recovery, but from the point of view of fully utilizing human and physical capacity, the economy stalled far short of its potential GDP. Thus, for mainstream economists at least part of the explanation for the success of the anti-inflation policy was the maintenance of a high level of unemployment and a low level of capacity utilization.

In addition, some economists in the mainstream tradition have been anxious to note that the rise of international competition during the late 1970s and especially the 1980s has made it virtually impossible for noncompetitive firms to raise prices in the face of declining demand. This argument suggests that it was not the Volcker-Reagan policy that defeated inflation but increased international competition. Many also believe that the success of the Volcker anti-inflation program was based in part on a "supply shock" of *falling* international oil prices after 1981. Just as many economists argued that the difficulties in the 1970s could be explained with reference to upward surges in oil prices, these same economists believed that the 1983–89 recovery's proceeding without rekindling inflation had more to do with the fall in oil prices than with the policies of the Federal Reserve.

The method by which inflation was reduced initially, namely the restraint of aggregate demand, required strong enough monetary restrictions that the fiscal stimulus would not become inflationary. This led, not only to high interest rates, but (because of the reduction of inflation) to historically high *real* interest rates. This helped create, according to this approach, the second half of the so-called twin-deficit problem. To understand this problem, we need to recall the discussion of crowding out in chapter 3. The idea is that the pool of available savings to be utilized by private-sector businesses for investment is the very same pool from which government borrows when it runs a deficit. If the Federal Reserve refuses to create enough new money to finance the deficit, interest rates rise, potentially crowding out private-sector borrowers.

However, the simple crowding-out analysis ignores the fact that international financing became more and more available in the 1970s and 1980s, in part as a result of the massive buildup of dollar holdings by certain OPEC countries, particularly Saudi Arabia, Kuwait, and the United Arab Emirates. When interest rates rose dramatically in the United States and inflation began to subside, holders of dollars overseas as well as holders of foreign currencies began to see financial investment in the United States as very attractive. Interest rates were high, and with inflation reduced, the long-term prospects for the international value of the dollar were good. Remember, if you're not an American, investing in a dollar denominated interest-bearing asset means risking a fall in the value of the dollar vis-à-vis one's own currency over the lifetime of the investment. The relative value of currencies can be quite volatile, as international holders of the dollar discovered in the middle and late 1970s. Thus, the decline in inflation and the seriousness with which the Federal Reserve pursued tight monetary policy reduced the risks of reigniting inflation and future falls in the value of the dollar.

So one reaction to the rise in interest rates in the United States was a big increase in the desire of foreigners to own assets denominated in dollars. This led to a rise in the international value of the dollar. Just as fears over the inability of the Federal Reserve to control inflation in the late 1970s had led to a decline in the value of the dollar, so belief that the Federal Reserve had gotten serious led in the 1980s to a rise in the value of the dollar. Note that that rise dates from the fourth quarter of 1980 and continued, with two short interruptions, till the value of the dollar against the currencies of the major industrial nations peaked in the first quarter of 1985.[14] Thus, this increase predates the impact of the tax-cut-induced fiscal deficit by two years.

As mentioned before, changes in the international value of the dollar have a major impact on the competitiveness of exports from the United States and competitiveness within the United States of imports from abroad. Just as the reduced value for the dollar improved the ability of U.S. producers to export and reduced Americans' willingness to buy foreign imports in the late 1970s, so the reverse occurred in the early and middle 1980s. A good measure of this is the merchandise trade deficit. In relation to GDP, it was less than 1 percent for 1979–82 and rose to 1.5 percent in 1983, 2.6 percent in 1984, 2.7 percent in 1985, and 3.0 percent in 1986.[15]

What Harm Was Done by the Twin Deficits?

The concern of mainstream economists throughout the 1980s centered on these twin deficits. The fear was that the large budget deficits would have two kinds of permanent consequences. The first was the straightforward crowding out of domestic investment. In fact, many argued that the relatively low percentages of gross domestic product devoted to investment after the boom year of 1984 can be traced to the high real interest rates engendered for most of the decade.[16]

The Gramm-Rudman-Hollings Act did not succeed in permanently reducing the federal deficit. Table 10 shows the deficit targets (for both versions of the act) as well as the actual deficit for those fiscal years.

For three years (fiscal 1987 to 1989) Congress and the president were able to approximate the targets of the 1987 law. In 1990 the recession destroyed all semblance of an effort to keep up with the Gramm-Rudman schedule. Just before that failure became apparent, the Council of Economic Advisers in their February 1990 report stated,

> *When viewed from a broad perspective, GRH has provided valuable control over Federal spending. . . .* A focus simply on the difference between GRH targets and annual budget deficits ignores important progress in controlling deficits. Since the adoption of GRH, the deficit has fallen steadily as a percentage of GNP. Moreover, deficits are far below the path projected prior to the adoption of GRH. . . . Furthermore, the rate of Federal debt accumulation has stabilized.[17]

TABLE 10. Goals, Successes, and Failures of Gramm-Rudman-Hollings

Fiscal Year	1985 Target	1987 Target	Actual Deficit
1986	171.9	171.9	221.2
1987	144.0	144.0	149.8
1988	108.0	144.0	155.2
1989	72.0	136.0	152.5
1990	36.0	100.0	221.4
1991	0	64.0	269.2
1992	0	28.0	290.4
1993	0	0	255.1

Source: Columns 1 and 2: ERP 1990, 72; column 3: ERP 1995, 365.

Economist Benjamin Friedman disagreed. He attacked the high deficits of the Reagan years in a 1988 book, *Day of Reckoning*. He argued that there is clear evidence of crowding out after 1984. He argued that Federal Reserve tight monetary policy initially caused the real interest rate to be quite high in 1981 and 1982.

> But even after monetary policy eased, real interest rates still remained high. Most of the drop in nominal interest rates merely reflected the slowing of inflation rather than a decline in the real cost of borrowing. . . . For the previous thirty years, the real interest rate on short-term business borrowing had averaged less than 1 percent. But it was over 5 percent in 1981, over 4 percent in 1986, and nearly 4 percent in 1987. Our new fiscal policy, generating ever larger deficits even in a fully employed economy, had long since replaced tight monetary policy as the reason for high real interest rates[18]

Note that his argument assumes that beginning in 1984, the economy was close enough to full employment for the deficit to begin crowding out private investors.[19]

The real interest rate can affect investment because it is part of the *cost* of productive capital investment. It is a cost in two senses. Explicitly, corporations and other businesses contemplating productive investment will usually have to resort to the capital market to borrow some if not all of the funds. The gross profit rate they receive must be sufficient to pay interest on those funds, pay taxes on the net profits, and still realize an acceptable after-tax rate of return. The tax changes introduced by the Reagan administration went a long way toward raising the after-tax profit rate, but, unfortunately, the rise in the real interest rate reduced the pretax profit rate.

The rise in the real interest rate also represents what economists call an *opportunity* cost. This means that even if the owners of businesses have accumulated sufficient internal funds to make investments without borrowing from the capital market, they still will take account of the rate of return their money could earn them if it were invested in interest-bearing assets. Productive investments that might be engaged in if the interest rate were 5 percent appear unattractive by comparison if the interest rate is, say, 8 percent. Even businesses with internal funds available will *choose* to put more of them into interest-bearing investments when rates rise.

The second cause for concern was that the increased foreign purchases of American dollars and the consequent rise in the international value of the dollar would result in a long-run decline in competitiveness. Overseas markets lost to American exporters would be hard to win back. American consumers who become used to buying imported products when they suddenly become cheaper as a result of the rise in the international value of the dollar will not automatically switch back to domestically produced products. This is true even if, as occurred after 1986, the dollar were to depreciate, removing the temporary advantages for foreign imports.[20] In addition, Robert Blecker pointed out,

> national firms could shift production overseas during the period of overvaluation, paying the fixed, sunk costs of relocation while they are low in terms of the home currency. Then, after the home currency depreciates, those firms can maintain foreign production as long as the operating costs abroad, converted to domestic currency, remain low enough to allow for profitable export back to the home country. In some product lines, little or no domestic production may remain after the overvaluation is reversed.[21]

Beginning in 1984 with the publication of the Brookings Institution's *Economic Choices* and continuing throughout the 1980s, mainstream economists and many political figures kept up a drumroll of complaint about the twin deficits.[22] In the mid-1980s, the Federal Reserve, acting in concert with central bankers in Europe and Japan, forced down the value of the dollar with some expansionary monetary policy. This led to a couple of years of falling real interest rates and rapid monetary growth.[23] The effect on the exchange rate was as expected. The international value of the dollar declined from its peak in the first quarter of 1985 till the end of 1987. Though it drifted downward from that point, the fall was slight.[24] Meanwhile, the trade deficit peaked in 1987 and began to decline as a percentage of GDP. However, by 1992, despite the fact that the value of the dollar had basically returned to its 1980 level, the trade deficit was a higher percentage of GDP than in 1980.[25]

The important element of this twin-deficits criticism of the 1980s prosperity is that financing significant levels of domestic investment and government deficits by borrowing from abroad *cannot go on forever.* In other words, using foreign savings to fuel the engine of growth is unsustainable. If the U.S. economy could generate sufficient domestic savings to finance both investment by the private sector and the politically desired excess spending by government, there would be no problem; in fact, in such a situation, the government deficit would be an essential element of aggregate demand and necessary to keep GDP as close to its potential as possible. But borrowing from overseas involves a trade deficit (by definition, the only way to borrow dollars from overseas is to first send more dollars overseas to buy imports) that has potential long-term consequences. Such borrowing also depends on the willingness of foreign investors to continue increasing the percentage of dollar-denominated assets in their investment portfolios. That increased percentage is going to reach some limit. When that occurs, the flow of funds from overseas will be reduced.

More significantly, the critics of the twin deficits argued that such borrowing is worthwhile only if the proceeds are invested productively so that repaying the loans is made easier. Here, analogies to individual borrowing and business borrowing are useful. Virtually everyone who owns a home takes out a mortgage to finance it. That is a perfectly legitimate way of consuming the services of housing. The benefits you get from owning your own home flow to you every year you live in it.[26] Thus, paying for it on time *as you utilize it* is totally acceptable. Obviously, if you suffer a financial reversal, say, you lose your job, you may not be able to sustain the mortgage payments and may have to sell the house and spend less on housing. But note that as long as you can afford to pay for utilizing the service of the house, that monthly mortgage payment is not cutting into your current consumption. Compare that with taking out a home equity loan and using it for a vacation. When the vacation is over, you must cut back on consumption of other items every month following the vacation for the life of that loan. And since this home equity loan was not invested in some enhancement of the home that increases the value to you of living in it, you get no benefits month after month to justify having to make those higher payments. In that situation, increasing the borrowing on your home creates a burden for yourself in the future.

Consider the same situation for a business. No one would argue that a corporation that issued twenty-year bonds to finance major construction projects to expand productive capacity was engaging in an irrational business practice. The newly constructed capacity should increase the revenue flow to the corporation over the life of the facilities, and that revenue should be more than sufficient to pay the interest on the loans. (If not, then financial officers will have made serious errors in calculation.) Now imagine, instead, that the corporation borrowed from the bond market and chose to buy a vacation retreat for top executives. Unless the increased ability of executives to "play and work together" in such a setting improves the productivity of the corporation, repaying those loans will have to come out of the revenue stream, thereby cutting into profits and dividends. Such a use of borrowed money would have negative consequences for the judgments of the corporation by both the stock and bond markets. A management team that authorized such use of borrowed money might very soon find itself the target of a takeover bid, unless, of course, it satisfied the investing community that executive vacations were a legitimate investment in the future well-being of the business.

The moral of these two examples is that borrowing for investment purposes is legitimate, but borrowing for current consumption is not. Of course, individuals do borrow for current consumption, but when that happens they must reduce consumption while they pay back the loan. Borrowing for investment, however, should produce increased flows of revenue out of which the loan and the interest can be paid back.

Returning to the problem of the twin deficits, we can note that the centerpiece of the criticism leveled by mainstream opponents of the policies of the 1980s is that such borrowing financed, not productive investment, but instead a "long consumption binge": "Between 1980 and 1987, consumer spending has grown almost 1 percent faster per annum than total spending in our economy."[27] In fact consumption as a percentage of GDP rose throughout the 1980s, rising from 64 percent of GDP in the depths of the recession of 1982 to 66 percent of GDP at the end of the decade.[28]

Benjamin Friedman also raised a point later echoed by H. Ross Perot. Friedman argued that after foreigners had accumulated large amounts of dollar-denominated financial assets, some began to cash in those assets to purchase real assets: factories, real estate, farmland, and so forth.[29] He warned that foreign ownership of American land and capital would be disadvantageous to the United States. Here he is in direct conflict with another member of the mainstream opposition to Reagan's program, the secretary of labor in Clinton's first term, Robert Reich. In his book *The Work of Nations,* Mr. Reich argued that the modern international enterprise has so many internationally interconnected parts that the nationality of the "ownership" of the corporation is virtually irrelevant.[30]

This is another very interesting issue. When politicians and academics in the 1960s and earlier argued that the spread of American and other advanced countries' businesses into the Third World was a modern version of imperialism, they were generally dismissed.[31] The argument was that in underdeveloped sections of the world, foreigners who obtain control of productive resources hire local factors of production, increase the output of the domestic economy, and, in the case of production for export, increase the foreign-exchange holdings of the economy, facilitating the importation of important capital goods. Foreign owners have access to foreign sources of capital and bring into the economy advanced technology. Since their goal is long-term profitable operations, their motivations will, according to this approach, be only marginally different from those of a local owner of the same business. The only potential problem is repatriation of profit, but that is counterbalanced by the inflow of financial capital for investment purposes.

The "imperialism interpretation" sees foreign ownership of local wealth as a method of exploiting local factors of production. The most extreme example of this is in so-called enclave economics, in which the advanced sector uses foreign factors of production to exploit domestic resources and the resulting products are then exported. The income from this successful business is mostly spent on compensating foreign owners, leaving little benefit to the domestic economy. Repatriation of profit, far from being compensation for inflows of foreign capital, often exceeds the inflows because many of the foreign-owned companies raise their (financial) capital locally instead of bringing it in from abroad.

The United States is not an underdeveloped nation with an advanced enclave more tied to the international than to the domestic market. The problem, however, is a similar one.

Becoming a nation of tenants rather than owners will jar sharply against our traditional self-perceptions. America will no longer be an owner, directly influencing industrial and commercial affairs abroad. At the same time, we will have to accept the influence and control exercised here by foreign owners. The transition is certain to be demoralizing and probably worse if potentially dangerous frictions also develop as the ordinary resentments of renters against landlords and workers against owners increasingly take on nativist dimensions. . . . World power and influence have historically accrued to creditor countries.[32]

Friedman argues that just as Britain was able to exercise considerable influence during the nineteenth century as an international creditor, the U.S.'s

influence as a genuine world power . . . gained further momentum when this country first became a major lender to Britain and France at the time of World War I and then dramatically gained maturity during and after World War II. . . . the political, cultural and social position that traditionally accrues to the foreign banker became this country's due. . . . Nations can lose influence as well as gain it. . . . The fiscal policy we have pursued in the 1980s has spawned just such a reversal. . . . the predictable consequences will inevitably follow, as America increasingly depends on foreign capital—a change that cannot help but alter America's international role.[33]

These arguments echo the views of radicals. The influence that Friedman sees accruing to creditors is the power that radicals emphasize. The fear of loss of national sovereignty emphasized by candidate Perot and others is part of this analysis, also. Stated as precisely and carefully as possible, the complaint seems to be that when the health of one's economy is dependent on the willingness of international bankers and foreign central banks to cooperate with your economy's needs, the national political structure must make its policy judgments not merely on the basis of what the majority of people in the country want, but on the basis of what will be acceptable to the international bankers and foreign central banks.

Suppose the majority of the people in the United States desired a policy of very low unemployment. In order to avoid the high interest rates that would follow from an excessively expansionary fiscal policy, suppose Congress were to order the Federal Reserve System to keep interest rates constant as the unemployment rate falls. Such a policy would entail rapid expansion in the money supply to finance the budget deficit to prevent crowding out and higher interest rates. Anticipated inflation would make investments in interest-bearing assets relatively unattractive, particularly to foreigners, who would see in the expected inflation and future decline in the international value of the dollar an unacceptably low rate of return *in their own currency*. The result would be a serious drain of financial capital from the United States. Not only would foreigners cash in their interest-bearing assets and move their capital to some safer haven, but Americans with money to invest might choose to put it into overseas interest-bearing notes. The decline in the value of the dollar and the acceleration of inflation might create a serious crisis of confidence in the business community, and investment might decline, even with the high levels of aggregate demand.

On the other hand, consider the same policy in the context of the United States as a net international creditor. The rise in government deficit-spending to finance the low-unemployment policy would merely divert funds that were previously flowing overseas to domestic spending. The position of an international creditor would give the economy a cushion from which to engage in a fully domestically oriented program without concern about an international collapse of the value of the dollar. Thus, becoming an international debtor does remove some of a nation's independence in setting economic policy.

The response, which comes not merely from supporters of the Reagan policy like Bartley but also from mainstream critics like Robert Reich is that whether or not one is an international creditor or debtor, the internationalization of production and capital markets has proceeded to such an extent that even a national economy as large and diversified as the United States must be concerned about international competitiveness and the judgment of international investors. In other words, it is not the debtor or creditor status that reduces national independence. National independence has already been reduced. The successful economies will attract international capital, and the unsuccessful economies will be punished by the judgment of international investors and consumers.

Despite this initial agreement, Reich and Bartley remain at opposite ends of the spectrum. Whereas Bartley sees the inflow of international capital as a judgment on the success of the Reagan policies of fostering incentives and rapid investment growth, Reich sees potential long-term erosion of America's economic strength due to the neglect of what he considers the most important roles for government, provision of good education and maintenance and extension of physical infrastructure.

Reich titled his book *The Work of Nations* in an effort to hark back to Adam Smith's *The Wealth of Nations.* To Reich, the wealth of a nation depends on the kind of work done by its people. If one does highly skilled, creative work of high value to the modern business enterprise, one will be handsomely rewarded. Other work will be rewarded at the lowest common international compensation rate, no matter how efforts at protectionism might try to delay or reverse that process. The key to locating business activity depends, according to Reich's analysis, on the availability of a pool of high-quality employees and good communications and transportation infrastructure. In addition, there must be a high quality of social infrastructure as well, so businesses can attract the high-quality employees they wish to hire to their current location. Thus, for Reich, the issue is not the inflow of foreign capital to purchase American assets that signals long-term economic difficulties. Instead it is the type of assets purchased that is crucial. If foreigners build facilities where researchers into product development, corporate leaders, inventors, and general researchers locate and produce their various "outputs" (often intangible), the nation is economically healthy over the long term. If foreigners buy up real estate or ongoing companies and reinvest the profits elsewhere, that is an indication that the infrastructure and skilled-educated labor force in the United States are not as advantageous as those available overseas. In such a situation, the alarm sounded by Friedman would be justified, but for a different reason.

To summarize the various elements of the mainstream critique, we can identify a number of points. The high budget deficits coupled with the Fed's severe anti-inflationary policies caused a much deeper than necessary recession and a less prosperous recovery. Particularly important was the relative sluggishness of productive investment in the private sector caused by the high real interest rates (crowding out occurred) and the reduced productive investment within the public sector (particularly infrastructure and education). The method by which crowding out was partially avoided, namely the financing of much investment by relying on overseas savings, contributed to a significant increase in the international value of the dollar, with serious consequences for the long-run competitiveness of American exports, producing significant permanent penetration of the domestic market by imports. The accumulation of the ownership of American assets in the hands of foreigners translates into a long-run decline in American economic independence, as defined by Benjamin Friedman and Ross Perot.

Thus, this critique boils down to identifying serious unsustainable elements in the post-1983 recovery. The high-interest-rate, high-government-deficit policy cannot be sustained because it ultimately involves borrowing indefinitely from overseas. The rise in government deficit spending over time increases the percentage of the government budget that must be devoted to interest payments. It also crowds out *some* private-sector investment. Government spending on the military, as opposed to projects that could be considered investments in the society's future, such as infrastructure and education, has long-run consequences for productivity growth As infrastructure and education deteriorate, the desire of international businesses to *locate* in the United States will decline. This is not something that will be noticed overnight, but over a decade or so, the decline will have serious consequences.

Radicals Respond to Conservative Economics

Those working in the radical tradition emphasize the exercise of power and the distribution of income in assessing the success or failure of an economic policy. As mentioned in chapter 4, radicals argued that for business and political leaders in the United States, the social safety net had become too expensive. The ability of labor to resist falls in the real wage rate had been the cause of the stagflation of the 1970s. The regulation and tax policy of the government had been too solicitous of low-income people, workers on the job, and the environment. It was necessary, from the point of view of the ruling circles in the United States, to reestablish the power of capital.

According to the majority of economists working within the radical tradition, the attempt to alter the balance of power within the economy in favor of investors and businesses and away from the population in general and labor in particular was an almost complete success. In *After the Wasteland,* Samuel Bowles, David Gordon, and Thomas Weisskopf argued specifically that the effort to reduce the regulation of business, to ease the tax burden on investment income, to redistribute income from the majority of the population to the top 20 percent (and even further to the top 5 percent), and to shift the priority of federal spending toward defense *all succeeded.*[34]

Just as the very nature of the success in the early postwar period created the seeds of future difficulty in the 1970s, so the methods used to bring success to the Volcker-Reagan program insured that these would not produce the expected results. The ultimate goal of the reassertion of power by business interests was to raise profitability sufficiently to stimulate productive capital investment, which would then feed on itself to produce further increases in profitability in a "virtuous circle" of profits, productivity growth, economic growth, more profits, and so on. Along the way, benefits of higher incomes and better jobs would trickle down to the rest of society.

It didn't happen. First of all, the benefits never trickled down. Inequality grew dramatically, as did poverty. Unemployment remained high for virtually the entire decade. Note that unlike the mainstream critique, which sees these results as *failures* of the Volcker-Reagan program, the radicals see the growing inequality and high unemployment rates as *keys to the success* of the program. Inequality and high unemployment constituted the stick that forced wages down as a way of fighting inflation while attempting to enforce increased productivity in the workplace, mostly through increasing the *effort* expended by workers. In analyzing this shift in the balance of power, Samuel Bowles and Juliet Schor have devised a measure known as the cost of job loss. When one loses a job, the best way to avoid a permanent reduction in income is to immediately get another job that is just as good. Obviously, the higher the rate of unemployment, the less likely finding that job is. So one aspect of the cost of job loss depends on the rate of unemployment. However, another important aspect of the cost of job loss is how much of the fall in income is *cushioned* by the social safety net—particularly unemployment compensation payments. Bowles, Gordon, and Weisskopf track this cost of job loss and argue that after declining significantly between 1966 and 1973, it rose only 1 percent on average between 1973 and 1979 and then only two more points between 1979 and 1989.[35]

This, and the shifting tax burden and shifting spending priorities, did increase the *share* of profits in the national income. From a class perspective, the rise in the share of income going to the "investing class" should raise investment. Here Bowles, Gordon, and Weisskopf identify important contradictions in the policy of business ascendancy. The very methods by which the *share* of profits rose tended to discourage, rather than encourage, investment. For example, they agree with

Benjamin Friedman and other critics of the twin-deficits problem in identifying high real interest rates as one of the culprits.

But there is another, even more significant by-product of the increased power of the business owners. The higher-than-average unemployment rate for the recovery was coupled with a lower-than-average capacity utilization rate. With a low capacity utilization rate, despite the rise in the share of profits, the expected rate of profit will not be sufficiently high to justify expansion of capacity. The reason should be obvious. What rationale is there for a business to expand capacity if present capacity is not being fully utilized? Making a productive investment does not depend solely on having the current profits to finance it; it depends crucially on the projection of *rising demand* for output that *current capacity* cannot meet. Until capacity utilization gets high enough to *force* businesses to increase that capacity in fear of losing customers to their competitors because of their future inability to expand output, expected rates of profit from such investment will not be high. Thus, the important tool of business success—the high unemployment and low capacity utilization—became the reason for the sluggish investment. Note that this analysis adds an important element to the mainstream critique, which was based, as we have seen, almost exclusively on the high real interest rate.

Another argument from the radical perspective is that reduced opportunities for productive investment, in part caused by high real interest rates, but also caused by the inherent stagnation tendencies in our economy, has resulted in a explosion in purely financial investments. With productive investment highly risky due to the overhang in excess capacity, purely financial investments in mergers, interest-bearing notes, real estate, and so forth permit high rates of return with much less risk.

Economist Robert Pollin has connected the long-run tendency toward stagnation to growing debt-dependency in the entire nonfinancial sector, not merely the government sector, as emphasized by Friedman.

> This can be seen when . . . we divide twentieth-century US financial activity into [long] cycles. . . . between 1897 and 1949, the net borrowing to GNP was remarkably stable at around 9 per cent for each long cycle. This relationship also held between 1950 and 1966. However, . . . between 1967 and 1986, this figure rose to 14.6 per cent, a 60 per cent increase over the historical average.[36]

Pollin believes that one of the results of the stagnant growth in incomes and profits has been the increased reliance of private households and businesses on credit. First this happens "to sustain expenditure growth in the face of declining revenues."[37] In addition, within the business sector, borrowing for speculative (purely financial) investments takes place for reasons mentioned above. The increased private-sector borrowing found investors not merely in the United States but abroad. "The US trade deficit . . . [was] instrumental in supplying foreigners with dollars which were then available to be recycled into the US financial market."[38] Note that this is not merely the result of high real interest rates but of a structural change in the borrowing habits of the entire nonfinancial sector, not only the government.

The combined impact of these structural changes that resulted from the long-run stagnation tendencies has been to weaken the ability of large budget deficits to stimulate the economy, as was possible in the past. The potential for crowding in as argued by Keynesians such as Robert Eisner depends on the expectations business leaders will have of profitability should they decide to create new assets. To the extent that stagnation tendencies have dampened profit expectations, the positive impact of budget deficits is reduced.

In addition, the entire period since World War II has seen the important role of budget deficits in countering downturns in the business cycle. This meant that unlike the period before World War II, business cycle downturns did not include any actual price deflation, and defaults were limited.[39] This might appear to be a positive trend, but not so. Michael Perelman points out in *The Pathology of the American Economy* that "market economies require strong competition and strong competition breeds depressions and recessions."[40] The ability of government deficits to prevent major recessions for much of the period after World War II has, in Perelman's view, changed our economy from "a strapling [*sic*], accustomed to the dangers and the rigors of a competitive jungle" to "a tragic bubble-boy who weakens daily in an atmosphere of loving care."[41] This weakness is what economist Hyman Minsky identified as financial fragility. In brief, this concept relates to the rising ratio of debt to assets in the private sector. Prior to World War II, recessions would enforce default on those firms that had borrowed too much. This periodic removal of the weakest businesses contributed to the strengthening of the financial structure of the entire economy. But as Pollin notes, "In the absence of debt deflations no automatic mechanism exists for discouraging the sustained growth in private debt financing."[42] This means that a higher and higher percentage of businesses increase their vulnerability to reductions in income. It stands to reason that a firm with a strong balance sheet can weather even a couple of years of low or negative rates of return by taking on more debt. On the other hand, a firm already deeply in debt will be stuck with a larger payment responsibility vis-à-vis income and be unable to tap the credit markets for new loans. Thus the argument from the mainstream that the growth in the period after 1983 was based on unsustainable forces is supplemented by the radical economists who emphasize that stagnant real growth leads to an explosion in purely financial investments that increases the financial fragility of the economy. That, too, is unsustainable, as the entire country discovered when the savings and loan crisis broke in 1988.

The International Aspects of the Radical Critique

In the international sphere, radicals identify another contradiction by which the very elements of success create the subsequent difficulties. One of the causes of the squeeze on profitability in the 1970s was the rise in the relative price of imports, particularly—but not exclusively—petroleum. The period of declining value for the dollar may have made exports competitive, but they also increased the cost of imports. With the *rise* in the value of the dollar in the first five years of the 1980s, the relative costs of imported products declined accordingly. However, the method of solving the problem of high prices for imports involved the same rise in the real interest rate that kept unemployment high and capacity utilization low. Another result of the appreciating dollar was the rise in the trade deficit. The trade deficit is another element of sluggish aggregate demand that keeps capacity utilization low and therefore interacts with the high real interest rate to dampen investment.

In addition, the Federal Reserve's monetary policy is constrained, not merely by the need to combat domestic inflation, leading to higher unemployment rates and lower capacity utilization rates, but because domestic credit markets have to attract foreign savings. The trade deficit makes dollars available to overseas lenders that could be sent back to the United States to purchase interest-bearing assets. However, that does not guarantee the willingness of foreign wealth-holders to purchase such assets. For that, they need expectations of high real rates of return denominated in their own currency. Thus, not only do they need a high enough interest rate to compensate for expected inflation in the United States, they need some assurance of the (relative) stability of the exchange rate between the U.S. dollar and their currency. This means that the Federal Reserve has to be extremely careful not to recreate the negative expectations many foreign wealth-holders formed during the period of "malign neglect."[43] This is the very same problem identified by Benjamin Friedman when he complained about the disadvantages of being a net international debtor.[44]

Thus, in a number of respects, those who believe that the basic problem confronting the United States economy in the past twenty-five years has been the emergence of a general tendency toward stagnation are relying on the same evidence Friedman used to argue that the irresponsible budget deficits of the Reagan era had harmed the economy. The difference is that Friedman blames the financial problems on the Reagan budget deficits, while radicals believe the budget deficits were a *result* of the tendency toward stagnation—a response to that tendency that did not fix the problem but merely increased financial activity and financial fragility.

Changing the Balance of Power in the Economy

Bowles, Gordon, and Weisskopf argue that the response to the difficulties experienced by the economy in the late 1970s led to a concerted attempt to increase the power of business. They argue that that effort was only an apparent success. The increased power was bought with self-destructive increases in the unemployment rate and the real interest rate. Unless more basic structural changes in the behaviors of workers and managers were to occur, profitability and productivity growth would become unacceptably low when the unemployment rate and real interest rate fell.[45] They conclude that there were no such basic changes despite the many successes of the Reagan Revolution.

Among the elements of the structure that Bowles, Gordon, and Weisskopf investigate is the intensity with which workers do their job. Recall that in chapter 2 we identified two different ways output per unit of labor can be increased. The first way enhances the ability of workers *using the same effort* to produce, the second involves increasing *intensity*.

If one can imagine conflicting desires on the part of workers and their supervisors as to how much intensity workers expend during the hours they are working, then the power of capitalists to push the level of intensity closer to its physical and mental maximum depends on their ability to cajole or bribe workers into willingly raising their levels of intensity or to threaten or punish workers if they refuse to raise their levels of intensity. Bowles, Gordon, and Weisskopf attempted to measure the elements that might cause workers to voluntarily raise their efforts with numbers like the index of worker satisfaction,[46] real spendable hourly earnings,[47] and the inverse of the industrial accident rate.[48]

They also attempted to measure the "stick" with which workers could be threatened for not working diligently enough. These numbers involved the cost of job loss, the amount of inequality among workers, and the percentage of supervisors involved in the production process. These require some analysis. The cost of job loss has already been developed. Suffice it to say that the higher the burden placed on a worker who loses a job, the more likely that worker will be anxious to work hard enough to please a supervisor. With a relatively modest social safety net and the prospect of a significant time spent unemployed, such a worker will be most anxious not to get fired. The attitude expressed in the 1970s by the country music song "Take this Job and Shove It" can quickly disappear when this job is the only one around and scores of unemployed people are dying to take it.

A higher percentage of supervisory personnel indicates that workers have a greater chance of being "caught" not working hard enough. Thus, for any given cost of job loss the probability of being forced to endure that cost increases if there are more supervisors. Most of the people who said, "Take this job and shove it" said it out of earshot of a supervisor. The more supervisors, the less likely they'll be out of earshot.

Finally, inequality is measured in order to capture the extent to which workers can band together to make it difficult for the owners and supervisors to enforce the speed and intensity they hoped for. There is tremendous evidence, going back to the early struggles over Taylorism,[49] that organized workers can thwart the efforts of owners to force them to work faster. One of the most dramatic episodes was the struggle in Lordstown in 1972.[50]

From this perspective, inequality among wage earners goes hand in hand with declining union membership.[51] Both play a role in eroding the ability of workers to resist increased intensity on the job. Thus, inequality should show up in increased productivity statistics. Arrayed against this is that fact that the median income of male year-round full-time workers actually declined over the decade from 1979 to 1989. The "cost of job loss" in that sense actually declined.[52] However, since the availability of unemployment compensation had been reduced and the average length of time one spent unemployed had increased, the decline in the cost of job loss due to declining wages was more than offset, but just barely.

This discussion of the intensity with which people work is just one element in Bowles, Gordon, and Weisskopf's attempt to see if long-term structural changes had come to the economy as a result of the Reagan Revolution. They conclude that they had not. The lower level of capacity utilization and the higher level of unemployment merely contributed to a rise in the "apparent power" of capital. If Bowles, Gordon, and Weisskopf are right, then the only way to preserve the profitability that did exist in the 1980s would be to permanently keep unemployment high and capacity utilization low. If they are right, recoveries must be stopped well short of any meaningful measure of "full employment."

In summary, radicals argue that since the Reagan-Volcker program did not solve any of the structural problems in the American economy, it is not surprising that it produced such disappointing results. The key point is that the apparent success was bought with such reductions in living standards, capacity utilization, and aggregate demand that profitability for productive investments was not restored sufficiently. The flight into purely financial investment was thus a symptom of the lack of attractiveness for the investment that would really have a positive impact on people's lives and long-run growth prospects in the economy.

How Do We Play Referee?

In the three strands of arguments on which we have focused in this chapter, certain issues keep rising to the forefront. All agree that inflation was reduced and contained, though some believe the cost of that victory was too high. A very interesting result of the reduction of, and containment of, inflation has been the historical destruction of the alleged link between budget deficits financed by money creation and the rate of inflation. As mentioned in chapter 3, when government budgets are financed by borrowing from the Central Bank rather than from the public, and when the Central Bank permits the money supply to rise sufficiently to cover that deficit, there is no crowding out of private-sector activity. Those who believe the words of Milton Friedman, "Inflation is always and everywhere a monetary phenomenon,"[53] conclude that the result of financing deficits with money creation will ultimately involve an increase in inflation. Yet even the most casual glance at the relationship between the government deficits of the 1980s, the rate of growth of money, and the rate of inflation should indicate how strongly the facts of 1983–90 contradict this proposition.[54] Perhaps because the pre-1980 budget deficits were relatively small as a percentage of GDP, the assertion that money-financed deficits were inflationary could be made on the basis of monetarist research alone. However, the experience of the large postrecession deficits that were paralleled by rapid expansion of the money supply in 1985 and 1986 but accompanied by declining rates of inflation should lay to rest the simplistic connection between deficits and inflation.

When it comes to identifying the impacts of the Volcker-Reagan program other than on the rate of inflation, there is tremendous disagreement. Was investment high and rising or low and stagnant? Did productivity growth rebound dramatically, or was it disappointing? What about employment? The unemployment rate? Once more we are faced with the question with which we began this investigation. What is the basis on which we can judge something a success or a failure? The next chapter attempts to use the historical experience to create a basis for judgment about whether the results of the Reagan-Volcker program can be considered a success or a failure.

8

Testing the
Various Assertions

Examining the disagreements between those who celebrate the Volcker-Reagan program and those who denigrate it, we find them speaking past each other when they describe what happened in the 1980s. As for the elements of a successful economy, they are clearly disagreeing about investment, the rate of growth of productivity, the rate of growth of real GDP, the level of unemployment, and the level of capacity utilization. However, the disagreement often comes down to different interpretations of the same numbers. For example, they all agree that a significant recession occurred, that inflation was reduced and did not reignite. Similarly, they recognize that profit rates were higher than in the period before 1979.[1] However, they interpret these facts differently. Specifically, their interpretations disagree over whether the sacrifices that accompanied the successful anti-inflation policy were justified, according to the other criteria of success identified in the previous chapters.

In order to make it absolutely clear what the basis of my conclusions is, I have collected quarterly information from 1960 through 1991. I use quarterly, as opposed to annual, data because many of the relevant periods we need to summarize are not complete years but, say, one or two quarters. The reader who wants to see the entire set of raw data is urged to refer to the tables from which the averages mentioned here are drawn.[2]

As discussed earlier, given the nature of our private enterprise economy, investment decisions by the private sector drive two processes at the same time. From the point of view of increasing economic growth, investment is the vehicle that fixes new technologies into the production process, part of the supply-side impact celebrated by Bartley and Lindsey. From the point of view of achieving our potential level of output, employment, and income growth, investment is a crucial component of aggregate demand. Consumption *responds* to increases in income. Government responds to political pressures. Outside of extraordinary periods such as all-out war, only investment growth can drive a recovery from recession into prosperity. The incentive effects of the totality of the Volcker-Reagan program were supposed to produce sufficient increases in investment to drive the recovery with increased aggregate demand while also sustaining the recovery with vigorous productivity growth. The productivity growth was supposed to play an important role in holding down inflation and maintaining our nation's international competitiveness. According to Lindsey and Bartley both of these occurred.

The success of the recovery in reducing unemployment rates (and raising capacity utilization rates), sustaining the rate of growth of real GDP, and doing so without rekindling inflation is heralded by those who believe the Volcker-Reagan program was a success. Thus, we believe that by focusing on the five sets of statistics collected in the appendix to this chapter, we will be answering the crucial questions about the economic impact of this program.

Starting with the recovery from the 1981–82 recession in the fourth quarter of 1982, we have thirty-one quarters of recovery through the peak in the third quarter of 1990. During that time, investment[3] as a percentage of GDP averaged 16.08 percent, civilian unemployment averaged 6.75 percent, capacity utilization averaged 80.92 percent, the rate of growth of real GDP per capita averaged 2.77 percent, and productivity growth averaged 1.35 percent. In addition, from its nadir in December 1982, the number of civilians working rose by over 19 million to its peak in May 1990.[4] When we ask whether these numbers represent success or failure, the answer, as always, involves another question, "Compared to what?"

An Investment Boom?

The way to answer that question is to actually compare the Reagan expansion to two other postwar expansions. A particularly useful comparison is the recovery from the 1974–75 recession, for this is the period that was considered such a failure by American policymakers. This was the period that the Reagan Revolution was reacting to. The recovery from the 1974–75 recession began in the second quarter of 1975 and peaked in the first quarter of 1980. Thus, this was a twenty-quarter expansion. Investment as a percentage of GDP averaged 17.18 percent for this expansion. What is interesting about this is that despite the alleged damage done to incentives by high and rising marginal tax rates, regulation of business, and destabilizing aggregate-demand management, the private sector's investment incentives were running quite strong until the Volcker policy of tight money to fight inflation regardless of cost was adopted in the fall of 1979.[5]

During the thirty-two-quarter expansion, 1962–69, investment as a percentage of GDP averaged only 15.63 percent. This raises an interesting question as to whether or not the 1960s were as good an experience for the private sector as is commonly assumed. If high marginal tax rates on individual and corporate income harm incentives, could lower investment rates between 1962 and 1969 be associated with higher taxation than in 1975–79?

First of all, nonfinancial corporations had lower tax liabilities in the earlier period than in the post-1975 period.[6] Turning to marginal federal income tax rates for a family of four at the median income, twice the median income, and half the median income, we discover divergent results. The median-income marginal tax rate stayed near 20 percent for most of both decades (1960–80), rising to 25 percent at the end of the period. Twice-the-median-income families, on the other hand, experienced big increases in their marginal tax rate. From 1970 through 1980, that rate rose dramatically, from about 18 percent to 43 percent. It is this increase that many economists focus on, because it is the incentives of people with higher incomes that are considered so crucial to generating a large volume of savings and investment. Meanwhile, families at half the median income actually experienced lower marginal income tax rates after 1970 than between 1960 and 1965.[7] Thus, it appears that the marginal income tax rates and the taxation of corporate income were not the cause of the relatively modest levels of investment registered in the 1961–69 recovery. This leads us to conclude that the rising marginal tax rates after 1970 did not damage investment incentives compared to the previous period of economic growth. The data also indicates that the changes introduced by the Reagan administration into the tax and regulation structure did not have the hoped-for dramatic effect on private-sector investment activity.

Before we move from this conclusion to the general statement that the incentive effects so crucial to what Lindsey called "the growth experiment" were apparently not as significant as the supporters of Reaganism had hoped, it would be useful to take some longer-run comparisons as well. Instead of comparing recoveries from recessions, we can take peak-to-peak comparisons for (roughly) all three decades as well as trough-to-trough comparisons. The advantage of these longer-run comparisons is that they encompass full business cycles. An analysis of a recovery could conceivably give a misleading result if the recession that precedes the recovery is particularly severe. To take just one example, the growth in jobs from December 1982 to May 1990 is quite impressive, but it did mask the decrease in over a million jobs from 1981 through 1982.

If the reader will recall the previous chapter, virtually all of the analyses in support of the Reagan program emphasize the unacceptable performance of the economy over a longer period than 1975–79. For example, many of the references are to 1973–81. We believe, however, that if one wishes to make long-term comparisons, it is essential to make them from the same phase of the business cycle.[8] This way, the analysis can give a sense of the long run developments in the economy without distorting the evidence. My three long-run comparisons roughly cover the 1980–90 decade (abbreviated VRB for Volcker-Reagan-Bush) the 1969–80 period (abbreviated NFC for Nixon-Ford-Carter) and the 1960–69 period (abbreviated KJN for Kennedy-Johnson-Nixon). Each comparison averages the investment ratio from the quarter immediately following the peak through the peak at the end of the period or the quarter immediately following the trough through the trough at the end. This information from the raw data tables is summarized in the appendix to this chapter to demonstrate these comparisons as well as the comparison with the 1975–79 recovery. In the thirty-eight-quarter period from 1960 to 1969 (peak-to-peak) investment as a percentage of GDP averaged lower than in the forty-one-quarter period from 1969 to 1980. In the forty-two-quarter period from 1980 through the peak in 1990, investment averaged less than in NFC, though more than in KJN.

There are two interesting aspects of this comparison. First, despite the fact that the 1970s and 1980s experienced more serious recessions than in KJN, investment still averaged higher in those quarters peak to peak. Second, measuring the long-run impact of the Volcker-Reagan program from peak to peak demonstrates conclusively that the success in defeating inflation did not translate into a significant increase in investment as a percentage of gross domestic product. The positive incentive effects of reducing inflation coupled with the positive incentive effects of decreasing government regulation, lower marginal tax rates, and less taxation of income from capital were insufficient to generate higher percentages of investment than the period (NFC) when all of these incentive effects were presumably having extremely negative consequences.

Put another way, the negative incentive effects of the 1970s—more regulation and taxation of business and higher marginal tax rates than *either* the period of the Volcker-Reagan policy *or* the previous period of the KJN prosperity—did not stop business from investing at a higher rate in NFC than in the other two. We have to conclude that something else must have been at work to override the incentive effects of the reduced inflation and taxation, or, alternatively, we will have to conclude that the incentive effects so emphasized by supply-side economics are not very important in practice. This latter point has particular resonance in the context of the tax law signed by President Clinton in August 1997. It is clear that a disproportionate share of the benefits go to high-income taxpayers. It also is important when we recognize that the law passed in 1995 to stop Congress from imposing unfunded mandates on state governments will have the effect of hindering the introduction of new government regulations. Many believe these changes will improve incentives—just as many asserted similar views about the changes wrought by the Volcker-Reagan program. Yet in fact the evidence is that since regulations increased dramatically between KJN and NFC and since investment actually was higher in the latter period, such regulations do not appear to have the negative impact that Weidenbaum and others have asserted.

The third comparison shows VRB closer to the period immediately prior. This involves taking the comparison from trough to trough over the decades rather than peak to peak. The defenders of the Volcker-Reagan policy have often argued that the recessions of 1980 and 1981–82 cannot really be blamed on that policy regime. Instead these recessions were the inevitable consequences of the failed policies of the 1970s. In addition, the Economic Recovery Tax Act did not begin to be effective in actually cutting tax rates until 1982. Thus, according to this view, the only fair comparison is to take as representative of VRB the long run from the recovery after 1982 through the trough of the 1990–91 recession. Thirty-three quarters are covered by this period. Surprisingly, investment averaged a lower percentage of GDP than in NFC, even though the earlier period experienced two severe recessions compared with one relatively mild one at the end of VRB. Again, the trough-to-trough ratio for KJN shows significantly lower investment percentages.

No matter how we attempt to make our comparisons, it appears that investment was not stimulated nearly as much as one might have expected.

What about Productivity Growth?

Lest the reader feel that the issue is settled, it is important to remember that Robert Bartley argued that investment was not necessarily the most important indicator of improved incentives. He emphasized the availability of venture capital, which in his view was increased by the expansion of the capital-gains tax preference in 1978 and its continuance up through 1986. The ferment in financial markets and the pressure on managements in any and all enterprises from the deal makers who created such intense publicity in the middle and late 1980s are positive things, according to Bartley. We believe that if his argument is true, we should see some evidence in productivity data.

Beginning with the recovery in 1983, output per hour of employed worker rose dramatically for two years and then slowed appreciably. For the entire thirty-one quarters, the average rate of growth of productivity was 1.35 percent. If we compare that to the twenty quarters of the 1975–79 period, 1975–79 nonfarm business productivity growth averaged 1.63 percent, *more* than in the thirty-one-quarter Reagan recovery.[9] If we compare it to the thirty-two-quarter KJN recovery, we note an average rate of productivity growth of 2.71 percent. This is particularly striking because in both 1962 and 1964, there were significant improvements in the incentives built into the tax code, and until the last years of the decade there was very little inflation. Thus, one would expect that if the Reagan incentive structure had reversed the negative effects of NFC, notwithstanding the lower levels of investment as a percentage of GDP, the rate of growth of productivity would, if anything, more closely resemble the KJN prosperity rather than the twenty quarters in the later 1970s. This does not appear to have been the case. Again we are forced to the conclusion that other tendencies counteracted the positive impacts of the incentives, or, alternatively, that the incentive impacts are relatively insignificant in a quantitative sense.

Looking at the long-run comparisons, the decade-long peak-to-peak analyses show a long-run decline in productivity growth. VRB averaged lower than the previous two periods. Looking at it trough to trough, the same long-run decline is apparent.

This conclusion can help us shed some light on the debate about the role of purely financial investment in enhancing the productivity of businesses by forcing management to defend against potential takeovers. If that defense had involved significant improvements in managerial and other efficiency, or if teams that successfully took over businesses were able to institute significant productivity-enhancing reforms, we should expect there to be some significant improvement in productivity growth during the decade when such pressures were at their maximum. It didn't happen. This is very general but significant evidence that the response of corporate management to the fears of takeover activity in the era of leveraged buyouts did not show up in measurable improvements in productivity. Perhaps the methods used in defending corporations against takeover had more to do with piling on heavy loads of debt and other efforts to make the company *unattractive* for takeover. In any event, we can safely conclude that the response of corporate managements to fears of takeover did not produce strong productivity growth, in comparison to the era of NFC as well as the earlier, KJN period.[10]

We should note in this context that improvements in efficiency at the managerial level and in fact overall *would* show up in the statistics. The Division of Productivity Research of the Bureau of Labor Statistics provides a note accompanying their data printout.

> Although the productivity measures contained in this listing relate output to the hours of all persons engaged in each sector, they do not measure the specific contribution of labor, capital, or any other single factor of production. Rather, they reflect the joint effects of many influences, including new technology, capital investment, the level of output, energy use, and managerial skills, as well as the skills and efforts of the work force.[11]

In other words, the rate of growth of productivity is not restricted to "labor productivity" but approximates the total productivity of the sector of the economy in question. Included in the improvements captured by these statistics are "managerial skills." A very rough piece of evidence for the potential improvement in productivity that results from increasing merger activity would be to observe the data for the period when mergers were on the increase and very much in the news. Since 1984 saw the first $100-billion-year's worth of merger activity and by 1985 there was much discussion in the press and among academics,[12] it is safe to say that the assumed incentive effects on management of the *threat* of takeovers would most certainly have been apparent by 1985. Taking the years 1985–88 (1989 was the year after the savings and loan crisis erupted), productivity in the nonfarm business sector rose a paltry 1.05 percent, significantly lower than the per quarter average for the entire recovery.[13]

Discussing the rise in productivity provides a useful lead-in to another bone of contention between the supporters of the Volcker-Reagan program and the detractors. Virtually all supporters of those policy changes point to the creation of new jobs as one of the hallmarks of its success. President Reagan, in his last *Economic Report,* noted that "nearly 19 million non-agricultural jobs have been created during this period [1982–88]"[14] One of the problems in identifying job creation as a success is that slow job creation often indicates high rates of growth of productivity, while rapid job creation can be evidence for slower growth rates. Thus, KJN had much more rapid productivity growth than either NFC or VRB but less job creation.[15]

Another point is that the longer a period, the more job creation would be expected to occur. Thus, the best way to compare the impact of the different policy regimes on job creation is by taking the per quarter average for job creation over the relevant period. When we do, we note that the recovery of 1975–80 created more jobs per quarter than the longer VRB recovery. It had a bit more productivity growth as well, providing evidence against our suggestion that there is an inverse relationship between productivity growth and job creation. However, when we compare the VRB recovery to the longer NFC recovery (1971–80), there is more job creation in the former, but productivity growth is greater in the latter. That inverse relationship also holds true for both the two long peak-to-peak comparisons and for the trough-to-trough comparisons.

Four of the possible five comparisons between NFC and VRB exhibited the inverse relationship. In addition, the strength of that inverse relationship is quite dramatic when any NFC or VRB period is compared with its counterpart in KJN. Thus, we believe it is important to stress that job creation in the 1970s and 1980s is perhaps more a result of sluggish growth in productivity than of successful policy. In the long run, it is only through productivity growth that incomes can grow, and it is only through income growth that job growth can be assured. Job growth associated with sluggish productivity growth is a prescription for an increase in jobs that do not bring good incomes.

Unemployment and Capacity Utilization

Sometimes, rapid job growth is insufficient to keep up with the rise in the labor force. When that occurs, job growth can be associated with unacceptable levels of unemployment. In theory, economists have no problem identifying unemployment as an unambiguous waste of human resources. However, there is a tremendous amount of controversy as to how much unemployment ought to be considered an acceptable minimum. If in fact the acceptable minimum level of unemployment has grown over the decades (particularly, as some have argued, when the labor force is expanding rapidly with many inexperienced workers),[16] then comparing the Volcker-Reagan period with the previous periods is not possible unless we have an agreed-upon analysis of how that acceptable minimum changed for the different periods.

In order to avoid getting tied up in this dispute, I have chosen to use the capacity utilization rate as the indicator of how poorly the economy is achieving its potential. There is no "natural rate" of capacity utilization comparable to the "natural rate of unemployment." High capacity utilization is usually a signal for businesses to make investments and expand capacity. It does not, in and of itself, create inflationary pressures, unlike the labor market, in which reductions in unemployment usually create upward pressure on wages.

In comparing VRB with the previous two periods, we begin as we have for investment and productivity with a comparison of the two recoveries. The thirty-one quarters after 1982 averaged 6.75 percent unemployment and 80.92 percent capacity utilization. This compares with 6.93 percent unemployment and 82.32 percent capacity utilization for the twenty quarters beginning in the second quarter of 1975. Here we see evidence of the success of the Volcker-Reagan program of *sustaining* the economic expansion much longer than was possible after 1969.

When we compare VRB with KJN, we get a different story. The thirty-two-quarter expansion in the KJN years averaged only 4.44 percent unemployment and a very impressive 86.42 percent in capacity utilization. However, by the end of the expansion, inflationary pressures had built up. Unemployment was below 4 percent for four straight years (1966–69), and inflation climbed from 1.6 percent in 1965 to 5.7 percent in 1970.[17] If we, therefore, restrict our comparison to the years before the rate of inflation exceeded 4 percent, the average unemployment and capacity utilization for the period from 1962 to 1967 (twenty-four quarters) were 4.75 percent and 86.27 percent respectively. These figures are hardly any lower than they were in the next eight quarters. This suggests that it is possible to have sustained periods of high levels of capacity utilization and low levels of unemployment without necessarily accelerating inflation.

However, others will argue that only the more vigorous efforts of the Federal Reserve in the late 1980s prevented the reduction in unemployment that occurred in 1988 and 1989 from reigniting inflation.[18] Thus, there is room for argument that the Volcker-Reagan program (with its higher unemployment and lower capacity utilization) "bought" a longer recovery than had been thought possible since 1969.[19] It also permitted the recovery to continue for thirty-one months; although the KJN recovery lasted longer, it had unemployment rates that were too low, and thus inflation occurred.[20]

Over the three long-run periods, measured peak to peak, we see the forty-two-quarter VRB period with higher unemployment and lower capacity utilization than the other two periods. Trough to trough the same order of results obtains.

One (Relatively) Bright Spot

What about GDP per capita? In this case, we need to measure a complete business cycle, either peak to peak or trough to trough. Measuring expansions will bias our comparisons. The deeper the recession, the more rapid the rate of growth *during* the recovery.[21] The peak-to-peak measures show a forty-two-quarter average of 1.69 percent for 1980 to 1990, which is less than the 1970–80 peak-to-peak measure, but only marginally less than the 1973–80 twenty-five-quarter period. The 1960–69 thirty-eight-quarter period had the most vigorous growth rate of all. The trough-to-trough measures are quite dramatic. Because of the stagflation of the 1970s and because the 1982 recession was the deepest since the 1930s, the per capita real GDP averaged only 1.62 percent in growth over the forty-eight quarters between 1971 and 1982. The rate of growth for the Reagan-Bush years was 2.34 percent for thirty-three quarters trough to trough, while in 1962–70, the thirty-six-quarter trough-to-trough average was higher.

Thus, we can conclude that about the only positive impact of the Volcker-Reagan program aside from the stifling of inflation was the good performance of the rate of growth of per capita GDP. Surprisingly, this was not caused by a dramatic increase in the ratio of investment to GDP, nor was it caused by dramatic improvements in productivity. Among the other components of aggregate demand, net exports averaged greater negative levels in the ten years from 1981 through 1990 than in the period from 1970 through 1980. (In the 1960s, net exports were positive).[22] Robert Blecker published a study in 1992 that argued that the increased trade deficit of the period after 1980 was not merely the result of the combination of expansionary fiscal policies with restrictive monetary policies between 1982 and 1985. Instead, he developed evidence that the persistence of the trade deficit even after the international value of the dollar began to fall could be attributed to a long-run decline in competitiveness.[23] Such a decline is consistent with relatively unimpressive rates of productivity growth.

The sluggishness of investment and productivity growth and the negative impact of the international sector on aggregate demand suggests the possibility that the growth in real per capita GDP might have resulted from the government sector and high levels of consumption. Since one of the goals of the supply-side policies was to change incentives so as to raise the rate of savings in the economy, if consumption in effect rose, that would be evidence that those incentives had changed in the *opposite* direction than predicted by the theory and the policymakers.

Consumption: The Record

In the raw data tables, we have collected quarterly data on consumption. We have organized it to observe two measures, the consumption-GDP ratio and the ratio of consumption to disposable personal income.[24] This latter concept reveals the behavior of all households in the economy. Each household has an income flow out of which it determines how much to spend. Some households have accumulated assets and that can also be spent. Finally, other households can increase their indebtedness in order to spend on current consumption items, though this practice obviously has limits. All income that is not spent is either used to pay off debt or increase the wealth of the household. Though many people speak of "investing" when they put unspent income into a certificate of deposit or a life insurance policy or the stock market, until a *new asset* is created that act of not spending is *saving,* not investing.

Households can really determine how much they wish to consume only after they have received their *disposable personal income.* This is the final dollar figure they receive after they have paid their taxes and after all transfer payments have been received from the government. To capture the impact of incentives on households, consumption divided by *disposable income* gives a much better measure than the consumption-to-GDP ratio. However, the calculation of the relationship of consumption to GDP helps demonstrate the impact of taxation and transfers. With this measure we go beyond the incentive effects captured when we use disposable income. When the consumption-GDP ratio behaves differently than the consumption-disposable income ratio, this indicates the impact of taxes and transfers on the level of income received.

If we observe the ratio of consumption to gross domestic product over time, we can see that no matter which subperiods we take, the average ratio never was more than 64 percent nor less than 60 percent between 1960 and the beginning of 1982. Between 1960 and the end of 1981, before the incentives of the Economic Recovery Tax Act would have taken effect, the ratio averaged 63.3 percent per quarter. When we measure the consumption-GDP ratio between 1982 and the second quarter of 1990 (before discussion of Bush's plan to raise taxes might have begun to harm incentives), we see an average ratio of 65.3 percent. This is 2 percent of GDP above the previous periods. Two percent of GDP was $93.8 billion in 1987. If consumption ratios had not been higher in this period and if nothing else had occurred to raise aggregate demand, there would have been at least a $187 billion reduction to overall GDP (assuming very conservatively a multiplier of two), which in 1987 was 4 percent of the actual GDP.

Interestingly, when we compare the pre-1982 period to the 1982–90 period in terms of the ratio of consumption to disposable income, we see much less of a difference. The average for 1960 through 1981 is 88.9 percent, while during the year of the first 10 percent tax cut (1982), the ratio of spending out of disposable income climbed, but only to 90.7 percent. What is important to note, however, is that in neither calculation do we see *any evidence* of the significant increase in the incentive to save that was promised by the theorists of supply-side tax cuts.[25] On the contrary, the evidence about the behavior of consumption in the period where the supply-side incentives were combined with the successful conquest of inflation supports the view that *rising consumption* was a major component of rising per capita GDP.[26]

The Reagan Deficits: A Final Judgment

When it comes to the role of government, we need to be very careful about our focus. From the point of view of aggregate demand, as mentioned chapter 2, we need to look not at the federal government but at the combination of spending and taxing by all three branches of government. We also have to look not at the absolute level of spending and taxation, not at the absolute level of the budget deficit, but at these quantities as a percentage of GDP. It is clear from even the most casual observation that VRB saw significantly higher deficits as a percentage of GDP than did the previous two periods. This is directly traceable to the activities of the federal government. Whereas during NFC, state and local surpluses significantly reduced the impact of the federal deficits, except in recession years, in the period after 1965 there were significant increases in deficit spending, and VRB saw such a massive increase in federal deficit spending that even relatively large state surpluses were not sufficient to offset them.[27]

At this point, we must confront head-on the argument about crowding out. The most extreme form of the crowding-out hypothesis suggests that every dollar borrowed by the government (that is, every dollar of deficit spending) represents a dollar that was not borrowed and therefore not invested by the private sector. Implied in this extreme view is the conclusion that, for example, if in 1985 the total government deficit was 3.2 percent of GDP and investment averaged 17.1 percent of GDP, then with a balanced national budget, investment would have been 20.3 percent of GDP. According to a more moderate analysis, to the extent that the total government deficit can be blamed for real interest rates higher than would otherwise exist, some investment that would have occurred at the lower real interest rate did not occur.

The opposing view is based on the argument that interest rates, whether real or nominal, are not the most important determinants of investment. Interest represents a cost to the investor, but the expectations of high and/or rising sales may increase the prospective investor's optimism about potential gross profits.[28] For example, if I know I have to borrow at the prime rate of 8 percent, and my best projections tell me I'm going to gross 20 percent, I might consider the net rate of return of 12 percent (and that's before I have to pay taxes) too low, given the risk. Over the next six months, if the economy starts moving at a faster pace and more of my potential customers are getting jobs and getting raises, I may revise my projected gross upward, perhaps as high as to 30 percent. If the prime rate, meanwhile, climbs to 10 percent (a quite dramatic increase for a six-month period), I still expect a net rate of return of 20 percent, significantly higher than the 12 percent of a half year ago. It is these kinds of calculations that lead many economists to question the impact of rising interest rates in response to government budget deficits. This is particularly true because as the government spends the money that is causing the budget deficit to grow, that money is finding its way into the pockets of government employees, businesses supplying the government with goods, and recipients of transfer payments. To those people, this government spending is income, and they spend a significant portion of it, increasing the incomes of other people, and so on. The multiplier effect from the rise in government spending, not balanced by a rise in government taxation, may at times have a very positive impact on the investment decisions of business, leading to crowding in rather than crowding out.

The discerning reader will already have sensed our problem. Those who believe that crowding out occurred as a result of the existence of deficits in the period after 1984 can assert that real interest rates would have been lower and therefore investment would have been higher if there had been lower deficits. Those who believe crowding in occurred can assert that the rate of growth of GDP would have been lower and therefore expectations of profitability would have become depressed and therefore investment would have been lower if there had been lower deficits. How can we tell which is correct? Both are making assertions about what is called a *counterfactual,* what would have happened in an imaginary world that in fact did not exist.

Here comparisons with previous periods are not useful, because the budget deficits were unprecedented (except in wartime) in the postrecession years of 1984–89. Instead, we believe that an examination of the course of real interest rates in those postrecession years in comparison to the year 1984 might give us some clues. The reasoning behind this view is that 1984 represented a very dramatic increase in investment from the previous year and, more importantly, the highest annual ratio of gross private investment to GDP for the entire recovery. Though we know that nominal interest rates fell from 1984 through 1987 and rose to below the 1984 peak in 1989,[29] many would argue that the key impact of budget deficits is on the real interest rate. Table 11 shows investment as a percentage of GDP and the two versions of the real interest rate for the six years 1984–89,[30] as well as the total government deficit as a percentage of GDP.

The government deficit as a percentage of GDP reached a peak in 1986 and then fell rapidly. If the crowding-out hypothesis were to be validated by these years, we would expect the real interest rate, especially the one based on expectations, to rise as the deficit is rising and fall while the deficit is falling. In fact, however, the expected real interest rate fell through 1986 and then rose. (Meanwhile the after-the-fact real interest rate fell through 1987 before rising.) We should also expect investment to fall as a percentage of GDP while the deficit is rising (responding to a predicted rise in the real interest rate) and then rise when the deficit starts to fall. However, in reality, investment as a percentage of GDP fell steadily for the entire period.

The result does not confirm the crowding-out hypothesis. The higher real interest rates were associated with lower budget deficits at both ends of the period. When those interest rates fell, they did not induce investment to rise. On the contrary, while real interest rates were falling, investment was falling, and when real interest rates started to rise (even though the deficits were falling), the investment decline continued. If these years constitute an important test of the assertion that high deficits crowd out private investment by causing increases in real interest rates and conversely that falling deficits stimulate rises in private investment by causing real interest rates to fall, then crowding out has flunked the test.[31]

This should not be surprising because, as many analysts have noted, American investors did not have to rely solely on domestic savings for their investments.[32] The best measure of foreign-savings flows to the United States is the net foreign investment column in the National Income and Product Accounts. Beginning with the 1983 recovery and continuing through 1990, there was a significant net flow of foreign savings to the United States. This added to the pool of

TABLE 11. Is There Evidence for Crowding Out?

Year	Total Government Deficit (% of GDP)	Real Interest Rate[a]	Expected Real Interest Rate[b]	Investment (% of GDP)
1984	3.0	8.14	5.47	18.34
1985	3.2	6.63	5.13	17.10
1986	3.5	5.63	4.53	16.33
1987	2.6	5.11	4.91	15.92
1988	2.1	5.62	6.29	15.32
1989	1.7	6.67	7.70	15.24

Source: Column 1: Department of Commerce, Bureau of Economic Analysis; columns 2–4: *ERP* 1996, 286, 360, 280.

[a]Prime rate minus rate of growth of GDP deflator
[b]Prime rate minus expected rate of growth of GDP deflator

domestic savings from which government and private-sector borrowers were drawing. Assuming that the private-sector depreciation funds were sufficient to cover the difference between gross and net investment, we note a significant rise in the percentage of the net domestic investment that could be accounted for with the contribution of foreign savers to the domestic savings pool.[33] As a result, the ratio of net borrowing to GDP actually was higher in the period after 1984 than in previous recoveries.[34] Thus, we believe we can safely conclude that the criticism of the decade of the 1980s based on budget deficits, to the extent that it predicted crowding out of private investment,[35] falls wide of the mark. On the contrary, given the persistence of high levels of unemployment, at least until 1988, and the relatively low rate of capacity utilization, we can be pretty confident that lower budget deficits would have produced a lower level of GDP and GDP growth.

Possible Explanations

Though the purpose of this book is an investigation of *what* happened as a result of the Volcker-Reagan program, it is useful to at least advance some tentative speculations as to *why* the 1983–90 period was so different from predictions by supporters of the program—especially in comparison with the previous periods. It is also interesting to examine why the 1960s were so much more successful than the following periods in terms of the rate of growth in income, despite lower investment than in the more recent decades.

Of all the suggestions propounded, the one that makes the most sense is the idea that the economy is a structure of interrelationships of income and job growth, spending, taxing, incentives, and expectations held together by a delicate balance of power. Between 1945 and the end of the decade of the 1960s, this structure produced significant rises in incomes for most members of society. As the years passed, the experiences of increased opportunity produced positive incentives. In explaining how productivity growth could have been so much higher in this period with significantly less investment than in the later periods, we need to remind ourselves that much of what shows up in the statistics as productivity growth is really evidence that workers are working harder, with more diligence, and with more esprit de corps. Perhaps the prospect of long-term secure employment—backed by what Bowles, Gordon, and Weisskopf called the capital-labor accord—and rising incomes led to an increase in the intensity with which people worked.[36]

Unfortunately, by the end of the 1960s, as we noted in chapter 4, the structural interrelationship began to break down. Higher wages, secure work, and rising incomes had generally led to growing markets, increased profitability, and rapid productivity growth, improving the incentives of both workers and investors. However, the long period of security on the job eroded work intensity, which in turn began to erode profits. This showed up in the turn of productivity growth from 3.4 percent in 1968 to 0.1 percent in 1969, which included negative levels for the final three quarters of that year, leading up to the beginning of the 1970 recession. It should not be too surprising that this falloff in productivity growth occurred during a period where the unemployment rate had been below 4 percent for two years, beginning in the first quarter of 1966, and averaged 3.5 percent for the year 1968.[37] All of this happened while investment as a percentage of GDP and the rate of growth of per capita income were still as robust as in the previous two years. In other words, it is important to focus on what we emphasized earlier, the *voluntary* nature of good, hard work. With unemployment rates low, the pressure on workers from the cost of job loss would be much lower.

Even if people do not find this analysis convincing as a cause of the initial productivity slowdown, the analysis is on much stronger ground as a potential explanation of the failure of the Volcker-Reagan policy regime to re-create the vibrant pre-1970 economy. Certainly, the early years of the Reagan-Volcker program significantly changed the balance of power within the workplace. Workers experienced a big increase in their cost of job loss, both in terms of the extent of unemployment and the reduction in the strength of the social safety net. It is not surprising, in this context, to note that the median income of year-round, full-time male workers actually declined between 1979 and 1989.[38]

The problem for investors, however, was not the ability to get workers on the job to work harder. The problem instead was the sluggishness of consumer demand. Aggregate demand just grew too slowly in the 1983–90 period, compared to the period between, say, 1962 and 1969. In other words, the success of forcing workers on the job to work with increased intensity occurred only because of the excess unemployment and underutilization of capacity. While the former raised potential profitability, the latter undermined the ability of investors to realize profits. The result was surprisingly lower investment ratios than in the 1970s and an inability of the investment to translate into higher measured productivity improvements than in the 1960s.

In the end, it may very well be that employees faced (on average) with stagnant or declining incomes responded with less esprit de corps and diligence than their counterparts did in the decade of the 1960s. Despite a decade of trying under Volcker, Reagan, Bush, and even Clinton, no new structure has emerged to produce success such as occurred before 1970. The loss in the sense of participation and solidarity on the part of average citizens in their places of work appears to have translated into more highly individualistic behavior that has severely impacted productivity. Perhaps the increased inequality in the distribution of income and wealth has had an impact on the economy as a whole—a negative impact.

Appendix

Table 12 summarizes the data for the comparative periods discussed in the text.

TABLE 12. Comparing Recoveries and Full Business Cycles, 1960–91

	Investment (% of GDP)	Civilian Unemployment Rate	Capacity Utilization Rate	Rate of Growth of Real GDP per capita	Rate of Growth of Productivity
1960 peak to 1969 peak (38 Q)	15.40	4.75	84.98	2.96	2.85
Recovery 1962– 1969 peak (32 Q)	15.63	4.44	86.42	3.23	3.16
1962 trough to 1970 trough (36 Q)	15.51	4.51	85.80	2.71	3.13
1969 peak to 1980 peak (41 Q)	16.63	5.22	82.63	2.12	2.01
Recovery 1971– 1980 peak (37 Q)	16.86	6.35	82.82	2.50	1.92
1971 trough to 1982 trough (48 Q)	16.80	6.80	81.90	1.62	1.56
1973 peak to 1980 peak (25 Q)	16.91	6.77	82.24	1.75	1.33
Recovery 1974– 1980 peak (20 Q)	17.18	6.93	82.32	3.15	1.63
1980 peak to 1990 peak (42 Q)	16.20	7.17	80.36	1.69	1.10
Recovery 1983– 1990 peak (31 Q)	16.08	6.75	80.92	2.77	1.38
1982 trough– 1991 trough (33 Q)	15.86	6.69	80.85	2.34	1.26

Source: Table 4 at the web site, <mars.wnec.edu/~econ/surrender>.

9

Failures, Real and Imagined

Beginning with the election campaign of 1984, opposition to the Reagan policies centered on the large and growing federal budget deficit. Walter Mondale, Democratic presidential candidate, argued that the deficit was so dangerous that it would be essential to raise taxes in order to reduce it. He made his honesty in promising to raise taxes a major campaign issue, in contrast to President Reagan's alleged dishonesty in not admitting that he would raise taxes.[1] With Reagan insisting that he would cut spending rather than raise taxes, and also that the United States could "grow out of" the deficit, Mondale suffered one of the worst defeats in history, carrying only the District of Columbia and his home state of Minnesota. In 1988, the Democrats continued to harp on the deficit. Vice presidential candidate Lloyd Bentsen was asked how he could criticize the Reagan-Bush administration's economic policies in the light of the long period of prosperity the nation had enjoyed since the end of the 1981–82 recession. His response was, "If you let me write billions of dollars of hot checks I'll give you an illusion of prosperity, also." Again, the public wouldn't buy the argument. George Bush was elected president in large part because he claimed he could control the deficit by imposing a "flexible freeze" on government spending without raising taxes.

Meanwhile, academic economists were hard at work attempting to warn of the dire long-run consequences of deficits and growing federal debt. Make no mistake about it, there was something different about the deficits experienced as a result of the Volcker-Reagan program. The Council of Economic Advisers noted that difference in early 1985.

> Federal borrowing as a share of GNP varied within a narrow range, except during World War II and recessions until the past several years [1981–84]. The ratio of the outstanding debt to GNP increased

sharply during the Great Depression and World War II, declined substantially through the 1970s, and has since increased sharply.[2]

The Alleged Burden of the National Debt

As mentioned in chapter 2, the absolute size of the national debt is probably meaningless when it comes to assessing its impact on the economy. What is important is the ratio of the outstanding debt to the GDP. The reason is clear. Whether one focuses only on the need to spend government revenue paying interest or whether one believes that ultimately future taxpayers will have to "pay off" the debt, the size of the GDP will determine the ability to make those payments. When H. Ross Perot warned in *United We Stand* that by the year 2000 we might have an $8 trillion national debt, he neglected to mention that by the year 2000 we would have a much larger GDP. In fiscal 1995, the national debt held by the public was about 50 percent of the GDP.[3] If GDP grows faster than the national debt between now and the year 2000, that $8 trillion national debt would be a smaller percentage of GDP. American taxpayers, thus, would pay a smaller percentage of their tax dollars toward interest on the debt than they do now.

Also despite the quadrupling of the national debt during the 1980s, interest payments remain a relatively small percentage of GDP and have not gone beyond 14 percent of the entire federal budget.[4]

It is true that over the period from 1979 to 1989, interest payments as a percentage of the federal budget almost doubled. This trend and the rising interest payments as a percentage of GDP cannot, of course, go on indefinitely. However, to suggest that the absolute level that has been reached *as a percentage of GDP* is unsustainable in just not true.

The other often-quoted part of the argument is the assertion that "our children" or "our grandchildren" will have to "pay off" the national debt with a crushing tax burden. Some economists talk of debt-financed government spending as an intergenerational transfer of wealth. The current generation borrows, and the future generation pays for it. This is total nonsense, and a moment's reflection should demonstrate that point conclusively. Individuals have to pay off debts because lending institutions know that sooner or later they will die, and if they die without sufficient assets to cover their unpaid debts, the lender will be stuck with a worthless asset—an uncollectible loan. Thus, lenders are very careful to assess the ability of potential borrowers to pay off their debts. Assets and income are the crucial elements.

If, however, a person accumulates assets, there is absolutely no limit to the amount of "deficit spending" they can engage in. For example, if you have a high enough income to make a down payment on a second house worth as much as your current one, your "deficit spending" to buy that house will double your personal mortgage debt. So long as your income is high enough to justify carrying that increased amount of debt, the bank will not worry about the size of your total debt because the value of your assets will have doubled also. We could continue this example. Suppose you bought a third, a fourth house, each with a mortgage. If your income were sufficient to meet the interest payments on the debt and if the value of the assets were greater than the total mortgage debt outstanding, no bank would refuse to make those loans. In other words, so long as the assets individuals own exceed their debts, and so long as their incomes permit them to make payments on those debts, individual "deficit spending" can continue indefinitely. It is only when the debt grows faster than the income, when the interest payments take a larger and larger percentage of the income that lenders begin to get concerned. And even then, if there are sufficient asset values to cover the new debts, the bank is assured of getting its money back.

The same thing is true of a business. There is no absolute limit to the amount of borrowing a business can engage in, so long as its assets remain greater than its liabilities. Unfortunately, lending to a business without specific assets to secure these loans (in contrast to home mortgages and loans to farmers) can be quite risky if bad business conditions suddenly devalue the firm's assets. Nevertheless, in general, businesses can (and do) expand their indebtedness as they accumulate more assets. Absolute levels of indebtedness, again, mean nothing in this context.

When we are talking about a corporation, we get close to approximating the ability of government to borrow and keep borrowing. Whereas individuals who take out mortgages and unincorporated business (including farms) that take out loans must repay these loans in their entirety because all individuals (including owners of unincorporated businesses) die sooner or later, a corporation can live forever. Individuals must have sufficient assets in their estate to cover their outstanding debts or their creditors will end up losing. This danger limits the willingness of lenders to permit individual borrowing to rise in absolute terms. Corporations only die from bankruptcy or merger.

Thus, lending institutions will often be willing to refinance corporate debt at prevailing interest rates, so long as the business remains with more assets than liabilities. In a sense, corporations that borrow money may *never* have to "pay off" those loans. When the corporate bonds come due, they can issue new bonds to pay off the old ones. This is called rolling over the debt.

Because government entities can live forever (like corporations), they too can repay old debt by issuing new debt. Some of the current national debt was initially borrowed to finance the Civil War. The last time that the U.S. government came close to paying off the national debt was before the Civil War.[5] The same is true of virtually every corporation. Some American corporations (particularly railroads) are over one hundred years old. During that period, they have *never* had zero outstanding debt. Debts contracted when the first tracks were laid have been rolled over. The Union Pacific Railroad, for example, has never had to pay off its initial debt. And with good reason. The value of its assets have increased so much over time through investment and growth that lenders have been willing not merely to lend them sufficient funds to roll over outstanding debt but to expand that debt. The same is true of the former United States Steel Corporation (now USX), the Standard Oil of New Jersey Corporation (now EXXON), and the American Tobacco Company (now American Brands). Can you imagine the laughter that would occur at a stockholders meeting of one of these corporations if someone opposed the issuance of new corporate debt by claiming that future stockholders would be poorer because they would have to pay it off. On the contrary, investments made with those borrowed funds will make future stockholders richer.

The real problem with the government debt is in fact not a problem of borrowing at all. As noted in chapter 2, the issue really is based on the idea that government borrows funds and then *wastes* the money. In short, this view is that there is no such thing as a *productive* government investment.[6] Starting with that presupposition, government debt is of course a dangerous thing because there is no corresponding valuable asset that results from that debt. Thus, unlike a business in which the productive asset acquired with borrowed funds will produce increased revenue in the future, making it easy to "pay off" the loan, a government entity will merely have a rising debt that will force taxpayers to pay higher amounts in the future, thereby decreasing these taxpayers' ability to enjoy the fruits of their own efforts.

The reason this is nonsense was stated very early in chapter 2. We noted the importance of private investment in creating both aggregate demand and economic growth. We also noted the appropriate role for government in providing education and basic scientific research. In chapter 3, we expanded our discussion of the role of government to include social goods and services such as infrastructure and national defense. We also noted its potential role in fighting recessions by increasing aggregate demand. In rereading the first report by the Reagan Council of Economic Advisers we note the agreement that there are certain functions that can only be appropriately undertaken by government. In other words, there are certain absolutely necessary inputs into the economy—education, basic scientific research, infrastructure, national defense. If we leave national defense out for a moment, we can observe that the other three activities increase the future capacity of the economy to produce, either by creating new physical capital (a bridge, road, tunnel, office building, school) or by enhancing the productivity of society (new discoveries, more educated citizens). In short, they play the exact same role that productive investment plays when engaged in by the private sector. In other words, the blanket dismissal of government spending as wasteful is a neat political slogan, but it is not based in reality.

Beyond the things that government produces that may be productive inputs into future production, there is also the aggregate-demand effect. This is particularly obvious during wartime, but it was also obvious during the period of the Cold War, when military spending was a significant percentage of GDP.[7] Though such spending rarely makes contributions to future production (with the possible exception of military research and development expenditures), to the extent that it puts people to work *who otherwise would have been unemployed* it raises GDP. Remember we noted earlier that unemployment wastes resources—output that could have been produced is not produced. Using government deficits to raise aggregate demand "gets back" some of that output that would have been lost had the deficits not occurred. This raises income in the present and therefore, the future incomes of the people who will have to pay interest on the debt contracted when the government raised aggregate demand. In other words, contracting debt today to raise aggregate demand creates more income in the future out of which can be paid interest on that debt. Such recession-fighting increases in debt need not create an unsustainable indefinite increase in the ratio of debt to GDP. Between 1969 and 1979, despite two recessions when the deficit rose as a percentage of GDP, the ratio of total debt to GDP declined from 38.6 to 33.2 percent.[8]

To summarize: the much lamented rise in the national debt during the Reagan era, though not sustainable indefinitely, appears to have done little damage to the U.S. economy. Interest payments as a percentage of GDP never got much above 3 percent, interest payments to foreigners never were above 1 percent of GDP. There appears to be little evidence of crowding out (as argued in the previous chapter), and in fact one might argue that the positive contribution of aggregate demand helped create a great deal of income growth that will, in the long run, make it easier for future generations to pay interest on the accumulated debt.

There is, however, one problem created by the large deficits of the Reagan years that does appear to have negative long-run consequences for the economy. This problem is not based on crowding out or any of the other candidates discussed above. It is a problem of political will in the 1990s. The intensity of the clamor to reduce these high deficits meant that when it was really necessary to raise the structural deficit in response to the next recession, Congress and the administration, who are together responsible for making fiscal policy, were unwilling or unable to do so.

We know that one of the most important tools for fighting recession is for government to supplement the actions of automatic stabilizers by raising the structural deficit to give the economy an aggregate-demand "kick" upward. The most dramatic examples of that occurred by design with President Ford's tax cut in 1975. The structural deficit went from an average of 0.70 percent of trend growth rate of gross national product[9] in the four quarters of 1974 to 2.83 percent in the four quarters of 1975. The actual deficit of total government operations as a percentage of GDP made an even bigger jump because of the workings of the automatic stabilizers. For the four quarters of 1974 it averaged 0.53 percent of GDP, and for the four quarters of 1975 it averaged 4.10 percent. In the recession year of 1982 and the first year of recovery 1983, the two full years of the Economic Recovery Tax Act played the same role. The structural deficit averaged 0.87 percent of trend gross national product in 1981, rising to 1.72 percent in 1982 and 2.67 percent in 1983.[10] The actual deficit for all government activity went from 1.00 percent of GDP in 1981 to 3.45 percent in 1982 and 3.95 percent in 1983.[11]

However, the structural deficit remained so high during the decade of the 1980s that there was no policy action comparable to the Ford or Reagan tax cuts taken in 1990. Worse, the budget agreement of 1990 went in the opposite direction. Meanwhile, the actual deficit as a percentage of GDP rose from 1.50 percent in 1989 to 2.50 percent in 1990, mostly as a result of the operation of the automatic stabilizers.[12] It is not surprising, therefore, that the only policy changes that acted to speed the recovery from the recession of 1990–91 were the Federal Reserve's efforts to lower interest rates. With no significant fiscal policy assistance as in 1975 and 1982–83, the recovery turned out to be the most sluggish of the entire postwar period.

This is a bit ironic. After complaining about the dangerous budget deficits in the 1984 and 1988 elections and getting soundly beaten by the Republicans both times, the Democrats (and H. Ross Perot) were able to combine the complaints about the deficit with an attack on the Bush administration for failing to do enough to fight the recession. If our analysis is correct, one of the reasons the Bush administration didn't do enough to fight the recession is that it and the previous administration had not controlled the deficit during the period of prosperity from 1984 through 1989. Had the actual budget deficit fallen to near balance (less than 1 percent of GDP) as it had in 1974 and 1979 and had the structural deficit fallen to 1 or 2 percent of trend gross national product as it had in 1974 and 1979 then there would have been plenty of leeway for a sharp increase (perhaps 2 percent) in both figures to give the economy the boost to aggregate demand that it needed. As it was, there was no leeway and no opportunity to administer the fiscal stimulus that might have worked. So in the end, the Reagan deficits played a role in defeating the Republicans, if only an indirect one.

Finally, there is the argument developed by economist Robert Pollin at the end of the 1980s. He argued that the historical processes over the past twenty to thirty years had changed the impact of budget deficits on the U.S. economy. As noted in chapter 7, he argued that rising debt for individuals and the nonfinancial business sector has paralleled the increase in government debt. These two factors, coupled with the increase in international competition and international flows of savings,

> weakened the demand-side stimulatory impact of any given-sized deficit, worsened the deficit's negative collateral effects, including its impact on financial markets and the after tax income distribution, and inhibited the Federal Reserve from pursuing more expansionary

policies. . . . the stimulatory effects of a given-sized deficit are [now] weaker and its negative side effects stronger.[13]

Thus, the American economy after 1984 was surprisingly sluggish, according to this interpretation, not because the deficit was too large, as Benjamin Friedman argued, but because the deficit does not play as dynamic a role as it did in earlier periods. To a certain extent this view accepts the international aspects of Friedman's arguments, namely that high fiscal deficits played a role in the rise in the U.S. trade deficit. However, the more significant elements are the continuing problem of economic stagnation, as evidenced by sluggish investment after 1984 and the rise in financial fragility as demonstrated by the savings and loan crisis, the stock market crash of 1987, and the increase in bank failures during the late 1980s.

Was Government Spending Wasteful?

The final battles of the Cold War were fought by military budget planners. As early as the 1950s, an idea developed within the U.S. government that high levels of military spending in the United States would force the Soviet Union to devote a much higher percentage of its resources to matching our military capabilities because it had a much smaller GDP than we did.[14] The Cuban missile crisis exposed Soviet nuclear inferiority, and the leadership in the post-Khrushchev period was determined to achieve parity with the United States no matter what. They spent the rest of the 1960s and most of the 1970s increasing their nuclear capacity and did achieve rough parity by the end of the 1970s. Meanwhile, improvements in accuracy became the watchword of American military technology beginning with the move to cruise missile technology in 1972. By 1980, the rough parity of the Soviet nuclear arsenal masked a technology gap in accuracy that began to create fears of a potential U.S. first-strike capability. This produced another big increase in Soviet defense efforts, just as the rest of the Soviet economy was being revealed as a stagnant house of cards. By the middle 1980s, the economic difficulties of the Soviet central planning system, in part exacerbated by the drain of defense spending, had convinced the new leaders of the post-Brezhnev era to opt for fundamental reform of the economic system. This set in motion the train of events that led, in 1991 to the breakup of the

Soviet Union and the repudiation of Communism and central planning. Though it is not possible to identify how much of the demise of the Soviet Union can be attributed to the perceived need to devote a high percentage of their resources to military production, it was probably a considerable factor.

That is the good news. The bad news is that heavy emphasis on military spending as the most appropriate activity for the federal government was not costless for the United States. A significant literature developed, beginning with the publication in 1963 of Seymour Melman's *Our Depleted Society,* that argued that the federal dollars spent on the military would have created more jobs and improved national productivity more if spent in other efforts.[15] Whereas in chapter 8 we argued that sometimes job creation and improvements of productivity trade off against each other, in this argument our nation could improve productivity *and* increase job creation by shifting federal expenditures from the military budget to many other alternatives—such as highway construction, aid to education, and basic (nonmilitary) scientific research.

Let me illustrate this with two hypothetical examples. The first involves canceling the purchase of state-of-the-art tanks and armored personnel carriers and applying the funds to repairing a stretch of highway. The second involves switching funds from research and development on attack helicopters to research and development on photovoltaic cells.

In the first instance, let us focus on job creation. State-of-the-art tanks and armored personnel carriers take a significant amount of skilled and semiskilled work to assemble, but they also take a great deal of high-tech planning and experimentation. In other words, the military purchases involve paying a small number of scientists, engineers, and technicians high salaries in addition to paying the going rate for assembly line work. It is also true that defense contractors usually work on a high profit margin because of the risks in developing new products on the cutting edge of the knowledge frontier. Thus, it would be likely that the percentage of the appropriation that goes for the profits of the company would be higher. With a fixed dollar amount, you hire fewer people when you pay higher salaries; you hire fewer people when less of the expenditure goes for wages as opposed to profits for the company.

Job creation doesn't stop with the initial company. There is a multiplier effect. However, we must remind ourselves that the higher one's income, the smaller the percentage of it that one spends. The size of the multiplier effect depends crucially on how much of the increased income (received by the assembly line workers, engineers, etc. and retained as profits by the company or paid in dividends to shareholders) is translated immediately into increased spending. With a smaller number of individuals receiving income from the defense appropriation, and with a significant percentage of those individuals receiving quite high incomes, it is likely that the multiplier effect would be smaller than if the money all went to pay assembly line workers' salaries.

The alternative spending on highways, by contrast, is very labor intensive, requiring virtually no high-tech inputs and very few high-priced engineers and scientists. Dollar for dollar, both initial employment increases and subsequent multiplier effects should be higher than if the same appropriation went to buy these new tanks and armored personnel carriers. In the 1980s there was a tremendous emphasis on modernizing our nuclear weapons: the development of the nuclear missile with many warheads on it, each capable of being individually targeted, the development of new generations of missile-carrying submarines, the beginning research on a nuclear shield (the so-called Star Wars proposal, called by the Reagan administration the Strategic Defense Initiative), efforts to "harden" computers against the presumed destruction that would occur from "nuclear pulse." This was very technology intensive, clearly leading to the employment of very few people per million dollars spent. Those people who were employed were for the most part very highly paid. The result was that during the 1980s, the percentage of the military budget that created jobs (expenditure on armed-forces personnel, personal equipment, maintenance, etc.) fell.[16] In 1983, the Congressional Budget Office compared the job-creating possibilities of defense spending with other types of government spending. Interestingly, it was in the area of defense *purchases* from industry (buying equipment rather than personnel expenses) that the difference emerged.[17]

Given the fact that job creation was less likely, would increased productivity be more likely? Unfortunately not. During the 1980s, the ability to translate military high-technology research into improvements in technology for the rest of the economy declined. That is because the specific technology problems confronted by military researchers were so narrowly focused on military needs (for example, getting a ten-ton missile to land within a ten-foot radius three thousand miles away) that the application to more general economic problems no longer was possible. In supersonic combat aircraft, it was essential that support functions (like toilets and coffeemakers) be able to withstand depressurization and sharp turns at two and three times the speed of sound. This required a lot of research and expenditure and led to scornful newspaper accounts of fourteen-hundred-dollar coffeemakers and three-thousand-dollar toilet seat covers. But those stories missed the point. These devices were so expensive because they were designed for extraordinary circumstances. The effort made to satisfy those needs was unnecessary and useless in toilets on civilian aircraft or the in-home coffeemaker.

Thus, when we turn to our second example, it should not be surprising for us to conclude that the improvements in productivity for the entire economy will be virtually nonexistent as a result of research-and-development spending on attack helicopters. The helicopter developments during World War II and even in Korea proved easily translatable into civilian use. However, beginning with the Vietnam era and continuing through the past twenty years, the specifications that military researchers attempted to match (increasing speed, ability to maneuver a *heavy* aircraft very quickly) were not important for the civilian sector. Photovoltaic cells, on the other hand, have incredible long-range possibilities in the era of rising costs (in the long run) of fossil-fuel-based energy. Research that would lead to reductions in the cost of generating electricity via photovoltaics would have far-reaching long-run consequences for the provision of energy to factories, office buildings, homes, and even vehicles. These reduced costs would spread throughout the economy, increasing productivity.

Research on photovoltaic cells in the end holds the promise of more job creation than does research into military attack helicopters. The research itself might not generate more jobs, but the indirect effects of the spread of the new technology definitely would, whereas in the case of the helicopters, there would be virtually no spread of the new technology into the rest of the economy, and therefore, no new job creation.

These two examples are presented to illustrate a perspective that has gained currency among many different economists and policy analysts: the heavy emphasis on military spending within our federal budget has caused United States employment growth and productivity growth to be lower than it would have been had the same amount of money been appropriated for civilian-oriented activities, such as building roads, basic scientific (civilian) research, education, and so on. Since the military budget grew as a percentage of GDP during the early 1980s, this fact might add another piece to the puzzle, helping to explain not only why the incentives of the Reagan Revolution produced such a relatively mild period of prosperity but specifically why an investment ratio higher than that of the 1960s produced a significantly slower rate of productivity growth.

Even more important, it is possible that the heavy reliance on military spending to bolster aggregate demand in the 1950s and 1960s was part of a long-run process of depleting the productivity-enhancing possibilities in the civilian sector of the economy. With top physicists, engineers, mathematicians, statisticians, and other valuable technical personnel devoting their energies to the military, civilian research efforts were less well served.[18]

Depleting Our Nation's Infrastructure

Concurrent with the rise in the military's share of total spending was the decline in the percentage of GDP devoted to infrastructure investment. Recall the arguments of Robert Reich, former secretary of labor, in *The Work of Nations*. He argued that infrastructure was a crucial determinant of what kinds of industrial activities would be located in a particular region. Though ownership of productive assets where high-quality, highly paid workers are hired is not very important to Reich (here he was arguing against both Benjamin Friedman and H. Ross Perot),[19] the location of these assets will determine income growth for a region (and therefore nation). Infrastructure investment is the kind of investment that, according to Reich, "enhance[s] the value of work performed by a nation's citizens. . . . such public investments uniquely help the nation's citizens add value of the world economy."[20]

What is infrastructure? It is the set of transportation and communications links that permits goods, people, and ideas to flow as quickly and cheaply as possible. It is the electrical, water, sewer and gas lines that connect our homes, offices, and other places of business. Some of these are provided by the private sector (such as electricity), many by the public sector. The Bureau of Economic Analysis in the Department of Commerce divides government investments in buildings and equipment into federal and state spending and then breaks it down further. Federal purchases of equipment and structures are divided into military and nonmilitary and then subdivided again. State and local structures are divided into three types of buildings and five types of structures.[21] I have chosen to count as infrastructure investment, spending on streets and highways, sewer and water systems, industrial buildings, conservation and development, utilities such as electricity and gas and nonmilitary mass transit, airports, and equipment. In addition to these kinds of investments, hospitals and schools, particularly public college and university facilities, make a major contribution to future productivity improvements.

Infrastructure investments as a percentage of GDP were much higher in the 1960s (and the 1950s) than they were in the 1970s. If we divide the twenty-eight years from 1961 through 1989 into roughly the same periods we identified in chapter 7 (KJN, NFC, VRB),[22] we note an average investment in what we have called infrastructure of 3.27 percent of GDP in KJN, falling to 2.52 percent in NFC and to 1.98 percent in VRB.[23] Some have argued that this time series is misleading because in the early period the interstate highway system was being built and by the 1970s much of that work had been completed. However, it is interesting to note that whereas the fall in street and highway spending as a percentage of GDP accounts for half of the decline in the infrastructure series between KJN and NFC, the reduction between NFC and VRB in street and highway spending accounts for only 41 percent of that decline. If the completion of the interstate highway system were the main reason for the decline in infrastructure spending, we should expect there to be virtually no reduction in such expenditure between NFC and VRB. We must remember that the spending on streets and highways includes ongoing maintenance and repair. This is a very important element in keeping our streets and highways productive, and it appears that such maintenance was significantly reduced during the VRB period.

In addition, public spending on hospitals and educational structures has lagged significantly.[24] As the need to educate a higher and higher percentage of our labor force at the postsecondary level has increased, and as the consumption of medical services, particularly of the growing elderly population, has also increased, the provision of the basic buildings to help produce these services has lagged again. Just as in the example of highways, we should not be mesmerized by the fact that in the context of the education of the baby boomers, school construction was particularly extensive in the 1950s and 1960s. The fact remains that a higher and higher percentage of the population *needs* to be serviced by postsecondary education. And buildings that are built still need to be maintained.

Economists David Aschauer and Alicia Munnell have argued that this decline in infrastructure investment has had a direct bearing on the rate of growth of productivity in the entire economy. They have argued that public capital investment is complementary with private capital investment and failure to maintain a sufficient stock of public capital ultimately reduces profitability in the private sector.[25] Thus, one element of supposed failure in the period of Reagan and Volcker is the failure of public capital expenditure to keep pace with gross domestic product.

Education

During the 1980s, there was a strong debate as to what had happened to American education. In 1981, the secretary of education created the National Commission on Excellence in Education with a mandate to report of the "quality of education in America."[26] The report was entitled *A Nation at Risk,* and it caused quite a stir, mostly with the following well-crafted, often-quoted sentence: "If an unfriendly foreign power had attempted to impose on America the mediocre educational performance that exists today, we might well have viewed it as an act of war."[27] The substance of the report was that educational achievement had stagnated, in fact declined. Aside from serious problems such as 23 million adults being functionally illiterate while 13 percent of seventeen-year-olds suffered from the same problem, there were a number of more subtle problems.

> Over half the population of gifted students do not match their tested ability with comparable achievement in school . . .
> College Board achievement tests . . . reveal consistent declines . . . in such subjects as physics and English . . .
> Both the number and proportion of students demonstrating superior achievement on the SATs (i.e., those with scores of 650 or higher) have . . . dramatically declined.
> Many 17-year-olds do not possess the "higher order" intellectual skills we should expect of them. Nearly 40 percent cannot draw inferences from written material; only one fifth can write a persuasive essay; and only one-third can solve a mathematics problem requiring several steps . . .
> Between 1975 and 1980, remedial mathematics courses in public

4-year colleges increased by 72 percent and now constitute one-quarter of all mathematics courses taught in those institutions.[28]

The commission called for a concerted effort to raise basic educational achievement of high school graduates and refocus efforts in higher education so that American workers would be able to compete in the global marketplace that was emerging. Specifically, they recommended requiring every high school graduate to have four years of English, three years of mathematics, three years of science, three years of social studies, and one-half year of computer science.[29] These subjects were referred to as the New Basics. They recommended more demanding programs in higher education with continuous achievement testing

> at major transition points . . . [to] *(a)* certify the student's credentials; *(b)* identify the need for remedial intervention; and *(c)* identify the opportunity for advanced or accelerated work.[30]

They recommended that more time be spent studying the New Basics, which might include lengthening the school year. Finally, they proposed seven recommendations to "improve the preparation of teachers or to make teaching a more rewarding and respected profession."[31]

To achieve these goals, the commission strongly recommended that citizens demand of their public officials a strong commitment to implementing the changes recommended, including the willingness to provide more financial resources. They concluded, "Excellence costs. But in the long run mediocrity costs far more."[32] State and local governments did continue to raise their expenditures on education through much of the decade of the 1980s, but the federal contribution toward those efforts declined.

Here it is important to distinguish between spending money on elementary and secondary education, on the one hand, and spending money on higher education. In the United States, higher education has been quite lavishly financed, both in the public and the private sectors. When state governments have had to cut back on providing larger appropriations for public higher education, the various federal student aid programs have helped more and more students pay (or borrow to pay) tuition at private institutions. Higher education also benefits tremendously from federal research grants. Thus, it is somewhat misleading to lump all education expenditures together when investigating how the United States measures up to the rest of the world in terms of public commitment to education.

To get around this, I have isolated the expenditure of federal and state and local monies on elementary and secondary education. This is the educational expenditure that can truly be identified as an appropriate role for government financing. As mentioned back in chapter 3, significant external benefits accrue to all members of society from the existence of a literate, knowledgeable population with crucial problem-solving and critical-thinking skills as well as the ability to communicate orally and in writing. Thus, it is appropriate that the entire society finance this basic level of education.

The data is pretty straightforward. After rising as a percentage of GDP in the 1960s and 1970s, reaching a maximum of 4 percent in 1975, the percentage of GDP spent on elementary and secondary education fell to 3.5 percent in 1981 and never was greater than 3.6 percent for the rest of the Reagan years.[33] This 0.4 percent difference in 1988 amounted to a total of $20 billion. The federal contribution to state and local governments specifically for elementary and secondary education rose to 0.22 percent of that spending in 1975, fell to 0.17 percent in 1981, and never was above 0.16 percent between 1982 and 1988.

One could argue that the earlier growth of spending was more a function of the rate of growth of compensation for the labor input (mostly teachers but also support personnel) rather than a true measure of the "supply" of the "education product" to students. However, it is important to note that teachers have skills that can be utilized elsewhere in the economy. A rise in the average salary in the 1960s probably had a lot to do with attracting and keeping capable teachers to and in the profession. As the relative incomes that teachers can earn outside of teaching rise, the attractiveness of the teaching profession and the enthusiasm with which teachers embrace their work is bound to decline.

Here again, we cannot stress enough the point made all the way back in chapter 2. A great deal of labor is the result of *voluntary* action on the part of the worker. It is true that people who supervise can set up criteria for measuring success and attempt to reward the successful and punish (that is, fire) the failures. However, when the "product" is a service that is delivered personally by a skilled professional, there is a tremendous amount of leeway between a barely adequate job for which you will not be fired and a major effort to do as good a job as possible. Surely it is not too great an assumption to suggest that (at least some) teachers who feel they are being paid fairly will make a more enthusiastic effort to be excellent than those who feel they are underpaid.

Health Care Costs

Despite the decline in overall inflation, one serious failure of the Volcker-Reagan period that we have already mentioned involved health care. The rise in health care costs and the rise in the consumption of health care services occurred because most people who "consume" health services do not pay for them out of pocket. Instead they pay for them indirectly by paying premiums to insurance companies or Medicare (part B). A very large number of individuals either have paid for their health care in the past through payroll taxes (Medicare part A) or receive medical care as an entitlement because their incomes are low enough to qualify for Medicaid.

If I have already paid my premium, or I already qualify for Medicare or Medicaid, then the cost of my immediate treatment is not relevant to me because I have already paid for it with my previous taxes or premiums. It is also true that my behavior in consuming expensive medical services will have a very small impact on my premium next year or five years from now. The premium will depend on the *group* behavior in consuming medical services. Even if I were not to use them at all, my premium would still go up if my group increases its utilization, or even if utilization stays the same but prices go up. Alternatively, I could use a tremendous amount of services, but if enough people in my group use little or none and if costs decline due to successful cost-cutting, my premium may stay the same or even fall next year.

Because the premium I pay is very tenuously connected to how much I use the insurance, I have little incentive to monitor my spending and consider less costly alternatives. Because I do not have that incentive, my health care provider does not either. A regular fee-for-service provider will know that I am not going to refuse a recommended course of treatment to save money because, in effect, it's not my money. Health maintenance organizations began to try and deal with the incentives from the providers side by created prepaid group practice. In effect all the personnel within a health maintenance organization get paid a fixed fee per enrolled patient, but when the patient needs treatment, except for a trivial copayment (a few dollars a visit), the patient pays nothing extra. Thus, the providers are encouraged to economize on treatment because they get no fee for each unit of service. In fact many have noted the similarity to the old Confucian view of the proper way to pay a doctor: the doctor gets paid while the patient is well, and gets nothing when the patient gets sick.

With the Reagan administration unable to make much headway in cutting Medicare and Medicaid, and with medical technology advancing at breakneck speed, it is not surprising that medical expenses rose dramatically throughout the VRB period.[34] Interestingly enough, this helped keep the standard of living of the elderly population well above the national average. Medicare cushioned the blow that increased health-care costs would have imposed on the population over sixty-five, leaving more disposable income for the elderly and their families. Medicaid played an extremely important role in covering a significant proportion of long-term nursing-care expenses. For many otherwise middle-class elderly, the ability to finance long-term care as a Medicaid recipient rather than out of pocket made the difference between passing on a legacy to their children and grandchildren and dying completely destitute. It is not surprising, therefore, that the elderly population, of all the demographic age groups, experienced the 1980s as a successful period. Those individuals who were able to supplement their retirement incomes with interest-bearing assets (such as long-term certificates of deposit) or stock were able to take advantage of the high real interest rates and the stock market boom for much of the decade.

In addition to the rising cost of Medicare and Medicaid, the rising cost of health insurance premiums began to affect the private sector. By the end of the decade, American business was beginning to recognize that buying health insurance as they had done in the past was unsustainable. The ratio of employer spending on private health insurance to private sector wages and salaries rose from 5.5 percent to 7.4 percent between 1980 and 1989.[35] This was despite the fact that a rising percentage of the population utilized health maintenance organizations. In response to this problem, government policymakers and business executives and health care providers began to attempt to figure out ways to reform the delivery and financing of health care.

Among the proposals were efforts to control the prices paid to providers. A form of managed care different from a health maintenance organization developed in the late 1980s and early 1990s, a *preferred provider organization*. A PPO, unlike an HMO, involves doctors and other health care providers contracting with the PPO to provide services to members of that PPO for discounted, fixed fees. The PPO promises the health care providers a guaranteed clientele and simplified billing. The business can get the PPO to offer a wide range of health care services in exchange for delivering to the PPO its entire workforce. Employees of a business that has shifted its health insurance coverage to a PPO may go outside of the PPO to purchase medical services, but they have to pay significantly more out of pocket if they choose to do so. By 1993, of the population purchasing private health insurance, over half were enrolled in some form of "managed care."[36] Nevertheless, as mentioned in chapter 7, the rising cost of medical care and the rising percentage of the population without any insurance represented a serious challenge to policymakers.[37]

One other important aspect of this problem was the increase in the amount of uncompensated care received by people at hospitals and other medical facilities either as a result of charity on the part of the health care provider or inability (or unwillingness) of patients to pay for their care. In 1980, the hospitals covered by the Medicare prospective-payments system absorbed $3.6 billion of uncompensated care that was partially offset by a $1 billion government subsidy. By 1989, that figure had risen to $10 billion with an offset of $2 billion. The actual trend was for uncompensated care to increase (in nominal terms) approximately 13 percent per year with government subsidies covering a declining proportion of that expense.[38] Uncompensated care is a symptom of the rise in the number of people who are not covered by health insurance. It is not that these people don't receive health care, but they usually wait until the situation is so desperate that they have to utilize a hospital.

This latter fact is borne out by the fact that when uninsured people are first admitted to hospitals their conditions lead to a higher probability of dying than people of the same age, sex and race with private health insurance. When the samples are compared with people who have identical conditions, it appears that care is not as good for the uninsured because they have a significantly higher probability of dying than their privately insured counterparts.[39] The rise in the numbers of uninsured people getting "late" treatment contributes to the overall increase in health care costs.

Meanwhile, hospitals find rising percentages of their operating expenses neither compensated by insurers or out of pocket by patients nor subsidized by government. Thus, they act to shift the cost of absorbing these patients onto those patients insured in the private sector by raising prices. This is the phenomenon known as cost-shifting, and it contributed by the beginning of the 1990s to the rapid escalation of health insurance premium costs. All in all, we must conclude that the escalation of health insurance costs, the tendency of government expenditures on Medicare and Medicaid to rise both absolutely and as a percentage of government spending, and the increasing numbers of Americans without health insurance were a major failure of the Volcker-Reagan period. It is important to note, however, that unlike the Bush and Clinton administrations, the Reagan administration never attempted to solve that problem. The failure was a failure of *omission.*

The Savings and Loan Meltdown

As mentioned back in chapter 5, the 1980 Depositary Institutions Deregulation and Monetary Control Act achieved the beginnings of financial deregulation while extending Federal Reserve control to all banks. This process was completed for the savings and loan industry with the passage of the Garn–St. Germaine Act of 1982. Deregulation of the savings and loan industry was a direct response to severe difficulties those institutions were experiencing trying to achieve a sufficient profit in their traditional markets. The problem for the thrift institutions was similar to the problem faced by commercial banks under Regulation Q.[40] When nominal interest rates rose in the 1970s in response to rises in the rate of inflation, the interest income of those institutions (mostly long-term mortgages) fell below the market interest rate that financial institutions were having to pay to attract borrowers. This was remedied, supposedly, by the removal of the ceilings on the rates savings and loans could pay borrowers. However, in the mortgage market, even as they began to issue higher-rate (and even variable-rate) mortgages, the thrifts found that the asset base of mortgages they had issued years earlier was falling in value.[41]

This fall in the value of assets coupled with the squeeze between income based on low-rate, long-term mortgages and costs determined by short-term, high-rate deposits led many savings and loans into what could only be termed *economic* insolvency. Though the mortgages carried on the books were valued by the agencies that regulated these institutions at their historical cost, in fact the amount the thrift could get if it tried to resell such a low-interest mortgage was much less. If institutions had been forced to write down the value of their assets by the depreciation in the mortgage, many would have proved insolvent.[42] Then, when interest rates started to fall in the 1980s, many people refinanced their high-interest mortgages. The Council of Economic Advisers noted in 1991:

In 1986 . . . nearly half of the mortgages originated by thrift institutions were refinancings. By 1989 the fraction of mortgage debtors who had refinanced was more than double its 1977 level. *Such refinancings reduced the costs to borrowers but also reduced the income of lenders.* Thus, S&Ls did not gain as much when interest rates fell as they lost when interest rates rose.[43]

The result of all this was that savings and loans, with their backs against the wall, took advantage of the deregulation and the expansion of insured deposits from forty thousand to one hundred thousand dollars to vigorously compete for deposits by offering higher and higher interest rates. They then turned around and invested as much as they could in the highest-risk investments possible. It was a no-lose proposition for managers and owners of savings and loan institutions that, but for the fake valuation of assets at historical costs, would already be bankrupt. If they succeeded in the high-stakes game,

> the owners retain the net worth of the S&L. If the investment fails, the deposit insurer will repay any losses on insured deposits. The closer an institution comes to insolvency, the more rewards become one-sided: Heads, the S&L owners win; tails, the deposit insurer loses.[44]

These high interest rates paid by savings and loan institutions attracted significant flows of deposits. A 1992 analysis by John Shoven, Scott Smart, and Joel Waldfogel showed that

> states with large numbers of thrift failures and/or sagging economies (Texas, Massachusetts, California) tend to be the states where high-rate thrifts are located. Furthermore, we observe abnormally high deposit inflows at thrifts in these states.[45]

They also argued that these high interest rates helped pull real interest rates in the rest of the economy up as well, because the insured certificates of deposit issued by high-rate savings and loans were good substitute for Treasury bills. Thus, the savings and loan debacle may have combined with the role of the Fed's tight monetary policies to keep real interest rates high during the period after 1984.[46]

Almost as soon as the election of 1988 was over, the federal government began to move on the insolvent savings and loan institutions. The Financial Institutions Reform, Recovery, and Enforcement Act of 1989 set up the Resolution Trust Corporation to quickly close insolvent thrifts and pay the insured depositors. The Justice Department began criminal investigations to punish those who had committed fraud.[47] Because this problem had been allowed to continue unchecked for virtually the entire decade, had in fact been exacerbated by the deregulation of 1980 and 1982, the cost to the taxpayers has been estimated at $130 to $176 billion if the payments were made all at once.[48] However, the Resolution Trust Corporation actually financed its activities by issuing bonds to the public. If one adds to the immediate cost the interest charges that are expected to be paid over the lifetime of the loans, the total cost is between $300 and $500 billion.[49]

One side effect of this crisis, was the intensity with which bank and other financial regulators began to scrutinize the lending policies of the surviving savings and loan institutions and banks in general. The law that set up the Resolution Trust Corporation "raised the minimum capital requirements for federally insured savings institutions, so that S&Ls will have to meet capital requirements no less stringent than those for national banks."[50] By the end of 1991 there was a sense that this intense activity on the part of regulators had gone too far. In 1992 the Council of Economic Advisers argued that "examiners have been discouraging banks and S&Ls from engaging in some sound lending opportunities." This was partially to blame for the fact that "growth of commercial and industrial bank loans slowed during 1990 and fell dramatically in 1991."[51] Since 1991 and 1992 were years of recovery from a recession during which monetary policy was expansionary, any unnecessary stringency introduced into the credit markets by gun-shy regulators would have a particularly unfortunate consequence. In fact, if one combines the view of the three economists who believe savings and loans' high-risk lending patterns had raised interest rates overall during the late 1980s with the view that tough regulations after 1989 slowed the growth of credit during the recovery from the 1990 recession, one quickly discovers that the $130 to $176 billion cost is just the tip of the iceberg. Shoven, Smart, and Waldfogel estimated the cost in extra interest charges paid by the government at between $53 billion and $366 billion by the end of the 1980s.[52]

One of the questions raised by the savings and loan debacle is what it tells us about deregulation and reliance on the "magic of the market" both in general and as it specifically applies to the banking system. There are many who seized on the insolvency of so many thrifts and the fact that this was exacerbated by deregulation to suggest that in certain sectors of the economy, deregulation is totally inappropriate. There are others who argued virtually the opposite, that the problem was that deregulation was only partial. From this latter point of view, the real villain was deposit insurance. Because of deposit insurance, depositors in banks do not have to acquaint themselves with the risks of entrusting their savings to a particular bank's management team. No matter how profligate the bankers are with my money, I know the United States government stands ready to make sure I don't lose it. As the Council of Economic Advisers noted in 1991, this had even begun to affect the commercial banking system. Deposit insurance did not initially encourage overly risky behavior on the part of banks and thrifts because they faced little competition from nonbank lending institutions, and thus the value to the owners of banks and savings and loans of their charters were quite high.

> As competition increased . . . profit opportunities for banks . . . eroded and the value of their charters decreased, causing a gradual decline of the economic capital in depository institutions. . . , [M]ost banks . . . remain well-capitalized. Nonetheless, losses in economic capital, due to the deterioration of charter values, combined with deposit insurance premiums that are insensitive to risk-taking, have given weak banks increased incentives to take undue risks.
>
> In most industries, incentives to take excessive risks are kept in check by the market. The cost of capital for firms pursuing risky strategies increases. This mechanism operates weakly in banking since banks are largely financed through insured deposits. . . . This lack of market discipline not only makes it easier for poorly managed institutions to operate, it also makes business difficult for prudent managers who compete with poorly managed institutions for both loans and deposits.[53]

One possible recommendation arising from this analysis is to *totally* deregulate banking and finance by removing deposit insurance. This would be akin to recommending a law *banning* the use of seat belts because wearing those belts gives drivers a false sense of security and causes them to speed more than they would without belts.[54] The reason for deposit insurance is to stop the failure of some poorly managed banks from creating panic among customers of well-managed banks, as happened during the Great Depression. The failure of a bank, because of its impact on the availability of credit and purchasing power for the economy in general, is much more serious than the failure of a nonfinancial enterprise of like size. Thus, there are extremely good reasons why government should commit the taxpayers' resources to insuring bank deposits. The alleged value of "market discipline" in an unregulated system pales to insignificance before the harm done by the possibility of spreading bank failures. The solution is not no regulation but smarter regulation.

We conclude that in the case of the savings and loan industry, deregulation created significant harm to the economy, harm that still had an impact more than halfway through the 1990s.

Rising Inequality?

At this juncture it is important to remember the implications of financial deregulation mentioned back in chapter 5. The end of both interest rate ceilings and the forced compartmentalization of the financial markets changed the nature of the impact of monetary policy. With interest rate ceilings, small increases in interest rates could produce almost a shutdown of the credit markets. When financial markets began to be deregulated, one of the results was that it would henceforth take much larger increases in interest rates to reduce the quantity of credit demanded. This certainly became apparent during the 1980s as real interest rates climbed to levels unprecedented in this century. All of this has been discussed in previous chapters. What has not been mentioned is one of the implications of this change, increased inequality in the distribution of income.

The connection is not obvious, but it is real. Rising interest rates raise the income of those who own large amounts of interest-bearing assets. For those people who receive less than 10 percent of their income as interest income, even doubling the rate of interest will only increase total income approximately 10 percent. According to the Census, between 1977 and 1990, only the people in the top 10 percent of the income distribution received more than 10 percent of their income as interest, dividends, and rents.[55] A family earning the median (real) income of $31,095 in 1980[56] averaged 4.5 percent of their income in interest, rent, and dividends. According to the Census, median income had risen to $31,717 by 1985, and a family earning that amount averaged 5.8 percent of income in interest, rent, and dividends. Thus, this median family increased its interest, rent, and dividend earnings from $1399 to $1839.[57]

Now let us compare that to someone in the top 5 percent of the income distribution, who received 19.3 percent of her or his income in rents, interest, and dividends. According to the Census Bureau, a family in that group averaged $54,060 in income in 1980. In 1985, the average income for someone in this category had risen to $77,706, of which 18.1 percent was in interest, rent, and dividends.[58] The much greater increase in overall income for this group was in part caused by the doubling of real interest rates and the persistence of historically unprecedented high real interest rates.

Another cause of rising income inequality was in the tremendous opportunities for capital gains, both because of a rising stock market and the proliferation of tax shelter schemes. The proportion of income received as capital gains for the top 5 percent of the population rose from 15.4 percent in 1980 to 21.2 percent in 1985. This change is even more striking if we examine the top 1 percent of the population. The share of their incomes derived from capital gains went from 26.9 percent to 35.2 percent over the same period.[59] The ability to take advantage of rising interest, dividend, and capital-gains income clearly depends on one's accumulation of wealth. As mentioned in chapter 4, wealth is much more unequally distributed than is income, and the decade of the 1980s increased this pattern.

According to the research of Edward N. Wolff,

> U.S. wealth concentration in 1989 was more extreme than that of any time since 1929.
>
> Between 1983 and 1989 the top one half of one percent of the wealthiest families received 55 percent of the total increase in real household wealth.[60]

Wolff notes that the only precedent for such a large increase in inequality of wealth was in the period leading up to the stock market crash of 1929, when artificially high stock prices increased the net worth of the very rich. What is remarkable about the trend between 1983 and 1989 is that the massive stock market decline in 1987 did not reverse it.

The improvement in the lot of the very wealthy was paralleled by the rise in the number of U.S. households that had either zero or negative financial wealth (except for equity in a home). The rise was from 25 to 29 percent of the population between 1983 and 1989.[61] Wolff notes that the increased wealth inequality can be attributed to rising income inequality as well as the higher rate of growth in stock prices as opposed to house prices. Owner-occupied housing is the main asset of the vast middle class, and when it falls in value in relation to stock prices, which mostly increase the wealth of the rich, wealth inequality will increase.[62]

With the passage of the Tax Reform Act, the advantages of receiving income as capital gains were significantly reduced, as were the opportunities to shelter income from taxation. The result was that capital gains represented only 10.7 percent of the income received by the top 5 percent in 1990, while rent, interest, and dividends increased slightly to 18.7 percent. For the top 1 percent, the shares were 17.3 percent in capital gains and 22.9 in rent, interest, and dividends. Yet overall inequality continued to increase. The reason is that not only was there a significant increase in interest, and other income received by owners of capital,[63] but during the entire decade there was a significant increase in the inequality among wage and salary earners.

Dividing wage and salary earners into five groups, the ratio of the real hourly wages received by the top fifth to the bottom fifth in 1979 was 2.46. By 1989, that ratio had increased to 2.77.[64] Another method of measuring wage inequality is to identify the percentage of jobs paying hourly wages below the poverty level, at the poverty level, 25 percent above the poverty level, twice the poverty level, three times the poverty level, and even higher. Between 1979 and 1989, the percentage of jobs paying less than three-quarters of the poverty level rose from 4.1 to 13.2 percent. Interestingly, the percentage of jobs paying between three-quarters of the poverty level and the poverty level actually fell from 21 to 14.8 percent. Combining those two, jobs paying the poverty level and lower rose from 25.1 to 28 percent. Between 100 and 125 percent of the poverty level, the percentage of jobs remained the same. The categories of jobs paying twice and three times the poverty level actually fell between 1979 and 1989, while all jobs paying more than three times the poverty level increased. It is in these divergent trends that we see again the increased inequality among wage earners.[65]

That increased inequality, by the way, did not develop because the wages of the highly paid workers rose dramatically. On average, even the hourly wage of the workers in the top 20 percent fell in purchasing power over the decade. Family incomes increased because workers worked more hours on average and because the number of wage earners per family increased. Meanwhile, as the evidence above shows, there was a dramatic increase in the number of low-wage jobs. This contributed to the increase in the number of people who could be characterized as the "working poor." In 1979, 33 percent of poor families with children provided the number of hours equivalent to three-quarters of a full-time worker. That percentage had risen by 1989 to 36 percent. Even among poor female-headed families with children, the percentage providing the equivalent of three-quarters of a full-time worker rose from 14.6 percent to 19.9 percent over that decade.[66]

This increase in inequality led many to suggest that there was a dangerous shrinkage of the middle class. To the slogan, "The rich got richer and the poor got poorer," could have been added the conclusion that "the middle class polarized in both directions." Among the people commenting on this phenomenon was the economist Paul Krugman. He proposed a measurement of how much of the average income growth between 1979 and 1989 accrued to the very rich, the top 1 percent of the income distribution. By his calculations, 70 percent of the rise in family incomes between 1977 and 1989 went to the top 1 percent of the population. The bottom 40 percent, by his calculations, actually lost income.[67]

Now before we explore this issue further, it is useful to recall our discussion back in chapter 4 about the significance of income distribution. The consensus among economists is that a tradeoff is created whenever government takes action to make the distribution of income more equal. That action reduces incentives and therefore reduces economic growth. We are then faced with a question of how much inequality we are willing to live with in order to make the economy operate most efficiently. However, there is also a recognition that too much inequality can have its own negative consequences for the economy. At the extreme examples, if a very high percentage of the population cannot afford to buy anything other than food, then the market for most consumer goods will be small, and *that* will damage business incentives. Thus, as mentioned in chapter 4, there is a range of possible income distributions that will avoid the extreme of massive poverty and destitution and avoid the extreme of too much interference with the market mechanism. It is the assertion of Paul Krugman, based on his calculation of what happened to the income growth between 1977 and 1989, that the failure of most of the population to share in the benefits of the economic growth of that period constituted a serious political challenge to the Republican Party in 1992.

> Supply-siders like Robert Bartley, the *[Wall Street] Journal*'s editorial page editor, believe that their ideology has been justified by what they perceive as the huge economic successes of the Reagan years. The suggestion that these years were not very successful for most people, that most of the gains went to a few well-off families, is a political body blow. And indeed the belated attention to inequality during the spring of 1992 clearly helped the Clinton campaign find a

new focus and a new target for public anger: instead of blaming their woes on welfare queens in their Cadillacs, middle-class voters could be urged to blame government policies that favored the wealthy.[68]

This same political point was made earlier by Kevin Phillips in *The Politics of Rich and Poor*.[69]

The Practice of Denial

Needless to say, there are two possible responses to the charges of Krugman, Phillips, and others. One possible response would be that the increase in inequality was necessary to create greater economic growth and there is no reason to alter policy at all. Even with increased inequality, "A rising tide lifts all boats," as the cliché goes. The other response was the one that Robert Bartley, Lawrence Lindsey, and Alan Reynolds took. They denied the facts as presented by Krugman and other government agencies.

Lindsey's discussion agrees that if the changes in the economy actually slanted income toward interest, dividends, and capital gains instead of wages and salaries, that would constitute a shift toward the rich (and very rich), as Krugman has calculated. Lindsey's response is to argue that most of the increase in interest income had occurred between 1977 and 1981.

> The interest share of personal income peaked in 1985 at 14.4 percent of income. Thus three-quarters of this windfall to the rich occurred before Reagan took office. Like the poverty rate, interest income as a share of personal income fell in the latter half of the Reagan presidency.[70]

Table 13 tracks personal income, personal interest income, and personal dividend income between 1970 and 1989. According to this information, interest and dividend income as a percentage of personal income declined by less than 1 percent between 1986 and 1988 and then jumped to a level above 1986 in 1989. It is important to note that the decline between 1986 and 1988 left that percentage much higher than it was when Ronald Reagan took office.[71] Thus, in contrast to the impression created by Lindsey's statement, the increase in interest income as a percentage of personal income stayed at historically high levels throughout the Reagan recovery, rising to its highest percentage in the last year of that recovery. This is not surprising because the key

TABLE 13. The Changing Share of Interest and Dividend Income, 1970–89

Year	Personal Income	Interest Income	Dividend Income	Interest (% of personal income)	Interest and Dividends (% of personal income)
1970	836.1	69.2	23.5	8.3	11.1
1971	898.9	75.7	23.5	8.4	11.0
1972	987.3	81.8	23.5	8.3	10.7
1973	1,105.6	94.1	27.7	8.5	11.0
1974	1,213.3	112.4	29.6	9.3	11.7
1975	1,315.6	123.0	29.2	9.4	11.6
1976	1,455.4	134.6	35.0	9.3	11.7
1977	1,611.4	155.7	39.5	9.7	12.1
1978	1,820.2	184.5	44.3	10.1	12.6
1979	2,049.7	223.6	50.5	10.9	13.4
1980	2,285.7	274.7	57.5	12.0	14.5
1981	2,560.4	337.2	67.2	13.2	15.8
1982	2,718.7	379.2	66.9	14.0	16.4
1983	2,891.7	403.2	77.4	13.9	16.6
1984	3,205.5	472.3	79.4	14.7	17.2
1985	3,439.6	508.4	88.3	14.8	17.4
1986	3,647.5	543.3	105.1	14.9	17.8
1987	3,877.3	560.0	101.1	14.4	17.1
1988	4,172.8	595.5	109.9	14.3	16.9
1989	4,489.3	674.5	130.9	15.0	17.9

Source: ERP 1997, 330.
Note: Except for percentages, figures are billions of dollars.

macroeconomic policy constant for the entire period from 1979 to 1990 was tight money imposed by the Federal Reserve. As shown back in chapter 8, the real interest rate rose in 1988 and 1989 as the Fed suggested that pursuit of a zero rate of inflation was not an unreasonable goal.

Robert Bartley introduced two major ways of challenging the general picture of increased inequality. First of all, he argued that even though income distribution might look very unequal, consumption expenditures by different groups within the income distribution were much more nearly equal than incomes. For example, in 1989, the lowest 20 percent received on average $5,720 in pretax income but on average spent $12,119. Bartley suggests that if we are concerned about the well-being of people, the amounts spent on consumption by each group in the income distribution would be a much better measure than the income figures.[72] He then attacks the trends in income distribution in the following way:

Between 1983 and 1989, the real income of the bottom quintile rose 11.8 percent, while the real income of the top quintile rose by 12.2 percent. By contrast, between 1979 and 1983, the real income of the bottom quintile fell 17.4 percent, while the real income of the top quintile rose 4.8 percent. Once the tide actually started to rise, in other words, it did lift all boats.[73]

In other words, he is arguing that the divergence of the income distribution is not the result of the Reagan administration policies but of the period between 1979 and 1983 when the anti-inflation policy of the Federal Reserve coupled with the 1981–83 recession caused all of the problems experienced by low-income people. The problem with this argument is that the criticism leveled by Krugman and others is of the long-term trends, which, as we have argued in chapter 8 must be measured from peak to peak of the business cycle. Even using Bartley's numbers one can note that despite the "seven fat years" of 1983 to 1989, the real income of people in the bottom 20 percent of the population had not risen enough to make up for the loss between 1979 and 1983. Meanwhile, those in the top 20 percent experienced increases in real income over the entire period, including the recession years.

One counterargument emphasized by Alan Reynolds of the *National Review* is that the evidence about the divergence between income groups is irrelevant because there is a great deal of social mobility between these groups. In other words, it doesn't matter if over a decade the ratio between the average income in the top group and the average income in the bottom group increases, if over the same period, a large number of individuals in the bottom group will have moved up to a higher group. Reynolds argued that based on a study by the Department of Treasury,

> 86 per cent of those in the lowest fifth in 1979, and 60 per cent in the second fifth, had moved up into a higher income category by 1988. . . . Similar research by Isabel Sawhill and Mark Condon of the Urban Institute found that real incomes of those who started out in the bottom fifth in 1977 had risen 77 per cent by 1986.[74]

The problem with the Treasury study is that it was restricted to people who paid taxes in all ten years. This clearly biases the sample toward those who are economically successful. The reference to Sawhill and Condon is only a partial report on what these Urban Institute scholars wrote in June 1992. It is true that the real income of the total sample of individuals in the bottom 20 percent in 1977 rose 77 percent by 1986. However, only half of the sample had actually raised their incomes enough to get out of the bottom 20 percent. The fact of social mobility does not contradict the trend toward increased inequality. The only way that would be possible would be if the amount of social mobility were to increase along with the inequality. Sawhill and Condon argued that there is no evidence of increased social mobility and hypothesized, therefore, that with inequality increasing and social mobility *not* increasing, *lifetime* incomes would become more unequal.

> To partially test this hypothesis, we averaged the total income of each individual in our sample over two ten-year periods, 1967–76 and 1977–86, and then ranked all individuals into five quintiles in both periods. . . . By averaging income over a ten-year period, we take account of each person's mobility over that period and get a more permanent measure of income. . . . In the second period . . . there was greater inequality. This finding suggests that lifetime incomes are becoming more unequal.[75]

They conclude,

> Although the poor can "make it" in America and the wealthy can plummet from their perches, these events are neither very common nor more likely to occur today than in the 1970s.[76]

This conclusion is in direct contradiction to the implications Reynolds attempted to draw from their data.[77]

For a final piece of evidence, it is useful to turn to the work of Timothy Smeeding, Greg Duncan, and Willard Rodgers. In order to determine whether the apparent polarization of the income distribution is, in fact, shrinking the middle class, the kind of data reported regularly by the census is insufficient because it does not capture what happens to the *same people* over time. The Sawhill-Condon analysis does attempt to do this, and their results are suggestive. However, the Smeeding-Duncan-Rodgers study, cleverly entitled "W(h)ither the Middle Class?" makes a major contribution to our understanding because it tracked adults between twenty-five and fifty-four years of age over a period of twenty-two years. The sample was the Panel Study of Income Dynamics, a yearly survey of a large number of adults from 1968 to the present. Smeeding Duncan and Rodgers surveyed the income changes experienced by individuals who remained within that age group between 1967 and 1988 (the income years reported by the 1968 and 1989 interviews).

They began by defining as middle class anyone whose income in a given year was above that received by the bottom 20 percent in 1978 and below that received by the top 10 percent in 1978 (the middle of the period). Thus, the middle class was defined by an absolute measure of income.[78] Smeeding, Duncan, and Rodgers then tracked their sample between 1967 and 1986. Between 1970 and 1977, the middle class was between 71 and 75 percent of the total sample. Beginning in 1977 and continuing through the rest of their survey years, the middle class does shrink. Between 1977 and 1981, this is largely due to the big increase in the percentage of the sample who are poor. After 1981, the reduction in the percentage that are poor does not counteract the increase in the percentage that are in the highest income group. On balance, before 1980 the poor had more chances of climbing into the middle class, while the middle class was less likely to fall into the lower income group than after 1980. People leaving the middle class before 1980 were just as likely to rise into the top income group as to fall into the bottom group, whereas after 1980 they were more likely to fall than to rise.[79]

In analyzing the most significant causes of the changing patterns after 1980, the authors identify the earnings of men as crucial.

> [T]he favorable transitions involving men's earnings . . . showed that they were . . . associated with higher rates of pay. . . . Downward transitions for men were more likely to result from changes in hours—job loss and unemployment—than declining rates of pay.
>
> The widening of the income distribution and the withering of the middle class are mainly associated with growing inequality in men's earnings—in particular wage changes.[80]

This supports the analysis presented in the reports of the Economic Policy Institute, *The State of Working America,* which were referred to above. Just as Paul Krugman and Kevin Phillips argued, the rising tide of the 1980s did not lift all boats.

One group of boats that had less chance of being lifted were those filled with African Americans. Between 1979 and 1989, the ratio of real median income of black men fifteen years or older to white men of the same age went from 61.9 percent to 60.4 percent. In absolute terms, black men earned less in 1989 than in 1979. For black women fifteen and older, the ratio to white women's income went from 91.1 percent to 80.3 percent, though both black and white women experienced absolute increases in median real income.[81]

When we focus on wage differentials, we see that the black-white earnings gap increased from 10.9 percent in 1979 to 16.4 percent in 1989, for an annual increase of 0.6 percent. Interestingly, even ominously, the most significant increase in the earnings gap occurred among college graduates. For this group, the earnings gap had declined between 1973 and 1979, only to rise at an annual rate of 1.6 percent for the next decade, from 2.5 percent to 15.5 percent.[82] In a study by John Bound and Richard Freeman, the rise in the earnings gap is decomposed into various causal factors.

> Among the workforce as a whole, the increase in blacks' wage disadvantage arises from the fact that the occupations and cities in which blacks are concentrated had lower wage growth, that blacks became relatively more concentrated in low-wage industries and nonunion settings, and that blacks were particularly disadvantaged by the failure of the minimum-wage threshold to keep up with inflation.[83]

Among the college graduates, 19 percent of the increased earnings gap can be attributed to the concentration of black college graduates in occupations experiencing lower than average wage growth. All other elements contribute 7 percent or less, leaving fully 59 percent of the earnings gap unexplained. The authors of the *State of Working America* suggest that "greater, or more potent, discrimination as well as weaker government enforcement of anti-discrimination laws may have played an important role."[84] They note that this rise in the racial wage gap occurred at the same time that the gap in test scores has been narrowing.[85]

This rise in black-white inequality is somewhat paralleled by the trend in black-white unemployment rates. The ratio of black to white unemployment in 1979 was 2.41, and in 1989 it had risen to 2.53. However, among men twenty years and older the ratio was unchanged.[86] Thus it appears clear that increased inequality between blacks and white is not caused by increased black unemployment but by an increase in the differences of earnings. As interest, dividends, and capital gains helped increase the inequality of income among the population as a whole, we should assume that the fact that the black population on average derives much less of its income from interest, dividends, and capital gains than the rest of the population played some role in the black-white income gap as well.

The increase in inequality between blacks and whites, especially among college graduates, suggests that one of the major complaints about the 1980s, namely that affirmative action programs had promoted blacks at the expense of whites, particularly in the professions, has no basis in reality. As a higher percentage of blacks with higher (test score) qualifications graduated from high school and college, they experienced a *decline* in earnings relative to their white counterparts, over half of which was unexplained by causes other than discriminatory behavior. We might also remind the reader that the decade of the 1980s saw *declining enforcement* of affirmative action and other antidiscrimination programs.

The Decline in Leisure

But how is it possible that declining hourly wages and increased inequality can be consistent with rising median incomes? Except for the bottom 20 percent, all families realized some increase in real income over the decade 1979–89 (though the second 20 percent experienced an increase of less than 1 percent over the entire decade!).[87] They experienced increases in real incomes because on average people worked more hours in 1989 than they did in 1979, and the participation of married women in the labor force continued to increase.[88] This actually marked the continuation of a much longer trend noted by the 1991 best-seller *The Overworked American* by Juliet Schor. Schor and her colleague Laura Leete-Guy discovered that after declining for almost one hundred years, the average work week began to rise in the 1940s and continued rising right up through the 1980s.[89] This trend led to such a decline in leisure hours for average working families that for the first time public opinion surveys showed that large percentages of the population would willingly give up part of their paychecks for more leisure time.[90]

The rise in the number of hours of work supplied by individuals to the marketplace in the face of declining hourly wages calls into question a fundamental premise of traditional economic analysis. The supply of any item, toothbrushes, cars, and the factor of production labor, is supposed to *fall* if the price paid for it (in the case of labor, that would be the wage) falls. Yet in the 1979–89 period we seem to have a perverse situation where declining wages are associated with rising numbers of hours supplied. The explanation is that the labor market is fundamentally different from other markets. In the case of most products, rising prices can attract new producers into the market, and falling prices can send producers leaving the market to produce and sell other things. In the case of the factor of production labor, most individuals have no alternative factors of production to sell if they cannot get enough for their labor. For most people, it is not possible to respond to declining wages by quitting and making a living selling something else. Some people with large amounts of assets that can be sold or invested do have the opportunity of "substituting" the supply of some other factor of production for their labor in the marketplace. These are a small minority of the population. Most people rely solely on their ability to work. If the wage they receive shrinks over time, many will respond by attempting to preserve their standard of living by working longer hours if they cannot switch to a higher-paying job.

This fact about the labor market explains why the big increase in the supply of labor from women (the labor force participation rate) occurred during the 1970s, years when the high marginal tax rates were supposedly discouraging women from entering the labor force. Though the participation of women in the labor force continued to expand during the 1980s, the rate of increase was much slower, despite the introduction of the supply-side incentives in ERTA in 1981.

There is another important fact about the labor market that the recent experience of the unwilling surrender of leisure highlights. People do not enter the labor market with the full freedom of other sellers. If I am a farmer, I have the right to determine how much of a crop I will grow and how much of my crop to offer for sale. The same is true if I am a retailer or a manufacturer. I determine how much inventory to stock and how much of a given product to produce and I determine when and in what quantities I bring them to market.

A worker offering to sell one's labor usually is faced with three choices: work full time, part time, or not at all. In addition, what constitutes full or part time will be decided by the employer (and a union in rare cases). The reduction in the average work week that occurred over the one-hundred-year period from the early nineteenth century through the 1930s occurred as a result of long, difficult, and concerted efforts by labor unions, sometimes aided by government policy, to force business *as a whole* to change what constituted full-time work. Beginning with the 1940s, the labor movement abandoned efforts to shorten the work week further, and by the end of the 1970s unions had become quite weak in setting national wage and hours policy.[91]

Meanwhile, American business appears to have decided that for a variety of reasons, it would be more profitable to hire three people to work eight hours than to hire four people to work six hours. One might wonder what the difference would be if the hourly wage were the same, but Schor makes some very telling points about the rationale of business. First, she suggests that mechanization and the need to train labor help explain the bias from business in favor of longer hours.

> Employers typically prefer to hire fewer workers and keep them on long schedules because they cannot count on finding additional workers of comparable quality and experience.[92]

The more complicated the machines, the higher the fixed costs involved in hiring and training and the more incentive there is to spread those fixed costs over more hours of work per worker.

Then there is the need to discipline labor that arises from the need to get workers to cooperate, as we have mentioned a number of times. One technique, which Schor traces to Henry Ford's famous five-dollars-a-day wage, is something traditional economics would find irrational, the creation of employment rent—in lay terminology, "overpaying" workers substantially. Technically, any payment over and above the wage necessary to get workers to join your company constitutes rent. Going back to David Ricardo, rent is a pure return to scarcity rather than an actual payment for a service. So what was so scarce about a semiskilled factory worker on Henry Ford's assembly line? Their willingness to stay on the job and work on an assembly line at its pace. The scarce item that earned the rent was docility. Once disciplined by overpayment (five dollars a day more than doubled the going wage rates in auto plants), workers could be subjected to speedups and other methods of boosting production. Schor concludes that "the development of employment rents played a major role in stabilizing and containing problems of labor discipline in twentieth century America."[93] Longer hours, with time and a half for overtime, raises the employment rent and ties workers even more completely to their jobs. In the post–World War II period, the rise of fringe benefits as a percentage of the cost of employee compensation introduces an even larger fixed cost of employing a worker beyond the training costs associated with mechanization. Three workers working eight-hour days is now much less expensive than four workers working six-hour days because that's one less package of fringe benefits.

Paradoxically, Schor notes that the decline in leisure has occurred as the inability of the economy to provide full-time employment for those who wanted work became more apparent. Since 1969, measured unemployment, discouraged employment, and involuntary part-time work has increased on average over each full business cycle. Schor argues that this has created another bias in the economy in favor of long hours for fewer workers. If workers reduced their hours on average, more jobs would be available. If this happened for the economy as a whole, the rate of unemployment would decline precipitously. From a supply-and-demand analysis, again, one might wonder why business would care (ignoring for a moment fixed costs like fringes). The answer, of course, is that very low unemployment rates lower the employment rent associated with any one particular job. This reduces the "club" that business can wield in the conflict-driven labor market. Schor notes that when American labor proposed a thirty-hour week during the depression, the business community mobilized all its political muscle to induce President Roosevelt to oppose the law that had already passed the Senate. The behavior of the business community and their supporters in the economics profession suggests that full employment is incompatible with American-style capitalism, and the push to extend the hours of those working that helps make some significant percentage of the work-force superfluous fits into that pattern.

Conclusion: What Were the Real Failures?

Of the major criticisms made of the Reagan-Volcker program, the most well known, the high deficit and debt, appear to have done no damage to the economy. However, government purchases in the defense area to the neglect of infrastructure and education do appear to have had a negative impact on productivity and income growth. The combination of deregulation and lax enforcement led to the disastrous savings and loan collapse, an example of how commitment to a principle (in this case the superiority of unconstrained markets over regulated ones) without considering the special nature of a particular market can create a serious failure of policy.

Inequality of income presents an interesting problem because there was some dispute as to whether inequality had increased. We believe the evidence establishes a significant increase in inequality and no parallel increase in social mobility. In fact, it appears that over the 1980s it became more likely that people in the middle of the income distribution would fall out into the poverty group rather than rise into the upper income levels. The second problem presented is whether in fact inequality mattered for any reasons other than political reasons. We believe the combination of increased income inequality, slow growth in median income, and decline in leisure led to an absolute stagnation in the incomes and well-being of a significant proportion of the population. The discontent of this group would be a significant element in the politics of the 1990s.

The Bush Presidency and Clinton's First Two Years

The End of Reaganomics?

George Bush was elected president in part because he promised to continue the Reagan program.[1] He is famous for his promise not to raise taxes no matter how many times the Democrats in Congress asked him to. Just as important was his commitment to using the tax system to stimulate investment. Every year of his presidency, he proposed a reduction in the rate of taxation on capital gains.[2] In the area of regulation, he set up the Council on Competitiveness with Vice President Quayle as the chair. This institution became a clearinghouse for discussions of how to reduce the burdens of regulation so as to increase the ability of American businesses to compete in an increasingly global marketplace. It also became a kind of "appeal of last resort" for business and other interests who felt that new proposed regulations would impose costly burdens not warranted by the benefits to society. In the international arena, he negotiated a free-trade agreement with Canada and then, together with Canada and Mexico, the North American Free Trade Agreement (NAFTA). Early in his presidency he reiterated his belief:

> Increased global competition is an opportunity for the United States and the world, not a threat. But we cannot remain competitive by avoiding competition. My Administration will therefore continue to resist calls for protection and managed trade.[3]

He succeeded in persuading the Congress to put NAFTA on a "fast track" for consideration. This meant that the negotiated treaty could only be voted up or down; in other words, Congress could not amend the treaty and force the administration to reopen discussions. The Bush administration also vigorously pursued a new round of negotiations for worldwide reductions in trade barriers under the General Agreement on Tariffs and Trade (GATT).

So far, there is nothing in these actions to distinguish the Bush administration from the rhetoric of the second Reagan administration. In fact, by promoting NAFTA and calling for a capital-gains tax cut, Bush was reversing Reagan, who had increased protectionism and signed the Tax Reform Act. Supply-siders like Robert Bartley and Lawrence Lindsey had disagreed with the part of the 1986 law that had ended the preferential tax rate for capital gains and had warmly approved of Bush's efforts to reinstitute it. So how was it that conservatives came to regard Bush as a counterrevolutionary, betraying the Reagan legacy? The short answer involves the Deficit Reduction Act of 1990. By signing a law that raised income taxes as part of an agreement to reduce the deficit, President Bush repudiated his "read my lips" promise not to raise taxes. Worse, according to Bartley and Lindsey, he reversed the incentive effects of the Reagan tax policy.

Replacing Gramm-Rudman-Hollings

In 1989, the Bush administration prepared its spending and revenue estimates for the fiscal year 1990. The amended Gramm-Rudman-Hollings Act of 1987 had provided for a deficit target of $100 billion,[4] but the administration estimated that the deficit would exceed that figure by more than the $10 billion margin permitted by the law. Therefore, the president ordered that $16.1 billion be cut (the legal term was sequestered) from federal spending. After months of conflict, Congress came up with a budget reconciliation bill that cut spending to within the Gramm-Rudman-Hollings limit for fiscal 1990, and the president released three-quarters of the sequestered funds. However, by the middle of 1990, it became apparent that the actual deficit for that fiscal year was going to exceed projections. The result was that President Bush and the congressional leadership entered into very intense negotiations aimed at really cutting the deficit. Just as President Bush had warned in his nomination acceptance speech at the Republican convention, the Democratic leadership of Congress insisted that raising taxes on the highest-income Americans so as to make the tax system more fair (in their opinion) was essential if they were to agree to any budget cutting. In addition, they insisted that the president explicitly support such a move so as to make the increase in taxes bipartisan. President Bush acquiesced, breaking his "read my lips" promise.

The Omnibus Budget Reconciliation Act of 1990 combined fairly stringent rules controlling spending with an increase in taxation. The top marginal tax rate on individual income was raised from 28 percent to 31 percent (the 33 percent "bubble" was abolished), and other tax increases were included as well. The Bush administration predicted that this law would reduce the federal deficit $500 billion over what it would have been if the law had not been enacted.[5] Unbeknownst to the congressional and administration negotiators, the economy had already slipped into recession in the third quarter of 1990.[6] As always occurs during a recession, tax revenues declined well below predictions, and automatic expenditures on transfer payments such as unemployment compensation rose above predictions. In 1991, the Bush administration calculated that even though the structural deficit (which reflects policy) as a percentage of GDP declined in 1990, the actual deficit (which reflects the economy) rose dramatically.[7] By the end of fiscal 1990, the deficit had ballooned to $221.4 billion, compared to the $100 billion target. This rising deficit during fiscal 1990 gave even more of a sense of urgency to the attempt to successfully conclude budget negotiations with Congress. A year earlier, we should remember, the president had invoked the automatic spending cuts (sequesters) in the Gramm-Rudman-Hollings Act and forced Congress to agree to cuts in appropriations. In the fall of 1990, he was focused on building an international coalition to fight the Gulf War against Iraq and winning congressional approval for the ultimate use of force in January 1991. Robert Bartley is of the opinion that the president might have refused to go along with the tax increases in the 1990 bill if he had not been personally focused elsewhere.[8] A number of antitaxation stalwarts in the congressional Republican delegation, including future Speaker Newt Gingrich, urged him not to support the bill in its final form and themselves voted against it. However, in the wake of Bush's successful prosecution of the Gulf War in early 1991 and his 85 percent approval ratings in the summer of 1991, objections to the 1990 tax increases were for the most part ignored.

In the *Economic Report of the President* for 1991, the 1990 law was hailed as a major step toward getting control of the budget. The report focused on how the new law had reformed the budget process. The law slowed the growth of entitlement spending and included a provision forcing Congress to "pay for" any future expansion in such entitlement spending (or other mandatory spending, such as agriculture programs) with cuts in some other mandatory spending programs. Similarly, any tax cut would have to be paid for by an increase in tax revenues from other sources.[9] With the administration basking in the glory of the victory in the Persian Gulf, and with most forecasters believing that the recession of 1990 would be short and shallow, the 1990 budget agreement seemed destined to continue the process of reducing the budget deficit as a percentage of GDP.

Did the Tax Increase Cause the Recession?

Two years later, as the presidential campaign was in the home stretch, there was a great deal of argument suggesting that President Bush's repudiation of his "no new taxes" pledge had caused the recession. It is certainly possible that the newspaper reports of his willingness to consider tax increases in June 1990 had changed enough expectations in the economy to trigger the recession. However, it appears very unlikely that such talk would have had such a profound impact, especially where there are many more obvious candidates, most notably, the Federal Reserve's tight-money policy, which slowed economic growth almost to a standstill in 1989.

At the March 1989 Federal Open Market Committee meeting, the approach of this very important body of the Fed was revealed quite clearly. Fear of accelerating inflation dominated the meeting, driving a policy of holding real growth below what was considered the economy's potential. Pressed by one of the governors as to why such a sustained period of below-potential growth was not expected to have a quicker impact on the rate of inflation, a staff member responded,

> MR. PRELL: . . . Let me say first that it takes a period of below potential growth in order for some slack to open up in the labor market in particular . . .
> MR. JOHNSON: I know, but there's a year of that kind of slack . . .
> MR. PRELL: But as you know, in our forecast that only brings the unemployment rate up to about 6 percent. The maybe "worst case" interpretation of the events of the last two years is that that's only getting us back to the natural rate.[10]

In a nutshell, there you have the focus of the Federal Reserve. While the Reaganites were celebrating the last two of the "seven fat years" because of the low unemployment and continued growth in per capita GDP, the Federal Reserve staff believed that unemployment had been too low. Staff member Prell stated, "All the anecdotal evidence over the past year or so suggests that in essence we have overshot a level of resource utilization that's consistent with stable inflation."[11] Even though the staff believed that without increasing interest rates, the rate of growth of the economy would slow down and the unemployment rate would edge up, they ended up recommending increases in interest rates in order to head off further rises in the rate of inflation. This was despite the fact that they acknowledged a danger of recession.[12]

When the members of the committee made their statements, there remained universal fear of further increases in the inflation rate, and explicit rejections of the recession danger. Vice Chairman Corrigan put it that "under the best of circumstances the near-term inflation numbers are going to be bad. And if the economy is simply pausing rather than trending down they could be terrible."[13] With only one dissent (Governor Martha Seger), the committee approved the following policy directive.

> In the implementation of policy for the immediate future the committee seeks to maintain the existing degree of pressure on reserve positions. Taking account of indications of inflationary pressures, the strength of the business expansion, the behavior of the monetary aggregates, the developments in foreign exchange markets, somewhat greater reserve restraint would or slightly lesser reserve restraint might be acceptable in the intermitting period. The contemplated reserve conditions are expected to be consistent with growth of M2 and M3 over the period from March through June at annual rates of about . . . 3 and 5 percent, respectively. The Chairman may call for Committee consultation if it appears to the Manager for Domestic Operations that reserve conditions during the period before the next meeting are likely to be associated with a Federal Funds rate persistently outside a range of 8 to 12 percent.[14]

In 1988 the rate of growth of real per capita GDP had been 2.8 percent. As a result of the interaction of Federal Reserve policy and general economic trends, it had fallen to 2.4 percent in 1989.[15]

Investment as a percentage of GDP fell more than one-half of a percent between the second and the third quarter of 1990, over $30 billion.[16] It is hard to believe that Bush's statement, coming at the very end of the second quarter, could have such an impact so quickly. When investment decisions change, investment spending changes only after a significant lag, so even decisions made during early July 1990 would be unlikely to impact the economy in less than three months. Though one might argue about the role of the budget agreement of 1990 in prolonging the recession, it appears to be a very difficult case to suggest that the prediction in June 1990 that there would be such an agreement including a tax increase had precipitated the recession. If anything, the Federal Reserve's single-minded focus on not permitting inflation to accelerate coupled with the exhaustion of the expansion combined to cause the recession.

Regulation

Reading the reports issued by the Bush administration Councils of Economic Advisers one is struck with the emphasis, over and over again, of the importance of reforming regulation. The 1990 *Economic Report* focused on environmental regulation, supporting market-oriented solutions over the traditional "command and control" methods of achieving pollution control.[17] In 1991, the report praises the 1990 revision in the Clean Air Act, which

> incorporated a flexible and innovative market-based system that will secure a substantial and permanent reduction in the sulphur dioxide emissions that cause acid rain. The reduction will be achieved at an estimated cost 20 percent lower than the cost of traditional, less flexible command-and-control regulation.[18]

In the same report, deregulation is celebrated and defended in the areas of energy and telecommunications.[19]

In January 1992, President Bush announced a new "regulatory reform initiative." Its goals were to

> revise (or repeal where appropriate) those regulations that clearly impose costs that exceed their benefits;

> ensure that regulatory goals are being achieved at the lowest possible cost;

> ensure that existing rules rely on market forces rather than command-and-control requirements to the extent feasible;

> and ensure that regulations provide clarity and certainty to the regulated community and do not promote needless litigation.[20]

The 1992 report devoted a whole chapter to issues in regulatory reform, focusing on the legal system, the environment, natural gas, electric power, the cable TV industry, and health and safety issues.[21] One proposal resulting from these initiatives, was described in the 1993 report.

> [T]he cost to an industrial polluter of reducing emissions by some amount through conventional controls may be $1000, but the owner of an old car that emits the same amount of pollution may be willing to sell the vehicle for $500. Under the EPA's proposal, the company could purchase the vehicle instead of directly reducing emissions from the plant. . . . The EPA's "cash for clunkers" program expands the notion of performance standards by permitting standards to be met through alternative means, such as eliminating sources of pollution other than those directly controlled by the polluter.[22]

The report provided a chapter entitled "Markets and Regulatory Reform" that went beyond a discussion of the regulatory-reform initiative and addressed reform of telecommunications regulation, the regulation of banking and finance, and the role of government in reducing environmental and health risks.

In the area of telecommunications, the report recommended removing restrictions on new competition. Interestingly, the recommendations made, even if very general, were all incorporated into the Telecommunications Reform Act passed by the House of Representatives in July 1995. The general approach was that since new technology made dramatic increases in competition possible, regulating rates and enforcing local monopolies (say on local telephone systems or on local cable TV systems) was no longer necessary. Thus, President Bush vetoed the cable TV reregulation act in 1992. Though passed over his veto, this act was repealed in the 1995 House bill.[23]

In the area of banking and finance, the report reached the conclusion that the laws passed in response to the savings and loan crisis (the FDIC Improvement Act and the Financial Institutions Reform, Recovery, and Enforcement Act) "may have created as many new problems as they have solved." The report actually blamed the law's stringency for the "shortage of commercial credit during the recent recession and recovery."[24] The 1993 report reiterated the reform proposals of 1991 that Congress had shown no interest in adopting. The issues that stymied the Congress and the president are similar to the problems involved in reforming telecommunications regulation: (1) How does one get the benefits of increased competition without permitting the rise of giant institutions that can make themselves immune to competition? and (2) How can a particularly crucial industry be prevented from becoming the cause of spreading and dangerous instability without being stifled by regulation?

In the case of dealing with health, safety, and general environmental risks, the 1993 report argued that there had been very significant progress in reducing health and other risks and that government regulations imposed significant costs when they attempted to reduce risks. At one point, the report seems to argue that the market system itself takes care of the problem of extra risks, say on the job, by paying workers "risk premiums" for more dangerous work, thereby creating incentives for businesses to minimize risks. However, the report continues by noting that this works only if workers are fully aware of the risks associated with a particular job, which obviously opens up an important function for government, insuring that all risks are known and publicized. The report does not acknowledge, however, that sometimes workers are stuck in highly risky jobs because they have few alternatives. That fact may seriously reduce the risk premium in their wages. This section of the report is filled with generalities, some of which seem contradictory. For the most part it suggests that modern industrial society has succeeded admirably in reducing risks of all kind, including pollution, with the implication that drastic governmental action to reduce risks is not necessary. Yet many of the examples of reduced pollution and risk are related to the period after 1970, when regulation to control health and safety on the job and air and water pollution were growing dramatically, as Weidenbaum's data from the 1970s and since clearly shows. The only consistent conclusion one can draw from this section of the report is that regulation had succeeded admirably between, say, 1970 and 1990 and therefore it was no longer necessary, because now all risk reduction was being purchased at too burdensome a cost—all of this, by the way, without quantitative data to relate costs and benefits of existing regulations. There is no question, after reading all the economic reports issued by the Bush Councils of Economic Advisers, that the general thrust of recommendations is in the direction of reducing regulations and changing the regulations that remain so as to use market incentives to achieve the goals of public policy.

The Americans with Disabilities Act

Despite his strong ideological commitment to reducing regulation and some significant practical steps taken in that direction, George Bush's presidency is in fact remembered most for increasing the regulatory burden on American business because he signed the Americans with Disabilities Act in 1990. Just as laws to counter racial and sex discrimination increased the costs of American business,[25] so did this law. The defense of such an act is presented in a very straightforward manner in the 1990 *Economic Report*.

> Inaccessible work-places and discrimination against disabled individuals have prevented many disabled persons who are able and willing to work from realizing their full economic potential. . . . Survey results . . . indicate that several million disabled individuals who want to work are unable to find employment.[26]

In addition to increasing the likelihood that businesses would utilize the labor of individuals with disabilities, the act also forced institutions such as schools and businesses to alter the delivery of services so they could serve people with disabilities In some cases, this merely means the installation of ramps so the business is accessible to customers in wheelchairs. In other cases, say a school, it can involve creating modifications in the way courses are taught so as to accommodate students with different kinds of disabilities as well as providing assistance in the form of sign language interpreters (for the hearing impaired) and readers (for the blind).

In order to force institutions to make modifications in their behavior immediately so as to truly open them up to access for all disabled people, this law included something that did not exist in previous civil rights legislation. Individuals who sued because they had been discriminated against in violation of the act were entitled, if they prevailed, to collect attorney's fees. With the passage of the Civil Rights Act of 1991, the ADA was amended to include compensatory and punitive damages.[27] This was a very important departure from other civil-rights legislation. Previous efforts to enforce civil rights for, say, ethnic minorities, were usually undertaken only by lawyers who specialized in such law, and in the absence of punitive damages and with the loser-pays provision for attorney's fees, lawyers could not expect to derive much income from lawsuits. Litigation under the ADA, however, permits attorneys to recover their fees from the loser. This aspect of the law made potential litigation an important club held over the head of businesses and other institutions.

Interestingly, using the threat of litigation to force changes in behavior is consistent with the market-oriented approach to regulation of business promoted by both the Reagan and the Bush administrations. The alternative method of enforcing a new civil-rights law like the ADA would be for government to issue direct commands to businesses and other institutions to modify their behavior so as to eliminate discrimination. As time passed, such an approach would produce reams of regulations designed to force business to conform to the spirit of the law. As various *Economic Reports* have pointed out, such an approach increases rigidity and often achieves the positive results sought at great cost.

The method created by the ADA permits private individuals to enforce the spirit of the law by finding other private individuals (lawyers) who are willing to take a chance on earning large fees by winning large settlements in lawsuits. Businesses and other institutions, fearful of such litigation (and perhaps observing some substantial judgments levied against violators of the law) will voluntarily adopt modifications in their behavior in order to insulate themselves from the danger of litigation. For many who believe in the role of the free market in enforcing behavior that the consumers and other participants desire, litigation and the danger of litigation is far preferable to government setting and enforcing the rules of conduct.

Paradoxically, in apparent contradiction to the reliance on the impact of litigation, an effort known as "tort reform" was under way that attempted to limit the amounts of punitive damages and attorneys fees that can be recovered as a result of injury, say from a defective product or because an institution violated someone's civil rights. The Bush administration proposed an Agenda for Civil Justice Reform in 1991 that was summarized in the 1993 *Report* as follows:

> capping punitive damages at an amount equal to a plaintiff's actual damages
>
> discouraging frivolous suits by adopting, in a limited set of Federal cases, a modified "English rule" in which the loser would pay the winner's legal expenses, up to a level equal to the loser's expenses;
>
> limiting the amount of free document requests, after which the requestor would have to pay the costs of providing the documents.[28]

The 1991 Civil Rights Act itself specifically limited punitive damages to three hundred thousand dollars for the largest business firms and fifty thousand dollars for firms with one hundred employees or less.[29] However, compared to previous civil-rights legislation, the existence of punitive damages coupled with the ability to recover attorneys fees made it likely that the passage of the ADA would lead to a big increase in litigation.[30]

Since the ADA is still a relatively recent act, there have been no national studies of its impact on business expenses. Nevertheless, we can assume that it imposes two sets of costs on American businesses. The first set involves one-time changes in personnel policies based on studying the ADA, altering job descriptions, and educating all decision makers in the organization about the behavior required by the ADA. These costs are significant, but once changes are in place, there is little ongoing expense other than monitoring within the organization to make sure the new way of doing things is actually carried out. This suggests that the Equal Employment Opportunity Commission was correct in predicting that the regulations issued to implement the ADA "will not have a significant economic impact on a substantial number of small business entities . . . based upon exiting data on the costs of reasonable accommodation."[31]

The second cost is imposed on places of public accommodation. It involves adjusting their delivery of service to accommodate consumers with disabilities. Take the case of colleges and universities. Here, the expenses involve some changes in the physical facilities in order to accommodate people with disabilities and reasonable accommodations in the programs offered so that students with physical and/or mental disabilities will be able to "consume" them. In a program presented by a consulting group to the College and University Personnel Association in April 1992, the administrators were admonished that the ADA required

> Providing assistance to disabled students or members of the public in order to provide them access to all services offered by the university;

> Eliminating discriminatory criteria on who can receive services, and practices that tend to screen out or adversely affect disabled persons;

> and Providing special equipment or services to persons with disabilities on request, when needed to allow them to use all of the services of the college on an equal basis.[32]

These requirements have caused colleges to hire sign-language interpreters for hearing-impaired students and to provide reading machines for vision-impaired students. According to the report, individuals offered these accommodations cannot be charged for them.

Another accommodation involves adjusting instruction in order to accommodate students with learning disabilities. Under the ADA, students applying for admission may not be rejected solely on the basis of any disability, including a learning disability. Once a student is admitted, a school must make "reasonable accommodation" for such students. This does not mean providing special classes and special support, as in special-education programs in public high schools. It does, however, mean making certain changes in how courses are delivered, such as permitting some students untimed testing. Many colleges are now creating an Office of Disabilities Services and are attempting to codify the various modifications that they believe the ADA will require them to make. This process is ongoing and at times involves delicate negotiations with professors about the methods of instruction and evaluation in their classes. Should individual faculty fail to make the adjustments deemed necessary and appropriate, the institution could be faced with a lawsuit from an already admitted learning-disabled student. At the very least, then, institutions are having to spend some resources in an ongoing program of accommodating students with learning and physical disabilities.

Title IV of the ADA applies to newly constructed facilities. It does not require complete retrofitting of existing facilities but does require that any changes made include improvements to make the facilities accessible to people with disabilities. On colleges and university campuses, this involves not merely making sure all buildings are accessible to the physically handicapped but also that connecting paths between buildings are similarly passable.

These costs of compliance are real, though as yet unquantifiable. Perhaps more significant have been litigation costs, which are likely to be substantial. However, just as in the case of fighting racial and gender discrimination, the end result of the changes envisioned by the ADA would be of great benefit to the entire society. A whole group of citizens, previously kept from utilizing their full productive capacity in the marketplace, now are adding to the society's GDP to the best of their abilities. Others with the same disabilities are fully participating as consumers in the marketplace for goods and services. The extra costs imposed on business, many of which are merely once-for-all transition costs, including the litigation costs that will establish important precedents, are more than compensated by the benefits to the entire society from expanding the scope of competition for jobs as well as increasing the size of the market for all products. The problem is that the benefits take time to appear, while the costs are felt immediately. In addition, the costs impact on specific businesses, while the benefits appear to accrue only to the disabled.

In fact, just as the reduction in racial discrimination benefited the entire society, not just ethnic minorities, there are benefits diffused throughout society that result from the more inclusive economy mandated by the Americans with Disabilities Act. On balance, the benefits of this law far outweigh the costs, but as the costs are real, it would not be surprising if many businesses and other institutions felt put upon by its passage and the new regulations issued by the Equal Employment Opportunities Commission. The same goes for the rising litigation costs of honest institutions attempting to comply with the law.

Civil Rights

In the area of civil-rights enforcement, the Bush administration, for all its intentions to limit the role of government in regulating business, found itself supporting a new civil-rights act that overturned a Supreme Court ruling that had reduced the burden of complying with previous civil-rights statutes. Up until 1989, the Civil Rights Act of 1964 had been interpreted by the Supreme Court as forbidding not only unfair treatment of individuals as a result of race, sex, or national origin, but

> practices that disproportionately burdened racial and ethnic minorities or women unless such practices could be shown genuinely to assess candidates' suitability for the job in question.[33]

Recall our discussion of affirmative action in chapter 5. If a device by which employers screen candidates has a disproportionate impact on racial or ethnic minorities or women and has no direct relationship to the requirements of a job (for example, requiring that candidates for an executive position be able to bench-press two hundred pounds would not identify an ability needed for the position and would discriminate against women), it is evidence of discrimination.

In 1989, the Supreme Court in *Wards Cove* overruled the prevailing precedent and held that the burden of proof now was, not on businesses to show that policies were necessary, but on the individual alleging discrimination to show they were unnecessary. Just this shift in the burden of proof removed a substantial expense from businesses. But it was seen by many in the civil-rights community as a step back from the policies that had been in place at least since 1971, when the original Supreme Court precedent was set.[34]

The result was that Congress passed legislation to reverse the Supreme Court decision. It could do so because the Court was interpreting certain sections of the Civil Rights Act of 1964, not declaring any part of that act unconstitutional. However, the first attempt by Congress was met by a veto from President Bush, who claimed that redirecting the burden of proof to businesses would induce them to adopt a system of hiring quotas to make them lawsuit-proof. Only after the bruising Clarence Thomas Supreme Court confirmation fight in 1991 did President Bush sign a modified version of the original bill.[35] Many in the business community saw no difference between the bill the president signed and the one he had vetoed in 1990. In their view, an effort to reduce a burden on business imposed by civil-rights legislation and previous legal precedent had briefly borne fruit with the Supreme Court decision of 1989 only to be rolled back when Bush caved in to the majority in Congress.

The Bush administration also presided over other significant expansion in the federal regulatory apparatus. If we assume that the $9.74 billion regulatory budget from 1989 was a holdover from Reagan, the four Bush years saw a 19.6 percent increase through fiscal 1993.[36] Melinda Warren of the Center for the Study of American Business noted that "since President Bush took office, the regulatory machine has grown considerably, but at a *slower rate* than in the last few years of the Reagan administration"[37]—another example of a "half full/half empty" dilemma. This raises the question of whether the Bush administration was improving upon the Reagan record or continuing a trend *reversing* the successes from Reagan's first term. If we follow the rule of thumb and multiply the explicit costs of regulation by twenty, the indirect impact of these increases was dramatic. And note, this is before the implications of the ADA had begun to be felt.

The Failed Recovery of 1991–92

If the increased cost of regulation and the violation of the "no new taxes" pledge created disaffection among some Republicans, the perceived failure of the Bush administration to create a strong recovery from the 1990 recession undoubtedly was the main reason for the defection of the so-called Reagan Democrats from the Republican Party in the presidential election of 1992.[38] Just as during the election of 1982 there was a significant falloff in support for President Reagan that led to large Democratic gains in the midterm congressional elections, in 1990, the slow pace of the recovery coupled with rising unemployment led to a tremendous reversal of fortune for President Bush.

With his popularity at an almost unbelievable 85 percent in the wake of the victory in the Gulf War, many of the so-called heavy hitters among Democratic politicians (Governor Mario Cuomo of New York, Senator Bill Bradley of New Jersey, Senator Edward Kennedy of Massachusetts, Representative Richard Gebhardt of Missouri) declined to enter the presidential sweepstakes. It was left to an obscure governor from Arkansas whose only previous national exposure had been an interminable nominating speech at the 1988 Democratic convention to become the "front-runner" as 1991 drew to a close.

But something extraordinary happened between the spring of 1991 and January 1992. The recovery that the National Bureau of Economic Research dated from the first quarter of 1991 did not translate into reduced unemployment and rising incomes. For the first time in all postwar recoveries, a full two years after the recovery began the unemployment rate was *higher* than when the recession presumably ended. The Bush administration and the Federal Reserve had been quite optimistic that the recession that began in the third quarter of 1990 would be short and shallow, ending with the "soft landing" that had eluded the Carter administration in 1979 and that the Federal Reserve had attempted to orchestrate in 1988 and 1989. They predicted that the rate of growth of real GDP would be 0.9 percent from the end of 1990 to the end of 1991, three times as fast as the rate of growth in the previous year. They also predicted that growth would be "robust" in 1992: "Business investment and construction activity are expected to be especially strong."[39] As a result of this optimism, there was no fiscal initiative to fight the recession in all of 1991. Meanwhile, the Federal Reserve permitted the Federal Funds rate to fall less than 1 percent over the first three quarters of 1991, and the prime rate fell less than 1 percent in the same period.

By the fourth quarter of 1991, the recovery that was dated from March of that year had seen none of the acceleration that the economy experienced in 1983 and 1976, for example.[40] The rate of growth of real

GDP from the first quarter of 1991 to the first quarter of 1992 ended up being 2.1 percent.[41] In per capita terms, the real GDP rose only 1 percent from the first quarter of 1991 to the beginning of 1992.[42] As mentioned above, the unemployment rate kept rising even though the recovery had begun. By the end of 1991, President Bush was in trouble, and the reason was the economy.

The Federal Reserve redoubled its efforts to ease monetary policy. The Federal Funds rate fell more between the third and fourth quarters of 1991 than in the previous three quarters combined.[43] This expansionary monetary policy continued throughout 1992 and 1993 as well. When interest rates finally stopped falling, the Federal Funds rate had fallen from 8.29 percent in June 1990 to 2.96 percent in December 1993, a decline of 64 percent.[44]

Belatedly, in January 1992, the Bush administration attempted to interject some fiscal stimulus into the economy. The major change that could be accomplished without the help of Congress was changing the rate of withholding on the personal income tax. In general, unless taxpayers make specific requests, the rate at which federal income taxes are withheld from salaries and wages is such that most taxpayers would be entitled to some refund when the time comes for final reconciliation. During the 1980s, approximately three-quarters of all taxpayers filed for refunds. The Bush administration hoped to increase spending by taxpayers as a result of this reduction because people received higher amounts of take-home pay. Of course, any increase in aggregate demand caused by this shift would be exactly balanced after April 15, 1993, when the extra amount not withheld would cause lower refunds. Nevertheless, increased spending in early 1992 might increase the optimism of businesses, which would then expand production and hire more people, and the recovery would begin in earnest. However, the result of the administration's effort was undetectable. The ratio of consumption to personal income was no higher in 1992 than in 1991. By contrast, the percent of personal income devoted to consumption rose more than 2.5 percentage points between 1982 and 1983 and rose 1.4 percentage points between 1974 and 1975. Both of these increases can be attributed to tax cuts that took effect in those years.[45]

Meanwhile, the actual (total government) deficit as a percentage of GDP only went up from 2.4 in the first quarter of 1991 to 4.5 in the third quarter of 1992. One area where the Bush administration departed from the approach of its predecessor was in extending unemployment compensation benefits.[46] Initially, in the early months of the recession, the Bush administration made no moves to extend benefits, and the first years after the downturn began saw no higher a percentage of the unemployed collecting benefits than in the first two years after the 1981–82 recession began. But during 1992, as a result of the laws passed in 1991, the percentage of the unemployed collecting compensation payments rose to 56 percent, fully 10 percent more than in the previous recession and in the early months of the recovery.[47]

In addition, the liberalization of access to welfare, food stamps, and Medicaid led to a virtual explosion of expenditures in these areas. Medicaid expenditures grew at the rate of 9.9 percent between 1983 and 1987, 13.7 percent between 1987 and 1990, and a whopping 28.1 percent between 1990 and 1992.[48] AFDC expenditures had grown only 1.3 percent between 1980 and 1990, but between 1990 and 1992 that growth was 11.7 percent.[49] Food stamps had grown on an average of 1.9 percent per year between 1980 and 1990, but between 1990 and 1992 that average rose to 17.2 percent a year.[50] Finally, SSI had increased on average 3.2 percent per year between 1980 and 1990, but between 1990 and 1992, the increase was 12.5 percent per year.[51]

It all begins with jobs. From the nadir of 1975, the economy created over six million jobs in the next two years. From the nadir of 1982, the economy created over five million jobs in the next two years. In the 1990 recession, the falloff in employment continued into 1991, and over the next two years fewer than three million jobs were created.[52] As the *State of Working America* pointed out, most of the jobs created during the recovery were low wage. One of the causes was declining defense spending. After reaching a peak as a percentage of GDP in fiscal 1986 (6.3 percent), defense spending slowed between fiscal 1987 and fiscal 1990 from 6.1 percent to 5.3 percent. Beginning in fiscal 1990, in recognition of the end of the Cold War, absolute dollars spent on defense began to decline, accelerating the fall as a percentage of GDP.[53] Though this decline reduced the federal budget deficit in the years after 1990, it made it harder for the economy to generate a good head of steam for the recovery. Equally important, employment in defense contractors also fell, with states like Connecticut and California experiencing much worse recessions than other parts of the country.

With few jobs created and good jobs in defense-related industries being lost, it is not surprising that the percentage of the population qualifying for food stamps and Medicaid would increase. Even with the efforts of some states to develop welfare to work programs pursuant to the Family Support Act of 1988, AFDC rolls increased rapidly as well. In just two years between 1990 and 1992, the number of families receiving AFDC rose from 4 million to 4.8 million, almost 2 million additional recipients.[54] One aspect of the Family Support Act that contributed to an increase in AFDC enrollment was the requirement that states offer an AFDC program to intact two-parent families in which the breadwinner was unemployed. Though numerically small relative to the traditional AFDC family (single parent with children), enrollment in this program (called AFDC-UP for "unemployed parent") rose 26 percent between 1990 and 1992 a direct result of the combination of the recession and the Family Support Act.[55]

While increased spending on Medicaid could in part be blamed on general inflation of medical costs, we should recall the significant liberalization of eligibility during the second half of the 1980s.[56] In Medicaid financing of nursing care, the cost per recipient rose quite rapidly between 1990 and 1992, partially as a result of the mandate to states imposed by the Budget Act of 1987 to increase the quality of care delivered. Higher-quality care meant higher prices, which meant higher costs to the states. The states, in turn, petitioned the Health Care Financing Administration for increased federal funds.[57]

The interaction of recession, slow job growth, and slow income growth in the period from 1989 through 1995 is very significant when we contemplate ways to solve the problems associated with public assistance. According to the proponents of the recently enacted welfare reform legislation, the main problem with the economy is the unwillingness of individuals to work. Forgetting for the moment that many of the people receiving food stamps and Medicaid are also working, note that if the explosion in the costs of means-tested entitlements after 1990 was caused by unwillingness to work, this unwillingness had arrived very suddenly. Just three years earlier, when the economy had not yet slipped into a recession, the costs of all these entitlements were growing much more slowly and the percentages of the population receiving them had not changed much since the previous recession. The timing and the speed with which the percentages of the population receiving these programs increased should suggest that something as basic as the "character" of the individuals receiving these transfers could not have caused such a significant shift. However, the cumulative impact of slowly growing incomes at the bottom of the income distribution over the entire decade and the increase in unemployment during and after the recession can explain these increases. It wasn't the people who had suddenly failed by revealing a terrible character defect. It was the economy that failed the people.

Enter H. Ross Perot

H. Ross Perot focused most of his on-again, off-again presidential campaign on the problem of the economy, exemplified, he argued, by the ballooning of our national debt during the twelve years of the Reagan-Bush administrations. As noted earlier, his rhetoric and published analyses argued that "Our first priority is to balance the budget."[58] Without discussing how the budget deficit and the national debt have caused the decline in productivity growth, the recession, and the slowdown in overall economic growth, he asserted the connection.[59] Many of his proposals in the presidential campaign; in his first book, *United We Stand;* and in *Not for Sale at Any Price,* which he wrote in 1993 are related to the need to eliminate the deficit and then begin to pay down the debt.[60] Some of his other proposals, to improve education, to stimulate investment, to fight poverty actually require reductions in revenue (as a result of tax credits) or increases in spending. He denies that any of his proposals require spending increases—in effect, better leadership and organization will create more efficient delivery of services such as education and health care. However, he does explicitly recommend tax credits for a number of goals and that clearly reduces government revenue.

The point of this is not to belabor the specifics of Ross Perot's program. What is important is that with his third-party candidacy for president in 1992 and his subsequent activities on the political front he put the problem of the budget deficit and the national debt at the center of the political debate. He also validated the criticisms made by Democratic nominee Bill Clinton of "trickle-down economics."[61] Since the economy was not rolling along as it had been in 1984 and 1988, it was impossible for the incumbent president to ignore the complaints about the deficit. Instead, President Bush was left defending his record by apologizing for signing the 1990 tax bill and promising never to do it again, while warning that if the Democratic candidate, Bill Clinton, were elected he would raise taxes even more. He also argued in vain that the economy was well on its way to recovery. Interestingly enough, the fourth quarter of 1992 saw the first dip in unemployment and a significant increase in the rate of growth of real per capita GDP. Unfortunately, these numbers came too late to help the president's reelection effort.

Meanwhile, commentators and others got into the act by focusing on Perot's proposals to raise taxes and cut the growth of entitlement programs.[62] This caused those who were not persuaded that the deficit was as dire a danger as Perot asserted to become fearful of the impact of a Perot deficit-reduction policy. Into this campaign stepped Bill Clinton. Emerging from the Democratic primaries with an insurmountable lead to win a nomination that most people thought would be a worthless prize just six months earlier, he discovered to his surprise that his message resonated in the country. He promised to get the economy moving again while making a strong effort to rein in the budget deficit. Though much attention was given to his promise of a "middle-class tax cut," he also promised to raise taxes on the wealthy who had benefited disproportionately from the years of Reaganomics. He also explicitly promised to use government spending to invest in education and infrastructure. President Bush's warnings that Bill Clinton was a "tax-and-spend Democrat" attempting to cloak his policy predilections with new rhetoric about "fairness" and "investment" could not overcome the disgust people felt with the failure of the economy to rebound from the recession.

One interesting area where Clinton did not join Perot in his criticisms of the Bush administration was in the area of trade agreements. While criticizing the Bush administration for not defending American interests against "unfair" Japanese competition, candidate Clinton supported the ratification of the North American Free Trade Agreement. In a sop to his labor and environmentalist supporters, Clinton promised that before submitting it to Congress for ratification he would negotiate some side agreements with Mexico so that labor rights would be protected and environmental laws would be enforced. He argued that without such agreements, the reduction of tariffs on imports from Mexico would permit Mexican industries (often American firms producing in Mexico) to cut costs and undersell American producers because they are ignoring Mexican environmental laws and underpaying Mexican workers. Perot, on the other hand, warned that if NAFTA were passed there would be a "great sucking sound" as American jobs vanished over the Rio Grande with American firms setting up plants just on the Mexican side employing cheap Mexican labor. Though the majority of Clinton's supporters probably opposed the ratification of NAFTA, it was not a major issue in the campaign once Clinton agreed to support it.

With Perot taking 19 percent of the popular vote, and drawing most of those voters from President Bush, Clinton was elected with only 43 percent of the popular vote but a commanding lead in the electoral college. He took office promising to "focus like a laser" on the problems of the economy. He also promised to propose a comprehensive reform of our health care system. In an economic-policy conference held in December 1992, he strenuously argued that it would be impossible in the long run to reduce the federal deficit if health care costs were not contained. The economy and health care, thus, were the major issues on the agenda as he took office in January 1993.

The 1993–94 Clinton Program: Attempted Reversal

When Bill Clinton was running for the White House, the "war room" of his campaign in Arkansas reportedly sported a big sign, "It's the economy, stupid!"[63] The point of course was that the economy was the major issue in the campaign. In a sense, though he didn't use the rhetoric, he was running the same kind of campaign that Ronald Reagan had run in 1980. Then, Reagan had asked the question, "Are you better off now than you were four years ago?" Just as many Americans responded to that earlier question by voting to throw President Carter out of office, there were an even greater number of Americans (62 percent of the popular vote) who voted to deny President Bush a second term because of his perceived failings in economic policy.

Reagan introduced his program for economic recovery early in his presidency. Following the same procedures, President Clinton presented his program in February 1993. He called it *A Vision of Change for America.* The change he contemplated was to correct the economic failures of the twelve years of the Reagan and Bush administrations. The failures he enumerated were (1) the anemic nature of the economic recovery from the 1990 recession, (2) stagnation in the standard of living for the majority of the population since the early 1970s, (3) increased income inequality and the shrinkage of the middle class, (4) the run-up of the national debt through the massive deficit spending during the previous twelve years, and (5) failure to use the borrowed funds productively during that same period, more specifically the neglect of infrastructure and education. Clinton's program attempted to deal with all of these problems at once, and he promised more long-term solutions to other problems such as health care access and costs and the need to reform the welfare system.[64]

1.   In order to accelerate the recovery that had been so disappointing up to the end of 1992, he proposed what was called a "stimulus package." This involved spending increases on various government projects, mostly having to do with infrastructure investment and job creation. It also involved some targeted tax credits to encourage private investment. Finally, it extended unemployment benefits to cope with the fact that unemployment kept rising for most of 1992 even though the recession was supposed to be over. This fiscal stimulus to the economy was to total $30 billion in spending and tax cuts and to occur during the fiscal year that had already begun, 1993 as well as 1994.[65]

2.   To raise the incomes of the majority of the population, it was essential to move toward full employment and even more important to make sure that the jobs people obtained were well-paid jobs. This required education and training for young people and workers. Such expenditures were the kinds of "investments" in people he talked about during his campaign, but given the necessity of reducing the budget deficit, very little could be attempted in this area early on. Nevertheless, his program did include a few proposals with these long-run goals in sight.[66]

3.   The reduction in inequality was to be accomplished via certain tax changes. During the campaign he had promised to reverse the Reagan tax approach by raising taxes on the wealthy and giving the middle class a tax cut. Though the specifically middle-class tax cut was abandoned, he did propose increased taxation on the well-to-do and a tax cut and wage subsidy for lower-income workers via a substantial expansion of the earned-income tax credit. As mentioned above, the EITC provided for reduced taxes (and if the credit exceeded the tax liability a direct payment) for individuals who worked and had at least one dependent child. When fully phased in, this expansion led to a tax cut for every wage earner, even one without children, who earned less than thirty thousand dollars a year. The middle class with incomes higher than this received no tax cut. Meanwhile, Clinton proposed increasing the top marginal income tax rate from 31 percent to 36 percent, with a 10 percent surcharge on top of that for taxpayers with greater than $250,000 of taxable income.[67] He also proposed raising the percentage of Social Security payments subject to taxes for retired

couples with more than thirty-two thousand dollars of income. Together, these changes did increase the tax burden on the top 20 percent of taxpayers.

Interestingly, the other sources of inequality identified in chapter 9 were presumably going to be reversed by increased training so that more working people could work at higher-paying jobs. Many people dubbed this the "field of dreams" version of good jobs, after the movie in which a man builds a baseball diamond on his farm and the stars of yesteryear appear in this field. Many doubted that creating more trained people would automatically attract the good jobs for which they were qualified, but the approach Robert Reich, whom Clinton named his secretary of labor, developed in *The Work of Nations* was that businesses have the whole world before them when they consider where to locate their operations. They will build the facilities that require highly skilled people where those people are. If we train the people, the argument goes, the jobs will come.

One other element of this approach was the firm Clinton administration commitment to free trade. In exchange for opening up the United States to imports that might tend to substitute for mass-produced products that employ semiskilled blue-collar workers, American businesses would receive access to foreign markets for more technology-intensive products, creating demand for more highly skilled workers. Thus, for example, the argument over NAFTA, though often conducted as if it were an argument about how many jobs on balance would be created or lost, really was about the *quality* of the jobs created as opposed to the quality of the jobs lost.

4. Even before he became president, Clinton was made aware that his most important priority was to "impress the financial markets" that he was serious about reducing the federal budget deficit. Journalist Bob Woodward describes a meeting between President-elect Clinton and the chairman of the Federal Reserve Board, Alan Greenspan, in December 1992. According to Woodward, Greenspan's main point to Clinton was that reducing the long-term interest rate was the best method of increasing economic growth. Unlike the Federal Funds rate (and other short-term rates), which were amenable to Federal Reserve control, long-term rates reflected the various financial-market fears of future inflation. Because deficits in the 1960s had produced double-digit inflation in the 1970s, investors feared that the increased deficits since 1990 (and for the foreseeable future) would translate into inflation sooner or later and thus were demanding a higher inflation

premium than in previous decades. According to Greenspan, the only way to get long-term interest rates to come down would be to enact a *credible* deficit reduction program.[68]

Notice how many controversial assertions are packed into this argument. First of all, deficits in the 1960s are dubious candidates for the main cause of the inflations of the 1970s. Oil price increases, dollar depreciation, and the short-term experience with price controls all played a major role in ratcheting up inflation between 1972 and 1974.[69] The 1979 inflationary surge followed two years of rather substantial deficits in 1975 and 1976, but during most of 1978 and 1979, the total government budget was actually in surplus.[70]

The spread between long-term interest rates and the Federal Funds rate had indeed reached unprecedented levels in 1992. Using the thirty-year Treasury bond as the example of a long-term interest rate, the gap had been in the 3 percent range during 1985, but in 1992 the gap had gone above 4 percent. However, in real terms, both the Federal Funds rate and the thirty-year rate had been higher in 1984–85 than in 1992.[71] Thus, the difference was not caused by the inflation premium that bondholders were insisting on before purchasing long-term debt instruments. Instead, the cause of the smaller spread in the 1980s (which actually turned negative in 1989) was the tight money policy of the Fed in the period after 1984 that kept the federal funds rate from falling as much as the long-term rate. By 1992, in contrast, the Federal Reserve was pursuing an expansionary monetary policy. The spread and both real interest rates fell over the later years of the 1980s *despite* the persistence of high structural deficits. With the sluggish recovery from the 1990 recession, the spread once again opened wider than in the past, even though the absolute level of the real interest rates remained lower than in the middle 1980s.[72]

Greenspan was arguing that a credible deficit reduction plan would reduce long-term rates, but in fact the 1990 budget agreement had been such a credible plan. It had failed to reduce the actual deficit because of the recession. What Greenspan didn't tell Clinton was that if *his* deficit reduction plan aborted the recovery and brought on a recession, the gap would stay wide, because the deficit would balloon again. Instead, Greenspan stressed that deficit reduction would cause the rates to come down and stimulate the economy. In other words, Greenspan was predicting that the only thing holding up private investments was high interest rates, and that lower long-term rates would be sufficient. Again, there is tremendous disagreement among economists as to how interest-sensitive investment decisions actually are.

5. Clinton responded by attempting to make deficit reduction *and* his investments (infrastructure, training, tax-based incentives) central to his plan. *A Vision of Change for America* included lots of details on specific kinds of investments as well as spending cuts aimed at deficit reduction.

Clinton's First-Year Program: An Assessment

In theory it would have been possible for most of these goals to coexist in the same package. Deficit reduction could occur with reductions in overall spending and increases in taxes on balance. Within the federal budget, however, spending could shift toward investments such as infrastructure and education and away from less productive activities, particularly defense. On the revenue side, the tax increases could be placed on well-off taxpayers and some of the middle class, and others could actually get some tax relief. Unfortunately, to accomplish both of these tasks would have required deep cuts in defense spending and steep increases in the tax burden of the well-off. Since the defense budget was already being cut according to a schedule designed by the Bush administration after the demise of the Soviet Union, and since those cuts were already producing significant layoffs within defense industries with important consequences for some states and localities, it is hard to imagine that speeding up those cuts or making them even deeper would have been politically feasible.

And regardless of the *possibility* of reconciling the policies of deficit reduction, middle-class tax relief, and increased public investment, it was impossible to reconcile deficit reduction and "stimulus." In fact this same problem confronted the Reagan administration and Paul Volcker in 1981. Volcker was jamming on the brakes with tight monetary policy in order to fight inflation while Reagan's tax cuts aimed at stimulating incentives were pressing on the gas, raising aggregate demand. Until Volcker's Fed ended the monetarist experiment and eased up on monetary policy, the brake pedal held and the economy experienced a long, wrenching recession. Clinton tried to finesse the contradiction by the timing of the stimulus package. According to *A Vision of Change for America,* in 1993 the stimulus package would temporarily increase the deficit. Beginning in 1994 the deficit reduction changes voted in 1993 would take over, and there would, in fact, be no more fiscal stimulus emanating from the federal budget.[73] The hope was that the short-run stimulus of 1993 would accelerate the recovery, leading to rising consumer spending. When the drag of decreased deficit spending occurred in 1994, private-sector investment spending would be expanding to take up the slack, both in response to that rising consumer spending and in response to the fall in long-term interest rates predicted by Alan Greenspan (and many others as well). Notice that this is very similar to the hope of the Bush administration that merely changing the timing of income tax collections in 1992 would provide a strategic push to aggregate demand.

Again, regardless of the potential rationality of such an expand-then-contract fiscal policy, the presumed need to reduce the deficit led many to question the economic rationality of attempting to stimulate the economy. How can you do something and its opposite at the same time? This problem was not lost on President Clinton, who himself observed that his administration was trying to stimulate the economy and reduce the budget deficit at the same time, something that had never been done before!

The importance of the stimulus package went beyond increasing aggregate demand. Candidate Clinton had made it abundantly clear that he was not merely criticizing the size and growth of the budget deficit, he was also arguing that the money borrowed by the federal government had not been invested productively. He implied that if less had been used to fund tax cuts and some of the defense buildup, it could have gone toward infrastructure investment and education reform. Here he was echoing Reich, who had argued that the key to the economic growth of a particular nation in the global marketplace was to have the infrastructure and the skilled, educated population that international corporations wanted. The government ought to be spending money on such items, according to candidate Clinton, and the Reagan and Bush administrations had seriously neglected such responsibilities.

His administration wanted to make a clean break with the Reagan-era conventional wisdom that all government spending is wasteful. We noted in chapter 1 that economic growth requires significant government assistance, if only in the education of the labor force. Later we noted the role of certain essential public works summarized under the heading infrastructure. Following on the campaign theme, many in the

Clinton administration were anxious to begin at least token investments as part of the stimulus package, even though the quantitative
impact would be minor, if visible at all. In the words of one of his aides,
quoted by Woodward, the stimulus package was not economic policy
but social policy.

In addition, the administration feared that the recovery had been
so lackluster that any move toward fiscal restraint associated with a
significant deficit reduction package would stop it in its tracks and create a new recession. Aside from the political and economic damage a
recession would do, it would also make deficit reduction virtually
impossible, as in the post-1990 period.

This two-part program was introduced into Congress as two separate bills, one for the stimulus package and one as the Omnibus
Budget Reconciliation Act of 1993. The latter made good on the Clinton campaign promise to introduce a serious deficit reduction package and to include in it income tax increases on those with high
incomes. However, President Clinton had to apologize on national
television for being unable to recommend a middle-class tax cut, such
as he had promised in the campaign, because the deficit was much
higher than he had thought during the campaign it would be. This
latter point was probably more wishful thinking than accurate
reflection of the information available in the fall of 1992, and many
people just shrugged it off as just one more politician's lie. Only
lower-income taxpayers received a tax cut through the expansion of
the earned-income tax credit.

The vehicle chosen to raise a significant amount of revenue as part
of the deficit reduction was a tax on business use of energy, called the
BTU tax. BTUs (British thermal units) measure quantities of energy.
As opposed to a broad-based sales tax, this tax was considered a useful
inducement to increased energy efficiency and reduced pollution. Businesses that used energy more efficiently would have less of a tax burden, and there was hope that businesses would begin to switch to more
energy-efficient methods. Though not exactly the same, this tax was
analogous to one that had been proposed by environmentally con-
scious economists for many years, the so-called carbon tax. Under a
carbon tax, each production and consumption activity would be taxed
according to the amount of carbon released into the atmosphere as a
result. The idea was to put pressure on businesses and consumers to
reduce the release of carbon, a major cause, it was argued, of global
warming. Though the BTU tax did not target carbon specifically, by

working to reduce consumption of fossil fuels, it would have an indirect effect of slowing the release of carbon into the atmosphere.

It is interesting that from the point of view of supply-side economics, this proposal is clearly superior to a progressive income tax. First of all, the marginal tax rate for an increase in income is zero under any tax on consumption, whether computed on the value of sales (as in most states), on the amount of fossil energy consumed by a product, or on any other form of consumption spending. Second of all, taxing these energy products would fulfill one important role of government developed in chapter 3, adjusting the composition of output to take account of social costs and benefits. Third, since the tax was on consumption, it should have some (probably small) positive impact on savings compared to an income tax that raised the same amount of revenue.

For all of these reasons, if the proposal had not come from a Democratic president, many conservative economists and politicians would probably have supported it. Conversely, if the proposal had come from a Republican president, few liberal Democrats would be willing to support it because as with all consumption taxation, the impact would be felt most by low-income people. The liberal Democratic approach is that the best way to raise revenue is through progressive income taxation that starts with a zero rate on low-income people. The Clinton proposal shows how far the debate had been shifted since the late 1970s. Returning to the progressive income tax rates of the pre-1980 period (see table 4) was clearly out of the question. In order to raise the revenue needed to create a credible deficit reduction program, a broad-based consumption tax was a necessity, even if it violated the equity principles Clinton was trying to reestablish with the increase in taxes on higher-income taxpayers and the expansion of the earned-income tax credit.

The Republicans refused to support the BTU tax because they were united behind the principle that all deficit reduction should come from spending cuts rather than tax increases. While this argument can make sense if one is adhering strictly to a supply-side argument about incentives and the tax in question raises marginal tax rates, it makes no sense whatsoever when one is talking about a consumption tax. In one aspect of the Clinton proposal, the argument that spending cuts are superior to tax increases reached absurd lengths. Recall that as part of the Social Security reform in 1983, Ronald Reagan had been persuaded to support the taxation of half of Social Security benefits for high-income recipients. The reasoning used by those who persuaded him was that it was not a tax increase but a net reduction in benefits. In fact, from that point onward, the Reagan administration had listed all income tax revenue collected from Social Security recipients as a *spending reduction,* not as a tax increase.

When the Clinton administration released its list of proposed spending cuts and tax increases, it followed the same (misleading) method and listed the increased revenue from expanded Social Security income taxation in the column of spending cuts. This brought howls of protest from those who had insisted spending cuts predominate over tax increases. The reason this whole discussion is ludicrous was spelled out clearly by economist Robert Eisner.

> Suppose social security benefit payments were reduced at the source by an amount corresponding to what would otherwise be taken away in taxes, probably by withholding, so that the checks would be the same. Would the amount spent by retirees be different?[74]

We might add a further question: would the incentives of retirees be any different? So aside from the need to score points against your political opponent, does taxing Social Security benefits differ in any meaningful way from reducing Social Security benefits for the same people the same amount?

Whatever the theoretical reasons for reducing the deficit using a BTU tax, in political terms this tax became a very hard sell. After passing the House, it was dropped from the Senate version of the deficit reduction plan in favor of adding a few cents per gallon to the gasoline tax. Meanwhile, just as the Republicans did not discriminate when it came to taxes (they were opposed to all of them), they did the same with the investments Clinton was trying to push with his stimulus package. A Republican filibuster blocked it in the Senate, and the administration gave up on it in April.

With that, the Clinton administration was left with only one economic strategy, deficit reduction. With the most extraordinary effort, over unanimous Republican opposition and with grudging support from many Democrats, the Omnibus Budget Reconciliation Act of 1993 squeaked through without a vote to spare. The deficit reduction actually accomplished by the act was only $3 billion less than the $148 billion reduction projected in *A Vision of Change for America.* The projected deficit reduction for 1998, compared to what would have occurred with no policy change, in OBRA 1993 was almost the same as called for in *Vision of Change,* even though the stimulus package had been abandoned.[75]

This victory actually masked the important fact that the Reagan Revolution had succeeded in shackling even a reform-minded Democratic president supposedly working with a like-minded Democratic majority in Congress. Even the modest stimulus package was hostage to charges of pork-barrel spending and the need to cut the deficit. Even though the tax increases were focused on very few Americans, those who had experienced dramatic increases in their incomes over the previous dozen years, they still barely won approval from that Democratic majority. This experience set the stage for the failure of health insurance reform a year later.

The Economic Impact, 1993–95

Though the financial community responded in a very positive way to the deficit reduction strategy,[76] 1993 was not a dramatic year for the economy. Real GDP did not grow in the first quarter and only at the rate of 1.9 and 2.3 percent in the next two quarters.[77] Investment stayed below 13.5 percent of GDP for the first three quarters, and productivity growth was negative for the first two quarters, averaging only .1 percent for the year.[78] Meanwhile, the civilian unemployment rate inched down from 7.1 percent in January to 6.7 percent in October. Recall that the unemployment rate had risen from the beginning of the recession to 7.7 percent in June 1992 before beginning to fall. Such a slow decline in unemployment coupled with a weak rate of economic growth produced stagnant incomes for large percentages of the population. However, the Clinton administration tried to put as good a face as it could on this result.

In the 1994 *Economic Report,* the Clinton Council of Economic Advisers pulled out all the stops in identifying deficit reduction as the key element in an economic program that would shift spending from consumption to investment, revive the economy, and raise the long-term rate of growth. Crucial to this argument was the assertion that credible plans for reductions in deficits had already significantly reduced long-term interest rates. The council argued that the very act of proposing a serious long-term deficit reduction plan caused interest rates to come down. They identified three ways actual deficit reduction can reduce real long-term interest rates.

Lower Federal borrowing reduces interest rates directly, by reducing demand for credit.

A more prudent fiscal policy reduces the likelihood that the Federal Reserve will need to pursue a restrictive monetary policy, and so reduces expected future short term rates. . . . increased national saving leads to an increase in investment. . . . the consequent increase in the capital stock reduces the marginal product of capital and therefore the interest rate.[79]

This reasoning appears pretty weak. The first point is clearly true, but the others are unlikely to influence long-term interest rates. We should recall that the whole point of Greenspan's earlier argument to Clinton was that Federal Reserve actions to alter short-term rates have *no impact* on long-term rates. Meanwhile, increases in the capital stock lower interest rates *only* if profit earned from capital investment is depressed by such an increase. If instead profits rise because the rate of growth of new technology or the efficiency with which the new capital is used increases *faster* than the capital-stock increases, the so-called marginal product of capital will actually *rise,* not fall.

The council went on to argue,

Because the [Clinton] plan had credibility, financial markets anticipated these effects. Since future expected short-term interest rates govern current long-term rates, long rates fell immediately in response to the proposal and enactment of the Administration's plan. There would have been no such market response if the plan had lacked credibility.[80]

A much more convincing explanation would have been that the financial markets, seeing a credible deficit reduction plan, believed that the likelihood of inflation in the medium future (five years or so) had been reduced. Instead of viewing future inflation dangers as contingent on the rate of growth of money, as a monetarist would argue, the financial-market decision makers were behaving as if the Keynesian vision of the world were more accurate. The way to prevent inflation was to prevent aggregate demand from growing too much. Deficit reduction, despite its potential long-term benefit if interest rates and international borrowing were to come down, has as an immediate consequence the stifling of aggregate demand, the maintenance of high levels of unemployment and excess capacity. In short, reducing the deficit banishes inflation fears by keeping the economy from getting near its potential output.

What appears to the average citizen as a *failure* of economic policy, the laboriously slow process of reducing unemployment from 7.1 to 6.7 percent, appears to the financial-market decision makers as evidence that unemployment will not get too low to threaten inflation in the foreseeable future. It's the prediction that accelerating inflation is not even on the horizon that causes the long-term interest rate to come down.

That's the theory. Unfortunately for the administration, the year 1993 was the only year of success in terms of reducing long-term interest rates. By the beginning of 1994, the Federal Reserve had become alarmed at how rapidly the economy was growing. In order to avoid spooking the financial markets, the Fed again engaged in a preemptive strike against inflationary expectations. They raised the Federal Funds rate rather dramatically during the course of 1994 and 1995. This was supposed to improve expectations in the financial markets and result in a further fall in the long-term interest rates, narrowing the spread between short- and long-term rates. Indeed, the spread did narrow, but only because the Federal Funds rate rose more than the thirty-year Treasury rate. Both in real and nominal terms, the long rate actually went up.[81]

In terms of the macroeconomy, 1994 and 1995 were pretty good years. The recovery continued through both years. Unemployment continued to decline on average. Inflation did not accelerate. Real GDP per capita was actually lower in the beginning of 1993 than it had been at the end of 1992. However, from that point to the end of 1994, growth in that measure averaged 2.4 percent per quarter.[82] The Council of Economic Advisers recognized that the decline in interest rates was carrying a much greater part of the policy burden than in previous recoveries.

> If we divide GDP into its interest-sensitive components (business fixed investment, housing, and consumer durables) and everything else, the data tell a fascinating story. While the three interest-sensitive pieces typically account for about 30 percent of GDP growth, in 1993 they accounted for virtually all of GDP growth. The rest of GDP barely increased over the year.[83]

They also recognized that deficit reduction could go too far. That is why the administration opposed a balanced-budget amendment to the Constitution and, in the summer of 1995, attempted to stretch out the deficit reduction program from the Republican seven-year goal of a balanced budget by the year 2002 for an extra three years.

The administration argued that deficit reduction of $140 billion or so over five years was all the economy could take without endangering the recovery.

> [L]arge spending cuts or tax increases at this time would require additional *large* declines in long-term interest rates to replace the lost aggregate demand. Should interest rates decline by less than the required amount, economic growth would slow and jobs would be lost.[84]

The council estimated that in order to move to a balanced budget, the fiscal package would reduce aggregate demand so much that it would take a decline of 3 percent in long-term interest rates to offset it.

> Since a 3-percent long-term interest rate [decline] seems quite unlikely, complying with a balanced budget amendment seems likely to harm the economy—perhaps severely.[85]

In the 1995 *Economic Report,* the council restated the importance of reducing the federal deficit but also noted that reducing the deficit to zero, thereby stopping the growth of the national debt, was not the primary policy goal.

> A . . . reason for reducing the deficit is to reduce the debt burden that the present generation will bequeath to future generations. . . . This legacy of debt is a real concern, yet it is important not to overstate the problem or to use it as an excuse to skimp on public investment. We also bequeath to future generations a stock of physical capital—highways, airports, and the like—as well as a stock of human capital and technological knowledge. Because these add importantly to future generations' productivity and well-being, these assets will somewhat reduce their debt burden.[86]

Other reasons given for reducing the deficit are instructive. The 1980s deficits had been financed, as we have noted in previous chapters, by significant borrowing from abroad. The near future should see significant demographic changes that will have a tendency to raise government spending on health and retirement programs for the elderly. Since such patterns will occur worldwide, the council warned that the foreign sources of savings that had financed government borrowing in the 1980s were not likely to be as available once those other countries find themselves devoting more and more of their national savings to financing their own budget deficits.

The third reason the council introduced actually acknowledges the fact that sometime in the future it may be necessary to *increase* the budget deficit.

> [A] large deficit hamstrings discretionary fiscal policy as a tool of macroeconomic stabilization. In the presence of a looming deficit, it is difficult for the Federal Government to respond to cyclical slowdown by cutting taxes or increasing spending. A gradual policy of reducing deficits can build a cushion in case the Federal Government needs to engage in countercyclical fiscal policy sometime in the future.[87]

This last argument is particularly significant since the GOP majority in Congress was at that very moment poised to pass a constitutional amendment mandating a balanced budget by the year 2002. The council revisited many of their arguments from the previous year, adding a major point about automatic stabilizers.

> A balanced budget amendment would throw the automatic stabilizers into reverse. The Congress would be required to raise taxes or cut spending programs in the face of a recession to counteract temporary increases in the deficit. Rather than moderate the normal ups and downs of the business cycle, fiscal policy would be forced to aggravate them.[88]

They argued that this would result in the Federal Reserve being the only source of macroeconomic stabilization policy. However, the decreased spending by the government in the face of a recession would require such big reductions in interest rates to counteract that recession that the resulting financial instability might cause the Fed to refrain from taking such dramatic action. If the Fed were to refrain, then every recession would have the potential of turning into a depression before the three-fifths majority of Congress necessary to temporarily suspend the requirements of the amendment could be put together.

Fortunately, Congress failed to pass the amendment, which fell one vote short in the Senate in 1995. This meant that even though Congress and the president have agreed on legislation creating a spending and revenue stream leading to budget balance in 2002, should a recession arise, the automatic stabilizers will be able to increase the budget deficit as a partial cushion to the decline in aggregate demand during the recession.

The successes noted by the administration involve deficit reduction, increased government investment in education, skills, science, and technology, the so-called reinventing government program, and a

vigorous promotion of export expansion both through bilateral nego-
tiation and strong support for multilateral trade barrier reduction as
with NAFTA and GATT. The consistent argument in the 1995 report
is that though government must spend less, it must also redirect its
spending to make it more effective and must revamp the way it delivers
its services so that fewer dollars purchase more. This is an attempt to
acknowledge the powerful force of the arguments by the proponents of
the *Contract with America* that government is too big and too wasteful.
However, it is also an attempt to introduce a nuance completely absent
from the Republicans' *Contract with America* and the sequel written in
the spring of 1995, *Restoring the Dream.* The latter two books make no
reference to anything valuable and useful that government can do
except provide national defense and engage in tough law enforcement.
Reading those books leaves one with the clear impression that those
are the only two actions that the federal government ought to be doing,
aside from providing cash transfers like Social Security and financing
Medicare. The Clinton administration spent virtually all of 1995 trying
to counter that position with the same points that were made in its *Economic Report:* government does do some things that are essential, and
indiscriminate cuts can do more harm than good even if they do reduce
the deficit. Except on the issue of Medicare spending, they seem to have
achieved a very small response from the public.

Meanwhile, despite the rise in long-term interest rates, 1994 was a
pretty good year. Investment as a percentage of GDP rose from 13.7
percent in the last quarter of 1993 to 14.7 percent in the last quarter of
1994. The unemployment rate continued to fall, reaching 5.6 percent in
that same quarter. The rate of growth of real GDP per capita averaged
2.2 percent for all of 1994, as opposed to 1.3 percent in the previous
year. Productivity growth continued to be a disappointment. After
averaging only .1 percent in 1993, it fell in two of the first three quarters
of 1994. Finally, despite the Fed's fears (or perhaps as a result of the
Fed's preemptive strike) there was no hint of inflationary pressure. The
rate of inflation in the GDP implicit price deflator actually fell from 2.6
percent in 1993 to 2.3 percent in 1994.[89]

11

The Republican Triumph and the Clinton Surrender

In the middle of 1994, a relatively good year for the economy, a record low percentage of the people went to the polls and voted to repudiate the Clinton administration and the Democratic Congress, thereby giving the Republicans a chance to deliver on their Contract with America. Why was such good economic news associated with such a massive repudiation? During the first two years of the Reagan administration, the changes Reagan began to implement combined with the Volcker anti-inflation policy to produce the 1981–82 recession. Republicans suffered heavily in those midterm elections. There was no similar dramatic economic failure in 1994, yet the voters reacted more negatively to the Clinton administration than they did to Reagan and the Republicans.

Perhaps we might gain some understanding of this if we compare the recovery since the first quarter of 1991 with the Reagan-Bush recovery of 1982–90 and with the 1971–80 and 1974–80 recoveries (see table 14).

The macroeconomic picture is very mixed. In terms of unemployment and capacity utilization, there is an improvement over the Reagan-Bush years, but not over the 1971–80 period. In measuring investment as a percentage of GDP, the rate of growth of real per capita GDP, and the rate of growth of productivity, the table reveals the worst averages of the recovery periods we have investigated. Perhaps the voters' anger reflects the cumulative effect of two decades of unacceptable economic performance. Even the best of the macroeconomic numbers from the period since 1991 have not compared favorably with the period that has come to be the standard for success, the postwar boom of 1945 to 1969, which included the period we have called KJN, the 1962–69 recovery.

TABLE 14. Comparing Five Recoveries

	Investment (% of GDP)	Civilian Unemployment Rate	Capacity Utilization Rate	Rate of Growth of Real GDP Per Capita	Rate of Growth of Productivity
Recovery 1962–69 peak (32 Q)	15.63	4.44	86.42	3.23	2.87
Recovery 1971–80 peak (37 Q)	16.86	6.35	82.82	2.12	1.92
Recovery 1974–80 peak (20 Q)	17.18	6.93	82.32	3.15	1.63
Recovery 1983–90 peak (31 Q)	16.08	6.75	80.92	2.77	1.35
Recovery 1991–94 (15 Q)	13.30	6.53	81.30	1.67	1.31

Source: Columns 1, 4: Department of Commerce, Bureau of Economic Analysis; column 2: Department of Labor, Bureau of Labor Statistics; columns 3, 5: Board of Governors, Federal Reserve System. For the raw data see tables 4 and 10 on the web site, <mars.wnec.edu/~econ/surrender>.

From the perspective of the public's disappointment with the overall performance of the economy, there are two alternative explanations for the failure of the Clinton economic policy. Was the policy a failure because it reversed Reaganomics, thereby continuing the disastrous Bush approach that raised marginal tax rates and imposed increased regulation while failing to get the budget deficit under control? Alternatively, was the Clinton policy a failure because it *did not* reverse Reaganomics, thereby continuing the disastrous trends of rising inequality, creation of more and more low-paying jobs, and reduction in the number of higher-paying jobs, despite the decline in unemployment?

Beyond these issues, there was also a growing feeling of insecurity among workers about their jobs as well as the increases in inequality and sluggish growth of real income. The pace of change, financial instability, corporate downsizing, increasing international competition, and awareness of the increasing percentage of the population without health insurance all combined to make the public feel less secure and more anxious about the future. This anxiety focused on the problems that politicians and opinion molders identified—the budget deficit, rising welfare rolls, wasteful, intrusive government activity. For many citizens, worries about layoffs, loss of health insurance, and falling values of homes became linked to the economic failures of government policy. Thus, the complaints of H. Ross Perot in the 1992 presidential campaign were echoed in the Republican criticisms of the Clinton administration. Poll after poll indicated that huge majorities of Americans believed it was essential to balance the federal budget, even if this required a constitutional amendment.

Two things are apparent from table 14. There is continued evidence for the relative unimportance of both marginal tax rates and regulatory burdens in determining the overall rate of productivity growth. We know that the marginal income tax rate did increase significantly (for some taxpayers, to 42.5 percent), and it is also relatively clear that the regulatory burden of the Americans with Disabilities Act was continuing to grow as legal issues were settled. Thus it would be safe to assume that from an incentive "supply-side" point of view, productivity growth ought to have been damaged by both the Clinton changes and the continued increase in regulatory activity begun in the Bush administration.[1] Yet the productivity numbers are only marginally different from those of the 1982–90 recovery.

In contrast to these public perceptions, the Clinton administration took a more positive stance. In 1995, a year after the Republican victory, the Council of Economic Advisers argued that its policies were already working quite well. They pointed to the lowest misery index in over twenty-five years,[2] an improvement in productivity and the creation of a significant number of jobs. The Republicans were blamed for the public discontent; they had worked to destroy the initiatives of the Clinton administration and then, in October 1994, complained to the voters that nothing could get done in Washington. This explanation fell on deaf ears, however, because the voters knew that both houses of Congress had Democratic majorities. Despite the continued efforts of the Clinton administration to identify economic successes and to place blame on Republican "demagoguery," the public's conclusion, voters as well as those from the core Democratic constituency too disillusioned to vote, was that the "economic policy" successes had not translated into any improvement in their lives.

Consider the creation of new jobs. Between January 1993 and December 1994, the economic recovery had increased total employment by 7.4 million jobs.[3] However, with the continuation of corporate downsizing, the shrinkage of federal defense spending, and pressure on state and local budgets, this net increase appears to have masked a further decline in the availability of well-paying jobs. Certainly the trends in wage inequality were not reversed during those first two years. Average weekly earnings, which had declined 3.5 percent between 1989 and 1993, rose a minuscule .7 percent in 1994.[4]

Failure of Health Care and Welfare Reform

The biggest failure of the Clinton administration was in the area of health care reform. After months of study, an administration task force headed by First Lady Hillary Rodham Clinton recommended a system of universal coverage through private insurance companies. All individuals would be required to buy health insurance. Except for those employed by large corporations who could negotiate packages directly with insurance companies, everyone not covered by Medicare would purchase coverage through regional "alliances" that would be able to bargain with health care providers for reduced rates of coverage. Every insurance package would have to offer the same set of comprehensive benefits. Certain practices of insurance companies designed to minimize their risks, such as refusing to enroll people with a "preexisting condition," or refusing to cover some highly expensive procedures or treatments, would be outlawed. The goal of this proposal was to eliminate the possibility that price controls in one area of health care financing (for example, in Medicare and Medicaid) would translate into higher prices in another area (such as group health insurance for the corporate sector). With everyone covered by insurance and all purchasers of coverage united in various alliances or large corporate entities, price inflation would be moderated as insurers vied for the lucrative contracts with various alliances and as providers vied for the lucrative contracts with insurance companies.[5]

This proposal illustrated the same contradictory impulses that had plagued the combined stimulus package and deficit reduction plan in the first months of the Clinton administration. The administration wanted to create a universal system of health insurance with a generous guaranteed package. At the same time they wanted to control inflation of medical costs. The Reagan Revolution followed by the 1990 recession and a sluggish recovery had bequeathed high budget deficits and, more importantly, a policymaker's consensus that deficit reduction was essential for future prosperity. Thus, increased spending without offsetting savings or revenue increases would not meet the "deficit neutral" test that had been imposed on policymakers. Unfortunately for reformers, using new tax revenue to finance significant increases in federal spending was also virtually impossible in the post-Reagan era. Even the 1993 tax increases that had been specifically targeted at deficit reduction had barely squeaked through Congress.

In order to make sure that there were significant cost controls in the reformed health care system, the proposal required the creation of regional health alliances, new regulatory bodies. Some form of taxation was needed to finance the coverage of the poor, whether employed or unemployed. Though the Medicaid program would become part of the comprehensive program, it was clear that the savings in Medicaid expenditure would be far less than the added expense of insuring all the uninsured. This approach would limit choice of physicians and even treatment availability. This last factor was already of growing concern within the health care delivery system as more and more companies began to shift their employees into "managed care." The Clinton program promised a significant acceleration of these moves into managed care.

The plan was an easy target for groups whose incomes would suffer as a result. Because of the cost constraints, average citizens saw many new regulations but no new infusion of federal dollars. Thus, it was hard for people who already had employer-provided health insurance to see benefits in this proposal for themselves and their families.[6] Early positive responses to the president's speech and the First Lady's testimony before Congress in support of the plan quickly faded as the insurance industry and other special-interest groups launched highly effective advertising campaigns with the theme, "There's got to be a better way." Members of Congress joined in, and, in the end, there was no consensus for comprehensive reform.[7]

Clinton would have had a better chance of success or, failing that, an opportunity to explain the reasons for his failure if he had presented a bold option for the creation of a Canadian style single-payer plan that *abolished* the role for private insurance in the financing of health care. The single-payer plan, introduced in Congress with a significant number of sponsors but never seriously discussed in the national media, would have financed all health care expenditures with a payroll tax and paid all health care providers according to prices negotiated by each state. Individuals would have had complete freedom of choice of physicians and hospitals who, in turn, would bill the state for all medical procedures at the prevailing price.

Such a system combines universal coverage with price controls.

The price controls are not, however, imposed externally to the market; they are negotiated between the purchaser (each state) and the seller. An individual "pays" for health care by simply running an identification card through a scanner. This type of system has worked quite well in Canada. The problem with such a system is that it takes billions of dollars in revenue away from the insurance industry and potentially reduces the income of specialists in the medical profession.[8]

In order not to provoke these powerful groups, the Clinton administration chose to propose the more complicated system.[9] They hoped the insurance industry and the medical profession would support their proposal over the more radical single-payer plan. Yet once the initial momentum in support of reform had run out and Congress proved incapable of uniting behind any version of the initial proposal, the opposition was able to raise the specter of "socialized medicine," successfully hoodwinking the public. Through public-opinion polls, people supported the *elements* in the Clinton reform, coverage for all, cost containment, private insurance, while at the same time voicing opposition to the "Clinton plan," the details of which they did not know. With the danger of a "worse deal" banished by a combination of media blackout and Clinton administration abandonment, the insurance industry and medical profession had no reason to accept the "better deal" the administration had proposed when they could settle for what they preferred, the status quo.

One side effect of the failure of health care reform was that Medicare and Medicaid costs were projected to continue rising faster than the rate of inflation. This forced the administration to propose a budget plan in 1995 that predicted no reduction in the federal deficit below $200 billion for the foreseeable future.

In the 1994 campaign, the Republicans were helped by the inability of Congress to reform health care. They were able to argue that the Democrats had had a chance with the presidency and control over both houses of Congress and had failed to accomplish anything except raising taxes. Once the new Congress arrived in January 1995, they set the agenda not just with moves to balance the budget but with an effort to "end welfare as we know it," Clinton's campaign promise.

The Clinton version of that proposal, which had never even reached the stage of congressional hearings, was one that attempted to move able-bodied welfare recipients into the labor force by imposing time limits on the receipt of AFDC payments. The problem with the Clinton version is that it increased expenditures for child care and job training.[10] The Republican proposal meant abolishing the federal guarantee of entitlement and turning AFDC over to the states. With a fixed federal block grant to help them finance their own versions of welfare, the states would be given great latitude in setting eligibility standards, time limits, and so on. That latitude only permitted *increasing* stringency. The Personal Responsibility Act promised to deny AFDC to women under eighteen who had children out of wedlock, and to force states to begin moving welfare recipients into the labor force after two years on aid. It also put a lifetime cap of five years on the receipt of AFDC.[11] The idea of turning over AFDC to the states had been prominently featured in Ronald Reagan's "New Federalism" proposal advanced in his State of the Union speech in 1982.[12] At that time governors were uninterested in taking on new responsibility without the federal cash to support it. Public-opinion polls also showed that citizens believed that it was a *federal* responsibility to set welfare standards.[13]

During the Clinton administration, basic federal responsibility to set standards and provide funding remained intact, while opportunities for states to experiment were greatly expanded, as provided by the Family Support Act of 1988. By 1996, forty of the fifty states had received some kind of waiver from the Department of Health and Human Services from the specific requirements of federal law in order to experiment.[14] Among the most prominent were the Wisconsin and Michigan reforms, in which Republican governors Tommy Thompson and John Engler were promoted as potential vice presidential nominees because of their alleged successes in reducing welfare rolls and finding employment for former recipients.

However, President Clinton vetoed the national Republican proposal in January 1996 because it was allegedly "too extreme" in the rigidity of its time limits, in its failure to provide child care and aid for disabled children, and in its removal of the federal guarantee of food and medical assistance. The Washington debates and the presidential vetoes once again masked a fundamental change. Through his approving of so many waivers, the president indicated that he would ultimately sign a law that ended "welfare as we know it" even if it did not contain the extra money that he originally thought was necessary to enact real reform. Despite the denunciations of some House and Senate Democrats that this was abolition, not reform, Clinton agreed to sign a modified bill in August. From the point of view of the administration, this bill was a marked improvement over the one Clinton had vetoed. The bill preserved the federal guarantees of food stamps and Medicaid even for those terminated from the AFDC program. It increased the budget for child care to assist welfare recipients who work. However, of much greater significance was the transformation of Clinton's original proposal to reform welfare by spending *more money* on child care and job training into a program that guaranteed cuts amounting to $55 billion over six years. Instead of reforming welfare, he had abolished it, turning it over to the states with inadequate funds to maintain services.[15]

In a December 1996 news conference, President Clinton acknowledged that

> there are not now enough jobs available, particularly in a lot of urban areas, for all the able-bodied people on welfare when they run out of their two-year time limit under the new law.

His solution was to

> provide special tax incentives and wage subsidies and training subsidies to employers to help hire people off welfare and to help the cities with a lot of welfare case load.[16]

He argued that his new fiscal 1997 budget plan included sufficient monies to fix this and other problems with the welfare reform bill. As part of the 1998 budget agreement with Congress, Mr. Clinton was able to restore $13 billion of the $55 billion spending reduction in the Personal Responsibility Act, most of it in restored SSI benefits to legal immigrants.[17]

The Final Surrender: Budget Balance by 2002

Unable to succeed with health care reform and appearing to be dragging its feet on welfare reform, the Clinton administration was battered for much of 1995 by Republican taunts that it had abandoned the fight for fiscal sanity by proposing a budget plan that saw deficits of $200 billion a year for the foreseeable future. This led the administration to abandon all of the arguments it had made in 1994 and 1995 that a push to balance the budget by a date certain would do more harm than good. In April 1995 it proposed its own version of a balanced-budget strategy. From then through November 1996, the major battles in economic policy were fought out over which path to a balanced budget was more realistic. The Republicans proposed tax cuts of approximately $230 billion over seven years and spending cuts approaching $480 billion over that same period to achieve balance by 2002.[18] The administration countered with a nine-year plan that cut taxes approximately $90 billion and cut spending a lot less than the Republicans to achieve balance by 2004. After November 1995, the Clinton administration proposed its own seven-year balanced-budget plan, accelerating the cut in spending but presenting more optimistic figures for revenue growth than the Republicans. By January, the administration had readjusted its figures to conform to the more pessimistic projections of revenue growth by the Congressional Budget Office.[19]

What is interesting about this debate is that there is nothing in the move toward a balanced budget that guarantees rising incomes for the vast majority of Americans, even if all the reduced aggregate demand from reduced government spending is countered by rising private investment.[20] The American economy had experienced significant levels of investment spending over the previous fourteen years. Yet between 1983 and 1997, the percentage of personal income received as wages and salaries fell from 58.1 percent to 56.4 percent. In manufacturing industries the fall was even greater, from 13.8 percent of personal income to 10.3 percent.[21] In 1989, the share of wages in personal income was 57.8 percent, only slightly lower than in 1983. The manufacturing share was 12.2. Thus, the increasing inequality through 1989 if anything had accelerated. Meanwhile, the share of corporate profits in national income went from 7.6 percent in 1983 to 7.9 percent in 1989 to 10.8 percent in 1996. After-tax corporate profits increased only a little less, falling from 4.9 percent in 1983 to 4.7 percent in 1989 and then rising to 7.2 percent in 1996.[22] As demonstrated in chapter 9, the rise in productivity that did occur after the 1970s was more unequally distributed than previous increases in productivity since World War II.[23] Much of that inequality has been the result of increasing wage inequality, not merely the rising share of profit and declining share of wages and salaries.[24]

In the 1995 *Economic Report* the Council of Economic Advisers identified four potential reasons for wage stagnation and rising inequality. One was the "shift in the demand for labor in favor of more highly skilled, more highly educated workers."[25] Two additional reasons were the decline in the percentage of the workforce that is unionized and the decline in the purchasing power of the minimum wage. Finally, in discussing increased international competition, the council cited studies that found that international competition played a relatively small role in the above-mentioned shift in demand for workers. However, it did acknowledge that the threat of international competition may have played a role in holding down wage increases, a problem that may increase as international trade grows in importance.[26]

The solution proposed was based on the argument that inequality has increased between those with college education and those without one. The proposal involved the expansion of educational opportunities for all Americans and institutional reforms designed to ease the transition from school to work and to facilitate retraining when workers change jobs.[27] Let us recall that the only way this will raise the number of high-pay, high-quality jobs in the United States is if we accept Robert Reich's proposition that the businesses of the world are creating such jobs at a very high rate and they will locate those jobs where a high-quality labor force exists. Otherwise, if there is no absolute increase in the rate of growth of high-quality jobs, then the only result of increasing the skill levels of the next generation of American workers will be to glut the market for such high-quality people and cause their incomes to become depressed.

Thus, Clinton's policies of omission failed to reverse the growth of inequality. The overall measurement of inequality called the Gini ratio (0.0 would be a perfectly equal distribution; 1.0 would involve only one person monopolizing all of the income or wealth or whatever was being measured) for both family and household income rose from 1991 through 1993 and fell very little through 1995.[28] By 1996, the issue of rising inequality actually forced its way into the presidential campaign. Republican candidate Patrick Buchanan used strident, populist rhetoric to attack free-trade policies, the financial bailout of Mexico, and immigration as causes of the stagnation in the living standards of American workers. In the context of highly publicized corporate downsizing and the apparent rise in the economic health of the largest corporate enterprises in the country with generous rewards received by CEOs of these businesses, these attacks seemed to be proposing what some saw as a dangerous revival of "class warfare," this time coming, not from the Democrats, but from a self-described conservative Republican.

The Clinton administration responded with a report from the Council of Economic Advisers that attempted to allay the fears of the average American. Despite the well-publicized shrinkage of employment in high-profile large corporations, there had been so much new job creation among small companies that on average there had been significant job creation. The council remarked that "nonfarm employment grew by 8.5 million (7.8 percent) between January 1993 and March 1996."[29] More to the point, a very high percentage of these new jobs were claimed to be in high-wage occupations: "Two-thirds (68 percent) of the net growth in full-time employment between February 1994 and February 1996 was found in job categories paying above-median wages."[30] Contrary to the view that much job growth involved involuntary part-time work, the council found that most of the newly created jobs were full time and that there was no increase in the percentage of the employed who held more than one job.[31]

Among the economic pundits, *Newsweek* columnist Robert Samuelson was particularly vocal in arguing that the average American actually was doing quite well economically. According to Samuelson, there had been no observable increase in job insecurity, and real family incomes had been rising decade after decade. In short, the rising feeling of insecurity was a psychological problem, not an economic problem.[32] Yet 1995 and 1996 were years where such anxiety continued to resonate. The Council of Economic Advisers' 1996 report acknowledged that the United States still faced the economic problems of slow productivity growth and rising income inequality.[33] These words were written fully three years after the Clinton administration took office with a blueprint summarized in *A Vision of Change for America* designed to deal with these problems. Though references were made to indications that "we may be beginning to succeed in sharing the benefits of growth and reducing poverty,"[34] much of the focus of the 1996 report remained on what needed to be done to deal with unacceptably low productivity growth and an unacceptably unequal distribution of income.

Putting the best face on the first three years the Clinton administration's economic policies, one could say that they *talked* a good game about reducing inequality through education. Their major achievement in helping low-wage workers was the expansion of the earned-income tax credit, and the *Economic Report* warned that efforts to cut that credit as part of the Republican balanced-budget plan were dangerously misguided. In the 1998 budget agreement, the Clinton administration could justifiably claim that it had succeeded in beating back those efforts. In fact, as the welfare reform bill began to be implemented during 1997, those former recipients entering the low-wage job market were able to benefit from expansions in the credit.[35]

However, the expansion of government infrastructure investment appears to have been mostly in the area of exhortation.

> The Administration has promoted public sector investments in technology through programs such as the Advanced Technology Program and the Manufacturing Extension Partnerships (at the Department of Commerce's National Institute of Standards and Technology) and the Technology Reinvestment Project (at the Department of Defense's Advanced Research project Agency).[36]

Later in its report, the council warned against deficit reduction via reductions in public capital investments.

In a departure from the previous calculations of the Department of Commerce's Bureau of Economic Analysis beginning with the 1996 *Economic Report,* the proportion of government purchases of goods and services that could be classified as investments rather than current expenditures is estimated. These investments do not include the intangible investments in people (education and training) and technology but only the most obvious investments as measured by the building of structures and production of equipment. The quarterly data for federal nondefense equipment and structures is shown in table 15.

It appears that the Clinton administration was unable to reverse the decline in real spending on structures. Equipment spending did rise from its nadir in the second quarter of 1994 and surpassed the level of real spending that had occurred in the first quarter of 1993 during 1997. Comparing the percentage of all federal purchases spent on civilian equipment and structural investments in 1992 with the percentage in 1997, we see a slight decline from 1.65 percent to 1.45 percent.[37] This is evidence that despite the rhetoric the Clinton administration had been unable to deliver on its promises to refocus government spending on investments. This is, of course, consistent with the information revealed by Woodward in *The Agenda.*

Completing the Volcker-Reagan Policy Change

Let us recall that even before Clinton became president he was forcefully told by his advisers and by the chairman of the Board of Governors of the Federal Reserve System, Alan Greenspan, that the key to his success was to "satisfy the bond market" if he was serious about cutting the budget deficit. Yet even with complete focus on reducing

TABLE 15. Nondefense Federal Investment, 1993–97
(in billions of 1992 dollars)

Year and Quarter	Structures	Equipment
1993:		
1	11.4	11.5
2	10.7	10.9
3	11.0	10.2
4	10.8	8.7
1994:		
1	9.9	9.2
2	9.3	8.7
3	9.4	9.0
4	11.1	9.6
1995:		
1	11.2	10.5
2	9.8	8.4
3	9.9	9.1
4	9.0	9.6
1996:		
1	9.9	11.0
2	10.2	10.6
3	10.0	11.9
4	10.0	10.7
1997:		
1	9.8	11.3
2	9.1	13.8
3	9.3	11.2
4	9.0	11.3

Source: ERP 1998, 305.
Note: Figures for the fourth quarter of 1997 were provisional.

the deficit, the Clinton administration was still faced with Fed policy that slowed down the economy in 1994 because the rate of unemployment was getting dangerously low and the rate of growth appeared "unsustainable." The result was that in 1995 the first two quarters saw a substantial slowdown in the rate of growth, to less than 0.5 percent. By contrast, the third quarter saw that rate jump to 2 percent.[38] Though the Clinton administration concluded in its 1996 report that "evidence suggested that the economy was once again growing at its potential rate,"[39] the evidence from capacity utilization and unemployment indicated a significant slowdown. Capacity utilization edged downward between January 1995 and the end of the year,[40] while the unemployment rate moved between 5.7 percent and 5.5 percent between April and December.[41]

The slowdown was so pronounced that the Federal Reserve actually reduced the Federal Funds rate from April 1995 through the end of the year after having raised it from 2.96 percent in December 1993 to 6.05 percent.[42] For 1996, the Fed adopted a wait-and-see attitude, taking action neither to ease the supply of credit nor to constrict it. In March of 1997, true to form, they raised short-term interest rates because the unemployment rate had remained below 5.5 percent since the previous July. Even though this did not succeed in slowing the economy, the Fed made no further restraining move for the rest of the year. However, they continuously indicated in public statements and leaked behind-the-scenes memoranda that they were very concerned that an unemployment rate below 5.5 percent was dangerously low, and that the rate of growth of the economy in excess of 2.5 percent was "unsustainable."[43]

The Clinton Administration never challenged the Fed's behavior nor the underlying view that a 2.5 percent growth rate was about as high as could be expected. Perhaps this was a more significant aspect of their policy posture than their effort to cut the deficit to appease the bond market early in their term.[44] They followed the pattern that began with President Carter's acceptance of Federal Reserve tight money in 1979 and 1980 and continued through President Reagan's cooperation with the Fed during the 1981–82 recession and President Bush's decision to leave to the Fed the entire burden of fighting the 1990 recession.

Active federal spending and taxing intervention to speed recovery from a recession is a thing of the past. The only role for fiscal policy, assuming supply-side tax-cutters don't have their way in the near future, would be to cut the budget deficit down to zero. It is now up to the Federal Reserve to determine how low unemployment will be allowed to go and, when the inevitable recession comes, how quickly and strongly to apply stimulus to the economy. Gone are the days when John F. Kennedy was able (in 1963) to tout a tax cut as a method of accelerating a recovery from a recession or when Gerald Ford could push through a substantial tax cut (in 1975) in the midst of a recession in order to start the recovery.

Let us look more closely at this sea change in policy responses to recession as well as the divergent results of those different policies. Recall the comparison between the U.S. government's response to the recession of 1974–75 and its policies since the 1990 recession.[45] In 1975, the tax cut, which was passed in an effort to combat the recession, resulted in a big jump in the federal budget deficit. By contrast, there was no tax cut at all in response to the recession of 1990. Though the budget deficit rose because of reduced revenues and some automatic spending increases, there was not as significant a change in the 1990–92 period as there was in 1975 and 1976.[46] In 1975, the year when the unemployment rate jumped to 8.5 percent, the percentage of the unemployed receiving unemployment compensation also increased from 50 percent to 76 percent. As the unemployment rate fell over the next two years, the percentage of the unemployed receiving those benefits also declined, averaging 56 percent for 1977.[47] In 1991 and 1992, by contrast, even though the unemployment rate rose from 5.6 percent in 1990 to 7.5 percent in 1992, the percentage of the unemployed receiving unemployment compensation increased only from 37 percent to 52 percent before starting to fall.[48]

Even though the full responsibility of fighting the second recession was borne by the Federal Reserve System, it was much slower to push interest rates down in response to the 1990 recession than it was in response to the 1974 recession.[49]

The different responses to these recessions by the federal government and the Federal Reserve produced dramatically different results, some of which have been documented in this and the previous chapter. The unemployment rate fell from 1975 through 1979, while the economy grew dramatically for three years, 1976 to 1978. During those four years of recovery, close to 13 million jobs were created. Since 1990, as we have seen, the recovery has been very slow. The rate of growth was actually negative in 1991 and was so slow in 1992 that the unemployment rate rose in the first two years of the recovery. Between 1990 and the end of 1996, this sluggish economy had only created 9 million jobs.[50]

After peaking in 1975 at 12.3 percent the percentage of the population living in poverty fell through 1978 to 11.4 percent. During this period, the number of individuals receiving AFDC cash assistance fell from a peak of 11.3 million to 10.3 million. In 1990, the percentage of the population living in poverty was at 13.5, and it rose through 1993. The number of individuals receiving welfare rose from 11.5 million in 1990 to 13.6 million in 1995. These numbers mask the fact that the percentage of children living in poverty covered by that program stayed above 70 percent for the period 1975–78 but stayed at or near 60 percent for the period 1991–94.[51] As we have mentioned, the response of Congress and the Clinton administration was to abolish this program entirely and leave the effort to fight poverty to the fifty states.

However, as we have also noted, the federal government and the Federal Reserve were not just sitting back and ignoring the economy. Far from it. In 1990, the Bush administration teamed up with the Democratic majority in Congress to push through a tax increase combined with spending controls in order to reduce the federal budget deficit. (The recession actually raised the deficit, as mentioned previously.) In 1993, the Clinton administration pushed through a major tax increase and controls on future spending. This time, these actions, combined with the quickening pace of recovery in 1992 and 1994, did lead to a fall in the federal deficit through 1997.[52] The Federal Reserve was not to be outdone. We have already seen that when economic growth threatened to be "too high," the Central Bank raised the Federal Funds rate from 2.96 percent in December 1993 to a peak of 6.05 percent in April 1995.[53]

The change in focus must be noted. Whereas economic policy in 1975 had been designed to increase the rate of growth, to reduce the level of unemployment, and to soften the blow of unemployment and poverty for those unable to find work and/or a decent level of income, after 1990 policymakers shifted focus to cutting the budget deficit and slowing the economy in order to prevent an inflation that hadn't even begun.

The drumfire of complaints about the deficits from the 1980s, left unchallenged by the press as well as by many economists, had achieved this singular result. Half the arsenal of aggregate-demand management had been mothballed, the half controlled by elected representatives of the people. The Clinton administration came into office promising "People First" with *A Vision of Change for America*. Instead it has as its legacy an abject surrender to an unelected group of people who represent the financial sector of the economy. No amount of political mudslinging related to the budget battles of 1995 and 1996 and the presidential election of 1996 should be permitted to blind the citizenry to the "true revolution" in American economic policy. Paul Volcker's and Ronald Reagan's goals from 1979 and 1981 have been largely achieved. The federal government will shrink relative to the economy. The amount of redistribution of income to the poor will decline. Fighting inflation will be much more important than reducing unemployment. In the language of the radicals, a new social structure of accumulation is being built, one in which the capital-labor accord is nonexistent; the social safety net is restricted to the elderly; and the most important thing that governments can do with taxpayers' money is to finance the defense department and a growing police and prison industry. This truly revolutionary transformation will continue as President Clinton and the Republicans "negotiate" the "reform" of Medicare and Social Security and poor women and children are left at the mercy of fifty parsimonious state legislatures.

So What Were They Fighting About?

We began this book with the victory of President Clinton and the reelection of the Republican majority in Congress. What apparently divided the Clinton administration from the Republican majority was the treatment of Medicare, the scope and nature of the tax cuts proposed, the changes in regulation, particularly environmental regulation, and the changes proposed in means-tested entitlements, particularly AFDC and Medicaid but also including the earned-income tax credit.

Yet President Clinton signed the "compromise" welfare reform bill before the election. After the election, the surprisingly rapid growth in the economy reduced the amount of spending cuts necessary, so the administration and Congress could put off the hard choices on how to reform Medicare. They even were able to restore some of the SSI benefits to legal immigrants that had been cut in the original bill. Nevertheless, it is safe to say that as the years go on, the trend toward fewer and fewer poor people receiving cash assistance will accelerate.

The euphoria of the strong economy at the end of 1997 and the beginning of 1998 led the Clinton Administration to propose a balanced budget for fiscal 1999, three years ahead of the schedule arrived at just six months previously. Nevertheless, the agreement made the previous summer still promises a series of spending cuts and tax decreases in the following years. These spending cuts will mostly be in the area of entitlement programs, particularly Medicare and Medicaid. However, as a result of welfare reform, there will also be limitations placed on expenditures for poor children under the state programs that replace AFDC, even though quantitatively that represents a tiny proportion of federal spending on entitlements.[54] The one area where Clinton's reelection has made a difference is in environmental regulation. A Republican president would probably have been more willing to acquiesce in the efforts by Congress to curtail regulatory activities in the cause of environmental protection.

As the Budget Deficit Shrinks to Zero, What Then?

When you add it all up, Clinton and Congress will continue the policy of fiscal restraint that was the hallmark of the first Clinton administration. Meanwhile, the Federal Reserve will continue to threaten higher interest rates to keep a hint of inflation from entering the expectations of lenders and borrowers. These policies promise a rerun of the 1980s without the deficits to stimulate growth and employment.

As has been mentioned above, the key to the arguments in favor of balancing the budget is to be found in the crowding-out analysis. If there is 100 percent crowding out, so that every dollar of the federal deficit is a dollar that has not been invested by the private sector, then a balanced federal budget will unleash a great surge in private investment. Another important assumption associated with this view is that the private-sector investment that would replace the government spending is a *better way* for those dollars to be spent. When government spends the money, the result is bureaucracy and "socialism," according to the rhetoric of, for example, former presidential candidate Senator Phil Gramm. When private investors spend the money, the result is private enterprise and "freedom"—and thus, obviously superior. Therefore, according to the supporters of budget balance by 2002, we should expect no decline in aggregate demand because the reduction in government spending will be completely offset by a rise in private investment. We also can expect more productivity growth because this private investment will be more productive than the government spending it replaces.

But can we really expect such a rise in private investment? Between 1993 and 1994, the rate of investment as a percentage of GDP rose from 13.4 percent (a very disappointing ratio considering the recovery that had been going on since 1991) to 14.5 percent, a very dramatic increase. Over the corresponding fiscal years, the federal budget deficit fell from 3.9 to 3.0 percent of GDP. This certainly appears to support the view that declining budget deficits will reduce interest rates sufficiently to stimulate more than enough investment to fill the gap. However, it is important to note that this occurred in the context of rising incomes and economic optimism. The deficit continued to fall to 2.3 percent of GDP over the next fiscal year, to 1.4 percent in fiscal 1996, and virtually disappeared by the end of 1997. Investment, however, rose only to 15.3 percent of GDP, a 1 percent increase in the face of a 3 percent fall in the deficit.[55]

This was in the context of Federal Reserve policy that saw the Federal Funds rate more than double from December 1993 through April 1995 despite the falling deficit/GDP ratio. Between April 1995 and the end of 1996, that rate fell less than 1 percent, even as the deficit/GDP ratio continued to fall.

With the budget at least temporarily in balance, private investment will have to rise another 2 percent of GDP to make up for the reduction in government spending's stimulus to the economy. Such rises are not unheard of—in fact between 1983 and 1984, the percentage of GDP invested rose by a greater amount. But the record of the last forty years indicates that such increases in investment usually occur during a recovery from a recession. The most recent experience of significant reduction in the federal deficit as a percentage of GDP occurred between 1968 and 1969, when the federal budget went from a deficit of 2.9 percent of GDP to a surplus of 0.3 percent.[56] Investment as a percentage of GDP went up less than one-half a percent, and the economy fell into recession in 1970.

The reasons this might be more likely to occur than the positive reaction anticipated by the proponents of a balanced budget are fairly straightforward. As in 1969, the economy at the end of 1997 was in outstanding shape. The economy posted the strongest rate of growth for the entire decade. The misery index was at its lowest point in over twenty-five years. Investment as a percentage of GDP was higher than it had been since before the recession. Yet this was an "old" recovery. The Asian financial crisis had already made investors very jittery, causing significant swings in the stock market since November 1977. In this context, investors are likely to be quite cautious about making long-term commitments, no matter what happens to long-term interest rates.

The experience of 1991 and 1992 supports this prediction. Beginning with the recession of 1990, the Federal Reserve Board pursued a policy of pushing interest rates down. Between June 1990 and January 1991, the Federal Funds rate fell from 8.29 percent to 6.91 percent. When the recovery proved extraordinarily sluggish, the Fed moved more vigorously and over the next two years cut the rate by over 50 percent (to 2.92 percent in December 1992). Meanwhile, the prime rate was 10 percent for most of 1990 and fell to 6 percent by August 1992, where it remained for over a year.[57]

Over the same period, the rate of growth in the GDP implicit price deflator fell from 4.4 percent in 1990 to 2.2 percent in 1993. Thus, the real Federal Funds rate fell during this period, while the real prime rate rose a bit. What was the impact on investment? Because of the sluggishness of the recovery from the 1990 recession, investment actually fell from 14.6 percent of GDP in 1990 to 12.2 percent of GDP before rising to 12.6 percent in 1992. True, the deficit as a percentage of GDP was rising, but the real burden of interest rates was not. We must recall once again that the only way a rising deficit can cause crowding out is by increasing interest rates, thereby choking off investment that would have occurred without the rise in the deficit.

What about the impact of the falling deficit? As the government budget moved toward balance by the end of 1997 without investment as a percentage of GDP rising sufficiently to fill the gap, why was there no recession in 1997? Consumption did not change much for the entire four-year period, remaining at approximately 68 percent of GDP. The trade deficit actually grew during this period so international demand for U.S. exports is not the source of the recent economic successes. The answer is that rising incomes raised tax revenues so much that government expenditures did not have to fall.[58] The decline to aggregate demand when significant government spending cuts were anticipated just did not materialize.[59] In addition, the rise in tax revenue did not decrease consumption because of the optimism of (mostly) high-income taxpayers whose increased capital gains, as a result of the stock market boom of 1996 and 1997, produced an unanticipated flow of revenue into the Treasury while giving them big increases in wealth as their stock portfolios all rose by over 30 percent. The problem with this scenario is the same with every stock market boom. When the bubble bursts, consumption will fall, and the failure to increase investment will be revealed as a major problem.

What If There Is a Recession?

As of January 1998, the Congressional Budget Office predicted a budget surplus by 2002 instead of a balanced budget as anticipated only five months previously. This prediction is based on an average growth of GDP of 2 percent a year in real terms. This average growth rate is quite conservative, being lower than the average for most comparable seven-year periods since 1960. In other words, the CBO is predicting that even if there is a recession during the period between the present and 2002, the low average predicted for the rate of growth of GDP should compensate for the temporary interruption in growth during the recession.[60] There's only one problem. When the recession hits (it is inconceivable that there will be no recession between now and 2002— that would create an eleven-year recovery, unprecedented in our history), revenues will drop and automatic spending increases will kick in. What will be the response of the president and Congress?

If they attempt to adhere to their programmed spending cuts, they will have to cut discretionary spending even more than planned to make up for the automatic increases in spending on unemployment compensation and the automatic decreases in receipts from income and payroll taxes. This will make the recession worse. However, such policy fortitude is unlikely. Even during the 1990 recession there was an extension voted in unemployment compensation by the Congress.[61] No matter how minor the extensions, they added up to more money spent than was previously expected. Such increased expenditures coupled with declining revenues were the main reasons the budget deficit ballooned after the 1990 budget agreement supposedly adopted policy changes to reduce the deficit. By comparison, the 1993 budget was followed by declining deficits because the recovery from the 1990 recession proceeded apace and finally accelerated.

In the *Economic Report of the President* in 1996 and again in 1997 and 1998, the Clinton Council of Economic Advisers argued that there is nothing inevitable about the end of economic expansions. In all three reports, the council identified increases in the core rate of inflation (the rate of inflation with food and energy price changes netted out due to their volatility), financial instability either in the banking sector or among households, or a significant increase in inventories as potential killers of the expansion. Both reports argued that since there is no indication that any of these three factors will be problems in the near future, there is no reason to expect the expansion to end anytime soon.[62] But of course that tells us nothing about what will happen after "soon" has passed. Perhaps the raging bull market that has caused Fed chairman Alan Greenspan to speak out more than once in warning will come crashing down sometime in 1998. Perhaps the Asian economic crisis will send a cold shiver of negative expectations over the business and financial community in the United States. Perhaps the Fed will not act swiftly enough to ease credit conditions in the United States in response to those expectations. After all, there are probably some inflation-hawks who still believe interest rates should have been raised in 1997 to cool the "over-exuberance" of the stock market. There are a whole host of factors that might trigger the next recession. What we can say with absolute certainty is that that recession will arrive well before 2002.

So what will Congress and the president do in late 1998 or 1999 or early 2000 after the recession hits? Will they support extended unemployment benefits? Will they increase block grants to the states whose welfare rolls will temporarily bulge with new clients? Will they increase block grants to the states for increased Medicaid expenditures? With unemployment rates rising and the increasing requirements that welfare recipients (even before they exhaust their family's cap of five years) enter the workforce, will there be a special appropriation from Congress to create public-service jobs for these people? If Congress and the president take any of these rather obviously necessary actions in the face of a recession, they will be abandoning their path to deficit elimination by 2002. If they do not, the recession will be longer and deeper than the 1990–91 version, and *that* will also make a zero deficit by 2002 an impossibility.

The answer to this question brings us full circle to the question with which we began this book, "How does one make an economy better?" According to the conservative diagnosis, you reduce government spending to a minimum, you reduce taxes, particularly the marginal rate of taxation, and you reduce regulations. According to mainstream approaches, you practice aggregate-demand management, redistribute income appropriately, and attempt to stimulate economic growth with targeted tax cuts and expenditures. According to radical analyses, if the system does not fit together so that the incentive structure reinforces economic growth despite its inequities and instability, no amount of tinkering will produce acceptable results. The mainstream approach clearly ran out of gas in the 1970s, and we had a full decade of conservative changes in economic policy between late 1979 and the 1990 budget agreement. After a half-hearted effort to reverse some of the policies of the 1980s during 1993 and 1994, the government of the United States appears poised for another round of 1980s-style conservative reforms.

If our historical analysis of the Reagan-Volcker period is correct, the reforms promised by the Republican Congress and acquiesced in by the Clinton White House will not stimulate a dramatic increase in private investment and productivity growth. And because the targeted "investments" so celebrated in "Putting People First" and *A Vision of Change for America* have not been forthcoming and the Federal

Reserve will probably permit unemployment to rise at least to 5.6 percent without taking action. The incomes of people at the bottom end of the income distribution will continue to stagnate; thus, inequality will continue to increase, further polarizing the middle class.[63]

Meanwhile, turning redistribution of income to the nonelderly poor over to state governments is a fait accompli. Neither does the administration appear interested in once again tackling comprehensive reform of the health care system. Thus, attempts to save money will continue to be ad hoc efforts aimed at reducing Medicare and Medicaid outlays without real reform. In other words, there will be some tinkering, but basic problems will be avoided as long as possible. Waiting in the wings are more radical plans to privatize Social Security and Medicare.

The "true revolution" in economic policy that began when Paul Volcker persuaded his colleagues to stamp hard on the monetary brakes in 1979 continued with the election and reelection of Ronald Reagan. The momentum of that revolution, reinforced by a drumfire of complaints about budget deficits, was so great it was able to turn back the tepid counterrevolutions of George Bush and the first two years of the Clinton administration, and the revolution is now complete. If history is any guide, the majority of people in the United States will benefit even less than they did during the Reagan era. At least then, the economy was driven forward by high budget deficits and put a lot of people to work. In a sadly ironic commentary on the poverty of economic policymakers, when the next recession hits, the only hope that the people will not be harmed even worse than in the 1980s is a return to "irresponsible" budget deficits to fight that recession.

Coda: "There Is No Alternative"

My intention in this book has been to use the lessons of recent history to illuminate the policy of the Clinton administration and Congress and to warn against the single-minded commitment to balance the federal budget that Nobel Prize–winner William Vickrey called "Financial Fundamentalism."[1] Many readers, even if persuaded by the evidence and arguments presented, will wonder if there are any viable alternatives to the policies of Volcker-Reagan and Greenspan-Clinton-Gingrich.

I believe that strategies aimed at increasing incomes and reducing unemployment are viable alternatives, not pie-in-the-sky absurdities. Serious proposals for a high-wage, high-employment strategy have been and continue to be developed by various academics and public-interest groups as well as by labor unions and other community-based organizations concerned about the incomes and futures of their memberships. I can merely sketch the elements of such a reform strategy and provide the readers with sources where they might pursue them further.

In 1985, at the high tide of the Reagan Revolution, the United States Conference of Catholic Bishops published a detailed pastoral letter on the economy entitled *Economic Justice for All.*[2] In it, the bishops proposed that the goodness of an economy should be judged by how well it takes care of the poorest and most downtrodden people. The specifications of the qualities of a good economy stemming from that ethical premise included recommendations that the economy guarantee certain things to people. These guarantees, according to the bishops, ought to go well beyond full employment and some minimal level of income. The bishops called for treating certain goods and services differently from mere commodities to be bought and sold in the market. Food, housing, and medical care were examples of necessities to which people were entitled as a matter of right, not just if they could afford them. The bishops topped off their analysis by calling for a requirement that all people affected by business decisions have a voice in those decisions, in effect calling for some official role in business decision-making by the people who work *for* businesses and by others affected locally (hence local governments), not only by those who *own* businesses.[3] This raises a serious question. Can an economy dependent on individual incentives for most investment (and therefore growth) decisions function well while maintaining full employment, promoting real wage increases, and guaranteeing food, housing, and medical care as well as education and public safety? Furthermore, is this likely to happen with an expanded role in corporate governance for employees and local citizens?

First of all, polling data indicates that the proposals by the bishops are not outside of the mainstream of public opinion in the United States. For example, the majority of Americans believe unemployment ought to be minimal and the economy should be growing faster. In fact the supposed support for the conservative economic agenda of cutting taxes, reducing regulation, and balancing the budget occurs because in the minds of most supporters, these will be means to the desired outcome of creating more jobs and increasing incomes. Support for the food stamps program and other efforts to guarantee nutrition to all Americans (such as the Women, Infants, and Children program) indicates that Americans also agree with the bishops about the right of all citizens to eat well. Similarly, as was clear during the failed campaign for the Clinton health insurance proposal, large percentages of the population believe health care is as much a right as is education. It appears that the only thing lacking is some coherent policy proposals for a high-wage, high-growth economy coupled with these guarantees. One could make the case that the public would react very favorably to such a set of proposals. It is the political and intellectual leadership of this country that seems to lack the will to make it happen.[4]

Throughout this century, whenever proposals have been made to constrain the operation of the private sector—for example, the introduction of mandatory collective bargaining and the Social Security system during the 1930s—the opposition has trotted out the tired old arguments that this is an effort to repeal the laws of nature. So it was when the bishops made their proposals in 1985. Former British prime minister Margaret Thatcher used to assert that "there is no alternative" to her (and by implication President Reagan's) policies of letting the market rule when it came to issues of poverty and unemployment.[5] The goals set by the bishops and other reformers could be accomplished, so the argument goes, only by a vast expansion of the role of government in the economy, and history shows that government involvement creates more harm than good. At the extreme, such reform proposals are ridiculed as "socialistic," and readers are reminded that the world has recognized the superiority of markets and freedom to the drab world of central economic planning under Communist dictatorships.

Of course neither the Catholic bishops nor any of the various public-interest and special-interest groups developing proposals for a high-wage, full-employment economy want to re-create the planned economy of even Brezhnev's Soviet Union, let alone Stalin's. What these groups are arguing is that a market economy can be constrained politically to guarantee certain economic rights to its citizens (such as food, education, medical care), to reduce unemployment to the bare minimum, and to speed up the rate of economic growth beyond that deemed sustainable by the current spokespeople for the financial sector.[6] Furthermore, they argue that such political interference will not necessarily harm the ability of the economy to function well.

The typical argument that such a strategy is economically impossible starts with the assertion that full employment (say a rate of 4 percent) would be inflationary. However, full employment would be inflationary only if production involved no improvements in productivity and if businesses had the freedom to raise prices at will. Neither of these need come to pass. Let us consider increasing productivity first. Full employment with significant government investment in reconstruction of roads, bridges, and schools will improve productivity.[7] Investments to wire every public school and public library for the Internet will likewise improve productivity. In the area of health care spending, guaranteed preventive health care for all Americans, including wholesale childhood immunizations and regular checkups to catch problems before they require emergency room treatment, will in the long run reduce health care expenditures and also increase the lifelong productivity of the average American. The same could be said for public investment spending to remove asbestos and lead paint from public buildings, particularly schools.

Such public-sector capital investment, many suggest, could best be accomplished by creating a separate capital account in the federal budget.[8] Robert Eisner, Alicia Munnell, and David Aschauer, to name just a few, have argued that it makes perfectly good sense to use public debt to finance public capital investments. The crucial problem, of course, is to clearly identify legitimate public capital investments. Many critics of the idea of a federal capital budget doubt the ability of the federal government to separate true public-capital investments from wasteful pork-barrel spending. The solution, however, is not to tie the government's hands because, as the "public choice" school argues, it always responds to special interests, not the general public interest. Instead, the solution is to increase public scrutiny of government activity and make politicians more responsive to general citizens' desires.

Here, of course, we see the important value of public financing of political campaigns and limitations on the ability of the very top of the income distribution to have disproportionate impact on the political process. One of the most shocking facts to come out of the campaign-financing scandals of the 1996 elections is that only *two-tenths of 1 percent* of the American population contribute two hundred dollars or more to political campaigns, and they are the people to whom politicians must cater. Ever since the Supreme Court ruled in *Buckley v. Valleo* that the First Amendment has guaranteed the right of anyone to spend as much money as they wish supporting political candidates,[9] the ability of the very rich to influence policy has accelerated. In a strong op-ed piece in the *New York Times,* lawyer-writer Scott Turow argued that only by restricting the campaign contributions of the very rich can we as a society "balanc[e] all citizens' First Amendment rights to speak and be heard."[10] When those with the largest agglomerations of wealth can seize and dominate the "public square" of debate on policy issues, all of those without the cash-megaphone are effectively silenced.[11]

It is clear that the obvious first step toward making democracy really work in setting government policy about capital budgeting (and everything else, for that matter) is to take large blocks of private money out of political campaigns and provide for complete public financing, as is done in Europe.

The other part of the alleged problem with full employment is the idea that wages will go up and therefore prices will go up, fueling a runaway inflation. First of all, let us recall we are in a very competitive world. American companies will not be able to lever their prices upward, even in response to rising wages, without reducing their competitiveness internationally. There are also a number of policies that governments can institute to control inflationary pressures directly. Some would go as far as to institute wage and price controls, but others lean toward more subtle forms of incomes policies, including the use of the tax system to create incentives to moderate price increases.[12] European governments were able to experience faster rates of growth than the United States in the early postwar period while holding unemployment near 2 percent by means of incomes policies that restrained inflation. Again, it requires political decision-making to craft policies that will restrain whatever inflationary pressures arise as a result of rising employment, rising economic growth, and rising wages. Even in the United States there are historical examples, such as World War II, when direct restraint on inflation proved possible and consistent with rising incomes and rapid growth.

However, what if such a policy were to reduce expected profitability? This might happen if the idea that people other than shareholders of corporations should have a say in corporate governance catches on. If wages were rising and full employment created a situation in which it was difficult to get increased intensity out of workers, and, further, if corporate managers now had to answer to workers and citizens as well as stockholders, American business might respond by cutting back on productive investment. Here again, political effort needs to be made to demonstrate that what American businesses lose in *control* over their workers might be more than compensated by the rising *productivity* of their workers as a result of increased job satisfaction.

However, let us assume there is a transition period during which the "business climate" does not appear good. What would the alternatives be for suddenly unwilling investors? They might choose financial investments. True enough, but that only points out another important element of this reform strategy. We would have to change the financial system to reflect the democratic desires of the majority rather than the desire of "the bond market," as is the current approach of the Central Bank. A democratically controlled Federal Reserve System could play the role of reducing long-term interest rates so as not to permit investors the "escape" from the productive sector into lucrative purely financial alternatives. Similarly, by asserting a new role of public credit allocation (much as Japanese and German banks do now) the Central Bank could fund important productivity-enhancing investment projects at low enough interest rates to overcome the reluctance of private-sector investors to pay the high wages that are the centerpiece of this new strategy.[13] In addition, redirecting credit to sectors usually served poorly and incompletely by existing capital markets would provide useful competition for the businesses liable to be participating in the investment slowdown. The Financial Markets Center, a public-interest organization devoted to increasing democratic control over the financial system, has argued for the development of a National Reinvestment Fund to help redirect the flow of credit.

Another way to reduce interest rates without buying bonds is to create money, as the government did during the Civil War when it issued paper currency known as greenbacks.[14] Had even 10 percent of the World War II deficits been financed by direct money creation rather than by borrowing from banks, over $22 billion in government expenditures on the war would have been interest free.[15] The value of making government payments by the direct creation of money rather than the indirect route of borrowing from banks or the Federal Reserve is that restricting the issuing of new government debt instruments contributes to increases in the price of those bonds, which reduces interest rates.

The next argument against high wages, full employment, and more democratic corporate governance is that investors will take their capital out of the country and create a depression in the United States. Some investors might want to do that, but physical capital in the form of buildings and machines cannot be taken out of the country. In a full-employment, high-wage economy, aggregate demand would be high and growing. Any private-sector firm that desired to close their factories would presumably want to sell its plants. With aggregate demand booming and public capital available from the Fed, it is hard to imagine that there would be no entrepreneurs willing to buy up these factories and machines and have a go at producing for this high-earning, high-spending population.[16] If the National Reinvestment Fund were in place, these factories and machines could be bought by community-based cooperatives and small start-up businesses.

Ah, but what if investors take their capital and invest it in overseas plants where wages are not high and then export the goods back to the United States? Here is where we would need a new system of international economic relations so that high wages and low unemployment do not translate into rising trade deficits and a flow of financial capital out of the country. A tremendous amount of activity worldwide is attempting to achieve that alternative, even as the conventional wisdom of economists and of public-policy people claims that in the face of "globalization" such efforts are nothing but pipe dreams.[17] The key elements of such a policy involve increasing rather than restraining aggregate demand, introducing significant rules into international

agreements to maintain and upgrade labor and environmental standards, and interfering with speculative flows of capital.[18] The creation
of a world in which private capital flows can damage a national policy
of full employment and rising wages has resulted from political decisions such as the new GATT agreements and NAFTA. Such a trend
can be stopped and even reversed by political decisions.

If this book is correct, the approach that builds prosperity through
budget balance and a shredded safety net will be exposed as a fraud
with the coming of the next recession. If this book is persuasive, the
public may yet begin to consider the alternatives that Thatcher, Reagan, and others have decried as impossible. When that time comes, let
us hope that all involved, caring, concerned citizens will begin the
effort to discover for themselves the appropriate alternatives and make
common cause to bring them about.

It Can Be Done

Consider the following facts from recent history. In 1964, presidential
candidate Barry Goldwater espoused an unabashed conservative philosophy of small government and honestly opposed even most sacred
cows of the welfare state as it then existed. He suffered one of the worst
defeats in presidential history. In 1965, recently reelected President
Johnson combined with a Democratic Congress to give a giant boost
to the welfare state with the passage of Medicare and Medicaid. The
growth in the redistributionist and regulatory components of the government's activity in the economy continued to grow through the two
Republican administrations of Nixon and Ford. The Nixon administration greatly expanded the food stamps program and created the
Environmental Protection Agency. The Ford administration engaged
in the most vigorous example of aggregate-demand management ever,
in fighting the recession of 1974–75 There was clearly a bipartisan
consensus, captured by President Nixon's comment, "We are all
Keynesians now." One could actually date the high tide of government
involvement in the economy to the Ford administration.[19]

The supporters of Barry Goldwater's philosophy did not give up
after their candidate's defeat in 1964. In conservative think tanks and
publications, they developed their analyses of why the course taken
by society during the 1960s and early 1970s was a disaster. A few
commentators and politicians popularized the message, none more

successfully than former governor of California Ronald Reagan, with a series of radio addresses and a vigorous, albeit unsuccessful, run for the Republican presidential nomination in 1976. When the economy turned sour in the 1970s, a whole body of analysis was waiting to be drawn upon for political proposals, such as the one by Representative Jack Kemp in 1978 for a three-year tax cut.[20] Meanwhile, in 1979, the Center for the Study of American Business came out with the conclusion that new social regulation was costing American businesses $100 billion per year.

Just sixteen years after Goldwater's defeat, Ronald Reagan won the presidency and the Republican Party took control of the Senate. The rest is the history we have just revisited in this book. It has been eighteen years since President Reagan's victory. Admittedly, those with ideas in opposition to the prevailing bipartisanship cannot draw on the same bottomless pits of money that institutions like the Heritage Foundation and the American Enterprise Institute, periodicals like the *Wall Street Journal* and the *Public Interest* have at their disposal. However, the vigor in developing new ideas is there in the Economic Policy Institute, the Jerome Levy Economics Institute at Bard College, the Center for Popular Economics, the Financial Markets Center, the education departments of various unions, including the umbrella AFL-CIO, and many other groups as well.[21]

The most difficult task for people who want to reverse the policies of the past eighteen years is to get their message through to the public at large and to press the agenda in Congress and state legislatures in ways that permit a concerned public to bring pressure to bear.

Let us once again recall that agenda. First and foremost, enforce the Humphrey-Hawkins Full Employment and Balanced Growth Act, which amended the Employment Act of 1946 to identify a target level of 4 unemployment as the end of policy. If this requires budget deficits, so be it. The sooner we Americans see through the absurd assertion that budget deficits almost always harm the economy, the better. Second, reform the financial sector to bring the Federal Reserve under the control of the elected representatives of the people with a clear mandate to allocate credit to socially productive activities such as housing, infrastructure, and research and development and to keep interest rates down. Third, get big money out of politics. Fourth, reform our international economic relationships to forestall massive capital flight and trade deficits.

This may seem like a tall order, but there are models from our own history and the experiences of Europe during the post–World War II period that indicate that these goals, in purely technical economic and legal terms, can be reached. In the end it will take a political struggle to make these changes, just as it took a political struggle to launch the Reagan Revolution. The major difference is that the Reagan Revolution ended up operating in the interest of at most 20 percent of the population, while these alternative reforms, as proposed by the Catholic bishops, the trade union movement, and various public-interest research groups, will benefit the other 80 percent. It is essential that that 80 percent come together to demand of our political leaders that they change course.

Notes

Chapter 1

1. The first shutdown lasted from November 14 to November 19, 1995 (*New York Times,* November 20, 1995, 1). The second began on December 16 (*New York Times,* December 17, 1995, 1; for details on what was shut and what wasn't, see p. 40). See also Congressional Budget Office, *The Economic and Budget Outlook: Fiscal Years 1997–2006* (Washington, DC: Government Printing Office, 1996), 9.

2. An article in the *Wall Street Journal* pointed out how much President Clinton had moved since the previous year. Whereas the previous year's (February 1995) budget proposal had projected deficits of $200 billion per year for the foreseeable future and contained five years of spending cuts totally $81 billion, the 1996 proposal had increased the projected cuts to $234 billion, permitting a deficit of zero by 2002 providing the economy remained at a steady rate of growth. With this reversal, President Clinton had surrendered to the Republicans. See Jackie Calmes, "Clinton's Fiscal '97 Budget Reflects Major Shift toward Ending Deficits and 'Big Government,'" *Wall Street Journal,* February 6, 1996, A16.

3. For details of that bill, see U.S. House of Representatives, Committee on Ways and Means, *1996 Green Book: Background Material and Data on Programs within the Jurisdiction of the Committee on Ways and Means* (Washington, DC: Government Printing Office, 1996), 1325–1418.

4. The most significant cuts in the 1995 budget that Congress had passed and that the president had vetoed were in the Medicare and Medicaid programs. To measure such cuts, the Congressional Budget Office (CBO) starts with a "baseline budget." This budget indicates how much it would cost to maintain current services over the period of time being considered, based on the CBO's estimates of costs and revenues, if no changes were enacted. Then the changes passed by Congress are measured against this baseline. This procedure is the source of the argument as to whether these are cuts or merely slowing the growth of spending. In fact, slowing the growth of spending makes it impossible to provide services at the current level to the growing population eligible for those services (the retired, the poor, the disabled in the case of Medicare and Medicaid) with the increased cost of providing those services over time. In December 1995, compared to the CBO baseline, recalculated according to the most recent predictions about the economy's next six years, the budget passed by Congress would have reduced federal spending by approximately $401 billion, of which approximately $359 billion would have been in Medicare and Medicaid. It also would have cut taxes approximately $229 billion (Jim Horney, "Memorandum: Updated Estimates of the Balanced Budget Act of 1995," Congressional Budget Office, December 13, 1995). The 1997 law, by

contrast, cut approximately $127 billion in toto while providing a modest $90 billion in tax reductions (and an additional $11 billion in refundable tax credits) through 2002 (see "Budgetary Implications of the Taxpayer Relief Act of 1997" and "Budgetary Implications of the Balanced Budget Act of 1997" in letter, June E. O'Neill, director, Congressional Budget Office, to Franklin D. Raines, director, Office of Management and Budget, August 12, 1997.)

5. For an analysis of Clinton's goals and methods on the road to this compromise see Martin Walker, "He Stoops to Conquer: Clinton's Budget Pact Shows His Messy Means to a Grand End," *Washington Post,* May 11, 1997, C1, C5. For initial coverage of the agreement, see the *New York Times,* July 30, 1997, A16, A17.

6. The Employment Act of 1946 states that

> it is the continuing policy and responsibility of the Federal Government to use all practicable means, consistent with its needs and obligations and other essential considerations of national policy with the assistance and cooperation of industry, agriculture, labor, and State and local government, to coordinate and utilize all its plans, functions, and resources for the purpose of creating and maintaining, in a manner calculated to foster and promote free competitive enterprise and the general welfare, conditions under which there will be afforded useful employment, for those able, willing, and seeking to work, and to promote maximum employment, production, and purchasing power. (Quoted in Stephen Kemp Bailey, *Congress Makes a Law* [New York: Columbia University Press, 1950], 228.)

The responsibility to "promote maximum employment" has been interpreted as requiring efforts to respond to the increase in unemployment that accompanies recessions. In 1978, this law was amended by the Full Employment and Balanced Growth Act to include a specific target of 4 percent unemployment.

7. There is a significant strand in economic analysis that suggests that paying the unemployed compensation may actually delay workers' finding new jobs because the benefit subsidizes the time without a job and reduces the urgency with which they look. See Martin Feldstein, "The Economics of the New Unemployment," *Public Interest* 33 (1973): 3–42. Similarly, there is a strongly held view, exemplified by the work of Charles Murray in *Losing Ground: American Social Policy, 1950–1980* (New York: Basic Books, 1984), that providing cash assistance to the poor as welfare actually *causes* poverty rather than reducing it. This point of view became the intellectual justification for the Republican proposals that led ultimately to the abolition of Aid to Families with Dependent Children, the program that provided a federally guaranteed cash grant to children in poor, single-parent families.

8. To give one example, total federal spending as a percentage of total economic activity (gross domestic product) stayed around 10 percent for the entire decade of the 1930s, rose to around 15 percent after World War II, hovered around 19 percent from the end of the Korean War till the late 1960s, and climbed to near 21 percent by 1979 (*Economic Report of the President* 1996 [Washington, DC: Government Printing Office, 1996], 368; henceforth these annual reports are abbreviated *ERP,* with the year indicated). Considering total government expenditures (including state and local outlays for things like police, fire, education, and public

assistance), we see an upward trend from 25 percent of total activity to 30 percent between 1960 and 1979.

9. The United States Central Bank consists of a system of twelve regional federal reserve banks whose actions are controlled by a seven-member Board of Governors in Washington appointed by the president (and subject to confirmation by the Senate) for fourteen-year terms. However, for the most important policy decisions, the controlling unit is the larger Federal Open Market Committee, which consists of the seven governors and the presidents of five of the regional banks (with the president of the New York Federal Reserve Bank always among the five). The actions of the Federal Reserve System are completely independent of the three branches of government, except that Congress may change the rules by legislation at any time. The president and secretary of the Treasury have no direct influence on Federal Reserve policy. All they can do is make speeches and attempt persuasion. A president wanting to force a change in policy would have to propose legislation to Congress. For a massive study of both the history and recent experience of the Federal Reserve System, see William Greider, *The Secrets of the Temple: How the Federal Reserve Runs the Country* (New York: Simon and Schuster, 1987).

10. A more detailed table, which goes back only to 1968, is provided in the *1996 Green Book*, 1321. Programs redistributing income on the basis of need for medical, food, and cash assistance went from 4.9 percent of the federal budget (in 1968) to 8.5 percent of the budget in 1978. Note that these are *fiscal* years, not calendar years. The fiscal year went from June of the previous year to the end of May of the numbered year until 1976; and from 1977 on, from October 1 of the previous year to the end of September of the numbered year. Thus, "fiscal 1968" was from June 1, 1967 to May 31, 1968. "Fiscal 1978" was from October 1, 1977 to September 30, 1978.

11. *ERP* 1997, 391.

12. The Congressional Budget Office analysis of the 1997 law shows a cut in Medicare spending of $115 billion in the years 1998 to 2002 over the predicted path of spending if no changes were to occur. See letter, June E. O'Neill, director, Congressional Budget Office, to Senator Pete V. Domenici, chairman, Committee of the Budget, United States Senate, July 30, 1997, table 4.

13. Daniel P. McMurrer and Isabel V. Sawhill, "Economic Mobility in the United States," Urban Institute no. 6722 (1996).

14. After the Republican success in the 1994 congressional elections, the *Contract with America* was published in book form, edited by Ed Gillespie and Bob Schellhas (New York: Times Books, 1994).

15. Representative Meek had asserted that

in 1980 a group of Republican candidates came to the Capitol steps and pledged that, if elected they would enact a supply-side miracle that would raise defense spending, cut taxes across the board, and still eliminate the deficit in 4 years. . . . They rammed their supply-side quick-fix through the Congress, and claimed it would solve all of our problems. . . . Their latest contract calls for: Another round of defense spending increases and a longer list of pie in the sky tax cuts.

What they do not tell us is that their contract will do two other things: First blow a $1 trillion hole into their balanced budget promise; and second, produce another tax windfall for the wealthy while leaving the middle class and the poor behind. (*Congressional Record* [September 29, 1994], 10254)

16. For example, see the following remarks by Speaker-designate Newt Gingrich on November 11, 1994: "It is impossible to take the Great Society structure of bureaucracy, the redistributionist model of how wealth is acquired, . . . and have any hope of fixing them. They are a disaster. They . . . have to be replaced thoroughly from the ground up" (*Contract with America*, 189).

17. It should be noted that some scholars and not a few citizens believe that this theoretical analysis is just a veneer behind which the true purpose of economic policy is to redistribute income and opportunity to those already in power, who have always been able to manipulate the political system to their ends. Thus, the role of government has always been rather extensive, and the cry for less government involvement always ignores the things government does to subsidize investments and profits of already large and successful enterprises. (On this point, note the *increase* in government activity and spending related to law enforcement, the punishment of criminals, and the defense establishment promised by the Republicans in the *Contract with America*, 37–64, 91–113.) This book will allude to this alternative point of view at times, but for the most part, we will conduct our discussion based on the mainstream analysis. The reason is that even if this alternative explanation of economic policymaking were true (and there is plenty in the historical record consistent with it), the changes in policy during the 1980–97 period are significant and worth exploring on their own terms. Second, the debates in the mainstream do not credit this alternative approach, and in the interest of dialogue with that mainstream, it is essential to accept some of the most basic premises, at least for the sake of the current discussion.

18. The federal budget deficit fell from $255 billion in fiscal 1993 to $22 billion in fiscal 1997. See Robert Pear, "Budget Heroes Include Bush and Gorbachev," *New York Times*, January 19, 1998, A12. See also *ERP* 1998, 372. Federal spending fell from 21.7 percent of total income to 21.1 percent between fiscal 1992 and 1996 (*ERP* 1997, 300, 391).

19. The economic proposals are contained in the following promised laws: "The Fiscal Responsibility Act . . . The Personal Responsibility Act . . . The American Dream Restoration Act . . . The Senor Citizens Fairness Act . . . The Job Creation and Wage Enhancement Act" (*Contract with America*, 9–10; see also 17–18). The specific proposals in these laws were a balanced-budget amendment to the Constitution, a denial of welfare to minor mothers, a rigid two-years-and-out limit on welfare eligibility and a cut in the dollars available for welfare, a five-hundred-dollar-per-child tax credit for all taxpayers making up to two hundred thousand dollars a year, an increase in the amount of money Social Security recipients can earn while collecting their pensions, a repeal in the 1993 tax increases on some Social Security income, a cut in taxes on business income including capital gains, and a reduction in government regulation of business and federal regulation of the states.

20. For the agreement, see Jerry Gray, "Congress and White House Finally Agree on Budget 7 Months into Fiscal Year," *New York Times*, April 25, 1996, A1, B13.

21. The marginal tax rate is the percentage of the next dollar you stand to

earn by, say, accepting a higher-paying job that you would have to pay in taxes. With a tax system that starts with some income free of taxation and then has a series of rising rates (such as our federal income tax system), the average tax rate is just the total level of taxes divided by total income. The marginal rate will always be higher than the average rate so long as some income is tax free (and therefore subject to a zero rate). It is the contention of some economists, including Lindsey, that high marginal tax rates discourage productive economic activity. See Lawrence B. Lindsey, "Simulating the Response of Taxpayers to Changes in Tax Rates," Ph.D. diss., Harvard University, 1985. For a concise, less technical discussion, see Lawrence B. Lindsey, *The Growth Experiment: How the New Tax Policy Is Transforming the U.S. Economy* (New York: Basic Books, 1990), 53–80.

22. This is the conclusion ultimately reached by Samuel Bowles, David M. Gordon, and Thomas Weisskopf in *After the Wasteland: A Democratic Economics for the Year 2000* (Armonk, NY: M. E. Sharpe, 1990). See especially pp. 121–69. For a short summary of the regressive tax changes, see Lawrence Mishel and Jared Bernstein, *The State of Working America, 1994–1995* (Armonk, NY: M. E. Sharpe, 1994), 93–108.

23. A supporter of Reagan-style tax cuts even before Reagan was elected president, Jude Wanniski wrote a book (*How the World Works* [New York: Touchstone/Simon and Schuster, 1978]) arguing that the ups and downs in all of world history can be traced to regimes of low versus high taxation.

24. See for example, Spencer Abraham, "The Real 1980s," *The World and I,* April 1996, 94–100. For counterarguments see Gary Burtless, "Tax-Cut Potions and Voodoo Fantasies," *The World and I,* April 1996, 100–102; and Michael Meeropol, "A Smoke Screen for Brutal Interest Rates," *The World and I,* April 1996, 102–3. See also Alan Reynolds, "Clintonomics Doesn't Measure Up," *Wall Street Journal,* June 12, 1996, A16.

25. Still others deny that the distribution of income has become more unequal.

Chapter 2

1. "Oeconomicus," *Xenophon in Seven Volumes,* trans. E. C. Marchant (Cambridge: Harvard University Press, 1968), vol. 4. The original conception of the ancient Greeks and Romans was very practically related to personal management of one's property (vii).

2. However, as noted in the previous chapter, income distribution is very important as a political issue. There is also an argument from the radical tradition in economics that the distribution of income and wealth has an important impact on economic growth. See pp. 59–63.

3. Of course this is in societies like the United States. In most traditional societies (and human beings lived in such traditional societies for hundreds of thousands of years before settled agriculture and civilization developed more complex organizations for producing food, clothing and shelter) cooperation occurs without modern-style leadership. True, there was a designated leader, but tasks were carried out based on tradition, not direct orders. Even in the United States and other modern economies, the leadership of certain organizations, such as cooperatives and partnerships, is not so hierarchical. Here voluntary cooperation

is much more explicit, and, in fact, in many cooperatives extensive rules govern that cooperation.

4. Harry Braverman, *Labor and Monopoly Capital* (New York: Monthly Review Press, 1974), 54–69 and 85–151.

5. In fact, even in the classic management literature, both the necessity of imposing order and maintaining control (the Marxist emphasis) and the fostering of a cooperative spirit coexist. For example, Henri Fayol, who published *Administration industrielle et generale* in 1916 (*General and Industrial Management,* trans. Constance Storrs [London: Isaac Pitman and Sons, 1949]), listed fourteen universal principles of management. Though most of the principles emphasize centralizing control over the work process (and therefore over the workers) in the hands of management (19–40), there is an intriguing fourteenth point, "Esprit de corps . . . Harmony, union among the personnel of a concern, is great strength in that concern" (40). In the late 1920s, the famous Hawthorne studies discovered (quite inadvertently) that varying physical surroundings of workers had much less important an effect on how well and hard they worked than did the attitudes of the workers themselves. Elton Mayo quoted from a private internal report on these studies as follows,

> The changed working conditions have resulted in creating an eagerness on the part of operators to come to work in the morning . . .

> The operators have no clear idea as to why they are able to produce more in the test room; but . . . there is the feeling that better output is in some way related to the distinctly pleasanter, freer, and happier working conditions . . .

> . . . much can be gained industrially by carrying greater personal consideration to the lowest levels of employment. (*The Human Problems of an Industrial Civilization* [New York: Viking, 1960], 65–67)

The inescapable conclusion of the Hawthorne Studies was that emotional factors related to morale were more important in determining the productivity of workers than physical factors.

Mary Parker Follet, lecturing in 1933, felt that she had discerned among the most forward-looking businesses the practice of developing collective responsibility, not only between different branches of the administration of a business, but down to the workers on the shop floor,

> wherever men or groups think of themselves not only as responsible for their own work, but as sharing in a responsibility for the whole enterprise, there is much greater chance of success for that enterprise . . . when you can develop a sense of collective responsibility then you find that the workman is more careful of material, that he saves time in lost motions, in talking over his grievances, that he helps the new hand by explaining things to him and so on. (*Freedom and Co-Ordination, Lectures in Business Organization* [New York: Garland, 1987], 73)

I am indebted to my colleagues Julie Siciliano and Peter Hess of the Department of Management at Western New England College for calling my attention to these sources.

6. In the context of environmental degradation and fears of world overpopulation, to state that growth appears to be have become permanent since the Industrial Revolution might be considered the height of hubris. I do not want to underestimate the dangers posed by environmental deterioration. However, it is a fact that the increased knowledge that has created the technology that is endangering our planet has also given us the *potential* information necessary to harness the technology and, in the words of the ecologist Barry Commoner "make our peace" with the planet (*Making Peace with the Planet* [New York: Pantheon, 1990]).

7. The importance of government in stimulating private investment with subsidies and other incentives should not be underestimated. For example, at the height of the laissez-faire approach to free enterprise during the nineteenth century, the U.S. government provided a tremendous subsidy to the railroads. First the government used the armed forces to defeat the Plains Indians and remove them from their land. Second, the government granted thousands of acres of land to the railroads along their right of way, land that the railroads were able to sell quite profitably. Virtually every major surge in investment in the United States can be traced to indirect or direct subsidies as a result of government activity, whether making war, building roads, or the like. Nevertheless, it is true that the actual spending of the investment funds is done by a private entity.

8. *Contract with America,* 23.

9. H. Ross Perot in *United We Stand* emphasized the interest burden on the federal taxpayer of the four-trillion-dollar national debt. He asserted,

> By 2000 we could well have an $8-trillion debt. Today all the income taxes collected from the states west of the Mississippi go to pay the *interest* on that debt. By 2000 we will have to add to that all the income tax revenues from Ohio, Pennsylvania, Virginia, North Carolina, New York and six other states just to pay the interest on that $8 trillion.

Central to the criticism leveled by Perot at the political leaders is a linkage between the unacceptable behavior of the economy in the 1990s and the ballooning national debt. In his very first chapter, he begins by mentioning some large layoffs. He then mentions the national debt and its growth every day as a result of the government deficit and concludes, "Does anyone think the present recession just fell out of the sky?" (*United We Stand: How We Can Take Back Our Country* [New York: Hyperion, 1992], 5)]. The reader is left with the inescapable conclusion that Perot wants us to believe the large debt *caused* the recession. We will explore these and other arguments about the alleged burdens of deficits and debt below. See pp. 43–44, 162–63, 170–74.

10. In *Restoring the Dream,* ed. Stephen Moore (New York: Times Books, 1995), 65–81, the House Republicans continue their arguments and promises made in the Contract with America. Their laments about the damage being done by budget deficits adds virtually nothing to what was said in the first volume. There is a reference to the absorption of national savings, the problem just referred to of "crowding out" private investment. The only other specific problems involve the increased percentage of federal spending devoted to interest payments on the debt and a reference to the fact that a rising percentage of the debt is held by foreigners. Both of these "problems" are not as serious as they make them out to be and are discussed on p. 170 and tables N-13 and N-14. Everything else in these pages is just

rhetoric. Readers skeptical of the assertions made here may want to consult any textbook on the principles of economics. There is usually a chapter on deficits and government debt. A more sophisticated but highly accessible analysis can be found in Robert Eisner's *The Misunderstood Economy: What Counts and How to Count It* (Boston: Harvard Business School Press, 1994), 89–119. See also James K. Galbraith and William Darity Jr., "A Guide to the Deficit," *Challenge,* July–August 1995, 5–12. For a recently published work that examines the intellectual history of American concern with budget deficits in great detail and argues for other damage that could potentially be done by some forms of deficit spending, see Daniel Shaviro, *Do Deficits Matter?* (Chicago: University of Chicago Press, 1997), esp. 28–150.

11. There is a school of economics known as the "public choice" school whose most prominent member, James Buchanan, received the Nobel Prize in economics in 1989. This school contends that there is an inexorable political pressure for government to expand its involvement in the economy based on the self-interest of government officials, elected and appointed, as well as the intensity of desire on the part of beneficiaries of government largesse. According to Buchanan, the future generations who must pay interest on the debt contracted before they were born have no political say in the decisions made by their grandparents, and thus the deck is politically stacked against them. In *Democracy in Deficit: The Political Legacy of Lord Keynes* (New York: Academic Press, 1977), Buchanan together with Richard Wagner blamed deficit spending for the ability of government to increase its spending in the economy. "Elected politicians enjoy spending public monies on projects that yield some demonstrable benefits to their constituents. They do not enjoy imposing taxes on these same constituents. The pre-Keynesian norm of budget balance served to constrain spending proclivities. . . . The Keynesian destruction of this norm . . . effectively removed the constraint" (93–94). Later on, they assert that the "bias toward deficits produces . . . a bias toward growth in the provision of services and transfers through government" (103). For a detailed examination of the "public choice" school, see Shaviro, *Do Deficits Matter?* 87–103.

12. This was baldly admitted by Murray Weidenbaum, the first chairman of the Council of Economic Advisers under President Reagan. At a discussion at the American Enterprise Institute, he candidly explained that concern over the deficit was necessary to counter pressure for increased government spending.

> DR. WEIDENBAUM: I'd like to offer, hopefully, some insight into the continuing concern . . . about deficits. I think the underlying concern is . . . to control the growth of government.
> And we measure that most conveniently by outlays. Surely the pressure for government spending growth is omnipresent. What is the counter pressure? In the legislative process . . . we're led back to the concern over deficits. . . .
> DR. STEIN [Herbert Stein, former chairman of the Council of Economic Advisers, then resident scholar at the AEI]: But aren't you worried that the whole trend of this discussion is reducing the inhibitions about running deficits, and therefore, weakening this restraining force against government spending.
> DR. WEIDENBAUM: Maybe that's why I made my comment.

DR. STEIN: Well, that's a good reason to make the comment but something more needs to be said then. That is, you need to reestablish some defensible reason for not having deficits. If you've now told us that they don't cause inflation, they don't crowd out. You see, it is not sufficient, as we know, for a group of economists to sit around and say, "Well, a deficit of a hundred billion dollars doesn't have these adverse effects," because you're dealing with a bunch of Congressmen out there, and if we say 100 billion is OK, they will ask why not 200 or why not 300.

They have a certain feeling about zero [that is, a balanced budget]. Zero is an intuitively appealing number. But we haven't found any other intuitively appealing rule, and that's what we've been missing. (American Enterprise Institute, "Public Policy Week," mimeo transcript, December 8, 1981, qtd. in Robert Bartley, *The Seven Fat Years* [New York: Free Press, 1992], 191–92)

13. See Milton Friedman, *Capitalism and Freedom* (Chicago: University of Chicago Press, 1962) and his collaborative work with Rose Friedman, *Free to Choose: A Personal Statement* (New York: Harcourt Brace Jovanovitch, 1980).

14. Qtd. in Conald Bedwell and Gary Tapp, "Supply-Side Economics Conference in Atlanta," *Economic Review of the Federal Reserve Bank of Atlanta* 57 (1982): 26.

15. See the quotations from Buchanan in note 11.

16. In fact there is another way a government can finance deficit spending, called "running the printing presses." It involves printing money and using it to pay for what the government needs. Such behavior had its origins in the days when governments collected precious metals and turned them into coins at the mint. In order to get more coins out of the precious metal, the mint was ordered to mix in some cheap metal with the gold or silver. This process was known as "debasing the currency," and the result was that the regime's coinage came into ill repute and individuals did not want to accept it at face value. Recent history has shown that wholesale resort to printing money to finance government expenditures leads to very rapid inflation—such as in Germany in 1922, when millions of marks were needed for a loaf of bread. This result has led many to argue that it is irresponsible to meet government spending needs by printing money over and above tax revenue. Printing bonds and selling them on the open market is considered more responsible because the rising national debt supposedly acts as a check on too much money creation. However, judicious printing of new money to finance some small percentage of the government budget might very well not lead to hyperinflation. This process, technically known as monetizing the debt, is frowned upon mainly because when the government borrows by issuing bonds, bankers make profits by placing them and investors have a secure place to invest funds. If the government just printed money at a slow enough pace not to accelerate inflation, the bankers would be out their cut.

17. The last time the federal government ran a surplus was in fiscal 1969 (*ERP* 1994, 359).

18. *Contract with America,* 23.

19. Eisner, *The Misunderstood Economy,* 51.

20. This is probably a good place to mention that much of the argument

against government spending in general is in reality aimed at government activity that redistributes income. As mentioned in chap. 1, the *Contract with America,* 91–113, called for increased government spending on national defense. The Republican majority in Congress has since 1994 attempted to reverse the decline in defense spending projected by both the Bush and Clinton administrations, while proposing dramatic cuts in Medicaid, Medicare, and transfer payments to the poor. Even those who rail against spending in general usually treat the defense budget as sacrosanct. Many have argued that this is because the defense budget is an indirect subsidy to large businesses, benefiting the kind of people who make large contributions to members of Congress and whose investment activity is the key to economic prosperity. See chap. 9, n. 18.

21. The National Bureau of Economic Research identifies recessions as periods during which the real GDP (that is, GDP corrected for inflation) falls for two consecutive quarters. Table N-1 combines the NBER's dating of post–World War II business cycles beginning with the 1948 recession. Each peak marks the end of a period of prosperity and the beginning of a recession. Each trough marks the point where a recession bottoms out and a recovery begins. Table N-1 shows the quarter before and after each peak and trough to give an idea of the way unemployment and capacity utilization rates behave around the peaks and troughs of business cycles. Later we will examine these and many other facts of recent economic history quarter by quarter in the years since 1960.

22. Thus, even though the recovery from the 1990 recession began in the first quarter of 1991, there was not one quarter during the rest of 1991 in which real GDP grew as fast as 2 percent (*ERP* 1997, 307). Thus, it is not surprising that the unemployment rate actually rose from 6.5 percent in the quarter the recovery began to 7.5 percent in the third quarter of 1992 before it began to decline. Similarly, the capacity utilization rate did not reach 80 percent until the fourth quarter of 1992. This made the 1991 recovery the most sluggish in the postwar period.

23. Note that this is a creation of something physical. Common usage often describes investment as any spending of money to acquire an income-generating asset. By that definition, investment includes buying stocks and bonds as well as physical assets like machines and buildings. For the purposes of describing the impact on aggregate demand, however, we restrict the meaning of investment to physical assets. Purely financial investments actually involve the transfer of ownership rights of already created physical assets and thus are not counted as part of the GDP. This is not to suggest that such financial investments are unimportant; far from it. See pp. 128, 156–57 for some discussion of the impacts of purely financial investments.

24. The public-choice field of economics analyzes that government decision making may not respond to an generalized "public interest" but to the narrow interests of particular constituencies. See James Buchanan, *The Demand and Supply of Public Goods* (Chicago: Rand McNally, 1968).

25. *ERP* 1997, 37, 38.

26. *ERP* 1996, 282.

27. *ERP* 1997, 389. These are fiscal years.

28. Real investment as a percentage of real GDP fell from 16 percent to 14 percent between 1984 and 1989 (*ERP* 1996, 282), the federal deficit fell from 5 percent of GDP in fiscal 1983 to 4 percent of GDP in fiscal 1986, and the national debt fell from 57.6 percent of GDP to 39.5 percent of GDP between 1960 and 1969. As a

TABLE N-1. Peaks and Troughs, 1948–91

Year and Quarter	Peak or Trough	Civilian Unemployment Rate (%)	Capacity Utilization Rate (%)
1948: 3		3.8	82.5
1948: 4	Peak	3.8	80.4
1949: 1		4.6	76.9
1949: 3		6.7	73.8
1949: 4	Trough	7.0	72.4
1950: 1		6.4	75.6
1953: 1		2.7	91.0
1953: 2	Peak	2.6	91.3
1953: 3		2.7	90.0
1954: 1		5.2	80.8
1954: 2	Trough	5.8	79.7
1954: 3		6.0	79.1
1957: 2		4.1	84.6
1957: 3	Peak	4.2	83.9
1957: 4		4.9	79.5
1958: 1		6.3	74.1
1958: 2	Trough	7.4	72.4
1958: 3		7.3	75.4
1960: 1		5.2	84.5
1960: 2	Peak	5.2	81.3
1960: 3		5.6	78.9
1960: 4		6.3	75.9
1961: 1	Trough	6.8	73.8
1961: 2		7.0	76.4
1969: 3		3.6	87.0
1969: 4	Peak	3.6	85.8
1970: 1		4.2	82.8
1970: 3		5.2	80.6
1970: 4	Trough	5.8	78.2
1971: 1		5.9	79.0
1973: 3		4.8	88.9
1973: 4	Peak	4.8	88.5
1974: 1		5.1	85.5
1974: 4		6.6	80.9
1975: 1	Trough	8.2	74.0
1975: 2		8.9	73.1
1979: 4		5.9	85.4
1980: 1	Peak	6.3	85.0
1980: 2		7.3	81.2
1980: 3	Trough	7.7	80.0
1980: 4		7.4	82.0
1981: 2		7.4	81.1
1981: 3	Peak	7.4	81.6
1981: 4		8.2	79.2
1982: 3		9.9	74.4
1982: 4	Trough	10.7	72.5
1983: 1		10.4	73.0
1990: 2		5.3	82.4
1990: 3	Peak	5.6	82.3
1990: 4		6.0	80.9
1991: 1	Trough	6.5	78.9
1991: 2		6.7	78.8

Source: Column 1: National Bureau of Economic Research; column 2: Bureau of Labor Statistics (Unemployment Rate, All Civilian Workers, quarterly data, seasonally adjusted, 1948–93); column 3: Board of Governors, Federal Reserve System, Utilization for Manufacturing, seasonally adjusted, 1948–66 (MFGUTL.B00004.S), Utilization for Total Index, seasonally adjusted, 1967–91 (MFGUTL. B50001.S).

percentage of GDP, this debt is much lower than was the much smaller absolute debt of $271 billion in 1946 (*ERP* 1997, 389). The ratio of debt to GDP was over 100 percent in 1945 and 1946; that is GDP was actually *lower* than the national debt in those years.

Chapter 3

1. The rate of growth averaged 4.07 percent between 1960 and 1969 and 2.85 percent between 1970 and 1979.

2. For the periods 1960–69 and 1970–79, productivity growth averaged 2.41 and 1.33 percent, respectively; unemployment averaged 5.58 and 6.21 percent, respectively; and capacity utilization averaged 84.86 and 82.58 percent, respectively.

3. Dean Baker, "Trends in Corporate Profitability: Getting More for Less?" Technical Paper, Economic Policy Institute, February 1996, table 1. A full business cycle begins with a peak and continues through the next trough to the next peak. Alternatively, it can begin with a trough and continue through the next peak to the next trough (see chap. 2, n. 21 and table N-1). The calculation of profit rates is made for the year before each cyclical peak, since the rate of profit usually turns down before the whole economy does. Thus, for example, using the profit rate of 1969 in the 1959–68 business cycle would have actually introduced profit data more appropriate for the next business cycle.

4. I use 1978 as the end point because in 1979 the Census Bureau changed data collections, and a spurt of unanticipated inflation caused median earnings of year-round, full-time workers to fall for that year. I did not want that one year's experience to skew the data. As it is, the change from the 1960s to the 1970s remains quite striking.

5. A variety of inflation rates are constructed and published by the various branches of the federal government. For the purposes of identifying the misery index, I have chosen the most widely publicized inflation rate, the consumer price index. Not all of the components of the consumer price index apply to all people; for example, a homeowning family with a fixed-rate mortgage is not affected by rising housing costs so long as the family stays put. As many economists will emphasize, however, the knowledge of general inflation has a discomforting impact on people even apart from those higher prices they actually pay.

6. Let's consider two numerical examples from the period of history covered in this book. Consider a mortgage loan entered into in 1965 with a ten-year maturity. The nominal interest rate in 1965 averaged 5.81 (*ERP* 1994, 352); the inflation rate (measured by the consumer price index) was 1.6 percent (*ERP* 1997, 370). If we assume that inflation rate was accurately anticipated by both lenders and borrowers, then the real interest rate these mortgage lenders were expecting was 4.21 percent. Within three years, when the rate of inflation had accelerated to 4.2 percent, the actual real rate of interest received by mortgage lenders was 1.61 percent. In 1969 it was 0.31 percent; in 1970 it was even lower (0.21 percent) because inflation was 5.7 percent. Beginning in 1973 and running through 1975, the rate of inflation was higher than the mortgage rate of interest contracted in 1965. This translated

into a *negative real interest rate.* The borrowers found the reduction in the real burden of their repayment of principal greater than the nominal interest rate they had to pay. The lenders lost real income on those loans.

Now let us consider a mortgage loan contracted in 1981. The nominal rate of interest for a ten-year mortgage averaged 14.7 percent and the rate of inflation in the consumer price index was 10.3 percent. This represented a real interest rate of 4.4 percent, assuming correct anticipation by lenders and borrowers. The rate of inflation deceleration after 1981 was so dramatic that the real burden of the mortgage interest rate rose in 1982 to 8.5 percent and only once fell below 10 percent for the rest of the time till maturity. In other words, borrowers were faced with a real interest burden more than twice as great as they anticipated when they contracted the loan.

7. Some businesses can set their prices and stick to them because they have few competitors, who will most likely match their price rather than provoke a price war. In the most general sense, the distinction needs to be made between businesses that are "price takers" and those that are "price makers." The earliest empirical work on the significant ability of certain firms to control prices was by Gardner C. Means. He identified industries that responded to the falloff in demand during the Great Depression by keeping prices relatively stable and reducing output. These industries he characterized as those with administered prices (that is, they were price makers) as opposed to those industries (such as agriculture) in which prices fell dramatically but output did not (in other words, price takers) (*Industrial Prices and Their Relative Inflexibility,* Senate Document No. 13, 74th Congress [Washington, DC: Government Printing Office, 1935]). This analysis was in opposition to traditional economic theory, which was built on the idea that most businesses (and sellers of factors of production) are price takers because they are subject to competition with a large number of competitors that sell roughly identical products (in the textbooks, the definition of this type of competition is even more restricted: they are all selling indistinguishable standardized products, like Class A corn, for example, or shares in AT&T). Beginning in the early twentieth century, economists began to recognize the significance of imperfectly competitive markets. Most textbooks now acknowledge the existence of competition among such a small number of firms that they are able to set prices. The technical term for this market structure is oligopoly. John Kenneth Galbraith referred to this sector of the economy as the "planning system" to identify the ability of these firms to plan output and control prices (John K. Galbraith, *The New Industrial State* [Boston: Houghton Mifflin, 1967], and *Economics and the Public Purpose* [Boston: Houghton Mifflin, 1973]). In one strand of the radical tradition, what Galbraith calls the planning system is called the "monopoly sector" of the economy, and the entire economy is identified as monopoly capitalism (see, for example, Paul Baran and Paul Sweezy, *Monopoly Capital* [New York: Monthly Review Press, 1966]; and John B. Foster, *The Theory of Monopoly Capital* [New York: Monthly Review Press, 1989]).

8. This would amount to a tax rate on my *real* income of 72 percent.

9. In actual experience, inflation induces most taxpayers to avoid taxable interest income. Instead, potentially taxable interest-bearing securities are bought by pension funds and other tax-exempt organizations and insurance companies and banks with very low effective tax rates. Individuals who wish the security of interest income buy tax-exempt bonds issues by states and municipalities. See

C. Eugene Steuerle, *Taxes, Loans, and Inflation: How the Nation's Wealth Becomes Misallocated* (Washington, DC: Brookings Institution, 1985), 9–18, 57–80.

10. Paying interest of $10,000 a year on a $100,000 loan with 5 percent inflation means the real burden of repayment is only $5,000 per year.

11. This would represent fully 72 percent of the real cost of my interest payments. Tax expert C. Eugene Steuerle argues that the interaction of inflation and the ability to deduct the full nominal interest paid induces unproductive investment activity, for example, excess construction of residences, office buildings, and shopping malls, just for the purposes of reaping the tax advantages. See *Taxes, Loans, and Inflation,* 57–114.

12. Let us assume a 36 percent tax rate. With no inflation, the tax of $36,000 is 36 percent of that real gain. Now let us assume inflation over five years causes an average increase in prices of 25 percent. The $100,000 gain is only $75,000 in increased purchasing power because $25,000 merely makes up for the inflation. But the tax burden is still $36,000, only it now represents 48 percent of the ($75,000) real gain.

13. To return to our specific numerical example, with a 50 percent exclusion and a 25 percent cumulative inflation over the five years, the real gain is $75,000, and the tax rate of 36 percent is applied to only $50,000. Thus, the tax is $18,000, which is only 24 percent of $75,000. If the real gain were only $50,000, applying the tax rate of 36 percent to half the dollar gain ($100,000) produces $18,000 in taxes, which is 36 percent of the real gain.

14. See chap. 1, n. 6, which quotes the Employment Act of 1946.

15. Fiscal policy is defined as all governmental decisions involving taxation and spending. Monetary policy consists of actions of the Federal Reserve System (often merely referred to as "the Fed") to change the rate of growth of money and/or to change interest rates. As mentioned above (chap. 1, n. 9), the United States has an independent Central Bank. The seven governors of the Federal Reserve Board are appointed by the president for fourteen-year terms to protect their independence. An expansionary fiscal policy would involve increased spending or decreased taxation or some combination of both. A restrictive fiscal policy would involve decreased spending or increased taxation or some combination of both. (For a variety of reasons, most economists believe that balanced increases of spending and taxation are expansionary and balanced decreases are restrictive, but that is quite controversial; see pp. 47–48 and chap. 3, n. 43.) An expansionary monetary policy increases the rate of growth of the money supply, aiming for a reduction in interest rates. A restrictive monetary policy decreases the rate of growth of the money supply, perhaps even contracting it, aiming for an increase in interest rates. How the alteration in money growth affects interest rates and the economy at large is the subject of a great deal of controversy. For an accessible and accurate summary of what he calls the monetary hydraulics, see Greider, *Secrets of the Temple,* 31–33. For a reasonable introduction to the controversy over how monetary policy works or does not work, see Richard Gill, *Great Debates in Economics* (Pacific Palisades, CA: Goodyear, 1976), 353–62.

16. Jude Wanniski's book *(How the World Works)* was published in 1978. The introduction of "supply-side" economics to the public at large occurred even earlier in his article "The Mundell-Laffer Hypothesis," *Public Interest* 39 (spring 1975): 31–57. In addition to the proposed cuts in the individual income tax, there

were major proposals for liberalizing depreciation deductions for businesses. For details of some proposals, see *ERP* 1981, 76.

17. See, for example, John N. Smithin, *Macroeconomics after Thatcher and Reagan: The Conservative Policy Revolution in Retrospect* (Aldershot, UK: Edward Elgar, 1990), 1–4, 8–24.

18. On this issue, see *Contract with America*, 125–41; *Restoring the Dream*, 37–52. On p. 41, the latter book has a diagram headlined "As Washington Grows, the Economy Slows." In the diagram the percentage of the economy covered by government spending is set against the rate of growth of real gross domestic product. Table N-2 reproduces the numbers in table form. Despite the rise in the rate of growth of GDP in the third period even as government spending rose, the long-run trend is obviously an inverse one.

19. Murray Weidenbaum, "America's New Beginning: A Program for Economic Recovery," in *Two Revolutions in Economic Policy*, ed. James Tobin and Murray Weidenbaum (Cambridge: MIT Press, 1988), 294. Note that the focus is on "excessive government spending," yet nowhere in this discussion are deficits blamed for the economy's problems. Instead there is a prediction that deficits will decline to zero and a passing reference to the "alarming trends" of rising deficits and rising spending over the decade of the 1970s (p. 302).

20. *ERP* 1981; *ERP* 1984.

21. See Friedman, *Capitalism and Freedom*, as well as *ERP* 1982, 27–33. For a more extreme superlibertarian view, see Murray Rothbard, *Power and Market, Government and the Economy* (Kansas City, MO: Sheed Andrews and McMeel, 1977).

22. In 1993, economic historian Douglass C. North won the Nobel Prize in economic science for his work on how institutions interact with economic actors to make it easier or harder for economic growth to occur. One can see the proposals in the Contract with America relating to increased spending on police and prisons, increased sentences for violent criminals, and legal reform to reduce the costs to business and individuals from "frivolous" lawsuits as an effort to re-create what Republicans see is an appropriate framework within which such a market economy can function (*Contract with America*, 37 64, 143–55).

23. William Baumol, J. C. Panzar, and R. D. Willig, *Contestable Markets and the Theory of Industry Structure* (New York: Harcourt Brace Jovanovich, 1982).

24. The *Contract with America* devotes an entire chapter to the proposition that the Clinton administration budget cuts have weakened the defense establishment to the point where the so-called hollow military of the late 1970s is in danger of being re-created (*Contract with America*, 91–113). The sequel volume, *Restoring the Dream*, 115–18, has proposed significant privatization of federally run activities such as the Naval Petroleum Reserve, the Air Traffic Control System, and certain Amtrak routes.

25. In the 1990s, there is an effort to take this principle even further. Areas of activity previously the sole responsibility of government, such as the running of prisons, have been proposed for privatization. Private companies contract with a state government to house a certain number of prisoners, getting paid a fixed fee and making their profit by delivering the "service" to the taxpayers at a lower cost than if the state paid the costs directly. With prison building on a dramatic upsurge in the past decade and prison populations rising dramatically, this is a great new frontier for profitable activity on the part of the private sector.

TABLE N-2. The Role of Government according to
Restoring the Dream

Period	Government Spending (% of GDP)	Annual Rate of Growth in Real GDP
1889-1919	10.0	3.9
1919-1948	15.0	3.0
1948-1973	27.0	3.7
1973-1992	36.0	2.3

Source: *Restoring the Dream,* ed. Stephen Moore (New York: Times
Books, 1995), 42.

26. *ERP* 1982, 30–31.

27. Given the incomes of all consumers, given the tastes and preference of these consumers, and given the capital and land and skills of the labor force available to be used by businesses as well as the state of technology, the satisfaction achieved by each and every consumer that is greater than or equal to the price they actually pay for what they buy exactly equals the sacrifice society has had to endure to produce the last unit of the product sold. If this occurs in every market, then this maximizes satisfaction for society as a whole. The problem of externalities is that the price paid by people does not equal the true cost to society; the satisfaction experienced by an individual does not equal the true benefit to all of society.

28. Economists would make the comparison by summing the present value of all expected net earnings of the farmer for the rest of his or her productive life. This would create what is called the capitalized value of the farmer's income stream. In reality, such a calculation would be very uncertain, because it actually depends on how one thousand dollars, say, five years from now is discounted to create its present value. In addition, farmers may place some kind of premium on maintaining their way of life, even if the dollar value of a lifetime in farming is lower than what could be obtained by selling out to a developer. Finally, the farmer's time horizon may include the projected incomes of his or her children and grandchildren.

29. Murray Weidenbaum, *The Future of Government Regulation* (New York: Anacom, 1979), 23. It should be noted that the Weidenbaum approach is not without its critics. Some have argued that his cost estimates are too high. See, for example, John E. Schwarz, *America's Hidden Success: A Reassessment of Public Policy from Kennedy to Reagan* (New York: Norton, 1988), 91–98. Others have attempted to measure benefits to show that the benefits do justify the costs. See, for example, Mark Green and Norman Waitzman, *Business War on the Law: An Analysis of the Benefits of Federal Health and Safety Enforcement,* preface by Ralph Nader, 2d ed. (Washington, DC: Corporate Accountability Research Group, 1981). However, it is not our intention to argue these points. It is important to develop the full conservative diagnosis of what ailed the economy because the solutions proposed and attempted by both the Reagan administration and the Republican majority in Congress since 1994 aims to change public policy to meet these alleged problems.

30. Monetarists believe that the rate of growth in the money supply is the cru-

cial determinant of the rate of growth of nominal GDP, that is, GDP uncorrected for inflation. They argue that deviations of the rate of growth of money from the current trend have a direct impact on GDP, but only after a lag of uncertain length. (They also believe that the actual division of the impact between price increases and output increases is unpredictable in the short run.) Therefore, the monetarists have argued against using discretionary changes in monetary policy to combat too much unemployment or inflation. To do so would just as likely be destabilizing as not. For a detailed monetarist historical overview, see Milton Friedman and Anna Schwartz, *A Monetary History of the United States, 1867–1960* (Princeton, NJ: Princeton University Press, 1963). See also Milton Friedman, "The Role of Monetary Policy," *American Economic Review* 58 (March 1968): 1–17.

31. For the original multiplier concept, see R. F. Kahn, "The Relation of Home Investment to Unemployment," *Economic Journal* 41 (1931): 173–93. The marginal propensity to consume and resulting multiplier are developed in all textbooks on the principles of economics. See, for example, N. Gregory Mankiw, *Principles of Economics* (New York: Dryden Press, 1998), 717–18; and Joseph E. Stiglitz, *Economics*, 2d ed. (New York: Norton, 1997), 674–77.

32. See Friedman, *Capitalism and Freedom*, chap. 5, esp. p. 81.

33. Ibid., chap. 5.

34. For some examples of some of the nonsense and their common-sense refutations, see Eisner, *The Misunderstood Economy*, 99–103. This is not to say that there are not some potentially negative consequences should deficits and debt rise *as a percentage of GDP*. When that happens, the increased percentage of government revenues devoted to paying interest would reduce the ability of government to spend on other needed activities. However, most of the claims about the evils of deficit spending and the national debt focus on the "necessity" of reducing deficits to zero and "paying off" the debt. See, for example, virtually any speech by any member of Congress beginning in March 1995.

35. See A. W. Phillips, "The Relation between Unemployment and the Rate of Change of Money Wage Rates in the United Kingdom, 1861–1957," *Economica* 25 (1958): 283–99.

36. Table N-3 presents the unemployment rate and inflation rate between 1951 and 1969.

37. *ERP* 1982, 51. Table N-4 brings the Phillips Curve data from note 36 from 1970 through 1979.

38. *ERP* 1982, 50.

39. Within the economics profession, this view became the basis of a whole new school. Known under the general rubric of "new classical" economics, it also goes by the name of the "rational expectations" school. Very briefly, this group of economists believes that the general economy tends to an equilibrium solution and that government efforts to alter, say, the rate of growth of the economy or the level of unemployment can only have short-run impacts because in the long run, other actors in the economy will take corrective action in response to government initiatives and the economy will end up back at the same equilibrium. Thus, they strongly support the view that there is an equilibrium ("natural") rate of unemployment toward which the economy is always tending. For a fascinating and readable analysis of this school, see Arjo Klamer, *Conversations with Economists* (Totowa, NJ: Rowman and Allanheld, 1984), 1–94. For criticism, see pp. 98–169.

TABLE N-3. A Phillips Curve for the United States, 1951–69

Year	Rate of Inflation (CPI)	Civilian Unemployment Rate
1951	7.9	3.3
1952	1.9	3.0
1953	0.8	2.9
1954	0.7	5.5
1955	−0.4	4.4
1956	1.5	4.1
1957	3.3	4.3
1958	2.8	6.8
1959	0.7	5.5
1960	1.7	5.5
1961	1.0	6.7
1962	1.0	5.5
1963	1.3	5.7
1964	1.3	5.2
1965	1.6	4.5
1966	2.9	3.8
1967	3.1	3.8
1968	4.2	3.6
1969	5.5	3.5

Source: ERP 1997, 346, 30.

TABLE N-4. No Simple Phillips Curve

Year	Rate of Inflation (CPI)	Civilian Unemployment Rate
1970	5.7	4.9
1971	4.4	5.9
1972	3.2	5.6
1973	6.2	4.9
1974	11.0	5.6
1975	9.1	8.5
1976	5.8	7.7
1977	6.5	7.1
1978	7.6	6.1
1979	11.3	5.8

Source: ERP 1997, 346, 370.

For one series of the NAIRU see Congressional Budget Office, *The Economic and Budget Outlook: Fiscal Years 1998–2007* (Washington, DC: Government Printing Office, 1997), 105.

40. This may seem contradictory, but it is not. One's marginal rate of taxation can rise even if the total percentage of one's income paid in taxes stays the same. Consider someone with an income of $50,000 paying one rate of 10 percent in income tax. That person's total tax is $5,000 and the marginal rate of taxation is 10 percent. Now, let us change the tax system into a two-bracket system with rates of zero percent on the first $25,000 of income and 20 percent on the second $25,000. Total taxes will still be 10 percent of income (20 percent times $25,000 = $5,000), but the marginal tax rate will have doubled. Beginning in 1964, there were a number of tax cuts that by raising personal exemptions and cutting tax rates other than the top marginal rate ended up keeping the average tax bite from rising while the marginal rate did rise.

41. It is important to understand that the tax rates shown in table 4 do not apply to the entire income of the taxpayer. Thus, someone making $25,000 in taxable income in 1980 would not owe $8,000 (32 percent of $25,000) on April 15, 1981. Instead, this person's income tax would be the sum of the tax owed on each level of income. The first $3,400 would be tax free. The next $2,100 would be taxed at 14 percent ($294). The next $2,100 would be taxed at 16 percent ($336). Subjecting the next $17,400 to tax rates of 18, 21, 24, 28, and finally 32 percent leads to a total tax bill of $4,633. The important incentive effect of the marginal tax rate is that the extra income an individual receives as a result of making an extra effort (to take a second job, to take a higher-paying job, to make a new investment) is equal to the increase in income *less* the marginal tax rate. If our imaginary taxpayer with an income of $25,000 got a pay raise of $4,000, he or she would get to keep only $2,720, paying $1,280 (32 percent of $4,000) more in income tax.

42. *ERP* 1982, table 5-4, p. 120.

43. Assume the government raises taxes and spending by $100 billion. All of the government's spending goes to buying military equipment, building roads, paying government employees, doing basic scientific research, thereby raising GDP. Meanwhile, some high percentage of the money paid to the government in taxes (say, $95 billion) represents a reduction in consumption expenditures, thereby lowering the GDP. But the other $5 billion in taxes paid is money that would not have been spent anyway. Thus, there is a net increase in spending of $5 billion, and that increase then is subject to the multiplier process as it ripples through the economy.

44. *ERP* 1982, 34–35.

45. *ERP* 1982, 35.

46. See, for example, Warren Shore, *Social Security, the Fraud in Your Future* (New York: Macmillan, 1975).

47. In 1979, 58.9 percent of the elderly would have been in poverty had they not received Social Security, unemployment compensation, and other cash payments also available universally. The other 41.1 percent with private-sector incomes above the poverty level also received Social Security. See Sheldon Danziger and Daniel Weinberg, "The Historical Record: Trends in Family Income, Inequality, and Poverty," in *Confronting Poverty: Prescriptions for Change,* ed. Sheldon Danziger, Gary Sandefur, and Daniel Weinberg (Cambridge: Harvard University Press, 1994), 46.

48. Though in the case of a millionaire, the unemployment compensation and Social Security check would (today) be subject to income taxation.

49. Leonard H. Thompson, "The Social Security Reform Debate," *Journal of Economic Literature* 21 (1983): 1425–67.

Chapter 4

1. This is not true about monetarism. There was a long and lively debate in 1965 around the publication of Milton Friedman and David Meiselman's study that sought to demonstrate the superiority of "monetarist macroeconomics" as an explanation for changes in the economy to the Keynesian multiplier. See Friedman and Meiselman, "The Relative Stability of Monetary Velocity and the Investment Multiplier in the United States, 1897–1958," in *Stabilization Policies,* ed. E. C. Brown (Englewood Cliffs, NJ: Commission on Money and Credit, 1963): 165–268. Friedman and Meiselman were challenged by many economists. See, for example, Albert Ando and Franco Modigliani, "The Relative Stability of Monetary Velocity and the Investment Multiplier," *American Economic Review* 55 (September 1965): 693–728; and Michael DePrano and Thomas Mayer, "Tests of the Relative Importance of Autonomous Expenditures and Money," *American Economic Review* 55 (September 1965): 729–51. The debate continued. See Friedman and Meiselman, "Reply to Ando and Modigliani and to DePrano and Mayer," *American Economic Review* 55 (September 1965): 753–85; Ando and Modigliani "Rejoinder," *American Economic Review* 55 (September 1965): 786–90; and DePrano and Mayer, "Rejoinder," *American Economic Review* 55 (September 1965): 791–92.

2. For a detailed analysis that goes beyond a discussion of supply shocks to explain accelerating inflation, see Alan Blinder, *Economic Policy and the Great Stagflation* (New York: Academic Press, 1979). See also *ERP* 1978, 141.

3. Barry Bosworth, "Economic Policy," in *Setting National Priorities: Agenda for the 1980s,* ed. Joseph Pechman (Washington, DC: Brookings Institution, 1980), 43. Bosworth goes on to argue, "The experience of recent recessions . . . suggests that at best an increase of 1 percent in the unemployment rate—about 1 million persons—if maintained over a two-year period would reduce inflation by only about 1 percentage point."

4. See Blinder, *Economic Policy and the Great Stagflation,* 146–52. For President Ford's two diametrically opposed requests see *New York Times,* October 9, 1974, 1, 24; January 14, 1975, 1, 20.

5. The government deficit as a percentage of GDP rose from less than 0.5 percent in 1974 to 3.4 percent in 1975 and 4.3 percent in 1976 (*ERP* 1997, 389).

6. The key barometer of Federal Reserve policy is the short-term interest rate that banks charge each other for overnight loans, the Federal Funds rate. In 1974, that rate had risen to 10.50. In 1975, the Central Bank pursued a vigorous policy to cut that rate down to 5.82, and the rate continued to fall till the first quarter of 1977 (*ERP* 1997, 382–83). See table W-1 on this book's web page, <mars.wnec.edu/~econ/surrender>.

7. The GDP deflator inflation rate was 5.6 percent in 1976 and rose to 9.2 percent in 1980 (*ERP* 1997, 306). The consumer price index rose at a rate of 5.8 per-

cent in 1976 to 13.5 percent in 1980 (*ERP* 1997, 369). See also the inflation rates in table N-4.

8. *ERP* 1981, 8.

9. For the budget deficit percentages, see *ERP* 1997, 389 (these are fiscal years). For the recession, see chap. 2, n. 21.

10. See *ERP* 1981, 156–58, for an explanation of the direction of fiscal policy during 1980. It is well known that Richard Nixon always believed that the Eisenhower administration's budget surplus in 1960 and subsequent recession was the chief cause of his narrow defeat by John F. Kennedy. Too late for Nixon, the Eisenhower administration permitted the budget to move into deficit in fiscal 1961 (0.6 percent of GDP), and the Kennedy administration raised that deficit in fiscal 1962 (1.3 percent of GDP) with the enactment of the investment tax credit combined with a five-billion-dollar increase in defense purchases. We already have seen how the Ford administration dealt with the recession of 1975. In 1970 and 1971 the Nixon administration took a number of small steps to raise the amount of fiscal stimulus. (Federal deficits rose to 2.1 percent of GDP in fiscal 1971 and stayed at 2.0 percent of GDP in 1972 [*ERP* 1997, 389].)

11. *ERP* 1997, 346. See also table N-4.

12. Between 1976 and 1979, the economy created over 10 million new jobs (*ERP* 1997, 340).

13. This point of view is summarized by President Carter himself in his report (*ERP* 1981, 3–5).

14. In 1981, the Brookings Institution's academic journal put out a special issue on the productivity slowdown. In the editors' summary, William Brainard and George Perry noted that the causes of this phenomenon "have remained largely a mystery. In the most comprehensive study to date, Edward Denison examined seventeen alternative hypotheses and concluded that alone or in combination they could explain no more than a fraction of the slowdown" (*Brookings Papers on Economic Activity* 1 [1981]: vii). See also Edward Denison, *Accounting for Slower Growth* (Washington, DC: The Brookings Institute, 1979). Interestingly, with much more hindsight, a team of economists under the direction of William Baumol of Princeton University discovered that the slowdown in productivity of the 1970s and 1980s was actually a return to the century-long trend that had been disturbed first by a tremendous decline in growth due to the depression of the 1930s and then a tremendous increase in growth in the period between 1945 and 1972. See Jeffrey G. Williamson, "Productivity and American Leadership: A Review Article," *Journal of Economic Literature* 29 (March 1991): 51–68.

15. Blinder, *Hard Heads, Soft Hearts: Tough-Minded Economics for a Just Society* (New York: Addison-Wesley, 1987), 24.

16. In the case of automobiles, the massive government subsidies to highway construction made automobile transportation of goods and people relatively attractive compared to rail travel and transport. There was also tremendous subsidy to housing dispersal into the suburbs with low-interest loans and tax deductions associated with home ownership. The aerospace and telecommunications industries' dependence on government seed money and extensive research and development funds is almost self-evident. Large government purchases often become the basis of concerted business efforts to cut the cost of new technological advances. One particularly significant example is noted by the *Economist*.

In 1961 . . . Fairchild and Texas Instruments found themselves sitting on a clever new invention, called the integrated circuit, which nobody could afford to buy. Then, the chips cost around $120 each. By 1971, the average price was less than $42. Why the change? Mainly because President Kennedy decided to send an American to the moon—a feat which led the federal government to buy more than a million integrated circuits and taught the semiconductor industry to build them at a fraction of the initial cost. ("Will Star Wars Reward or Retard Science?" *Economist*, September 7, 1985, 96.)

The Internet is only the latest government-created product that is now available virtually free of charge for use by the private sector.

17. The stagnation school is associated with the work of Paul Baran and Paul Sweezy in *Monopoly Capital*. The basic conclusion of this school is that capitalism in the twentieth century is subject to a permanent tendency for aggregate demand to fall short of potential GDP. The result is that more and more government intervention is necessary to stave off economic depressions, and even with such intervention, a tendency toward secular stagnation sets in.

This school explains the post–World War II sustained growth by stating that the massive expansion of the military during World War II had ended the depression. Then there was a short postwar consumer boom as people made up for hard times since the early 1930s. The years 1950–53 saw the Korean War, and even with the end of the war demand hardly slackened because the economy was into the suburbanization-automobilization that by the midsixties had put almost two cars in every garage and built thousands of miles of interstate highways. By the end of the 1960s, another shooting war was going on, and the economy actually pushed unemployment below the 4 percent level. With the slowdown in military spending associated with the reduction in U.S. activities in Indochina came the sluggishness of the 1970s. This was counteracted with other kinds of government spending and the creation of mountains of consumer and corporate debt, but it was not enough. The economy slipped into stagnation, and the efforts to fight it only created inflation to go along with the basic problem. For this school, the economy is successful only so long as special events, usually military spending or wars, are counteracting the basic tendency of the economy to settle into stagnation.

18. The various writers in this tradition have presented different version of this post–World War II structure (see, for example, Bowles, Gordon, and Weisskopf, *After the Wasteland*, 48). The text presentation is my own version based on a reading from a variety of sources as well as discussions within the Center for Popular Economics on the postwar period. The main difference between this group and the Baran-Sweezy stagnation school is that the latter sees the economy as always in danger of falling into a stagnant or worse situation absent extraordinary surges in aggregate demand. The long-swing group suggests that when a coherent structure, a social structure of accumulation, is in place, the economy generates a fairly long period of decent growth with short, mild interruptions.

19. *ERP* 1994, 320, 323.

20. In 1953, an American CIA operative led a joint British-American effort to overthrow the elected Iranian government, which had moved to nationalize international oil companies. That government was replaced by a monarchy headed by the shah. In 1954, the elected government of Guatemala had attempted to nation-

alize some of the land owned by the United Fruit Company. Under cover of protecting the hemisphere from Communist influence (the Guatemalans had bought some military equipment from Czechoslovakia), the United States again organized a coup (Bowles, Gordon, and Weisskopf, *After the Wasteland,* 50–51). See also Kermit Roosevelt, *Countercoup: The Struggle for the Control of Iran* (New York: McGraw-Hill, 1979); and Steven Schlesinger and Steven Kinzer, *Bitter Fruit* (Garden City, NY: Doubleday, 1982).

21. The stagnation school, by contrast, believes that the economy had just run out of causes for surges in aggregate demand, and so the natural tendency to stagnation reasserted itself.

22. Arthur Okun, *Prices and Quantities: A Macroeconomic Analysis* (Washington, DC: Brookings Institution, 1981), 83–126. On pp. 127–30 he analyzes the inflationary bias that collective bargaining may add to the process.

23. Gary Bryner, president, Local 1112, United Auto Workers, qtd. in Studs Terkel *Working* (New York: Pantheon Books, 1974), 192–93.

Chapter 5

1. The rate of increase in the GDP deflator had averaged 6.3 percent in 1977 and 7.7 percent in 1978. In 1979, the first three quarters saw the annual rate of inflation rise to 8.6 percent and stay at 8.7 percent for the next two (*ERP* 1997, 306). Quarterly rates from Bureau of Economic Analysis, Department of Commerce.

2. *ERP* 1997, 422.

3. The best measure of the international value of the dollar compared to our major trading partners actually rose slightly between 1973 and 1976 before beginning to plummet (*ERP* 1997, 422).

4. The price of gold is per troy ounce. The monthly series for the price of gold is published by *Metals Week* and available from the Branch of Metals, U.S. Bureau of Mines.

5. The printout of monthly gold prices from the U.S. Bureau of Mines has the highest, lowest, and average price of a troy ounce of gold per month beginning in 1968 and continuing up to the present. Robert Bartley, quoting Roy W. Jastram, noted that "when one nation shows economic and political turbulence, its currency will decline as holders seek safe havens in other currencies. 'But what happens when danger is sensed in every direction? There is one "currency" with no indigenous difficulties—gold. The cautionary demand for it is really a short position against all national currencies'" (Bartley, *The Seven Fat Years and How to Do It Again* [New York: Free Press, 1992], 109). Meanwhile, the *Monthly Review,* operating in the radical tradition, published an editorial identifying the spike in the price of gold as "Capitalism's Fever Chart" ("Gold Mania: Capitalism's Fever Chart," *Monthly Review,* January 1980, 1–8).

6. *ERP* 1996, 280.

7. Greider, *Secrets of the Temple,* 109–16.

8. Greider, *Secrets of the Temple,* 109–23. Interestingly, in other analyses of the Fed's policy reversal, much emphasis is placed on Volcker's trip to an international bankers' conference in Belgrade, Yugoslavia, which occurred *after* the decision of the Board of Governors but *before* the ratification of that decision by the Federal Open Market Committee. This has led some commentators to suggest that

Volcker was responding to pressure from foreign central bankers, which of course was not true, since the decision had already been made. See, for example, Bartley, *The Seven Fat Years*, 85–86 and Blinder, *Economic Policy and the Great Stagflation*, 77.

9. "Statement by Paul A. Volcker, Chairman, Board of Governors of the Federal Reserve System, before the Joint Economic Committee of the U.S. Congress, October 17, 1979," *Federal Reserve Bulletin* 65 (November 1979): 889.

10. Both nominal and real Federal Funds rates 1970–91 are collected in table W-1 at the book's web site, <www.mars.wnec.edu/~econ/surrender>.

11. Actually, these yearly figures mask some significant variations during the year. In 1980, in particular, the rate of growth of money started out at 6.7 percent (last quarter of 1979 to first quarter of 1980) but then turned negative as the economy experienced a sharp but very short (one-quarter) recession (the rate was −3.4 percent). The shrinkage of the money supply was not, of course, what the Federal Reserve had promised when it adopted monetarism. In response, the Fed shifted to an expansionary monetary policy. The rate of growth of money shot up to 15 percent in the third quarter before subsiding to 10.9 percent in the fourth. By the first quarter of 1981, the rate of growth had fallen further to 4.6 percent. Data of the Federal Funds rate and the money supply (M1) available directly from the Board of Governors of the Federal Reserve System.

12. "Monetary Report to Congress," *Federal Reserve Bulletin* 66 (March 1980): 177.

13. *ERP* 1994, 347. This is evidence for the charge by Greider and others that the so-called monetarist experiment was merely a political cover for interest rates high enough to wring inflation out of the economy no matter how much unemployment would be necessary. Interest rates rose high enough to get the job done, and it didn't matter whether the growth rate of M2 or M3 slowed.

14. Beginning at 13.82 percent in January 1980, it rose to 17.61 percent in April, then fell to 9.03 percent in July (the second quarter was the time when there was a short but sharp recession), before rising to a peak of 19.08 percent in January 1981. Over the next two months it fell to 14.70 percent before rising to 19.1 percent in June. Monthly averages for the Federal Funds rate are available from the Federal Reserve Board, table J1–1. For a quarterly time series of the Federal Funds rate, see table W-1 at the web site.

15. Federal Reserve Board, table J1–1.

16. *ERP* 1997, 377.

17. Using annual data, both the consumer price index and the GDP implicit price deflator had the highest rate of increase in 1980 (*ERP* 1997, 306, 369). Using quarterly data, the first quarter of 1981 experienced the highest rate of increase in the implicit price deflator (*Survey of Current Business*, September 1993, 54), while for the consumer price index (urban consumers) the first quarter of 1980 experienced the highest rate of increase (Bureau of Labor Statistics, Consumer Price Index All Urban Consumers, U.S. city average 1982–84 = 100).

18. *ERP* 1984, 299. The prime rate is the interest rate banks charge their best business customers. The mortgage rate listed here is for a conventional mortgage with a ten-year repayment period.

19. The "true" real interest rate must somehow create a measure of the *expected* rate of inflation that the "average" borrower and lender have agreed

upon when making the "average" loan agreement. There are a number of conventions that have been established to measure the expected rate of inflation. One of the simplest is to take the average of the preceding three years and assume that that is what borrowers and lenders expect inflation to be in the coming year(s). I have created such a table using the average inflation rate in the preceding twelve quarters for the "expected" rate of inflation in each quarter. In effect this attempts to measure what borrowers and lenders *believe* to be the real interest rate upon which they are agreeing. One might think of this as the planned real interest rate. To measure the actual impact on the economy of the real interest rate, I believe it is useful to concentrate on the actual burden of interest in terms of lost purchasing power. Thus, I also measure the real interest rates by subtracting the actual inflation rate in each quarter from the nominal interest rate. One might think of this as the experienced real interest rate. The inflation rate used in the appendix and throughout this book when identifying the real interest rate is the rate of increase in the GDP implicit price deflator unless otherwise noted. I choose this over the better-known consumer price index because we are looking for the generalized impact of inflation on interest rates throughout the entire economy, not just on consumers. It should be noted that no matter which way we attempt to measure real interest rates, there will always be limitations. Every individual experiences inflation differently because each person buys different types of products and "sells" different types of products, all of whose prices are changing at different rates than the average, no matter how that average is measured.

Both versions of the real interest rate peaked in 1981, fell during the recession, and then rose in 1984 as the Fed demonstrated its commitment to keeping inflation in check long before unemployment got anywhere near the 1980s version of the "natural" rate—6 percent. See tables W-2 and W-3 at the web site for details, <mars.wnec.edu/~econ/surrender>.

20. Bartley, *The Seven Fat Years,* 145; Greider, *The Secrets of the Temple,* 155–80.

21. A supply curve plots alternative prices against the quantities of the good or service businesses are willing and able to provide based on the scarcity of the resources involved. If the true scarcity of all resources used in a production process, including some, such as air and water, that aren't bought by the producers, is accurately reflected in the costs to the businesses, we can say that the supply curve accurately measures the *sacrifice* made by society in producing the various quantities of that product. The demand curve plots alternative prices against the quantities of a good or service consumers are willing and able to purchase. If the true satisfaction derived by the consumer is accurately reflected in the price he/she is willing and able to pay, *and* if there are no spillover costs and/or benefits to non-involved consumers, then we can say that the demand curve accurately measures the *satisfaction* experienced by society in consuming the various quantities of that product. Note that the "ifs" about true scarcities and absence of externalities conceal a whole host of exceptions, as even the Reagan administration's first Council of Economic Advisers acknowledged (see pp. 39–41). For supply-and-demand curves, see any textbook on the principles of economics. For example, Mankiw, *Principles of Economics,* chap. 4, and Stiglitz, *Economics,* chap. 4, devote entire chapters to introducing these concepts.

22. A minimum wage does not permit the price to fall to its equilibrium. This deprives some of the "suppliers" (in this case workers) of the opportunity to offer

their labor for sale at a wage they would be willing to accept. It also deprives some "consumers" (in this case businesses seeking to hire workers) of the ability to purchase some wage-labor at a wage they would be willing to pay. The result is an artificial reduction in the amount of labor hired and, therefore, a reduction in output. This was the major argument developed by the members of Congress, such as Majority Leader Richard Armey, himself a Ph.D. economist, against the recent increase in the minimum wage.

Table N-5 is an imagined table of alternative wages and quantities of labor offered for sale restaurants by workers and desired to be hired by businesses (the "quantity" is measured in person-hours per week). Let us assume this labor market refers to fast-food restaurants, a typical job for low-wage workers. If the minimum wage were to be set at $5.50 per hour or higher, a significant number of individuals will attempt to find work and will either be hired for fewer hours than they want or will not be hired at all. Only at the "market wage" of $5.00 an hour in this imaginary example will all workers who want to work at that wage find work. Raising that wage to $6.00 per hour would cause businesses to cut back hiring from six hundred hours a week to five hundred hours, thereby causing some people to lose their jobs. For two textbook treatments of the minimum wage, see Mankiw, *Principles of Economics,* 118–20, and Stiglitz, *Economics,* 828, 833.

23. Greider, *Secrets of the Temple,* 177.

24. Bartley, *The Seven Fat Years,* 224.

25. *ERP* 1982, 23.

26. "President's News Conference on Foreign and Domestic Affairs," *New York Times,* February 19, 1982, 20.

27. *ERP* 1982, 23.

28. *ERP* 1982, 109.

29. U.S. House of Representatives, Committee on Ways and Means, "Overview of Entitlement Programs," *1993 Green Book: Data on Programs within the Jurisdiction of the Committee on Ways, and Means* (Washington, DC: Government Printing Office, 1993), 1497.

30. *1993 Green Book,* 1528–29.

31. See C. Eugene Steuerle, *The Tax Decade: How Taxes Came to Dominate the Public Agenda* (Washington, DC: Urban Institute Press, 1992), 186–87.

32. *ERP* 1982, 141.

33. *ERP* 1982, 142.

34. Paul R. Portney, "Natural Resources and the Environment: More Controversy Than Change," in *The Reagan Record,* ed. John L. Palmer and Isabel V. Sawhill (Cambridge: Ballinger Publishing, 1984), 146–47.

35. To take a fairly extreme example, the Birmingham, Alabama, fire department didn't hire its first black firefighter until 1968. A seven-year lawsuit between 1974 and 1981 finally ended with the city entering a consent decree (like a plea bargain in a civil lawsuit). To remedy the effects of past discrimination, the city agreed that if any black candidates for either appointment or promotion were qualified, all hiring and promotion would have to be split fifty-fifty between whites and blacks.

In 1983, two firefighters took the exam for lieutenant. Both passed. Under the consent decree the black firefighter got the promotion. The problem was that though both passed the exam, the white firefighter got the higher score. Right here we see one of the cores to the battle over affirmative action. By the standards of the

TABLE N-5. Supply and Demand for Low-Wage Labor (invented data for illustrative purposes)

Wage Rate	Person-Hours Demanded per Week	Person-Hours Supplied per Week
$6.50/hr	400	900
$6.00/hr	500	800
$5.50/hr	600	700
$5.00/hr	650	650
$4.50/hr	700	600
$4.00/hr	800	700

job, both men were qualified. According to the supporters of the white firefighter, the scores on the test showed who was more qualified. The fact that there had been previous discrimination was irrelevant to the alleged injustice done to the white individual involved. From the other point of view, once the individuals involved are judged capable of doing the job, basic fairness involves permitting black candidates for jobs and/or promotion to be compensated for the disadvantages illegally imposed on people like them in the past. People who have higher test scores today are building on the ill-gotten gains of past discrimination (Thomas B. Edsall and Mary D. Edsall, *Chain Reaction: The Impact of Race, Rights, and Taxes on American Politics* [New York: Norton, 1992], 125–26). There is one other extremely important issue that builds strong support for affirmative action policies, even in the 1990s. That is the view that the desire to discriminate on the basis of race and gender has not disappeared just because it has been made illegal. In order to *force* decision makers to behave in a nondiscriminatory manner, some program needs to be in place. The victims of current discrimination cannot rely on goodwill and/or inability to cover up discriminatory behavior to protect their rights in the job market.

36. Ibid., 188.

37. Ibid., 191.

38. D. Lee Bawden and John L. Palmer, "Social Policy: Challenging the Welfare State," in Palmer and Sawhill, *The Reagan Record,* 204.

39. Ibid., 205.

40. This is not the place to engage in a detailed debate about affirmative action. Two very significant affirmative action cases were decided by the Supreme Court in the late 1970s. For the legal issues and facts, see "Regents of the University of California v. Bakke," *Preview of United States Supreme Court Cases,* October 1977 Term, No. 4 (September 26, 1977), 1–3; and "United States Steelworkers of America v. Weber," "Kaiser Aluminum & Chemical Corp. v. Weber," and "United States v. Weber," *Preview of United States Supreme Court Cases,* October 1978 term, no. 31 (April 5, 1979), 1–3. The important issue is to understand that regardless of whether affirmative action programs are a good idea or not, having the chief civil-rights enforcement organizations in the country more concerned with fighting "reverse discrimination" against white people than with remedying the sorry state of affairs for black Americans sends a powerful message to those

who have always resented civil-rights enforcement and the businesses who have always resented any government intrusion into how they conduct themselves.

41. *ERP* 1980, 118–19.

42. *ERP* 1982, 163–64. See also William Niskanen, *Reaganomics: An Insider's Account of the Policies and the People* (New York: Oxford University Press, 1988), 119–20. Note, however, that in this book Niskanen voices some complaints about regulatory changes that were blocked. Particularly interesting is the following comment:

> In 1983, the FCC proposed to relax the "financial interest and syndication rules," which restrict the right of the TV networks to develop original programming and to syndicate reruns. These rules in effect protect Hollywood from competition by the networks. Although this proposal was broadly supported within the administration, the "California mafia" in the White House ruled in favor of Hollywood, and the proposal was withdrawn. (120)

43. In real (1987) dollars, the total regulation budget went from $4 billion in 1970 to $8.31 billion in 1981. In 1984, the number was $8.23 billion (a 1.0 percent decline) (Melinda Warren, "Mixed Message: An Analysis of the 1994 Federal Regulatory Budget," Occasional Paper 128, Center for the Study of American Business, Washington University, St. Louis, 1994, 6).

44. 53.6 percent in 1970, 56.7 percent in 1975, 55.7 percent in 1980 (*1993 Green Book,* 616).

45. See ibid., 619, for the changes in the rules. For the numerical example, see p. 621.

46. Ibid., 738.

47. Ibid., 1312–13.

48. By contrast, the percentage of individuals in poverty receiving AFDC was 42.8 percent in 1975. Three years later that percentage stood at 42.4 percent (ibid., 471, 1225).

49. Ibid., 1622.

50. Ibid., 1632.

51. Table N-6 shows the participation in the food stamp program in absolute numbers and as percentages of the total population as well as the population living in poverty between 1975 and 1991.

52. Palmer and Sawhill, *The Reagan Record,* 370.

53. Teresa A. Coughlin, Leighton Ku, and John Holahan, *Medicaid since 1980: Costs, Coverage, and the Shifting Alliance between the Federal Government and the States* (Washington, DC: Urban Institute Press, 1994), 20. According to the *1993 Green Book,* 1659, the per capita real dollar spending on children and AFDC adults declined from 1981 through 1984. This was at a time where other areas of Medicaid expenditure were rising in real terms, so that the overall per capita real spending rose over 9 percent.

54. Palmer and Sawhill, *The Reagan Record,* 370.

> Since 1981, the administration has proposed more cuts in Medicaid, including an extension of reduced matching payments and a requirement that states charge beneficiaries at least a nominal amount for services received. Congress has rejected most of these proposed cuts because they would shift costs to the states or reduce service to the poor.

TABLE N-6.   Food Stamps Utilization, 1975–91

Year	Number of Food Stamp Participants (in millions)	Food Stamp Participation (% of total population)	Food Stamp Participation (% of poor population)
1975	16.3	7.6	63.0
1976	17.0	7.9	68.1
1977	15.6	7.2	63.1
1978	14.4	6.5	58.8
1979	15.9	7.2	61.0
1980	19.2	8.4	65.6
1981	20.6	9.0	64.7
1982	20.4	8.8	59.3
1983	21.6	9.2	61.2
1984	20.9	8.8	62.0
1985	19.9	8.3	60.2
1986	19.4	8.0	59.9
1987	19.1	7.8	59.1
1988	18.7	7.6	58.9
1989	18.8	7.6	59.6
1990	20.0	8.0	59.8
1991	22.6	9.0	63.3

Source: 1993 Green Book, 1622.

Note the use of the term *gross national product* rather than GDP. GNP differs from GDP only slightly. It adds to GDP the income Americans earn abroad and subtracts from GDP the income foreigners earn in the United States. American national income accounts shifted from GNP to GDP in 1992, so researchers who wrote before then used gross national product as their measure of total national output.

55. Robert B. Carlson and Kevin R. Hopkins, "Whose Responsibility Is Social Responsibility?" *Public Welfare* 39 (fall 1981): 10, qtd. in Bawden and Palmer, "Social Policy," 192n. This rather vague definition obscures a centuries-long debate as to who constitutes the "truly needy." For a historical survey, see Richard A. Cloward and Frances Fox Piven, "The Historical Sources of the Contemporary Relief Debate," in Fred Block, Richard A. Cloward, Barbara Ehrenreich and Frances Fox Piven, *The Mean Season: The Attack on the Welfare State* (New York: Pantheon Books, 1987), 3–43. In practice, since the beginning of the Reagan administration "truly needy" has come to refer to people who are not physically or mentally able to work.

56. *1993 Green Book,* 867.

57. Ibid., 836–37.

58. Bawden and Palmer, "Social Policy," 201.

59. *1993 Green Book,* 66.

60. Ibid., 70.

61. The percentage of unemployed workers receiving compensation averaged 50 percent in 1974, 76 percent in 1975, and 67 percent in 1976, the first full year of recovery (ibid., 491).

62. The percentages in 1981 and 1983 were 41 and 44 percent respectively (ibid., 491).

63. In addition to the explicit changes in federal government policy, there were a number of changes adopted that encouraged states to tighten eligibility. For details, see Marc Baldwin and Richard McHugh, "Unprepared for Recession: The Erosion of State Unemployment Insurance Coverage Fostered by Public Policy in the 1980s," Briefing Paper, Economy Policy Institute, 1992, esp. 4–7.

64. See *ERP* 1982, 33–34, for an analysis of why government "insurance" against low or no income is necessary because private-sector insurance will always leave some group uninsured as "bad risks."

65. Martin Feldstein, "Social Security, Induced Retirement and Aggregate Accumulation," *Journal of Political Economy* 82 (1974): 905–25. See in rebuttal Dean Leimer and Selig Lesnoy, "Social Security and Private Saving: New Time-Series Evidence," *Journal of Political Economy* 90 (1982): 606–29; and Robert Eisner, "Social Security, Saving, and Macroeconomics," *Journal of Macroeconomics* 5 (1983): 1–19.

66. David Stockman, *The Triumph of Politics: Why the Reagan Revolution Failed* (New York: Harper and Row, 1986), 181–93. See also Niskanen, *Reaganomics,* 37–38.

67. *1993 Green Book,* 30–35. According to estimates from 1994, the retirement trust fund of the Social Security system will begin running deficits in 2015 and will have absorbed all of the built-up surplus by the year 2036 (C. Eugene Steuerle and Jon M. Bakija, *Reforming Social Security for the 21st Century* [Washington, DC: Urban Institute Press, 1994], 51). These estimates change with every report from the trustees of the Social Security system. More recent reports place the year when deficits will begin earlier and the exhaustion of the surpluses significantly earlier than 2036.

68. Bawden and Palmer, "Social Policy," 191.

69. Steuerle and Bakija, *Reforming Social Security,* 237.

70. For the Medicare spending, see *1996 Green Book,* 133–34. For Social Security spending and total federal spending see *ERP* 1997, 391, 389. (Once again, these are fiscal years.)

71. Bawden and Palmer, "Social Policy," 191. For details, see *1993 Green Book,* 147–48. Note that the data presented in the table on p. 235 in the *1996 Green Book* is clearly in error. A spending reduction of less than one-half billion dollars resulting from the change in hospital reimbursement is much too low. Similarly, the changes from the 1982 Tax Equity and Fiscal Responsibility Act described on pp. 223–25 could not have ended up reducing expenditures by $23 billion between 1983 and 1987, in part because the changes in the 1983 bill superseded the hospital reimbursement changes in the 1982 act.

72. For calendar years 1980–83, the actual level of intergovernmental grants was $88.7, $87.9, $83.9, $87.0. Note that this is in a context of a rising overall federal budget (*ERP* 1994, 365). By contrast, such grants rose in absolute terms in both 1974 and 1975 (*ERP* 1980, 289).

73. George E. Peterson, "Federalism and the States: An Experiment in Decentralization," in Palmer and Sawhill, *The Reagan Record,* 219–20.

74. Ibid., 224.

75. Table N-7 shows the relationship of individual and corporate income tax receipts to gross domestic product from 1979 to 1985. Ignoring the recession years of 1981 and 1982 and the first recovery year of 1983, even in 1984 and 1985, the ratio

TABLE N-7. Decline in Individual and Corporate Tax Collections as Percentage of GDP as a Result of ERTA

Fiscal Year	GDP (in billions of dollars)	Individual Income Tax Receipts	Corporate Income Tax Receipts	Total Income Tax Receipts (% of GDP)
1978	2,212.6	181.0	60.0	10.9
1979	2,495.0	217.8	65.7	11.4
1980	2,718.9	244.1	54.6	11.0
1981	3,049.1	285.9	61.1	11.4
1982	3,211.3	297.7	49.2	10.8
1983	3,421.9	288.9	37.0	9.5
1984	3,812.0	298.4	56.9	9.3
1985	4,102.1	334.5	61.3	9.7

Source: ERP 1997, 389, 391.

of income tax collections to GDP had remained a full percentage point lower than in 1978 and 1980 and one and a half percent lower than in 1979.

Chapter 6

1. *ERP* 1997, 389. Recall (see above, pp. 23–24) that the absolute level of the budget deficit does not tell us anything about its impact on aggregate demand. For that we need to express it as a percentage of GDP.

2. As noted in note 54 to the previous chapter, the Department of Commerce switched from gross national product to gross domestic product for their measurement of total economic activity. However, the Bureau of Economic Analysis tables for the fixed-unemployment GNP have not been so transformed.

3. Data supplied by the Bureau of Economic Analysis, Government Division, Department of Commerce, calculations by Michael Webb. The calculation is based on government expenditures and revenues calculated using the rules of payments and taxation and applying those rules to the estimated GNP with 6 percent unemployment. The structural deficit so calculated continued to rise through 1985. See table W-1 at this book's data web site, <mars.wnec.edu/~econ/surrender>.

4. Though we are here focusing on the federal deficit, it is important to note that the actual impact on aggregate demand is created by the total government deficit (or surplus). In table W-1 at the web site, a series of the total government deficit/surplus as a percentage of GDP is included along with the structural deficit as a percentage of gross national product.

5. Monthly money stock information is available from the Federal Reserve Board. See table W-1 at the web site for quarterly data on the rate of growth of M1.

6. This is not, of course, how the strong defenders of the incentive policies of the Reagan administration see it.

With the Phillips curve, the Keynesians found themselves trying to hit two birds [inflation and unemployment] with one stone. To fight inflation, you needed one lever. And to fight stagflation, you need a second one. . . . the answer was clear: You fight inflation with monetary policy. . . . And you fight stagnation, you stimulate the economy, with incentive-directed tax cuts. (Bartley, *The Seven Fat Years,* 59)

7. I don't want to be misunderstood. I personally believe that the pain and suffering inflicted on people during a recession is a terrible blot on our economic system. For some impressionistic details, see Greider, *Secrets of the Temple,* 450–71. The reason I choose not to belabor this issue is that from the point of view of long-run policy, the success or failure of the Reagan-Volcker program is to be judged not by the existence of the recession but by the nature of the recovery. Those are the terms on which the architects of the policy wished to be judged, and those are the terms on which history must make the judgment.

8. See Isabel V. Sawhill and Charles F. Stone, "The Economy, the Key to Success," in Palmer and Sawhill, *The Reagan Record,* 82–90, for some simulations of how a different policy mix might have avoided the depth and severity of the recession and still brought inflation down (though not as far down as actual policy). See also Blinder, *Hard Heads, Soft Hearts,* 79.

9. For details of this point of view, see Bowles, Gordon, and Weisskopf, *After the Wasteland,* 80–96.

10. This concept is explained fully in the useful textbook *Understanding Capitalism,* by Samuel Bowles and Richard Edwards (New York: Harper Collins, 1993), 433–39.

11. See, for example, Bowles, Gordon, and Weisskopf, *After the Wasteland,* 187–233.

12. For example, in his account of the Reagan years Robert Bartley of the *Wall Street Journal* argued that the recession was caused by a failure to concentrate the supply-side incentives in the first year of the Economic Recovery Tax Act, coupled with the Federal Reserve's inconsistent monetary policy. Bartley would have preferred a "commodity" standard to anchor the value of the dollar rather than the restrictive monetary policies of Volcker's Fed. See Bartley, *The Seven Fat Years,* 103–33.

13. For example, despite the very low unemployment rates in 1967 and 1968, the federal deficit as a percentage of GDP only reached 2.9 percent in fiscal 1968. See *ERP* 1997, 390.

14. If we are interested in the impact of policy, the structural deficit of the federal government is important. However, if we want to observe the impact on aggregate demand, we have to observe the actual deficit of all levels of government, federal, state, and local. Thus, in table W-1 at the web site we have tracked the total government deficit as a percentage of GDP.

15. These are calculations of the after-the-fact real interest rate. The real rate generated with a series of expected rates of inflation shows a similar qualitative difference in general between the post-1983 years and the period of the 1970s, but it does experience high levels in both 1970 (averaging 3.23 percent) and 1974 (averaging 5.03 percent). The rate of growth of the money supply tells a different story. Except for 1984, the rate of growth of M1 was quite high from the abandonment of monetarism in the last quarter of 1982 through 1986. Beginning in 1987, the Fed tightened up on the rate of growth of money. What is interesting is that through most of the decade of the 1980s, the impact of the rate of growth of money on the

real interest rate and on the rate of growth of nominal GDP was hard to identify. For quarterly details, see table W-1 at the web site, <mars.wnec.edu/~econ/surrender>, for the rate of growth of M1 and the after-the-fact measure of the real interest rate. Tables W-2 and W-3 at the web site have two measures of the expectations-generated real interest rate.

16. Congressional Budget Office, *Defense Spending and the Economy* (Washington, DC: Government Printing Office, February, 1983), 35–36.

17. This decision and the White House and bond market reactions are reported in Greider, *Secrets of the Temple,* 611–24.

18. (*ERP* 1986, 292). Note that these figures are percentages of the entire labor force and are therefore not completely comparable to the figures in table W-4 on the web site because those figures are for the civilian labor force only.

19. Steuerle, *The Tax Decade,* 42.

20. Ibid., 186. For GDP, see *ERP* 1997, 300.

21. Steuerle, *The Tax Decade,* 186. For details see pp. 58–61.

22. Interestingly, Steuerle argues that part of the reason those first efforts failed was not merely that Social Security had a strong and politically potent constituency.

> During 1981, the administration held some internal meetings on Social Security reform: with some political officials from the White House, the Department of Health and Human Services and the Social Security Administration. In attendance were many new political appointees with strong but sometimes unchecked views on what was wrong with the system. The newcomers were so distrustful of the entire civil service that they prevented many of the most talented individuals in the executive branch, including top analysts from the Social Security Administration, from attending these meetings. Valuable information was thereby precluded through inadequate use of staff. The controversy that surrounded the proposals that were tentatively released, therefore, was due not simply to the difficulty and sacredness of the Social Security issue; it was also due to bad planning and the forwarding of some poorly designed proposals. (*The Tax Decade,* 62)

23. This last item ultimately reduced payments by $39.4 billion between 1983 and 1989. This may seem strange because it is only a onetime delay. However, if there had been no delay, the cost-of-living increase would have been paid six months early *every year after 1983 as well.* Thus, the total cost of the delay to the recipients (and thus the savings to the Social Security trust funds) adds up year after year. See *1993 Green Book,* 34. See also Steuerle, *The Tax Decade,* 62–63.

24. See *1993 Green Book,* 30–31, for data and some numerical examples.

25. John H. Makin and Norman J. Ornstein, *Debt and Taxes* (New York: Times Books, Random House, 1994), 222–23.

26. *1993 Green Book,* 34. Focusing only on tax increases, not benefit changes, Steuerle comes up with the number $110.5 billion (*The Tax Decade,* 65). Steuerle's total is approximately $20 billion lower than the *1993 Green Book*'s figure, but since he used the 1990 *Green Book,* I assume the figure in the text to be more accurate.

27. See Steuerle, *The Tax Decade,* 49, for an example of how a 9 percent real loss on an investment could translate into a positive profit of 3 percent for a tax-

payer who borrowed the money, depreciated the asset at the accelerated post-1981 rate, and took the investment tax credit. Steuerle also notes that by 1984

> "tax straddles" . . . had become too popular for the legislature to ignore anymore. A person could essentially buy and sell rights to future commodities in a way that created equal gains and losses—like flipping a coin and betting on both heads and tails. The taxpayer would then take losses on whichever "leg" of the straddle generated a loss, use that loss to offset other capital gains that otherwise would be taxable, and then defer recognition of the "leg" with a gain to future years. (67)

28. Ibid., 92.
29. Ibid., 186.
30. Ibid., 112.
31. Ibid., 122.
32. The effective rate of taxation is defined as the ratio of actual taxes paid to the broadly defined tax base (ignoring preferences for the moment). Recall that the rate of inflation changes the real value of the depreciation allowances as well as the real value of interest deductions. (See ibid., 151, for some alternative calculations at different inflation rates.) Other variations in effective tax rates have to do with whether or not the particular industry devotes most of its investment dollars to equipment purchases that would then trigger the investment tax credit.
33. Under pre-1986 law, the capital-gains exclusion would have made only forty thousand dollars taxable, in this case *overcorrecting* for inflation.
34. Steuerle, *The Tax Decade,* 145
35. Bartley, *The Seven Fat Years,* 157.
36. The original idea of the Tax Reform Act was to have two positive rates as well as a "zero bracket." These rates ended up being 15 percent and 28 percent. However, to raise more revenue, at a certain level of income (seventy thousand dollars in 1987, thereafter indexed for inflation), the benefits of the zero bracket and lower rate of 15 percent were phased out at the rate of 5 percent of income over that threshold. This had the effect of raising the marginal tax rate temporarily to 33 percent until all the benefits of the zero bracket and 15 percent rate had disappeared. At that point (in 1987 at an income of $127,000, thereafter indexed) the marginal tax rate reverted to 28 percent.
37. This changed the definition of "long-term" capital gains from one year to a year and a half. Allegedly this was designed to reduce the tax advantage for purely speculative investments—to give the preference to those making some kind of a "commitment" to their investments. See "Highlights of Some Provisions Covering Taxes and Tax Credits, Capital Gains," *New York Times,* July 30, 1997, A16.
38. Murray Weidenbaum, *Rendezvous with Reality: The American Economy after Reagan* (New York: Basic Books, 1988), 9.
39. Niskanen, *Reaganomics,* 125.
40. Real spending levels were $8.23 billion in 1984, $8.42 billion in 1985, $8.23 billion in 1986, $8.99 billion in 1987, $9.56 billion in 1988, and $9.73 billion in 1989 (Warren, "Mixed Message," 25).
41. Coughlin, Ku, and Holahan, *Medicaid since 1980,* 104.
42. *ERP* 1989, 196.
43. *ERP* 1989, 198.
44. *Contract with America,* 135. See also the arguments on pp. 139–41.

45. See p. 207 and pp. 212–14 for a discussion of the Bush administration's activities in this area.

46. In the first four months under the 1984 law, the AFDC grant would be cut 43 cents for every dollar of earnings. During the next eight months, the benefit reduction rate climbs to 63 cents out of every dollar. This is lower than the cut under OBRA, 1981, but it is still high enough to reduce the monthly cash grant in the median state to zero. After twelve months on welfare, the grant is reduced by approximately 70 cents for every dollar of earnings. Under the 1988 law, each of these rates is slightly reduced. The numbers are 36, 62, and 67 cents per dollar of benefits for the same three durations. Again, after four months the net benefits in the median state have been reduced to zero (*1993 Green Book*, 621).

47. Ibid., 625. See pp. 630–33 for details on which states offered which programs as of 1993. For participation requirements, see pp. 627 28.

48. Ibid., 640–44.

49. Ibid., 668.

50. *1996 Green Book*, 467.

51. *1993 Green Book*, 688.

52. Table N-8 shows the percentages for 1984 through 1990.

53. Gary Burtless, "Effects on Labor Supply," in *The Economic Legacy of the Reagan Years: Euphoria or Chaos?* ed. Anandi Sahu and Ronald Tracy (New York: Praeger, 1991), 58. The data is collected in a table on p. 57.

54. *Contract with America*, 65–77. See also *Restoring the Dream*, 53, 163–72.

55. For the trend in the poverty threshold for different-sized families, see *1993 Green Book*, 1310. By 1989, the three-person family needed $9,885 per year to escape from poverty, over 40 percent above the income of a year-round, full-time worker receiving minimum wage.

56. Ibid., 1630: "The across-the-board benefit increase in maximum benefits (above normal inflation adjustments) called for by the act was 0 65 percent in fiscal year 1989, 2.05 percent in fiscal year 1990, and 3 percent in later years."

57. For data on enrollment and expenditures by eligibility groups, see Coughlin, Ku, and Holahan, *Medicaid since 1980*, 20–21.

58. Ibid., 35.

59. Ibid., 46–53.

60. Ibid., 58–59.

61. For details see *1993 Green Book*, 261–62, especially the footnote on p. 261.

62. See Coughlin, Ku, and Holahan, *Medicaid since 1980*, 105.

63. Medicaid was $78.2 billion in 1990. National spending on nursing-home care was $53.3, of which approximately 47 percent was paid by Medicaid (*1993 Green Book*, 266, 1647, and 259). Elsewhere the *Green Book* gives a percentage of 27 percent of Medicaid spending for fiscal 1991. This is lower than the figure in the text because it excludes nursing homes for the retarded. Whatever the percentage, the following information is quite relevant: "In 1991, Medicaid nursing home payments amounted to 60 per cent of total Medicaid payments for all services for all elderly beneficiaries" (ibid., 261).

64. For the Medicare spending, see *1996 Green Book*, 134. For Social Security spending and total federal spending see *ERP* 1997, 391, 389.

65. This result was obtained by comparing the average annual benefit per aged person in 1980 and 1990 (*1993 Green Book*, 138) and deflating both numbers by the consumer price index (*ERP* 1995, 341). The more rapid escalation in the costs

TABLE N-8. Aid to Families with Dependent Children, Coverage of All Poor and Coverage of Poor Children, 1984–90

Year	AFDC Caseload (in millions)	AFDC Caseload (% of population in poverty)	Children on AFDC Caseload (in millions)	Children on AFDC Caseload (% of children in poverty)
1984	10,645	31.6	7,017	52.3
1985	10,672	32.3	7,074	54.4
1986	10,850	33.5	7,206	56.0
1987	10,841	33.5	7,240	55.9
1988	10,915	34.4	7,328	58.8
1989	10,799	34.2	7,287	57.9
1990	11,699	34.8	7,922	59.0

Source: *1993 Green Book*, 688, 1312.

of Part B should not be surprising, since hospital reimbursements had been subject to a form of price controls since 1983. This result also demonstrates one of the problems health care policymakers began to discover during the 1980s: price controls in one part of the system merely encourages price to rise all that more rapidly in other parts of the system. If we deflate the average annual benefit per aged person by the consumer price index for medical care, the real benefits still have risen, but by less than 10 percent for Medicare Part A and a bit less than 80 percent for Part B. This demonstrates that the rising price of medical care was not the only reason for increased spending, that there was an increase in the real amount of services delivered. Again, the difference between Part A cost increases and Part B relates to the imposition of price controls.

66. See *1993 Green Book*, 266.

67. In *Restoring the Dream*, 133—40, the Republican members of the House of Representatives describe how they will save Medicare from bankruptcy and offer senior citizens more choice than they now have while avoiding coercing Medicare beneficiaries "into mandatory health alliances such as those proposed in Clinton's 1994 health-care proposal." They do this without proposing any comprehensive health care reform, and in fact they imply that such a reform is unnecessary because "Market-based reforms have reduced the inflation rate in private-sector spending to 4.7 percent" (139). Republicans and Democrats did cooperate in passing a very modest health reform bill, the Kennedy-Kassebaum Act of 1996.

68. Robert Pear, "$24 Billion Would Be Set Aside for Medical Care for Children," *New York Times*, July 30, 1997, A17. This change would permit states to extend insurance to over 2 million previously uncovered children and retain coverage to over 1 million who would have lost Medicaid coverage as a result of the welfare law changes. See O'Neill, letter to Raines, 48–50.

69. *1993 Green Book*, 491.

70. Blinder, *Hard Head, Soft Hearts*, 103.

71. Ibid., 221n. 41.

72. Blinder claims that this occurred because of "accounting gimmicks and budget trickery that gave the appearance of compliance with Gramm-Rudman without the reality" (ibid., 104).

73. Automatic reductions occurred only if the budget as adopted projected a deficit $10 billion above the target set by the law during the first two weeks. An incorrect projection does not trigger the automatic cuts when it is proven wrong later in the fiscal year (*ERP* 1990, 70; see also Blinder, *Hard Heads, Soft Hearts,* 104).

74. "[I]f the projected deficit exceeds the target by more than [$10 billion] the Administration calculates automatic spending cuts (or sequester) needed in each program to meet the . . . deficit target. If legislation does not achieve this reduction by the end of the second week of the fiscal year, the President orders a sequester" (*ERP* 1990, 71).

75. Whereas the 1990 report of the president's Council of Economic Advisers described the workings of the Gramm-Rudman-Hollings Act (pp. 69–73), the 1991 report doesn't even mention it, focusing instead on the OBRA of November, 1990 (*ERP* 1991, 46–49).

76. It is important to note, however, that the Reagan administration made no moves toward a more competitive international trade stance. Despite the rhetoric of conservative economics in favor of "free trade," the administration supported the profitability of the top American industries, particularly the automobile industry, "presid[ing] over the greatest swing toward protectionism since the 1930s" (Shafiqul Islam, "Capitalism in Conflict," *Foreign Affairs* 69 (1990): 174). This judgment, which is echoed by the work of Patrick Low in *Trading Free* (New York: Twentieth Century Fund, 1993), 271, 270ff., is consistent with the view that the *real* role for government in our kind of society is to rig the market in favor of those who already have an advantage and that the "principles" of conservative economics that we identified in chapter 3 and that we have used as yardsticks for the Reagan administration's policy initiatives are routinely ignored whenever it serves the higher purpose of increasing the wealth and power of the already wealthy and powerful. Though I find significant evidence for this general point of view, I reiterate that the analysis of this book reaches a different conclusion. Whatever the motivations of policymakers and their intellectual supporters, the changes identified in the previous two chapters do constitute a qualitative shift in the role of government in the American economy. In addition, as we will see in the following chapters, despite the increase in protectionism, U.S. industry was subjected to increased international competitive pressure throughout the two Reagan terms.

Chapter 7

1. "The Real Reagan Record," *National Review,* August 31, 1992, 25–62.

2. Bartley, *The Seven Fat Years,* 141–42.

3. Jeffrey Davis and Kenneth Lehn, "Securities Regulation during the Reagan Administration: Corporate Takeovers and the 1987 Stock Market Crash," in Sahu and Tracy, *Economic Legacy of Reagan,* 8.

4. "Who Business Bosses Hate Most," *Fortune,* December 4, 1989, 107, qtd. in Bartley, *The Seven Fat Years,* 140.

5. Bartley, *The Seven Fat Years,* 140.

6. *ERP* 1985, 187–89. There remains a significant debate as to the long-run consequences for the actual productivity of firms that are successfully targeted for takeover. Compare Davis and Lehn, "Securities Regulation," 131–34, with Robert

T. Kleiman, "'Securities Regulation during the Reagan Administration': Comment," in Sahu and Tracy, *Economic Legacy of Reagan*, 141–42. See also William F. Long and David J. Ravenscraft, "Lessons from LBOs in the 1980s," in *The Deal Decade: What Takeovers and Leveraged Buyouts Mean for Corporate Governance*, ed. Margaret M. Blair (Washington, DC: Brookings Institution, 1993), 222–24.

7. *ERP* 1989, 39. Note again the reference to gross national product rather than GDP.

8. *ERP* 1989, 56–57.

9. *ERP* 1989, 62.

10. Note this differs from the depreciation businesses are permitted to deduct from taxable income. The government-measured capital consumption allowance is based on fixed service lives for each type of capital equipment in use and is measured by deducting the total value of the investment divided by that service life every year.

11. The unemployment rate fell from 9.4 percent in the third quarter of 1983 to 7.5 percent in the second quarter of 1984 (U.S. Department of Labor, Bureau of Labor Statistics, Current Population Survey). Real GDP per capita grew at the rates of 7.9 percent, 6.1 percent, 6.3 percent, 8.1 percent, and 5.2 percent from the second quarter of 1983 through the second quarter of 1984. Investment as a percentage of GDP rose from 14.3 percent in the first quarter of 1983 to 16.6 percent in the third quarter of 1984 (U.S. Department of Commerce, Bureau of Economic Analysis). For all the quarterly numbers, see table W-4 at the web site, <mars.wnec.edu/~econ/surrender>.

12. *ERP* 1997, 390.

13. For the quarterly Federal Funds rate, see table W-1 on the web site. Monthly rates available from the Federal Reserve Board, FFR, effective rate averages of daily figures, October 4, 1994, table J1–1 (monthly values of FFR 1964–September 1994). For the capacity utilization rate and unemployment rate, see table W-4 on the web site.

14. *ERP* 1989, 109.

15. *ERP* 1996, 280–81. It is also important to note that during this period, the macroeconomic policies pursued by our major trading partners, particularly West Germany and Japan, were much less expansionary. For details, see Robert Blecker, *Beyond the Twin Deficits: A Trade Strategy for the 1990s* (Armonk, NY: M. E. Sharpe, 1992), 37–40, especially the table on p. 39.

16. As Benjamin Friedman writes,

> The chief counterpart of our overconsumption in the 1980s has been underinvestment. On average during the prior three decades, we invested 3.3 percent of our total income in net additions to the stock of business plant and equipment. . . . Thus far [1987] during the 1980s, the average has been just 2.3 percent. (*Day of Reckoning: The Consequences of Economic Policy under Reagan and After* [New York: Random House, 1988], 28–29).

Note, however, that this decline in net investment is not matched completely by a decline in gross investment. See table 12.

17. *ERP* 1990, 70–71.

18. Friedman, *Day of Reckoning*, 174.

19. See table 11 for evidence as to whether or not this was in fact true.

20. "This idea of *permanent* or *irreversible* effects of a temporary exchange rate changes has become known as "hysteresis" . . . temporary but large appreciation of a nation's currency induces foreign firms to enter the domestic market as long as they can still make a profit over their operating costs in their own currency in spite of the home currency's depreciation. Thus the market structure of the home country is permanently altered" (Blecker, *Beyond the Twin Deficits,* 48). For a detailed model see Richard E. Baldwin, "Hysteresis in Import Prices: The Beachhead Effect," *American Economic Review* 78 (September 1988): 773–85.

21. Blecker, *Beyond the Twin Deficits,* 49.

22. See Friedman, *Day of Reckoning;* Peter Peterson, "The Morning After," *Atlantic Monthly,* 260 (October 1987): 43–69; Alice Rivlin, ed., *Economic Choices, 1984* (Washington, DC: Brookings Institution, 1984); and Henry J. Aaron et al., *Economic Choices, 1987* (Washington, DC: Brookings Institution, 1986).

23. The Federal Funds rate averaged below 7 percent in 1986 and 1987; the rate of growth of M1 went from a low of 5.7 percent in 1984 to 12.4 percent and 17 percent in 1985 and 1986 respectively before falling back to 3.5 percent in 1987. For the Federal Funds rate see Federal Reserve Board, table J1-1, available from the Federal Reserve Board. For the rate of growth of M1 see *ERP* 1989, 385. The real Federal Funds rate, though remaining at a historically high rate, did fall below 3 percent for two quarters in 1986 and the first quarter of 1987.

24. *ERP* 1994, 241.

25. In 1980, the merchandise trade deficit was 0.9 percent of GDP, while the 1992 deficit was 1.5 percent of GDP (*ERP* 1996, 392, 280). The full balance on current account (which is the usual statistic reported in the press as the "trade deficit") went from surplus in 1980 to a deficit of close to 1 percent of GDP.

26. Economists say you are "receiving" an "implicit income"—the rent you do not have to pay because you own your own home. It is not as outrageous as it sounds. When you live in a house or apartment you are "consuming" the services of that structure, whether you pay rent or not.

27. Friedman, *Day of Reckoning,* 151.

28. *ERP* 1996, 280.

29. Friedman, *Day of Reckoning,* 64–67. Some examples from Friedman: "In 1984 Nestle . . . paid $3 billion to buy Carnation. In 1986 Unilever . . . paid $3 billion for Chesebrough-Pond's, and Hoechst . . . paid $2.8 billion for Celanese. In 1988 Bridgestone . . . paid $2.6 billion for Firestone" (66).

30. Robert Reich, *The Work of Nations: Preparing Ourselves for 21st Century Capitalism* (New York: Knopf, 1991), 136–68.

31. An exception is the serious but critical study of modern radical analyses of imperialism by Benjamin J. Cohen, *The Question of Imperialism* (New York: Basic Books, 1973). For his discussion of whether poor countries are exploited by foreign domination, see pp. 145–227.

32. Friedman, *Day of Reckoning,* 76.

33. Ibid., 79–80.

34. Bowles, Gordon, and Weisskopf, *After the Wasteland,* 123–31.

35. Ibid., 159.

36. Robert Pollin, "Budget Deficits and the US Economy: Considerations in a Heilbronerian Mode," in *Economics as Worldly Philosophy: Essays in Political and Historical Economics in Honour of Robert L. Heilbroner,* ed. Chatha Blackwell and Nell Blackwell (New York: St. Martin's, 1993), 128.

37. Ibid. This is what Pollin calls "necessitous" demand for credit. See Robert Pollin, "The Growth of US Household Debt: Demand-Side Influences," *Journal of Macroeconomics* (spring 1988): 231–48.

38. Pollin, "Budget Deficits," 130.

39. "In earlier historical phases, the rise of private debt financing was checked and reversed when credit bubbles were burst by severe debt deflations and widespread defaults, which in turn forced the economy's aggregate rate of debt financing sharply downward. In the contemporary period, cyclical deficits counteract the debt deflation process by increasing the level of aggregate income in the short run" (ibid., 133).

40. Michael Perelman, *The Pathology of the American Economy* (London: Macmillan, 1993), 6–7.

41. Ibid., 9.

42. Pollin, "Budget Deficits," 133.

43. See pp. 70–72.

44. See pp. 138–39.

45. This structure is termed the "underlying power of capital" and developed and measured in Samuel Bowles, David M. Gordon, and Thomas Weisskopf, "Business Ascendancy and Economic Impasse: A Structural Retrospective on Conservative Economics, 1979–1987," *Journal of Economic Perspectives* 1989 (winter): 107–33. See especially the table on p. 117 and pp. 122–30.

46. The job satisfaction index is derived from polls conducted by the Opinion Research Corporation. Bowles, Gordon, and Weisskopf counted the percentage of employees who answered the question "How do you like your job—the kind of work you do?" with either "Very much" or "A good deal" (Bowles, Gordon, and Weisskopf, *After the Wasteland*, 102).

47. This is a measure that takes the gross hourly wage of nonsupervisory workers, adds the fringe benefit of medical insurance, and subtracts Social Security and personal income taxes. See Thomas Weisskopf, "Use of Hourly Earnings Proposed to Revive Spendable Earnings Series," *Monthly Labor Review,* November 1984, 38–43.

48. Bowles, Gordon, and Weisskopf, *After the Wasteland,* 102.

49. F. W. Taylor developed a system he called "scientific management" in the early years of the twentieth century. He urged business leaders to recognize that initially the workers monopolized the knowledge of the production process and, following their obvious self-interest, attempted to make the job as easy as possible for themselves. Taylor started by *studying* the processes and then attempted to force the workers to work harder. He had an extraordinarily difficult time but ultimately succeeded in the experiments he carried out. This whole process is described in great detail in Taylor's autobiographical works. See, for example, F. M. Taylor, *The Principles of Scientific Management* (New York: Harper and Brothers, 1916), 42–52.

50. See p. 67.

51. See Bowles, Gordon, and Weisskopf, *After the Wasteland,* 126, for a particularly dramatic illustration. Union membership was above 20 percent of the workforce and had fallen to 15 percent by the end of the decade.

52. The point is, I would fear being fired from a job that paid me what I considered a good wage more than I would fear being fired from a job that paid me what I considered a very low wage. If I were in a job in which I got no raise over a

TABLE N-9. Relationship between Deficits, Money Growth, and Inflation

Year	Total Government Deficit (% of GDP)	Rate of Growth of Money Supply (M1)	Rate of Growth of Money Supply (M2)	Inflation Rate (GDP deflator)
1983	4.2	9.9	12.0	4.2
1984	3.0	6.0	8.7	3.9
1985	3.2	12.3	8.3	3.3
1986	3.5	16.8	9.5	2.7
1987	2.6	3.5	3.6	3.1
1988	2.1	4.9	5.5	3.7
1989	1.7	1.0	5.0	4.2
1990	2.8	4.1	3.5	4.3

Source: Column 1: Department of Commerce, Bureau of Economic Analysis; columns 2 and 3: *ERP* 1994, 347; column 4: *ERP* 1997, 306.

five-year period during which inflation had eroded some of my real purchasing power, my attitude toward my job would undoubtedly decline.

53. Milton Friedman and Rose Friedman, *Inflation: Causes and Consequences* (New York: Asia Publishing House, 1963), 17.

54. Table N-9 gives annual information on deficits, money supply growth, and inflation. As deficits fell as a percentage of GDP, the rate of growth of money (both the broader and the narrower measure) tended downward as well. In the two years when the trend was reversed (1985 and 1986) the rate of growth of money increased as well. But the rate of inflation continued to trend downward during those two years of rising deficits and rising rate of money growth, and when the deficit increase and money growth reversed themselves between 1986 and 1989, the rate of growth of inflation began to increase.

Chapter 8

1. The profit rate in the nonfarm business sector averaged 4.1 percent between 1980 and 1988, reaching 4.6 percent in 1988. This is in contrast to the 1974–79 period, when the profit rate averaged 2.42 percent and reached 2.94 percent in 1979. See Baker, "Trends in Corporate Profitability," tables 6 and 7. The after-tax profit rate of nonfinancial corporations rose from 4.26 percent in 1974–79 to 4.75 percent in 1980–88, reaching 5.82 percent in 1988 (see ibid., tables 1 and 2).

2. Tables W-4 and W-5 at the web site, <mars.wnec.edu/~econ/surrender>, provide the quarterly data from 1960 through 1991. The raw data for table W-4 is summarized in table 12, the appendix to this chapter.

3. We should remember that in this discussion we are using the term *investment* in the same way we introduced it in chapter 2: as a real, tangible, creation of a capital asset. In the National Income and Product Accounts of the United States it is called *Gross Private Domestic Investment* and includes all construction of new structures, all new business equipment, and net additions to business inventories.

We will discuss the potential roles of purely financial investments (such as business merger activities, the buying and selling of corporate stocks and bonds) on pp. 156–57.

4. *ERP* 1986, 288; *ERP* 1994, 307.

5. Investment as a percentage of GDP actually averaged 17.1 percent for the six quarters following the peak in the first quarter of 1980. For the next six quarters (five of which constituted the recession of 1981–82), investment as a percentage of GDP averaged 15.6.

6. Steuerle, *Taxes, Loans, and Inflation,* 29.

7. Steuerle, *The Tax Decade,* 24–25.

8. Though the National Bureau of Economic Research identified the third quarter of 1973 as a peak and the third quarter of 1981 as a peak, the 1981 peak was the result of a very short and not very dynamic recovery from the equally short recession of 1980, which actually only lasted one quarter. The unemployment rate at the peak in 1973 was 4.8 percent and the capacity utilization rate 88.5 percent, while the unemployment rate at the 1981 peak was 7.4 percent and the capacity utilization rate 81.6 percent. These were hardly improvements over the trough values for 1980 of 7.7 percent unemployment and 80.0 percent of capacity utilization. Thus, a peak-to-peak comparison of 1973 to 1981 is very misleading. Either one should use the period from the peak of 1973 to the peak of 1980, or as we do in the text, take the longer periods from 1969 to 1980 or 1970 to 1982.

9. It is important at this point to recognize that these average rates of productivity growth are not the same as the *compound* rate of growth. Let me illustrate. If over a ten-year period, productivity grows 10 percent, the average is 1 percent per year. But the compound rate of growth is actually a bit less (0.96 percent). Thus, for any given change over a period of years, the cumulative compound rate is always *lower* than the average rate. If we try to compare productivity growth over different length periods of time, the longer the period, the lower the relationship between the compound rate and the average rate. So if productivity were to grow 20 percent over two years, the average would be the same as for a 10 percent growth over ten years, but the compound rate would be lower (0.92 percent). Thus, the appropriate comparison for productivity growth over different length periods of time is the average per period rather than the cumulative compound rate. This same principle applies to the rate of growth of per capita GDP.

10. See Robert Kuttner, *Everything for Sale: The Virtues and Limits of Markets* (New York: Knopf, 1996), 178–88, and especially his argument that

> the claim that target firms are poorly managed underperformers is not borne out by the facts. . . . Many of the takeovers, in hindsight, turned out to be bad deals. . . . There is a long catalogue of cases in which the acquiring firm . . . knew less about what it was buying than the established management, and proved to be an even worse manager. Several recent studies confirm that hostile takeovers . . . tend to depress the performance of the raiding firm. (183–84)

11. Division of Productivity Research, Office of Productivity and Technology, Bureau of Labor Statistics, "Computer Printout of Industry Analytical Ratios for the Business Sector, All Persons" (available from Bureau of Labor Statistics).

12. Note the previously mentioned chapter (chap. 6) in *ERP* 1985. The $100 billion figure is from p. 193.

13. Office of Productivity and Technology, Bureau of Labor Statistics (BLS), "Industry Analytical Ratios for the Nonfarm Business Sector, All Persons," December 4, 1997 (available from the BLS).

14. *ERP* 1989, 7. Actually, in the statistical tables in that same report, the total number of nonagricultural jobs at the end of 1988 was only 17 million above the nadir at the end of 1982. The growth in the total number of jobs was also only 17 million (*ERP* 1989, 345; *ERP* 1986, 288). The 19 million figure in the text was based on job growth through May 1990.

15. Compare the first three rows in table N-10 with any comparable rows from the NFC or VRB periods. The table compares the average rate of productivity growth in the various periods with the average nonagricultural jobs created per quarter. In some cases, total employment peaks and troughs do not correspond to the turning points in the business cycle, but I have used those business cycle turning points as the comparative benchmarks.

16. This point is emphasized in John E. Schwarz, *America's Hidden Success: A Reassessment of Public Policy from Kennedy to Reagan,* rev. ed. (New York: Norton, 1993), 115–26. According to the Congressional Budget Office, the NAIRU, which approximates the minimum level of unemployment that is sustainable, rose from 5.9 percent in 1970 to 6.3 percent in 1973 before starting to fall in 1981 (*Economic Outlook, 1998–2007,* 105).

17. This is the consumer price index (*ERP* 1994, 339). The GDP deflator rose from 2.0 percent to 5.4 percent in the same period (*ERP* 1997, 306).

18. Unemployment fell below 6 percent in the fourth quarter of 1987 and kept falling through 1989. See table W-4 at the web site, <mars.wnec.edu/~econ/surrender>.

19. Recall in this context the quote from Barry Bosworth cited in chap. 4, n. 3.

20. The thirty-two-quarter expansion from 1962 to 1969 is longer than the Reagan-Bush expansion of 1983–90. Nevertheless, since at least three of the earlier years coincided with the heaviest American involvement in the war in Indochina (1966–69), it is correct to call the Reagan-Bush years the longest *peacetime* expansion since World War II. The view that it is so important to avoid the acceleration of inflation that 5.5 percent unemployment is about the lowest the economy can sustain now permeates virtually the entire policymaking establishment. When President Clinton nominated Alan Blinder to be a governor of the Federal Reserve System, the financial markets demonstrated unease because Blinder is known as a Keynesian who sees reducing unemployment as a major priority, at least until inflation appears immanent. Meanwhile, the policy of the Federal Reserve System beginning in 1984 has been to engage in "preemptive strikes" of tight monetary policy in order to keep inflationary pressures from even appearing on the horizon. The result has been the remarkable specter of the Federal Reserve reacting to the first really prosperous year of the recovery, 1994, by attempting to stifle that recovery with seven increases in the interest rate. See Robert D. Hershey Jr., "Federal Reserve Raises Its Rates Seventh Time in a Year," *New York Times,* February 2, 1995, A1, D4.

21. From the depths of the 1982 recession to the peak in 1990, the economy averaged a 2.77 percent annual growth rate per quarter in per capita GDP. This compares favorably with the period from 1971 to the peak in 1980, when the average was 2.50 percent. The 1962–69 period and 1975–80 period each had higher rates.

TABLE N-10. Job Growth and Productivity Growth, 1960–91 (in billions of dollars)

Period	Rate of Growth of Productivity	Total Non-Agricultural Jobs Created (in thousands)	Average Job Creation per Quarter (in thousands)
1960 peak to			
1969 peak (38 Q.)	2.87	13,391	352.4
Recovery 1962–			
1969 peak (32 Q.)	2.71	12,726	397.7
1962 trough to			
1970 trough (36 Q.)	2.73	12,680	352.2
1969 peak to			
1980 peak (41 Q)	2.01	19,795	475.5
Recovery 1971–			
1980 peak (37 Q)	1.92	19,721	533.0
1971 trough to			
1982 trough (48 Q)	1.56	19,306	402.2
1973 peak to			
1980 peak (25 Q)	1.33	12,711	508.4
Recovery 1974–			
1980 peak (20 Q)	1.63	13,464	673.2
1980 peak to			
1990 peak (42 Q)	1.09	19,222	457.7
Recovery 1983–			
1990 peak (31 Q)	1.35	18,662	602.0
1982 trough–			
1991 trough (33 Q)	1.23	17,396	527.2

Source: Column 1: see table W-4 at the web site, <mars.wnec.edu/~econ/surrender>; column 2: Bureau of Labor Statistics.

22. *ERP* 1996, 281.

23. See p. 134. Blecker, *Beyond the Twin Deficits,* claims three types of evidence for this conclusion.

> [T]he real value (purchasing power) of the dollar which would enable the United States to balance its trade has decreased steadily over time. . . . the response of U.S. exports to foreign income growth is much smaller than the response of U.S. imports to domestic income growth. . . . U.S. nonoil imports have grown by roughly $98 billion more in the past ten years [1980–90] (measured in constant 1982 dollars) than can be accounted for by changes in import prices, exchange rates, and national income. (58)

The details are provided on pp. 58–70.

24. See table W-5 at the web site, <mars.wnec.edu/~econ/surrender>.

25. For evidence that the percentage of personal income saved did not rise as a result of the alleged incentive changes in the early 1980s, see *ERP* 1997, 332.

26. In a study for the Economic Policy Institute, Robert Blecker decomposed the increase in consumption into a number of sources and found that 60 percent of the increase in consumption was explained by increases in interest income, wealth, cash receipts from successful business takeovers, and the rise in transfer payments.

Except for the rise in transfer payments, virtually all of the rest of the increases accrue to high-income individuals. See *Are Americans on a Consumption Binge? The Evidence Reconsidered* (Washington, DC: Economic Policy Institute, 1990), 27.

27. See table W-1 at the web site, <mars.wnec.edu/~econ/surrender>; column 2 gives the total government deficit beginning in 1970. For the federal deficit in fiscal years, see *ERP* 1997, 390.

28. This is another form of the mainstream argument against supply-side or "incentive-based" economics. The key to the incentive of private investors is to be found in overall aggregate demand and growth in the economy, not in the tax rate on profits or the burden of government regulation. See pp. 51–52.

29. See *ERP* 1997, 382, for annual values for both the prime rate and the Federal Funds rate.

30. In column 2 we measure the real rate after the fact by subtracting the prime rate from that year's rate of increase in the GDP deflator. In column 3 we follow convention by taking each year's expected rate of increase in the GDP deflator as an average of the three previous year's rate of increase in that variable.

31. In a detailed summary article of many of the issues related to the crowding-out controversy, economists from the Treasury Department and the Congressional Budget Office analyzed forty-two separate studies of the relationship between federal deficits and interest rates. Seventeen showed that federal deficits caused interest rates to rise, nineteen showed that they either had no statistically discernible impact or caused interest rates to fall, while six produced "mixed" results (James R. Barth, George Iden, Frank S. Russek and Mark Wohar, "The Effects of Federal Budget Deficits on Interest Rates and the Composition of Domestic Output," in *The Great Fiscal Experiment*, ed. Rudolph G. Penner [Washington, DC: Urban Institute Press, 1991], 71–141; for the table see pp. 98–102). Note, however, that the appropriate crowding-out impact can only be measured against the *total government* deficit because if state surpluses counteract federal deficits, the credit markets are not drained as much as a focus on the *federal* deficit would indicate.

32. See, for example, Bartley:

> With the Federal Reserve tied up keeping money tight to fight inflation, wouldn't it [the budget deficit] 'crowd out' investment? How could it be financed?
> [Robert] Mundell, . . . brushed away the issue, 'The Saudis will finance that.' . . . [T]hey did. (*The Seven Fat Years*, 59)

Bartley was, of course, referring to the great increase in dollar balances controlled not just by Saudi Arabia but by a number of oil-rich nations who had received giant windfalls throughout the 1970s as a result of the rise in the relative price of oil. This point is actually a bit flip, because in the mid-1980s, Saudi Arabia and other oil-rich nations were facing declining revenues due to a near free-fall in oil prices. Most of the net foreign investment during the middle 1980s came from Japan.

33. Table N-11 shows the rising importance of foreign savings between 1983 and 1990.

34. See table N-12. Total private-sector borrowing averaged 88.6 percent of GDP between 1962 and 1969, 96.5 percent of GDP between 1971 and 1973, and 99.5

TABLE N-11. Foreign Savings of Increasing Importance, 1983–90

Year	Net Foreign Investment	Gross Private Domestic Investment	Net Private Domestic Investment	Ratio of Net Foreign Investment to Net Domestic Investment (%)
1983	37.3	547.1	149.3	24.0
1984	91.5	715.6	304.7	30.0
1985	116.9	715.1	282.7	41.4
1986	142.9	722.5	263.1	54.3
1987	156.4	747.2	264.0	59.2
1988	118.1	773.9	258.0	45.8
1989	92.4	829.2	277.3	33.3
1990	78.6	799.7	223.9	35.1

Source: Columns 1 and 2: *ERP* 1996, 302, 280; column 3: Department of Commerce, Bureau of Economic Analysis.

percent of GDP between 1976 and 1979. Beginning in 1983, total private-sector borrowing averaged 118.9 percent of GDP through 1989. The average was even *higher* after 1984 (123.7 percent).

35. As did Benjamin Friedman, for example. (see p. 133). Yet Friedman, himself, acknowledged that business was able to borrow record amounts, which is evidence against the role of budget deficits in making borrowing more difficult. See Friedman, *Day of Reckoning,* 264–65.

36. Bowles, Gordon, and Weisskopf tried to document this in "Hearts and Minds: A Social Model of U.S. Productivity Growth," *Brookings Papers on Economic Activity* 1983, no. 2:381–441. See also their *After the Wasteland,* chap. 7.

37. For the productivity data, see Bureau of Labor Statistics, "Industry Analytical Ratios for the Nonfarm Business Sector," January 4, 1998. The quarterly unemployment data from the BLS averages 3.5 percent. The yearly figure in the *ERP* 1997, 355, is 3.4 percent.

38. Bureau of the Census, Current Population Reports, Series P 60, "Year-Round, Full-Time Workers—Median and Mean Earnings."

Chapter 9

1. Mondale asserted, "Let's tell the truth. Mr. Reagan will raise taxes, and so will I. He won't tell you. I just did" (*Washington Post,* July 20, 1984, 18).

2. *ERP* 1985, 65. Note the use of GNP rather than GDP. The trend of the debt/GDP ratio is exactly the same as that described by the council. The absolute value of the ratio might vary slightly.

3. Perot, *United We Stand,* 8. In terms of the burden on taxpayers to service the debt with interest payments, the only really meaningful measure of the national debt is the amount held by the public. A fairly substantial proportion of the total national debt is held within the United States government by various trust funds, including the Social Security trust funds and by Federal Reserve banks.

Table N-13 measures the national debt held by the public and the total

TABLE N-12.   Rising Private-Sector Indebtedness, 1960–89

Year	GDP (in billions)	Household Debt (in billions)	Business Debt (in billions)	Private Debt (% of GDP)
1960	526.6	211.7	204.3	79.0
1961	544.8	228.0	218.7	82.0
1962	585.2	249.5	237.1	83.2
1963	617.4	275.6	257.1	86.3
1964	663.0	304.4	279.6	88.1
1965	719.1	332.3	309.7	89.3
1966	787.8	354.5	344.5	88.8
1967	833.6	374.9	379.8	90.5
1968	910.6	404.5	420.9	90.6
1969	982.2	434.5	471.2	92.2
1970	1,035.6	453.3	518.5	93.8
1971	1,125.4	495.5	569.9	94.7
1972	1,237.3	553.4	639.1	96.4
1973	1,382.6	624.1	731.7	98.1
1974	1,496.9	674.9	829.4	100.5
1975	1,630.6	728.2	871.6	98.1
1976	1,819.0	815.5	940.2	96.5
1977	2,026.9	948.3	1,053.9	98.8
1978	2,291.4	1,108.2	1,187.2	100.2
1979	2,557.5	1,273.2	1,351.8	102.6
1980	2,784.2	1,391.1	1,487.3	103.4
1981	3,115.9	1,500.5	1,657.8	101.4
1982	3,242.1	1,569.7	1,800.1	104.0
1983	3,514.5	1,732.9	1,979.5	105.6
1984	3,902.4	1,946.7	2,290.6	108.6
1985	4,180.7	2,259.9	2,562.5	115.4
1986	4,422.2	2,516.9	2,874.4	122.0
1987	4,692.3	2,777.7	3,097.6	125.2
1988	5,049.6	3,067.9	3,370.8	127.5
1989	5,438.7	3,346.6	3,630.8	128.3

Source: Column 1: *ERP* 1997, 300; columns 2–4: "Total Net Borrowing and Lending in Credit Markets," Flow of Funds Accounts, Federal Reserve System. (I am indebted to Robert Pollin for sharing his data set with me.)

national debt both in absolute figures and as a percentage of gross domestic product. The data is for fiscal years, and thus the GDP measures will not correspond to calendar years. In 1977, the fiscal year changed from beginning on July 1 to beginning on October 1. Thus for fiscal 1976, the GDP departed much more from calendar year GDP ($1,819 billion, as opposed to the number in table N-13) than in 1977 ($2,026.9 billion, as opposed to the number in table N-13).

4. Table N-14 shows the increased interest payments of the federal government over the last three decades.

5. When I was told this over the phone, I was actually surprised. I had always assumed the Treasury had paid off the Civil War debt in its entirety sometime in the late nineteenth century. Not true, according to the Bureau of the Public Debt. In a *1979 Report of the Secretary of the Treasury* (table 19), available on the Web at <www.publicdebt.treas.gov>, the total gross public debt, which stood

TABLE N-13. The National Debt, 1960–96

Year	GDP	National Debt Total	National Debt Held by Public	National Debt (% of GDP) Total	National Debt (% of GDP) Held by Public
1960	518.3	290.5	236.8	56.1	45.7
1961	530.4	292.6	238.4	55.2	45.0
1962	567.3	302.9	248.0	53.4	43.7
1963	599.0	310.3	254.0	51.8	42.4
1964	639.8	316.1	256.8	49.4	40.1
1965	686.8	322.3	260.8	46.9	38.0
1966	752.7	328.5	263.7	43.6	35.0
1967	811.9	340.4	266.6	41.9	32.8
1968	868.0	368.7	289.5	42.5	33.4
1969	948.1	365.8	278.1	38.6	29.3
1970	1,009.4	380.9	283.2	37.7	28.1
1971	1,077.4	408.2	303.0	37.9	28.1
1972	1,177.0	435.9	322.4	37.0	27.4
1973	1,306.8	466.3	340.9	35.7	26.1
1974	1,438.1	483.9	343.7	33.7	23.9
1975	1,554.5	541.9	394.7	34.9	25.4
1976	1,730.4	629.0	477.4	36.4	27.6
1977	1,971.4	706.4	549.1	35.8	27.9
1978	2,212.6	776.6	607.1	35.1	27.4
1979	2,495.9	829.5	640.3	33.2	25.7
1980	2,718.9	909.1	709.8	33.4	26.1
1981	3,049.1	994.8	785.3	32.6	25.8
1982	3,211.3	1,137.3	919.8	35.4	28.6
1983	3,421.9	1,371.7	1,131.6	40.1	33.1
1984	3,812.0	1,564.7	1,300.5	41.1	34.1
1985	4,102.1	1,817.5	1,499.9	44.3	36.6
1986	4,374.3	2,120.6	1,736.7	48.5	39.7
1987	4,605.1	2,346.1	1,888.7	51.0	41.0
1988	4,953.5	2,601.3	2,050.8	52.5	41.4
1989	5,351.8	2,868.0	2,189.9	53.6	40.9
1990	5,684.5	3,206.6	2,410.7	56.4	42.4
1991	5,858.8	3,598.5	2,688.1	61.4	45.9
1992	6,143.2	4,002.1	2,998.8	65.2	48.8
1993	6,470.8	4,351.4	3,247.5	67.3	50.2
1994	6,830.4	4,643.7	3,432.1	68.0	50.3
1995	7,186.9	4,921.0	3,603.4	68.5	50.1
1996	7,484.7	5,181.9	3,733.0	69.2	49.9

Source: ERP 1997, 389.

at $75.5 million at the end of 1790, fell to a negligible $37,513 (less than one penny per person) in 1835. It was above $10 million from 1841 to the Civil War and above $1 billion from 1863 to World War I (with 1892 and 1893 as exceptions—it dipped just below $1 billion in those years). At the end of World War I it stood at $24 billion. At the eve of World War II it was $40 billion. At the end of World War II it was $269 billion, which exceeded the GDP.

6. When then-governor Clinton ran for president, he tried to argue that government spending for investment purposes (education, infrastructure) would be

TABLE N-14. The Impact of Interest Payments on the Federal Budget and of Interest Payments to Foreign Creditors

| | Federal Interest Payments | | | Federal Interest Payments (% of GDP) | |
Year	Total	To Rest of World	As a Percentage of Federal Spending	Total	To Rest of World
1960	6.8	.3	7.3	1.3	0.06
1961	6.3	.3	6.2	1.2	0.06
1962	6.8	.3	6.2	1.2	0.05
1963	7.3	.4	6.4	1.2	0.07
1964	8.0	.5	6.7	1.2	0.08
1965	8.4	.5	6.7	1.2	0.07
1966	9.2	.5	6.4	1.2	0.06
1967	9.8	.6	5.9	1.2	0.07
1968	11.3	.7	6.2	1.3	0.08
1969	12.7	.8	6.7	1.3	0.08
1970	14.1	1.0	6.8	1.4	0.10
1971	13.8	1.8	6.2	1.3	0.16
1972	14.4	2.7	5.8	1.2	0.22
1973	18.0	3.8	6.7	1.3	0.28
1974	20.7	4.3	6.8	1.4	0.29
1975	23.0	4.5	6.3	1.5	0.28
1976	26.8	4.5	6.8	1.5	0.25
1977	29.1	5.5	6.8	1.5	0.28
1978	34.6	8.7	7.4	1.6	0.39
1979	42.1	11.1	8.1	1.7	0.45
1980	52.7	12.7	8.6	2.0	0.47
1981	71.7	17.3	10.3	2.3	0.57
1982	84.4	19.3	11.0	2.7	0.61
1983	92.7	19.0	11.0	2.7	0.56
1984	113.1	21.2	12.7	3.0	0.56
1985	127.0	23.0	13.1	3.1	0.57
1986	131.0	24.1	12.7	3.1	0.56
1987	136.6	25.3	12.8	3.0	0.56
1988	146.0	30.2	13.2	3.0	0.62
1989	164.8	35.9	14.0	3.1	0.68

Source: Calculated from information provided by the U.S. Department of Commerce, Bureau of Economic Analysis.

Note: Except for percentages, figures are in billions of dollars.

extremely important. President Bush ridiculed that idea, claiming that "they call it investment, but it's the same old government spending." In short, it's the same old *wasteful* government spending.

7. In fiscal 1948, before rearmament, defense purchases as a percentage of GDP fell to 3.6 percent. They rose to 4.9 percent in fiscal 1949 and 14.2 percent at the height of the Korean War (in fiscal 1953). Despite the end of the war, military purchases remained over 10 percent of GDP for the rest of the 1950s (*ERP* 1997, 389, 391).

8. These numbers are for fiscal years and refer to total federal debt. Federal debt held by the public as opposed to other government agencies fell from 29.3 percent in 1969 to 25.7 percent in 1979 (*ERP* 1997, 390).

9. Recall from chapter 6 that the Bureau of Economic Analysis calculated the structural deficit as the deficit that would exist if unemployment were 6 percent and expressed that deficit as a percentage of that potential level of gross national product. The switch to GDP as a measurement of total output occurred after these structural-deficit numbers were calculated. As mentioned above, the difference between GDP and gross national product is quantitatively quite small. The Congressional Budget Office has calculated a different measure of potential GDP for those years based on the view that 6.2 percent is the appropriate measure of the NAIRU. By their measure, the increase in the structural deficit is not as dramatic, from 1.2 percent in fiscal 1974 to 2.4 percent in fiscal 1975 (but recall that the tax cut was passed in early 1975, fully halfway through that fiscal year—the full effect of the tax cut was felt in fiscal 1976 when the structural deficit was 3.1 percent of GDP). See Congressional Budget Office, *Economic Outlook, 1998–2007,* 105.

10. The Congressional Budget Office measure rose from 1.8 percent of potential GDP (NAIRU of 6.2 percent) in fiscal 1981 to 2.0 percent in fiscal 1982 to 3.7 percent in fiscal 1983. (In the latter year, the NAIRU was estimated to have fallen to 6.1 percent). See Congressional Budget Office, *Economic Outlook, 1998–2007,* 105.

11. See table W-1 at the web site <mars.wnec.edu/~econ/surrender>. The federal deficit as a percentage of GDP went from 2.6 percent in fiscal 1981 to 4.0 percent in fiscal 1982 to 6.1 percent in fiscal 1983 (*ERP* 1997, 390).

12. See table W-1 at the web site. Note that the structural *federal* deficit was larger than the total government deficit in the mid-to-late 1980s and the early 1990s because unemployment was actually below the 6 percent benchmark, and state and local governments were once again counteracting some of the federal deficit with surpluses. Because the 1990 tax increases were phased in over time and because fiscal 1990 actually ended before the tax increase went into effect, the Congressional Budget Office's measure of the structural deficit actually rose from 2.8 percent of GDP in fiscal 1989 to 3.1 percent in fiscal 1990 to 3.3 percent in fiscal 1991. This is a far cry, however, from the changes between 1974 and 1976 and from 1981 to 1983. See notes 9 and 11 to this chapter.

13. Pollin, "Budget Deficits," 109.

14. In 1950, the United States National Security Council drafted a document, NSC 68, that argued that a large-scale military buildup was necessary to fight international communism *and* that such a buildup could also prop up domestic aggregate demand. Washington resident Gore Vidal remembers hearing Secretary of State John Foster Dulles "predict that this policy would lead to an arms race that the Soviets were certain to lose because they were so much poorer. As a result, the Soviet economy would suffer irreparable harm" (qtd. in Perelman, *Pathology of American Economy,* 62).

15. Seymour Melman, *Pentagon Capitalism* (New York: McGraw-Hill, 1970), and *The Permanent War Economy: American Capitalism in Decline* (New York: Touchtone, 1974). See also Perelman, *Pathology of American Economy,* chap. 4.

16. Between 1973 and 1984, employee compensation fell from 49.8 percent of total defense spending to 35.2 percent (Rebecca Blank and Emma Rothschild,

"The Effect of United States Defense Spending on Employment and Output," *International Labour Review* 124 [November–December 1985]: 679).

17. Congressional Budget Office, *Defense Spending and Economy*, 42–44. While $10 billion in additional defense spending and government nondefense spending (exclusive of transfer payments) were both calculated to create approximately 250,000 new jobs, if all of the $10 billion were devoted to defense purchases, the job creation would have been 20 percent less

18. Judith Reppy estimated in 1985 that 42 percent of the scientific personnel in the United States were employed in defense-related work ("Military R & D and the Civilian Economy," *Bulletin of the Atomic Scientists* 41 [October 1985]: 11). This is probably an important place to acknowledge that there is a counterargument to the position articulated in this section. That argument is given by James Cypher in "Military Spending, Technical Change, and Economic Growth: A Disguised Form of Industrial Policy?" *Journal of Economic Issues* 21 (March 1987): 33–59. Cypher argues that the military has always been a important prop to technological progress. He supports this argument with aggregate data (pp. 40–43) as well as references to case studies (pp. 43–47). He approvingly quotes Robert Reich:

> Large-scale defense and aerospace contracts provided emerging industries in the United States with a ready market that let them quickly expand production and thus gain scale economies and valuable experience. The Pentagon's willingness to pay a high premium for quality and reliability, moreover, helped emerging industries bear the cost of refining and "debugging" their products. (Reich, *The Next American Frontier* [New York: Times Books, 1983], 102, qtd. in Cypher, 44)

Cypher continues by citing "the military's role in promoting the U.S. semi-conductor and aircraft industries—both of which exhibited world leadership through the mid-1970s" (44). He approvingly quotes Merritt Roe Smith:

> The military has been an important agent of technological and managerial innovation. By linking national defense with national welfare, it has sponsored all types of research and development and has served as an important disseminator of new technologies. Just as it helped to inaugurate the industrial revolution in America, it continues to alter the structure of industrial society today. (Smith, *Military Enterprise and Technological Change* [Cambridge: MIT Press, 1985], 36, qtd. in Cypher, 45)

Cypher asserts that military programs played significant roles in numerous technological advances, including standardization, metalworking, steel modernization, the spread of Taylorism, and the Ford style mass production technology (p. 45).

The point Cypher and others make in response to the analysis in the text is that the huge military spending of the United States government has been the conduit through which the funds necessary to drive the incentives of the private sector toward technological advancement have come. To assert as Melman and others have that military spending has sapped productivity growth is to miss that fact that absent military spending, American private enterprise would have had *less* incentive to produce the technological progress that has occurred. Note, by the way, that this point of view fits with the argument raised very early in this book (see chap. 1, n. 17) that the role of government has been to subsidize particular enterprises and to make sure the low-risk profits flow to those already powerfully situated. As we mentioned then, this is an intriguing position, made stronger by the historical studies that have backed it up. (Reich's and Smith's examples in the works cited by Cypher are two cases in point.) Nevertheless, this writer believes on balance that in the most recent period, the expansion of military spending has probably done more harm than good to American productivity growth. In any event, a dispute over *what* has caused productivity growth to be so slow in the 1980s does not change the fact that despite the changes instituted by the supplysiders, productivity growth did not revive.

19. See pp. 136–37.

20. Reich, *The Work of Nations*, 266.

21. The federal nonmilitary structures include industrial, educational, and hospital buildings plus an overall category ("other") that includes office buildings, courthouses, auditoriums, garages, and airline terminals. Other structures are highways and streets, conservation and development structures (like dams), and electric and gas facilities, transit systems, and (civilian) airfields. The state and local structures are divided among educational and hospital and "other" buildings. The "other" category includes the same types as under the federal rubric plus police and fire stations. Nonbuilding structures include those already mentioned under the federal government plus sewer systems and water supply facilities. See Bureau of Economic Analysis, Department of Commerce, *Fixed Reproducible Tangible Wealth in the United States, 1925–89* (Washington, DC: Government Printing Office, 1993), 421, 423.

22. We begin in 1961 since that is the starting point for KJN in the previous chapter. However, we end the period with the data from the Department of Commerce through 1989 because that is the final year in which Reagan administration decisions had an impact. I have summarized this information in table W-6 at the web site, <mars.wnec.edu/~econ/surrender>.

23. These calculations are based on 1961–69 for KJN, 1970–80 for NFC, and 1981–89 for VRB. Changing NFC to 1970–81 changes the ratio of infrastructure spending to GDP to 2.47 percent. VRB changes to 1.99 when we shorten the period to 1982–89. Since this analysis deals only with the spending priorities of different administrations, it seems appropriate to begin VRB with the first budget in which Reagan priorities had an impact. As is clear from chapter 5, there was an effort in the early months of the administration to reverse some of the budget decisions already made for fiscal 1981. There was no such activity on the part of the Nixon administration, and thus it is appropriate to begin NFC with the year 1970. For details see tables W-7 and W-8 at the web site <mars.wnec.edu/~econ/surrender>. A less precise estimate has been available from the Bureau of Economic Analysis since 1996. They give figures for expenditures on nondefense equipment and structures by the federal government and on equipment and structures by state and local governments (*ERP* 1997, 321). The ratios are 3.38 percent for KJN, 2.47 percent for NFC, and 2.04 percent for the Reagan years. The data is collected in table W-9 at the web site.

24. The percentages of GDP devoted to this area of infrastructure investment fell from 0.70 in KJN to 0.53 in NFC to 0.25 in VRB.

25. David A. Aschauer, "Is Public Expenditure Productive?" *Journal of Monetary Economics* 23 (1989): 177–200. See also Alicia Munnell, "How Does Public

Infrastructure Affect Regional Economic Performance?" *New England Economic Review* (September–October 1990): 11–32.

26. National Commission on Excellence in Education, *A Nation at Risk* (Washington, DC: Government Printing Office, 1983), iii.

27. Ibid., 5.

28. Ibid., 8–9. For more details, see pp. 18–23.

29. Ibid., 24. This is spelled out in detail on pp. 24 25.

30. Ibid., 28.

31. The four major recommendations with numerous implementing recommendations are in ibid., 24–31.

32. Ibid., 33.

33. Table N-15 shows the data from 1960 through 1988.

34. The Congressional Budget Office estimated total national health expenditures at $247 billion in 1980 and $697 billion in 1990. This represented an increase from 8.9 percent to 12.1 percent of GDP (*Economic Outlook, 1998–2007*, 126).

35. The information in table N-16 has been collected by the Employee Benefit Research Institute (web address <www.ebri.org>). Unfortunately, there are significantly different numbers for employer spending on health insurance premiums and employer spending on private health insurance. I have included both data sets in the table. It is conceivable that the difference between the ratios has to do with the fact that column 3 was updated more recently. The important point is that both ratios rise significantly over the decade.

36. Karen Davis, Gerard Anderson, Diane Rowland, and Earl Steinberg, *Health Care Cost Containment* (Baltimore: Johns Hopkins University Press, 1990), 134.

37. Health expenditures as a percentage of GDP rose from 9.2 percent in 1980 to 13.2 percent in 1991. By 1989, 14 percent of the population was not covered by any health insurance (Mishel and Bernstein, *State of Working America, 1994 95*, 298, 305).

38. *1993 Green Book*, 307, 305

39. Mishel and Bernstein, *State of Working America, 1994–95*, 312. The data is from a study by Jack Hadley, Earl Steinberg, and Judith Feder, "Comparison of Uninsured and Privately Insured Hospital Patients: Condition on Admission, Resource Use, and Outcome," *Journal of the American Medical Association* 265 (1991): 374–79.

40. See pp. 75–78.

41. "[I]n 1980 . . . thrifts earned an average yield of 9¼ percent on outstanding mortgages, while the prevailing rate on newly issued mortgages was about 12½ percent. Since the market value, or price, of a fixed-rate asset falls as the interest rate rises, the sharp increase in mortgage interest rates slashed the value of the outstanding mortgages held by S & Ls" (*Economic Report of the President, 1991*, 168).

42. "By 1980, the net worth of the entire industry measured at market value was actually negative" (John B. Shoven, Scott B. Smart, and Joel Waldfogel, "Real Interest Rates and the Savings and Loan Crisis: The Moral Hazard Premium," *Journal of Economic Perspectives* 6 [1992]: 159).

43. *ERP* 1991, 170.

44. *ERP* 1991, 172.

45. Shoven, Smart, and Waldfogel, "Real Interest Rates," 165.

TABLE N-15. The Changing Public-Spending Commitment to Elementary and Secondary Education, 1960–88 (in billions of dollars)

Year	GDP	Total Government Expenditures on Elementary and Secondary Education[a]	Federal Grants to State and Local Governments for Elementary and Secondary Education[a]	Elementary and Secondary Education Expenditures (% of GDP)[a]	Federal Grants (% of total expenditures on elementary and secondary education)
1960	526.6	14.919	.252	2.83	0.05
1961	544.8	16.335	.262	3.00	0.05
1962	585.2	17.379	.278	2.97	0.05
1963	617.4	18.944	.287	3.07	0.05
1964	663.0	20.971	.343	3.16	0.05
1965	719.1	23.043	.394	3.20	0.05
1966	787.8	26.362	1.787	3.35	0.23
1967	833.6	29.186	1.762	3.50	0.21
1968	910.6	31.958	1.895	3.51	0.21
1969	982.2	35.248	1.830	3.59	0.19
1970	1,035.6	39.286	2.143	3.79	0.21
1971	1,125.4	43.538	2.265	3.87	0.20
1972	1,237.3	47.470	2.840	3.84	0.23
1973	1,382.6	52.029	2.519	3.76	0.18
1974	1,496.9	57.947	3.189	3.87	0.21
1975	1,630.6	66.322	3.660	4.07	0.22
1976	1,819.0	71.800	2.742	3.95	0.15
1977	2,026.9	76.993	3.532	3.80	0.17
1978	2,291.4	83.242	4.000	3.63	0.17
1979	2,557.5	92.526	4.775	3.62	0.19
1980	2,784.2	101.129	5.235	3.63	0.19
1981	3,115.9	108.342	5.209	3.48	0.17
1982	3,242.1	116.259	5.108	3.59	0.16
1983	3,514.5	124.267	4.258	3.54	0.12
1984	3,902.4	134.888	5.888	3.46	0.15
1985	4,180.7	145.128	5.953	3.47	0.14
1986	4,422.2	157.042	5.953	3.55	0.13
1987	4,692.3	168.831	5.464	3.60	0.12
1988	5,049.6	181.484	6.731	3.59	0.13

Source: Column 1: *ERP* 1997, 300; columns 2 and 3: *National Income and Product Accounts of the United States, 1959–88,* 2:124–48.

[a]In billions of dollars.

46. Ibid., 161, 165–66.

47. "By the end of 1990, the Department of Justice had obtained nearly 400 convictions in major fraud cases in connection with the S & L crisis" (*ERP* 1991, 173).

48. The 1992 report of the Council of Economic Advisers noted, "The expansion of deposit insurance that did not account for the riskiness of an institution's

TABLE N-16. Health Insurance Fringe Benefits as a Percentage of Employee Compensation, 1980–89 (in billions of dollars)

Year	Compensation of Employees (wages and benefits)	Employer Spending on Wages and Salaries (non-government)	Employer Spending on Private Health Insurance	Employer Spending on Health Insurance Premiums	Private Health Spending (% of wages and salaries)	Employer Spending on Private Health Insurance (% of compensation of employees)
1980	1,653.9	1,116.4	61.0	47.9	5.5	2.9
1981	1,827.8	1,232.0	71.7		5.8	
1982	1,927.6	1,286.7	82.6		6.4	
1983	2,044.2	1,360.3	91.5		6.7	
1984	2,257.0	1,507.5	100.3		6.7	
1985	2,425.7	1,622.1	107.4	83.9	6.6	3.5
1986	2,572.4	1,720.0	113.7		6.6	
1987	2,757.7	1,849.5	122.9		6.7	
1988	2,973.9	2,003.2	138.7		6.9	
1989	3,151.6	2,118.7	157.2	122.8	7.4	3.9

Source: Columns 1 and 2: *ERP* 1997, 328; column 3: *EBRI Databook on Employee Benefits,* updated table 10.10 (May 1996); column 4: ibid., table 10.14.

investments enabled weak banks and S & Ls to stay open and to overinvest in risky assets without losing depositor confidence" (*ERP* 1992, 25).

49. In support of the first set of numbers as the more accurate, the Council of Economic Advisers argues, "The [larger] estimates are obtained by adding up all the future repayments. . . . Such an estimate would be akin to claiming that a 10-percent 30-year, $100,000 home mortgage costs $315,925, which in fact is the undiscounted sum of the repayments required by that mortgage" (*ERP* 1991, 173). The word "undiscounted" is key, here. Income you receive in the future is worth less than the same amount of money received today—that's why lenders demand, and borrowers are willing to pay, interest. Repayments in the future cost less in today's dollars than they will when they have to be paid because, in anticipation of having to make that payment, one could invest a smaller sum and watch it grow to the amount needing to be paid out.

50. *ERP* 1991, 174.

51. *ERP* 1992, 26.

52. The wide range of estimates is based both on the wide range of possible impacts on the rate of interest (anywhere from 0.5 percent to 2.5 percent) paid by the government on its outstanding debt as well as the time rate of discount used to collapse the cost into present value terms. See Shoven, Smart and Waldfogel, "Real Interest Rates," 266.

53. *ERP* 1991, 177.

54. This argument has been facetiously taken to its logical conclusion with the suggestion that the way to guarantee safe driving is to mandate that every steer-

ing wheel come equipped with a permanent harpoon aimed at the chest of the driver to guarantee that the driver will not collide with anything!

55. *1993 Green Book,* 1525.

56. That's real income, calculated in 1993 dollars. See Bureau of the Census, Current Population Reports, Series P 60, table H-1.

57. *1993 Green Book,* 1530–31. For median income, see U.S. Bureau of the Census, table H-1.

58. *1993 Green Book,* 1530–31.

59. *1993 Green Book,* 1531. Interest, dividend, and rental income for the top 1 percent went from 24.6 percent of their total income to 21.8 percent in 1985, not so much because their received less interest, dividend, and rental income but because their ability to receive income in capital gains increased so dramatically.

60. Edward N. Wolff, "The Rich Get Increasingly Richer: Latest Data on Household Wealth during the 1980s," Briefing Paper, Economic Policy Institute, 1992, 1.

61. Ibid.

62. Wolff calculates that between 1922 and 1989 (with twenty separate observations), three-fifths of wealth inequality can be attributed to income inequality and two-fifths to relative increases in stock prices to home prices (ibid., 12–13).

63. With such ownership concentrated heavily in the top 5 percent of the population. For the years 1980, 1985, and 1990 the income from capital for the top 5 percent and 1 percent of the population is detailed in table N-17.

64. Lawrence Mishel and Jared Bernstein, *The State of Working America, 1992–93* (Armonk, NY: M. E. Sharpe, 1993), 140.

65. Ibid., 146.

66. *1993 Green Book,* 1326.

67. Paul Krugman, "The Right, the Rich, and the Facts," *American Prospect* 11 (fall 1992): 23–24. Note that the base year is 1977, not 1979, because the data set he used was a Congressional Budget Office study that did not collect information for 1979.

68. Ibid., 25.

69. Kevin Phillips, *The Politics of Rich and Poor* (New York: Random House, 1990).

70. Lindsey, *The Growth Experiment,* 82.

71. In 1990, both ratios began to fall, dominated by the decline in nominal interest rates that actually reduced total personal interest income in absolute terms between that year and 1993 (*ERP* 1997, 330).

72. See Bartley, *The Seven Fat Years,* 272–73.

73. Ibid., 278.

74. Alan Reynolds, "Upstarts and Downstarts," *National Review,* August 31, 1992, 26.

75. Isabel V. Sawhill and Mark Condon, "Is U.S. Income Inequality Really Growing? Sorting Out the Fairness Question," *Policy Bites* (Urban Institute), June 1992, 3–4. Tables N-18 and N-19 include the information referred to in their article.

76. Ibid., 4.

77. This battle still raged three years later. See, for example, "Dick Armey's Research" letters from U.S. Representative Dick Armey (R.-TX) and a response by Michael Lind, *New York Times Book Review,* August 20, 1995, 27.

78. "The lower and upper boundaries are $18,500 and $55,000, respectively, in

TABLE N-17. Interest, Dividends, and Capital Gains for High-Income Families

Year	Percentage of Rents, Interest, and Dividends Received by Top 5 Percent of Families	Percentage of Capital Gains Realized by Top 5 Percent of Families	Percentage of Rents, Interest, and Dividends Received by Top 1 Percent of Families	Percentage of Capital Gains Realized by Top 1 Percent of Families
1980	46.8	75.5	26.0	57.6
1985	45.4	84.9	26.4	68.1
1990	49.8	84.7	30.5	68.5

Source: 1993 Green Book, 1528-29.

TABLE N-18. Social Mobility between Quintiles, 1977–86

Family Income Quintile in 1977	Family Income Quintile in 1986 (%)					
	Bottom	Second	Third	Fourth	Top	Total
Bottom	10.6	5.0	2.2	1.3	0.8	20.0
Second	4.3	6.0	5.1	2.9	1.7	20.0
Third	2.9	3.8	5.9	4.8	2.6	20.0
Fourth	1.0	2.9	4.3	6.8	5.0	20.0
Top	1.2	2.2	2.5	4.1	10.0	20.0
Total	20.0	20.0	20.0	20.0	20.0	100.0

Source: Isabel V. Sawhill and Mark Condon, "Is U.S. Income Inequality Really Growing?" 2.

TABLE N-19. Real Family Incomes of Individuals Averaged over Ten Years

Quintile	Average Family Income (in dollars)		
	1967–77	1977–86	Percentage Change
Bottom	$18,293	$18,579	2
Second	32,785	34,084	4
Third	42,636	46,082	8
Fourth	54,100	60,594	12
Top	83,486	101,286	21
All	46,260	52,125	13

Source: Isabel V. Sawhill and Mark Condon, "Is U.S. Income Inequality Really Growing?" 2.

1987 dollars and are applied to all years using the CPI-UXI price index" (Timothy Smeeding, Greg Duncan, and Willard Rodgers, "W[h]ither the Middle Class?" Policy Studies Paper No. 1, Metropolitan Studies Program, Income Security Policy Series, Maxwell School of Citizenship and Public Affairs, Syracuse University, February 1992, 5). The specifics of the index used need not concern us here. The important point is that once they have established an absolute standard of what constitutes the "middle class" the authors adjust that standard to take account of inflation for all the other years in the survey. This permits them to see if people who were in the absolutely defined middle class in 1967 *stayed* there over the next twenty-one years. Note that it is essential to have an absolute standard because if we merely identified the same ratio (between the lowest 20 percent and the top 10 percent) we would have the *same number* of households (70 percent of them) each year! Smeeding, Duncan, and Rodgers use another measure of the middle class that adjusts for family size. In this case, the middle class consists of families with incomes from two times to six times the family's "poverty threshold," which varies according to family size (in 1990 it was thirteen thousand dollars for a family of four). Their results show similar patterns for this measure and the original one. (I am indebted to Professor Smeeding for sending me this paper.)

79. Smeeding, Duncan, and Rodgers, in "W(h)ither the Middle Class?" created table N-20, which they title "Percent of Adults Making Key Income Transitions." The high-income transitions involve either a middle-income individual moving above the high-group threshold of income, or someone from that group "falling out" into the middle class. The low-income transitions involve either a middle-income person falling below the middle-class threshold or a person from that low-income group "climbing out" into the middle class. One should not be misled by the high percentages of high-income people "falling out" compared to the seemingly low percentage of middle-income people "climbing out" because, remember, the middle-income group represents close to 70 percent of the population, while the high-income group to begin with represents only 10 percent of the population, while the lower-income group is only 20 percent. In absolute numbers 6.7 percent of 70 percent of the population is much higher than 29.1 percent of 10 percent of the population. (If there were one thousand people in the population, 6.7 percent of 70 percent would be about forty-seven people, while 29.1 percent of 10 percent would be twenty-nine people!) Instead, the most important numbers above are the differences between the probabilities of social mobility before 1980 and after 1980.

80. Smeeding, Duncan, and Rodgers, "W(h)ither the Middle Class?" 24.

81. Bureau of the Census, Current Population Reports, Series P 60, table P-4, "Race and Hispanic Origin—Persons 15 Years Old and Over, by Median and Mean Income, and Sex: 1947–93," 5–6. The ratio of median incomes for women of all races to men of all races over fifteen went from 36.9 percent in 1979 to 48.4 percent.

82. Mishel and Bernstein, *State of Working America, 1994–95,* 188.

83. Ibid., 189.

84. Ibid.

85. Ibid., 150.

86. *ERP* 1995, 321.

87. *1993 Green Book,* 1405.

88. In 1979, American workers averaged 43.6 weeks per year of work and 38.6 hours per week. By 1989, those numbers had grown to 45.2 and 39.0 respectively (Mishel and Bernstein, *State of Working America, 1994–1995,* 112). Working wives' contributions to the income of married couples increased from 26 percent in 1979 to 29 percent in 1989 (ibid., 62).

89. For details of the research as applies to 1969–89, see Juliet B. Schor and Laura Leete-Guy, "The Great American Time Squeeze: Trends in Work and Leisure, 1969–1989," Briefing Paper, Economic Policy Institute, 1992. See also Juliet B. Schor, *The Overworked American: The Unexpected Decline in Leisure* (New York: Basic Books, 1992).

TABLE N-20. Percentage of Adults Making Key Income Transitions

	All Years	Before 1980	1980 and After
High income transitions			
Percentage of middle-income individuals climbing out	6.7	6.3	7.5
Percentage of high-income individuals falling out	29.7	31.1	27.1
Low-income transitions			
Percentage of low-income individuals climbing out	33.6	35.5	30.4
Percentage of middle-income individuals falling out	7.0	6.2	8.5

Source: Smeeding, Duncan and Rodgers, "W(h)ither the Middle Class," 13.

90. According to Schor,

A 1989 poll found nearly two-thirds expressing the desire to give up an average of 13 percent of their current paycheck for more free time. Eight of ten respondents indicated they would forego a faster career track for a slower one which would allow them more time to spend with their families. A second survey found that 70 percent of those earning $30,000 a year or more would give up a day's pay each week for an extra day of free time. Surprisingly, even among those earning only $20,000 a year, 48 percent said they would do the same. . . . even a decade ago, only a very small percentage of Americans preferred to give up income for time. (Schor and Leete-Guy, "The Great American Time Squeeze," 1)

The surveys were reported in Robert Half International, "Family Time Is More Important Than Rapid Career Advancement: Survey Shows Both Men and Women Support Parent Tracking," press release, San Francisco, June 28, 1989; and Carol Hymowitz, "Trading Fat Paychecks for Free Time," *Wall Street Journal,* August 5, 1991, B1.

91. See Schor, *The Overworked American,* 72–82.

92. Ibid., 60.

93. Ibid., 194

Chapter 10

1. Actually, his election was pretty much guaranteed by the good economy in 1988. Except for 1952, 1968, and 1976, since World War II the party in power has lost the presidency only if there is a recession during the election year. The recession of 1960 appears to have cost Richard Nixon the presidency his first time around, and the recession of 1980 clearly was the cause of President Jimmy Carter's failure to win reelection. In the years 1956, 1964, 1972, and 1984 the incumbent had

no trouble winning—in fact we could characterize all four elections as landslides. In 1952, the candidate was General Eisenhower, a highly popular figure running against a relative unknown in the middle of an unpopular war. In 1968, the Democratic Party was considered the party of the unpopular Vietnam War. In 1976, Gerald Ford was running for reelection in the aftermath of both Watergate and the recession of 1975—and he had pardoned Richard Nixon.

2. His Council of Economic Advisers' first *Economic Report* argued,

A key item on the Administration's economic agenda, reducing the tax rate on capital gains, will enhance all types of investment. Cutting the capital gains tax rate will lower the cost of investment funds and thus stimulate investment. Much of the reward to entrepreneurial activity, such as generating new technology and bringing it to market, comes in the form of an increase in the value of businesses. Reducing the capital gains tax rate will thus reward these efforts and encourage invention and innovation. (*ERP* 1990, 25)

In his last State of the Union address (January 1992) Bush was still insisting that he "must" have a "capital gains tax cut" as part of his policy to stimulate growth (*ERP* 1992, 4).

3. *ERP* 1990, 7.

4. See chap. 7, table 10.

5. *ERP* 1991, 63. For details on the act, see pp. 64–65.

6. See table N-1.

7. The Bush administration's assertions about a slight fall refer to fiscal years, not calendar years (*ERP* 1991, 66). The Congressional Budget Office calculation identifies a rise in the structural deficit from 2.8 percent of GDP in fiscal 1989 to 3.1 percent in fiscal 1990 and 3.3 percent in fiscal 1991 (Congressional Budget Office, *Economic Outlook, 1998–2007,* 105). Clearly, the administration was using a different standard for measuring the structural deficit than the CBO. Between fiscal 1989 and fiscal 1990, the actual federal deficit rose from 2.8 percent of GDP to 3.9 percent of GDP (*ERP* 1997, 390).

8. Bartley, *The Seven Fat Years,* 281.

9. Spending over which Congress has year-to-year control (discretionary spending) was grouped into three categories: domestic, defense, and international. Each of these areas of the budget was capped for 1991 through 1993, after which all three areas would be merged for fiscal 1994 and 1995. The law then reintroduced the G-R-H automatic mechanism. If discretionary spending were to exceed the caps, that would trigger a sequester in that part of the budget. If mandatory spending or tax cuts were voted that were not "paid for" elsewhere in the budget, that, too, would trigger a sequester (ibid., 66). When fiscal 1997 ended on September 30, the federal deficit had fallen to a minuscule $22 billion. In a news analysis published in January 1998, Robert Reischauer, who headed the Congressional Budget Office from 1989 to 1995, is quoted as concluding that the spending constraints and tax increases in this bill accounted for the largest single contribution to deficit reduction in the seven years from its passage until the middle of 1997 (see Pear, "Budget Heroes Include Bush and Gorbachev").

10. Transcript, Federal Open Market Committee Meeting, March 28, 1989, 13, available from the Federal Reserve Board, Freedom of Information section.

11. Ibid., 14. The report given by this staff member predicted that as a result

of price pressures in the first quarter of the year, the Fed expected the consumer price index to rise more than 5 percent in 1989, justifying increased tightening of monetary policy. See Michael J. Prell, "FOMC Briefing—Domestic Economic Outlook," appendix, Staff Papers to the Federal Open Market Committee meeting, 2.

12. Transcript, Federal Open Market Committee Meeting, 21.

13. Ibid., 28.

14. Transcript, Federal Open Market Committee Meeting, 42. In fact, the Fed hit the M2 target almost exactly; the increase between March and June was 2.97 percent on an annual basis. M3 grew slower than planned, at 3.23 percent (Money Stock: Federal Reserve Board). The Federal Funds rate stayed within the target range, rising from 9.65 percent in March to 9.84 in April and trending downward to 9.53 in June (*ERP* 1991, 369).

15. Bureau of Economic Analysis, Department of Commerce (per capita gross domestic product in chained 1992 dollars). The Bush administration identified the recession as beginning in the fourth quarter of 1990, contradicting the NBER, which dated it from the third. The Bush Council of Economic Advisers also tried to blame the recession on the "oil price shock, the sudden drop in consumer and business confidence, and the uncertainty about when the Persian Gulf crisis would end" (*ERP* 1991, 22) but then immediately acknowledged that the Federal Reserve had initiated a more restrictive monetary policy in the spring of 1988 to ward off an increase in the underlying inflation rate. The lagged effects of this policy also slowed the economy in 1989 and 1990, as higher interest rates discouraged spending (p. 23).

16. *ERP* 1997, 300.

17. *ERP* 1990, 187–207.

18. *ERP* 1991, 32–33.

19. *ERP* 1991, 97–98, 143–45.

20. *ERP* 1991, 158.

21. *ERP* 1992, chap. 5

22. *ERP* 1993, 175. The report noted that automobiles manufactured before the 1980 model year were only 29 percent of vehicles on the road but caused 53 percent of hydrocarbon and 51 percent of carbon monoxide pollution. Buying up old vehicles still on the road, therefore, was a fruitful way of reducing air pollution.

23. Note that this is the same argument exemplified by the conservative economists' view that vigorous antitrust prosecutions are unnecessary anachronisms. The opposition, of course, argued that without regulation "free competition" would lead to a few giants winning and controlling unacceptably high percentages of the communications media. The Clinton administration agreed with the congressional majority on a telecommunications reform bill, which was finally passed in 1996 (*ERP* 1997, 200–202).

24. *ERP* 1993, 199.

25. See pp. 62–65.

26. *ERP* 1990, 176–77.

27. College and University Personnel Association, "The ADA and The Civil Rights Act of 1991," tab 4, part 2, 1. Photocopy.

28. *ERP* 1993, 173.

29. ADA Compliance Manual, 2.

30. "The EEOC has estimated that 10,000–12,000 disability discrimination

charges will be filed in the first year after the law goes into effect, an increase of *15–20 percent* in its caseload" (Robert L. Duston, "What Every College and University Administrator Needs to Know about the ADA, and Why," conference manual for the College and University Personnel Association conference on the Americans with Disabilities Act, April 11–12, 1992 [available from Robert L. Duston, Schmeltzer, Aptaker & Shepard, P.C., Washington, DC], table 4-2).

31. U.S. Equal Employment Opportunity Commission and the U.S. Department of Justice, "Americans with Disabilities Act Handbook," EEOC-BK-19 (October 1992), 1–19.

32. Duston, "What University Administrator Needs," 18–19.

33. Drew S. Days, "Civil Rights at the Crossroads," *Debating Affirmative Action, Race, Gender, Ethnicity, and the Politics of Inclusion,* ed. Nicolaus Mills (New York: Delta, 1994), 267.

34. The vote was five to four, with the three Reagan appointees (O'Connor, Scalia, and Kennedy) joining Chief Justice Rehnquist and Byron White for the majority. See *Wards Cove Packing Co. v Atonio* 490 U.S. 642 (1989). For the previous precedent, see *Griggs v Duke Power Co.* 401 U.S. 424 (1971).

35. It is thought by many that this agreement was won due to the strong efforts of Senator James Danforth (R.-MO), who was Thomas's principal supporter in the Senate and cosponsor of the Civil Rights Act of 1991.

36. Warren, "Mixed Message," 25. There was a 15.2 percent increase in the Reagan regulatory budget between fiscal 1985 and 1989.

37. Melinda Warren, "Regulation on the Rise: Analysis of the Federal Budget for 1992," Occasional Paper 89, Center for the Study of American Business, Washington University, St. Louis, 1991, 10.

38. The "Reagan Democrats" are longtime Democratic voters, blue-collar workers, and other middle-class people who voted in increasing numbers for Ronald Reagan in 1980 and 1984 and stayed with George Bush in 1988—this despite the fact that in state and congressional elections they continued to vote for Democrats.

39. *ERP* 1991, 71. They concluded by predicting that unemployment would decline in that year, a prediction that appeared almost foolproof since such a decline had occurred in all previous postwar recoveries.

40. The real GDP in 1976 ended up 5.6 percent higher than in the previous year. The real GDP in 1983 ended up 4.0 percent higher than in 1982 (*ERP* 1997, 302).

41. *ERP* 1997, 302.

42. In real dollars, GDP per capita was $24,033 in the first quarter of 1991, at the trough of the recession. In the first quarter of 1992, it was $24,280. For the first eight quarters after the trough in 1991, growth in real GDP per capita averaged 1.2 percent per quarter. By contrast, the first eight quarters after the trough in 1982 produced an average rate of growth of 5.3 percent. The first eight quarters after the trough in 1975 produced an average of 4.0 percent (Bureau of Economic Analysis, Department of Commerce, "Per Capita Gross Domestic Product—Chained (1992) Dollars,") unpublished data.

43. The same held for the prime rate and for the real Federal Funds and prime rates (calculated using the expected rate of inflation).

44. *ERP* 1995, 359.

45. *ERP* 1997, 332.

TABLE N-21. Defense Expenditures, 1986–93

Fiscal Year	GDP (in billions)	Federal Expenditures	Defense Expenditures	Defense Purchases (% of GDP)	Defense Purchases (% of federal spending)
1986	4,374.3	990.5	273.4	6.3	27.6
1987	4,605.1	1,004.2	282.0	6.1	28.1
1988	4,953.5	1,064.5	290.4	5.9	27.3
1989	5,351.8	1,143.7	303.6	5.7	26.6
1990	5,684.5	1,253.2	299.3	5.3	23.9
1991	5,858.8	1,324.4	273.3	4.7	20.6
1992	6,143.2	1,381.7	298.4	4.9	21.6
1993	6,470.8	1,409.4	291.1	4.5	20.7

Source: ERP 1997, 389, 391.

46. *1993 Green Book*, 521–22.

47. *1993 Green Book*, 491.

48. Coughlin, Ku, and Holahan, *Medicaid since 1980*, 16.

49. *1993 Green Book*, 1993.

50. *1993 Green Book*, 1609.

51. *1993 Green Book*, 815.

52. *ERP* 1995, 314.

53. There was a brief uptick in fiscal 1992. Table N-21 shows the trend in defense spending as a percentage both of GDP and of federal spending during this period. The Congressional Budget Office has a significant rise in defense spending in fiscal 1991, and some of its figures differ from the figures in the *Economic Report*. Perhaps the CBO included funds that were contributed by our allies toward the Gulf War, while the *Economic Report* did not. See Congressional Budget Office, *Economic Outlook, 1998–2007*, 114.

54. Coughlin, Ku, and Holahan, *Medicaid since 1980*, 38.

55. Ibid., 39. On the AFDC-UP program, see *1993 Green Book*, 623–24.

56. See above, pp. 118–19.

57. Coughlin, Ku, and Holahan, *Medicaid since 1980*, 104.

58. Perot, *United We Stand*, 35.

59. In a more detailed description of what was wrong with the U.S. economy between 1980 and 1992, Perot seems to be blaming a decline in savings, the budget deficit, the national debt, and a decline in competitiveness. Carefully perusing the relevant pages in *Not for Sale at Any Price* provides lots of good information about the failures of the U.S. economy since the early 1970s but no real analysis of why that failure occurred. Losing out to foreign competition is mentioned, and there is a quote attributed to a "friend in Japan": "In Japan we think ten years ahead, in the United States you think ten minutes ahead" (64). That hardly passes for explanation. See *Not for Sale*, 32–95.

60. *United We Stand*, 34–56.

61. Clinton would be expected to criticize the economic policies of the current administration. Mondale had tried the same in 1984, as had Dukakis and Bentsen

in 1988. The combination of the recession and Perot's criticisms made Clinton's appear less partisan (that is, fake) and more accurate. For a Perot assault on "trickle-down economics" see *Not for Sale,* 69–77.

62. For some details, see Perot, *United We Stand,* 40–51, and *Not for Sale,* 101–10.

63. In fact, according to Bob Woodward's "insider" account *The Agenda: Inside the Clinton White House* (New York: Simon and Schuster, 1994), the sign had three lines listing the "three-pronged message" of the Clinton campaign: "Change vs. more of the same. The economy, stupid. Don't forget health care." The version in the text and the public consciousness is in fact a slightly incorrect version of only one-third of the sign. See *The Agenda,* 54, and the accompanying note.

64. Office of Management and Budget, *A Vision of Change for America* (Washington, DC: Government Printing Office, February 17, 1993).

65. Ibid., 29. Details of the stimulus package are spelled out on pp. 29–39.

66. There are over twenty pages of proposed increases in public investment and education efforts, both with direct expenditures and tax incentives (ibid., 41–48, 61–63).

67. In addition, the 2.9 percent payroll tax for Medicare was extended to all wage, salary, and self-employment income instead of leaving it capped at $135,000 in 1993. Thus, for people paying the new 36 percent marginal tax rate on income plus the 10 percent surcharge (39.6 percent), if they received wages, salaries, and/or self-employment income in that bracket, the actual marginal tax rate would have risen from 31 percent to 42.5 percent. Note that the 2.9 percent payroll tax for Medicare does not apply to income from interest, rent, dividends, and, most importantly, capital gains.

68. Woodward, *The Agenda,* 69–71.

69. Blinder, *The Great Stagflation.* Anyway, measured as a percentage of GDP, the total government deficit was only above 1 percent from the first quarter of 1967 through the middle of 1968. For the six quarters from the end of 1968 through the first quarter of 1970, the total government was in surplus. To assert that these two years would produce the run-up in inflation in 1973 and 1974 is dubious indeed.

70. *ERP* 1996, 371. In calendar year 1978 the total government ran a surplus of $20.9 billion, while in 1979 that surplus totaled $33.8 billion.

71. For the Federal Funds rate, see Board of Governors, Federal Reserve System, table J1-1. For the thirty-year Treasury bill rate, see table J1-10. For the structural deficit, see W-1 at the web site, <mars.wnec.edu/~econ/surrender>.

72. See table W-9 at the web site <mars.wnec.edu/~econ/surrender> for the details.

73. The full projection in *A Vision of Change for America* involved a net increase of $13 billion in spending in 1993. In 1994 deficit reduction cuts and revenue increases would be $66 billion, but the rest of the stimulus coupled with the beginning of new public investments would reduce that, resulting in a net deficit reduction of $39 billion. Between 1993 and 1998, the plan called for an initial deficit reduction of $704 billion combined with increased public investments, tax reductions (and the stimulus package) totaling $231 billion, for a net deficit reduction of $473 billion. See p. 22 for details. As a percentage of GDP, the deficit was projected to fall from 5.4 percent in 1993 to 2.7 percent in 1997. Absent reform in health care,

the Clinton administration predicted an increase in the deficit for 1998, which would increase the deficit as a percentage of GDP to 3.1. In fact the rapidly growing economy in 1996 and 1997 coupled with the August 1997 agreement led to a virtual disappearance of the deficit by the beginning of fiscal 1998 (see Pear, note 9 in this chapter).

74. Eisner, *The Misunderstood Economy*, 198–99.

75. *A Vision of Change for America*, 22; and *ERP* 1994, 32. The Reischauer analysis quoted by the *New York Times* (see Pear, note 9 in this chapter) gives significant credit for succeeding—in fact, improving on these targets—to the 1993 deficit reduction package but not as much as to the 1990 one.

76. Between January and December 1993, the thirty-year Treasury bond yield fell from 7.34 percent to 6.25 percent. The gap had fallen to 3.29 by December, despite continued declines in the Federal Funds rate (Board of Governors, Federal Reserve System, table J1-10).

77. *ERP* 1997, 303.

78. Ibid., 300. For productivity growth, it is necessary to ignore the data in the 1997 economic report and utilize the industry analytical ratios for the nonfarm business sector from the Bureau of Labor Statistics because they recalculated productivity data during 1997.

79. *ERP* 1994, 35.

80. Ibid.

81. The thirty-year Treasury bond yielded 6.25 percent in January and reached 8.08 percent in November. Thereafter it began to fall, though it did not get below 6.25 percent till December 1995 (Board of Governors, Federal Reserve System, table J1-10). In real terms, it was at 3.75 percent in the first quarter of 1994 and rose to almost 5.5 percent by the end of the year before beginning to fall slowly in 1995.

82. See U.S. Department of Commerce, Bureau of Economic Analysis, "Per Capita Gross Domestic Product—(Chained (1992) Dollars)."

83. *ERP* 1994, 34.

84. Ibid., 38.

85. Ibid., 38.

86. *ERP* 1995, 27.

87. *ERP* 1995, 27. This was exactly the point I made above (see pp. 174–75) about the inability to give the economy a fiscal stimulus to fight the 1990 recession due to the high deficits that had persisted during the 1980s.

88. *ERP* 1995, 30.

89. For the details, see tables W-10 through W-12 at the web site, <mars.wnec.edu/~econ/surrender>. They present quarterly data from 1991 to the present and will be updated from time to time.

Chapter 11

1. In terms of regulatory burdens, the Center for the Study of American Business estimated that Clinton's first budget proposal reversed a slight reduction in federal regulatory spending that had occurred with the last Bush budget (fiscal 1993) and continued to increase actual staff in the various regulatory agencies. See Warren, "Mixed Message," 4.

2. The misery index, we should recall, sums the unemployment rate and the rate of inflation. Taking the rate of inflation in the consumer price index, we see a misery index of 9.9 percent in 1993, 8.7 percent in 1994, and 8.4 percent in 1995 and 1996. The last time the index had been that low was in 1968 (*ERP* 1997, 370, 346).

3. *ERP* 1995, 314; *ERP* 1996, 318.

4. *ERP* 1997, 352. In 1995 the fall resumed, leaving average weekly earnings less than one-half dollar above the 1993 figure in purchasing power.

5. The proposed Health Security Act is described in detail in *ERP* 1994, chap. 4.

6. Historian Theda Skocpol has written a postmortem on the failure of Clinton's health care reform. In the following passage she stresses the point we have made herein:

> Historically, Americans have been perfectly happy to benefit from federal government spending, and even to pay higher taxes to finance spending that is generous and benefits more privileged groups and citizens, not just the poor. Such benefits are especially appealing if they flow in administratively streamlined and relatively automatic ways. But Americans dislike federal government regulations not accompanied by generous monetary payoffs. (*Boomerang: Clinton's Health Security Effort and the Turn against Government in U.S. Politics* [New York: Norton, 1996], 167)

7. Ibid., chap. 5.

8. The opposition to the Canadian system produced significant amounts of propaganda by anecdote to make it appear that Canadians were all flocking to the United States for operations that the Canadian system routinely refused to perform. This despite the fact that Canadians routinely expressed high levels of satisfaction with their health care system, in much higher percentages than did Americans.

9. Skocpol argues that the political constraints under which Clinton operated precluded his offering a single-payer proposal. Particularly she argues that such a proposal "could easily have been caricatured by fiscal conservatives . . . as a 'budget buster,' a new 'entitlement' that was bound to get out of control. . . . threatened stakeholders and the populist right would . . . have carried on a devastating scare campaign about a 'government takeover' of medical care" (*Boomerang,* 179). While she is no doubt correct that support for a single-payer plan would have gone against Mr. Clinton's pro-private-sector instincts, the ability of the groups mentioned to caricature and misrepresent *any* comprehensive reform suggests that supporting an easily described, easily defended system would have been *better* than the overly complicated proposal that was also labeled "socialized medicine" by the opposition.

10. It was estimated that the original Clinton proposal would have added approximately $10 billion to the cost of welfare (Todd S. Purdum, "Clinton Remembers Promise, Considers History, and Will Sign," *New York Times,* August 1, 1996, A22).

11. *Contract with America,* 66–67.

12. See pp. 96–97.

13. Advisory Commission on Intergovernmental Relations, *Changing Public Attitudes on Governments and Taxes, 1981* (Washington, DC: Government Printing Office, 1981).

14. The *1996 Green Book* provides this account:

> According to an HHS compilation, by mid-February 1996, all but 10
> States . . . had approval to test departures from specified provisions of
> AFDC. . . . AFDC waiver projects can be classified broadly as restricting
> or liberalizing some elements of the program. Examples of the former
> include:
>
> Place time limit on benefit duration (24 States);
>
> Tighten work requirements (31 States);
>
> Link benefits to school attendance/performance (26 States)
>
> Limit benefits for additional children (14 States);
>
> Reduce benefits based on relocation (2 States);
>
> Require fingerprinting as a condition of eligibility (1 State).

Major waiver provisions that liberalize some terms of the program include:

> Treat earnings more generously (30 States)
>
> Expand eligibility for 2-parent (unemployed) families (25 States)
>
> Increase resource limit (28 States);
>
> Increase vehicle asset limit (25 States);
>
> Expand transitional medical and child care benefits (21 States).

(434–45)

15. Purdum, "Clinton Remembers Promise." See also "Points of Agreement, and Disagreement, on the Welfare Bill," *New York Times* August 1, 1996, A22.

16. "Excerpts from the President's News Conference at the White House," *New York Times,* December 14, 1996, A1.

17. $9.5 billion was restored in SSI benefits to legal immigrants, $2 billion in increased Medicaid for these individuals, and $2.7 billion in increased grants to states to help people receiving welfare under the two-year limitation find work. See O'Neill, letter to Raines, 54–55.

18. These are Congressional Budget Office estimates made in December 1995 based on the provisions of the Balanced Budget Act that President Clinton had vetoed. See CBO Memorandum, "The Economic and Budget Outlook: December 1995 Update," 27–28.

19. Congressional Budget Office, *Economic Outlook, 1997–2006,* chap. 3. It was this readjustment that had so impressed the reporter from the *Wall Street Journal* in early February 1996 (Calmes, "Clinton's Fiscal '97 Budget").

20. Defenders of the Clinton administration will no doubt point out that they had rallied virtually the entire Democratic congressional caucus to support their proposed minimum-wage increase and that their drumfire of support for the proposal and scorn for the Republicans who opposed it ultimately led to enough Republican defections from the leadership to pass a $.90 per hour increase in the summer of 1996 (Jared Bernstein and John Schmitt, "The Sky Hasn't Fallen: An Evaluation of the Minimum-Wage Increase," Briefing Paper, Economic Policy Institute, 1997, 1). The first thing to note about this is that when the Democrats had

the majority in Congress, the Clinton administration never made *mention* of the need to raise the minimum wage. The second is that this increase will still leave the minimum wage 20 percent below its level in 1979 in purchasing power. It is too early to tell if the increase in the minimum wage has helped reverse the increasing inequality among wage earners. That will be the key issue.

21. *ERP* 1998, 314.

22. *ERP* 1998, 312–13.

23. For a particularly useful visual picture, see Krugman, "The Right, the Rich."

24. "[L]evels of wage inequality for men have been greater in recent years than at any time since 1940. Women received wage increases throughout the wage distribution, but the gains were concentrated at the top" (*ERP* 1995, 176).

25. *ERP* 1995, 181.

26. Ibid.

27. *ERP* 1995, 184–95.

28. For families, the Gini ratio had peaked at .401 in 1989, fell slightly to .390 in 1991, rose to .401 in 1992. and jumped to .429 in 1993 before falling slightly to .421 in 1995. See Bureau of the Census, Incomes Statistics Branch/HHES Division, Current Population Reports, Series P-60, Table F-4, "Gini Ratios for Families, by Race and Hispanic Origin of Householder: 1947–1995." For Households, the peak of inequality in 1989 was at .431. The Gini ratio then fell to .428 in 1991, rose to .434 in 1992 and jumped to .454 in 1993. It fell slightly to .450 in 1995. See ibid., table H-4, "Gini Ratios for Households, by Race and Hispanic Origin of Householder: 1967 to 1995." We should note that in 1993, the method of collecting the census information was expanded, and much of the measured increase in inequality is probably due to the changed method of data collection. The most crucial point of all this information is that the increase in inequality between 1979 and 1989 was not been reversed despite the long recovery and despite the Clinton administration's alleged efforts. For the most recent information (as this book goes to press), see *ERP* 1998, 127.

29. "Job Creation and Employment Opportunities: The United States Labor Market, 1993–1996," report by the Council of Economic Advisers with the U.S. Department of Labor, Office of the Chief Economist, April 23, 1996, 1.

30. Ibid., 4. This is not definitive evidence about the actual nature of the jobs created because though the "job category" paid "on average" above-median wages, there is a wide variation in wages within each job category. It is possible the newly created jobs would pay less than average for that job category.

31. Ibid., 7–8.

32. Robert J. Samuelson, *The Good Life and Its Discontents* (New York: Times Books, 1995), esp. chap. 4.

33. *ERP* 1996, 23. It is interesting to note that one of the results of the revision in how the Department of Commerce's Bureau of Economic Analysis computed the gross domestic product was to substantially reduce the initial rates of productivity growth for the 1990s. For a quick comparison, check out the *Economic Report of the President* for 1995 and 1996, table B-46, productivity.

34. *ERP* 1996, 22.

35. According to the Congressional Budget Office analysis of the combined tax cut and balanced-budget plan passed in the summer of 1997, the Taxpayer Relief Act will increase expenditures under the earned-income tax credit and the

(smaller) child care credit by a total of $11.5 billion through fiscal 2002. See O'Neill, letter to Raines.

36. *ERP* 1996, 33.

37. *ERP* 1998, 304. These are percentages of government purchases. It does not include transfer payments.

38. See table W-9 at the web site, <www.mars.wnec.edu/~econ/surrender>.

39. *ERP* 1996, 45.

40. *ERP* 1997, 359.

41. *ERP* 1997, 346.

42. *ERP* 1996, 361. We might note that such a reduction in the Federal Funds rate was accompanied by an actual shrinkage in M1 throughout 1995, once again demonstrating that the rate of growth of M1 was an unreliable guide to monetary policy. M2 growth was accelerated during 1995 (*ERP* 1996, 355).

43. For the actions of the Fed in 1997, see *ERP* 1998, 44. For the unemployment rate month to month, see ibid., 330. By the middle of 1997 the reason for the Fed's behavior became apparent as insider newsletters were reporting a rising fear that the economy might "overshoot" the target of zero inflation and experience deflation. By the end of 1997, with the Asian financial crisis making investors nervous, there was even talk that the Fed might have to *lower* interest rates despite the fact that unemployment had fallen below 5 percent and that the economy had been growing faster than 3 per cent for much of 1997.

44. The 1998 *Economic Report of the President* actually attempted to reconcile the existence of a NAIRU (nonaccelerating inflation rate of unemployment) of approximately 5.5 percent with the experience of 1997 when inflation actually *fell* while unemployment dived below 4 percent (see ibid., 54–63). The council also forecast that the economy would snap back from its "unsustainable" high growth rates of 1996 and 1997 to 2.0 percent from fourth quarter to fourth quarter in 1998, 1999, and 2000 (see ibid., 78–87). The Congressional Budget Office makes a similar prediction:

> Despite low unemployment and high output, which CBO estimates exceeded its potential (the amount that can be produced without accelerating inflation), the rate of inflation . . . fell . . . CBO believes that factors such as falling import prices have masked the inflationary pressures that have built up over the past two years. CBO expects that inflation will begin to increase during 1998 . . .

> The rise in inflation, together with low unemployment is expected to lead to slightly tighter monetary policy in 1998. Along with the effect of the Asian financial crisis on U.S. exports, an increase of 0.2 percentage points in short-term interest rates is expected to slow economic growth to a sustainable pace by early 1999. (Congressional Budget Office, *The Economic and Budget Outlook: Fiscal Years 1999–2008,* xvii–xix)

45. See above, pp. 1–2.

46. The federal deficit as a percentage of GDP rose from less than 0.5 percent in fiscal 1974 to 3.4 percent in fiscal 1975 and 4.3 percent in fiscal 1976. By contrast the rise from fiscal 1989 to fiscal 1992 was from 2.8 percent to 4.7 percent. Remember, the key to using the government to raise aggregate demand is in the *rise* in deficit spending (*ERP* 1997, 389).

47. The unemployment rate was 5.6 percent in 1974. It fell to 7.7 percent in 1976. Unemployed receiving compensation fell to 67 percent in the same year. For unemployment, see *ERP* 1997, 346. For the percentage of the unemployed receiving compensation, see *1996 Green Book,* 332.

48. *1996 Green Book,* 332.

49. In 1974, the Federal Funds rate rose to 10.50 percent. In 1975, the Central Bank pursued a vigorous policy to cut that rate down to 5.82, and the rate continued to fall till the first quarter of 1977. By contrast, in 1991 the rate was only cut from 8.10 the previous year to 5.69. In 1992, however, the Federal Reserve did push that rate even lower; it fell below 3 percent in the last month of that year (*ERP* 1997, 382–83). See also table W-1 at the web site, <mars.wnec.edu/~econ/surrender>.

50. The rate of growth of real GDP was 5.6 percent in 1976, 4.9 percent in 1977, and 5.0 percent in 1978. In 1979 that rate fell to 2.9 percent. In 1991, the rate of growth was –1.0 percent. In 1992, 1993, and 1994 it was 2.7 percent, 2.3 percent, and 3.5 percent. In 1995 it fell back to 2.0 percent (*ERP* 1997, 307). For the creation of jobs, see *ERP* 1997, 340. In 1997 close to three million jobs were created (see *ERP* 1998, 324), but remember, that is "unsustainable."

51. For the percentages of the population in poverty see *1996 Green Book,* 1226. For the total population receiving AFDC, see p. 467. For the percentage of poor children receiving AFDC, see p. 471.

52. Remember that according to the Reischauer study referred to by the *New York Times* (Pear, "Budget Heroes Include Bush and Gorbachev") the Bush changes were more significant than the Clinton changes in contributing to the virtual disappearance of the deficit by the end of 1997.

53. *ERP* 1997, 383.

54. In 1993, the House of Representatives Ways and Means Committee projected federal spending on AFDC for fiscal 1996 at $1.5 billion, approximately 1 percent of all federal expenditures and 6.6 percent of the total federal expenditure on "income security" (*1993 Green Book,* 679; *ERP* 1997, 391). In fact the expenditure for fiscal 1996 was actually closer to $1.3 billion, an even lower percentage of the federal budget (*1996 Green Book,* 459). The projected reductions in expenditures between fiscal 1997 and 2002 as a result of the abolition of AFDC and other aspects of welfare reform come mostly from cuts in SSI and food stamps, not the AFDC replacement called Temporary Assistance for Needy Families (TANF) (*1996 Green Book,* 1332–33). As mentioned above, some of these cuts have since been repealed. See O'Neill, letter to Raines, 58–61.

55. For investment, see *ERP* 1998, 280; for the federal deficit, see *ERP* 1998, 374.

56. *ERP* 1997, 390.

57. *ERP* 1995, 359.

58. Federal revenues actually *rose* as a percentage of GDP in fiscal 1997, a year in which GDP itself grew quite rapidly (see *ERP* 1998, 373). Federal spending did not quite keep pace with GDP, but total government purchases of goods and services did (ibid., 280–81).

59. Recall that the budget that was passed in 1995 provided for over $1.5 trillion in spending cuts between 1996 and 2002.

60. By its own admission, Congressional Budget Office projections do not

incorporate business cycle impacts on revenue and expenditures beyond the next two years. Thus, in the spring of 1996, seeing no sign of a recession in either 1996 or 1997, they developed their 1998–2006 projections without attempting to estimate the impact of a recession.

> [T]he projections are designed to approximate the level of economic activity on average, including the possibility of above-or below-average rates of growth, inflation and interest. CBO uses historical relationships to identify trends in fundamental factors underlying the economy, including growth of the labor force, the rate of national saving, and growth of productivity. The projections of variables such as real GDP, inflation, and real interest rates are then based on their historical norms (Congressional Budget Office, *Economic Outlook, 1997–2006,* 12).

In 1997, the CBO was able to revise upward their revenue estimates based on strong economic growth so far that year. That also permitted projecting rates of growth of real GDP of 2.2 percent for 1997 and 1998 (Congressional Budget Office, *Economic and Budget Outlook, 1998–2007,* 1, 12–16). Even these projectious proved too pessimistic, and in 1998 they again raised their predictions of real growth for 1998 (Congressional Budget Office, *Economic and Budget Outlook, 1999–2008,* p. 2).

61. The Emergency Unemployment Compensation Act of 1991 temporarily extended benefits. This act was amended a number of times, and extended benefits ended up being available through October 2, 1993 (*1993 Green Book,* 521–22).

62. *ERP* 1996, 65–69; *ERP* 1997, 45–61, 74–85, 87–91; and *ERP* 1998, 85–87.

63. The Clinton Council of Economic Advisers devoted a chapter in the *Economic Report of the President* for 1998 to "The Economic Well-Being of Children." They noted that between 1993 and 1996 the number of children in poverty had declined by over two percentage points. However, the chart they present (92) shows that the current level is much higher than before the Volcker-Reagan revolution and isn't quite as low as it was at the end of the Reagan recovery in 1989. At the end of 1996, 13.7 percent of the entire population lived in poverty, still well above the figures for 1980 and 1988 (320). They also acknowledged that overall inequality has increased since the 1970s (127).

Coda

1. When Professor Vickrey won the Nobel Prize for economics in 1996, he was ecstatic because he believed he could use that "bully pulpit" to present his strong arguments to the general public against single-minded pursuit of budget balance. Unfortunately, he died within a week of receiving the prize, and the public is left only with his writings to support his and others' position against the current policy consensus. For a summary of his views, see *Fifteen Fatal Fallacies of Financial Fundamentalism,* October 5, 1996, available on the Columbia University Department of Economics web site at <www.columbia.edu/cu/economics>.

2. National Conference of Catholic Bishops, *Economic Justice for All: Pastoral Letter on Catholic Social Teaching on the U.S. Economy* (Washington, DC: U.S. Catholic Conference, 1986).

3. There has been a long debate in the specialist literature as to which group

actually controls the behavior of corporations, the shareholders who are the legal "owners," or the managers who carry out the day-to-day activities of the business. See Adolph A. Berle and Gardner C. Means, *The Modern Corporation and Private Property* (New York: Commerce Clearing House, 1932), for the argument that by 1929, a high percentage of corporations were effectively controlled by their top managers. In 1966, in *The New Industrial State,* John Kenneth Galbraith identified the middle-level "technostructure" that, due to its monopoly on the expertise (accounting, marketing, engineering) necessary to make the business run successfully, effectively controlled corporate decision-making. In the discussion of the value to society of a vigorous market for corporate control (see pp. 127–28) the Council of Economic Advisers argued in 1985 that managers are forced to act in the interest of their shareholders by credible threats of outside takeovers. The bishops' view has recently gained significant currency in the literature on the appropriate form of corporate governance, most prominently in the work of Margaret Blair (*Ownership and Control* [Washington, DC: Brookings Institution, 1995]). Blair supports the view that "corporate policies that generate the most wealth for shareholders may not be the policies that generate the greatest total social wealth" (p. 13). This is actually nothing more than a variation on the view that private rates of return and private costs do not always reflect social benefits and costs, a fact acknowledged by the 1982 report of the first Reagan Council of Economic Advisers (see above, pp. 39–41). Blair concludes, as do the bishops, that longtime employees bear significant risks, perhaps more than the shareholders, when they commit themselves to a particular company and should therefore have some say in corporate decision-making (see particularly chaps. 7 and 8).

4. A less benign version of this point is that political and intellectual leaders are very well aware of what the public wants and spend all their time giving the public false impressions of policies designed to help the very richest at the expense of everyone else (how the supply-side tax cuts and other elements of Reaganomics were sold as a way to raise economic growth and employment, when in the end all they did was redistribute income upward) while warning (falsely as well) that the proposals of reformers are "impossible." For an analysis of how public opinion is thwarted by the capture of the political process by big money, see Thomas Ferguson, *Golden Rule: The Investment Theory of Party Competition and the Logic of Money-Driven Political Systems* (Chicago: University of Chicago Press, 1995).

5. Let us recall that when it came to subsidizing business, Reagan was perfectly happy to spend billions on the Star Wars defense system even though the scientists assured the Department of Defense that it would never work, and perfectly happy to force the Japanese to restrain auto exports to protect Detroit producers. Both of these activities overruled "the market" for some "greater good." Recall the summary statement by the editor of *Foreign Affairs* and the argument about the role of the Pentagon in directing investment spending (see chap. 6, n. 76 and chap. 9, n. 18).

6. For an argument that it is, indeed, possible for the economy to grow faster than the 2.3 percent identified in the 1997 *Economic Report of the President* as the long-term sustainable rate (pp. 85–87), see Barry Bluestone and Bennett Harrison, "Why We Can Grow Faster," *American Prospect* 34 (September–October 1997): 63–70. For a contrary view that supports the administration, see Alan Blinder, "The Speed Limit: Fact and Fancy in the Growth Debate," *American Prospect* 34 (September–October 1997): 57–62.

7. See Munnell, "Public Infrastructure," and Aschauer, "Output and Employment Effects." For an argument that high wages and a new approach to labor-management relations also can increase productivity, see Perelman, *Pathology of American Economy,* chap. 8.

8. One such proposal is contained in National Jobs for All Coalition, "A Growth Agenda That Works: A Program for Sustainable Economic Growth and Development" (available from National Jobs for All Coalition, 474 Riverside Drive, Suite 832, New York, NY 10115, email: njfac@ncccusa.org), 27. For their discussion of public capital expenditure, see pp. 8–12.

9. *Buckley v. Valleo,* 424 U.S. 1 (1976).

10. Scott Turow, "The High Court's 20-Year-Old Mistake," *New York Times,* October 12, 1997, sec. 4, 15. Turow continues, "As long as politicians must approach the well-to-do on bended knee to secure their chances for election, it is inevitable that the concerns of that narrow segment of the society will have a disproportionate influence on national policy."

11. The Supreme Court argued that one could not abridge someone's First Amendment rights in order to assure someone else's First Amendment rights (see *Buckley v. Valleo*). If this logic were applied to actual speech, an individual who monopolized the floor at a public meeting and continually shouted down the efforts of everyone else in the room to be heard could not be silenced!

12. National Jobs for All Coalition, "Growth Agenda That Works," 21.

13. For details of such a reform of the Fed, see Robert Pollin, "Public Credit Allocation through the Federal Reserve: Why It Is Needed; How It Should Be Done," in *Transforming the U.S. Financial System,* ed. Gary Dymski, Gerald Epstein, and Robert Pollin (Armonk, NY: M. E. Sharpe, 1993), 321–52. More generally, the organization devoted to analyzing and reforming the way monetary policy is conducted today is the Financial Markets Center (PO Box 334, Philomont, VA 20131, email: finmktctr@aol.com). Their key reform strategies involved "leveling the regulatory playing field upward—by evenly applying prudential standards, financial guarantees and reinvestment standards across the entire financial system." On the Federal Reserve, they argue that "the Fed must be far more accountable to the citizenry" (Tom Schlesinger, "A Financial Market Strategy for Working Americans," presented to the National Consumers League Conference, May 7, 1996, Los Angeles, 5; see also Sheldon Friedman and Tom Schlesinger, "Fed Follies: Why Alan Greenspan Won't Let American Workers Get a Raise," *WorkingUSA,* July–August 1997, 30–36). The vehicle for many of their proposals is the idea of a National Reinvestment Fund to "build a financial infrastructure for businesses and communities lacking access to affordable credit and capital." See *National Reinvestment Fund and Key Federal Reserve and Credit Guarantee Reforms Achieved through the National Reinvestment Fund* (Philomont, VA: Financial Markets Center, 1996). See also Jane D'Arista and Tom Schlesinger, "The Emerging Parallel Banking System," in *The Financial Services Revolution,* ed. Clifford Kirsch (Chicago: Irwin, 1996), 500–501.

14. By January 1864, $449 million of these had been issued. By 1867, greenbacks in circulation represented close to one-third of all currency (Friedman and Schwartz, *Monetary History,* 15–25, especially the table on p. 17). There is nothing mysterious or magical about this process. Instead of creating government bonds that are then sold to banks or the Fed, increasing the Treasury's accounts with Federal Reserve banks, the Treasury would merely order the Fed to increase their

account balances. The difference is that after the Treasury writes checks to pay government workers and suppliers and recipients of transfer payments with borrowed funds, the government must allocate interest payments to bondholders, even if the bonds are merely held by the Federal Reserve System.

15. If these deposits had merely been created without the issuing of a bond, once the money is spent and circulating in society, the government owes no interest to anyone. Between 1940 and 1946, the national debt of the United States rose from $42.9 billion to $269.4 billion (*1979 Report of the Secretary of the Treasury,* 63). Ten percent of that increase is $22 billion. Even a 1 percent interest rate translates into a saving to the Treasury of $220 million a year through the entire life of those bonds.

16. See Pollin, "Public Credit Allocation," 347–48, on ways of preventing financial intermediaries from evading Federal Reserve control by using foreign-controlled assets.

17. See, for example, Robert Kuttner, "Managed Trade and Economic Sovereignty," in *U.S. Trade Policy and Global Growth,* ed. Robert Blecker (Armonk, NY: M. E. Sharpe, 1996), 3–35. See also Gerald Epstein, James Crotty, and Patricia Kelly, "Multinational Corporations and Technological Change: Global Stagnation, Inequality, and Unemployment," mimeo, University of Massachusetts, Amherst, February 1997, 30–34.

18. The simplest of these latter proposals has come to be known as the "Tobin tax," after Nobel Prize winner James Tobin. The proposal is to place a rather small (say 1 percent) tax on unproductive speculative security transactions in order to discourage large movements of funds in and out of particular stocks or particular currencies just to capture a tiny short-term advantage. Even a relatively small tax will discourage these highly speculative activities. For the specific proposals to cut down on destabilizing international currency movements, see James Tobin, "A Proposal for International Monetary Reform," *Eastern Economic Journal* 4 (1978): 153–59, and "A Tax on International Currency Transactions," United Nations *Human Development Report* (1994).

19. For the vigorous aggregate demand management of the Ford administration see pp. 1–2, 255–56. For the expansion of the specifically redistributionist aspect of federal spending see Michael B. Katz, *In the Shadow of the Poorhouse: A Social History of Welfare in America,* rev. ed. (New York: Basic Books, 1996), 269–82.

20. This later became the basis of ERTA. Much of this story can be traced in Bartley, *The Seven Fat Years,* chaps. 2–6. See also Sidney Blumenthal, *The Rise of the Counter-Establishment: From Conservative Ideology to Political Power* (New York: Times Books, 1986), for a discussion of the role of conservative foundations and think tanks in developing and disseminating the conservative critique of what Speaker Newt Gingrich later called the "Great Society redistributionist model."

21. The Economic Policy Institute's work has been referred to and quoted throughout this book. The institute is located at 1660 L Street, NW, Suite 1200, Washington, DC, 20036. Their web site is <http://www.epinet.org>. The Levy Institute's work has also been quoted in this book. It can be reached at Blithewood, Annandale-on-Hudson, NY, 12504; the web site is <http://www.levy.org>. The Center for Popular Economics can be reached at Box 785, Amherst, MA, 01004. Their e-mail address is cpe@econs.umass.edu. The center collaborated with

the Labor Relations and Research Center at the University of Massachusetts at Amherst on a curriculum for internal education at the AFL-CIO, *Common Sense Economics: A Study Group Manual* (Washington, DC: AFL-CIO, 1997). For information about this manual, call the AFL-CIO education department at 202–637–5142. The Financial Markets Center is referred to above in note 13. The left wing of the Democratic Party has also attempted to bestir itself. See, for example, Stanley Greenberg and Theda Skocpol, eds., *The New Majority: Toward a Popular Progressive Politics* (New Haven, CT: Yale University Press, 1997).

References

Government Documents and Publications

Advisory Commission on Intergovernmental Relations. *Changing Public Attitudes on Governments and Taxes, 1981.* Washington, DC: Government Printing Office, 1981.

Buckley v Valleo. 424 U.S. 1 (1976).

Bureau of Economic Analysis, Department of Commerce. "Per Capita Gross Domestic Product—Chained (1992) Dollars." Unpublished data.

Bureau of Labor Statistics. Division of Productivity Research. Office of Productivity and Technology. "Computer Printout of Industry Analytical Ratios for the Business Sector, All Persons." Available from Bureau of Labor Statistics.

Bureau of the Census. Incomes Statistics Branch/HHES Division. *Current Population Reports.* Series P 60.

Congressional Budget Office. *Defense Spending and the Economy.* Washington, DC: Government Printing Office, 1983.

———. *The Economic and Budget Outlook: Fiscal Years 1997–2006.* Washington, DC: Government Printing Office, 1996.

——— *The Economic and Budget Outlook: Fiscal Years 1998–2007.* Washington, DC: Government Printing Office, 1997.

——— *The Economic and Budget Outlook: Fiscal Years 1999–2008.* Washington, DC: Government Printing Office, 1998.

Congressional Record. House. September 29, 1994. 10254.

Council of Economic Advisers with the U.S. Department of Labor, Office of the Chief Economist. "Job Creation and Employment Opportunities: The United States Labor Market, 1993–1996." April 23, 1996.

Economic Report of the President (ERP). Washington, DC: Government Printing Office, various years.

Federal Reserve Board. Table J1-1. Available from the Federal Reserve Board.

Federal Open Market Committee. Meeting transcript, March 28, 1989. Available from the Federal Reserve Board, Freedom of Information section.

Griggs v. Duke Power Co. 401 U.S. 424 (1971).

Horney, Jim. "Memorandum: Updated Estimates of the Balanced Budget Act of 1995." Congressional Budget Office, December 13, 1995.

Joint Committee on Taxation. *General Explanation of the Economic Recovery Tax Act of 1981.* Washington, DC: Government Printing Office, 1981.

Means, Gardiner C. *Industrial Prices and Their Relative Inflexibility.* Senate Document No. 13, 74th Congress. Washington, DC: Government Printing Office, 1935.

National Commission on Excellence in Education. *A Nation at Risk.* Washington, DC: Government Printing Office, 1983.

1979 Report of the Secretary of the Treasury. Washington, DC: Government Printing Office, 1979.

Office of Management and Budget. *A Vision of Change for America.* Washington, DC: Government Printing Office, February 17, 1993.

U.S. Department of Commerce, Bureau of Economic Analysis. *Fixed Reproducible Tangible Wealth in the United States, 1925–89.* Washington, DC: Government Printing Office, January 1993.

————. *National Income and Product Accounts of the United States.* Vol. 2, 1959–88. Washington, DC: Government Printing Office, 1992.

————. *Survey of Current Business* 73 (September 1993).

U.S. Equal Employment Opportunity Commission and the U.S. Department of Justice. *Americans with Disabilities Act Handbook.* EEOC-BK-19. October, 1992.

U.S. House of Representatives, Committee on Ways and Means. *Overview of Entitlement Programs, 1993 Green Book, Background Material and Data on Programs within the Jurisdiction of the Committee on Ways and Means.* Washington, DC: Government Printing Office, 1993.

————. *1996 Green Book: Background Material and Data on Programs within the Jurisdiction of the Committee on Ways and Means.* Washington, DC: Government Printing Office, 1996.

Wards Cove Packing Co. v. Atonio. 490 U.S. 642 (1989).

Unpublished Manuscripts

Aschauer, David A. "Output and Employment Effects of Public Capital." Working Paper 190, Jerome Levy Economics Institute, 1997.

Baker, Dean. "Trends in Corporate Profitability: Getting More for Less?" Technical Paper, Economic Policy Institute, February 1996.

Baldwin, Marc, and Richard McHugh. "Unprepared for Recession: The Erosion of State Unemployment Insurance Coverage Fostered by Public Policy in the 1980s." Briefing Paper, Economic Policy Institute, 1992.

Bernstein, Jared, and John Schmitt. "The Sky Hasn't Fallen: An Evaluation of the Minimum-Wage Increase." Briefing Paper, Economic Policy Institute, 1997.

Center for Popular Economics and Labor Relations and Research Center, University of Massachusetts, Amherst. "Common Sense Economics: Study Group Manual." Washington, DC: AFL-CIO, 1997.

College and University Personnel Association. "The ADA and the Civil Rights Act of 1991." Photocopy.

Duston, Robert L. "What Every College and University Administrator Needs to Know about the ADA, and Why." Conference manual for the College and University Personnel Association conference on the Americans with Disabilities Act, April 11–12, 1992. Available from Robert L. Duston, Schmeltzer, Aptaker & Shepard, P.C., Washington, DC.

Epstein, Gerald, James Crotty, and Patricia Kelly. "Multinational Corporations and Technological Change: Global Stagnation, Inequality, and Unemployment." Mimeo. University of Massachusetts, Amherst. February 1997.

Financial Markets Center. *Key Federal Reserve and Credit Guarantee Reforms Achieved through the National Reinvestment Fund.* Philmont, VA: Financial Markets Center, 1996.

——. *National Reinvestment Fund.* Philmont, VA: Financial Markets Center, 1996.

Lindsey, Lawrence B. "Simulating the Response of Taxpayers to Changes in Tax Rates." Ph.D. diss., Harvard University, 1985.

McMurrer, Daniel P. and Isabel V. Sawhill. "Economic Mobility in the United States." Urban Institute, December 1966.

National Jobs for All Coalition. "A Growth Agenda That Works." November 1995. Available from National Jobs for All Coalition, 475 Riverside Drive, Suite 832, New York, NY 10115.

Robert Half International. "Family Time Is More Important Than Rapid Career Advancement: Survey Shows Both Men and Women Support Parent Tracking." Press release. San Francisco, June 28, 1989.

Schlesinger, Tom. "A Financial Market Strategy for Working Americans." Paper presented to the National Consumer's League Conference, Los Angeles, CA, May 7, 1996.

Schor, Juliet B., and Laura Leete-Guy. "The Great American Time Squeeze: Trends in Work and Leisure, 1969 1989." Briefing Paper, Economic Policy Institute, 1992.

Smeeding, Timothy, Greg Duncan, and Willard Rodgers. "W(h)ither the Middle Class?" Policy Studies Paper No. 1, Metropolitan Studies Program, Income Security Policy Series, Maxwell School of Citizenship and Public Affairs, Syracuse University, February 1992.

Vickrey, William, *Fifteen Fatal Fallacies of Financial Fundamentalism.* October 5, 1996. Columbia University Department of Economics web site, <www.columbia.edu/cu/economics>.

Warren, Melinda. "Mixed Message: An Analysis of the 1994 Federal Regulatory Budget." Occasional Paper 128, Center for the Study of American Business, Washington University, St. Louis, 1994.

——. "Regulation on the Rise: Analysis of the Federal Budget for 1992." Occasional Paper 89, Center for the Study of American Business, Washington University, St. Louis, 1992.

Wolff, Edward N. "The Rich Get Increasingly Richer: Latest Data on Household Wealth during the 1980s." Briefing Paper, Economic Policy Institute, 1992.

Articles

Abraham, Spencer. "The Real 1980s." *The World and I,* April 1996, 94–100.

Ando, Albert, and Franco Modigliani. "Rejoinder." *American Economic Review* 55 (September 1965): 786–90.

——. "The Relative Stability of Monetary Velocity and the Investment Multiplier." *American Economic Review* 55 (September 1965): 693–728.

Aschauer, David A. "Is Public Expenditure Productive?" *Journal of Monetary Economics* 23 (1989): 177–200.

Baldwin, Richard E. "Hysteresis in Import Prices: The Beachhead Effect." *American Economic Review* 78 (September 1988): 773–85.

Barth, James R., George Iden, Frank S. Russek, and Mark Wohar. "The Effects of Federal Budget Deficits on Interest Rates and the Composition of Domestic Output." In *The Great Fiscal Experiment,* ed. Rudolph G. Penner. Washington, DC: Urban Institute Press, 1991.

Bawden, D. Lee, and John L. Palmer. "Social Policy: Challenging the Welfare State." In *The Reagan Record,* ed. John L. Palmer and Isabel V. Sawhill. Cambridge, MA: Ballinger, 1984.

Bedwell, Conald, and Gary Tapp. "Supply-Side Economics Conference in Atlanta." *Economic Review of the Federal Reserve Bank of Atlanta* 57 (1982): 25–35.

Blank, Rebecca, and Emma Rothschild. "The Effect of United States Defense Spending on Employment and Output." *International Labour Review* 124 (November–December 1985): 677–98.

Blinder, Alan. "The Speed Limit: Fact and Fancy in the Growth Debate." *American Prospect* 34 (September–October 1997): 57–62.

Bluestone, Barry, and Bennett Harrison. "Why We Can Grow Faster." *American Prospect* 34 (September–October): 63–70.

Burtless, Gary. "Effects on Labor Supply." In *The Economic Legacy of the Reagan Years: Euphoria or Chaos?* ed. Anandi Sahu and Ronald Tracy. New York: Praeger, 1991.

———. "Tax-Cut Potions and Voodoo Fantasies." *The World and I,* April 1996, 100–102.

Carlson, Robert B., and Kevin R. Hopkins. "Whose Responsibility Is Social Responsibility?" *Public Welfare* 39 (fall 1981): 8–17.

Cloward, Richard A., and Frances Fox Piven. "The Contemporary Relief Debate." In Fred Block, Richard A. Cloward, Barbara Ehrenreich and Frances Fox Piven, *The Mean Season: The Attack on the Welfare State.* New York: Pantheon, 1987.

———. "The Historical Sources of the Contemporary Relief Debate." In Fred Block, Richard A. Cloward, Barbara Ehrenreich, and Frances Fox Piven, *The Mean Season: The Attack on the Welfare State.* New York: Pantheon, 1987.

Cypher, James. "Military Spending, Technical Change, and Economic Growth: A Disguised Form of Industrial Policy?" *Journal of Economic Issues* 21 (1987): 33–59.

Danziger, Sheldon, and Daniel Weinberg. "The Historical Record: Trends in Family Income, Inequality, and Poverty." In *Confronting Poverty: Prescriptions for Change,* ed. Sheldon Danziger, Gary Sandefur, and Daniel Weinberg. Cambridge: Harvard University Press, 1994.

D'Arista, Jane, and Tom Schlesinger. "The Emerging Parallel Banking System." In *The Financial Services Revolution,* ed. Clifford Kirsch. Chicago: Irwin, 1966.

Darity, William, Jr., and James Galbraith. "A Guide to the Deficit." *Challenge,* July–August 1995, 5–12.

Davis, Jeffrey, and Kenneth Lehn. "Securities Regulation during the Reagan Administration: Corporate Takeovers and the 1987 Stock Market Crash." In *The Economic Legacy of the Reagan Years: Euphoria or Chaos?* ed. Anandi Sahu and Ronald Tracy. New York: Praeger, 1991.

Days, Drew S. "Civil Rights at the Crossroads." In *Debating Affirmative Action:*

Race, Gender, Ethnicity, and the Politics of Inclusion, ed. Nicolaus Mills. New
York: Delta, 1994.

DePrano, Michael, and Thomas Mayer. "Rejoinder." *American Economic Review*
55 (September 1965): 791–92.

———. "Tests of the Relative Importance of Autonomous Expenditures and
Money." *American Economic Review* 55 (September 1965): 729–51.

"Dick Armey's Research." *New York Times Book Review,* August 20, 1995, 27.

Eisner, Robert. "Social Security, Saving, and Macroeconomics." *Journal of
Macroeconomics* 5 (1983): 1–19.

Feldstein, Martin. "The Economics of the New Unemployment." *Public Interest*
33 (1973): 3–42.

———. "Social Security, Induced Retirement, and Aggregate Accumulation."
Journal of Political Economy 82 (1974): 905–25.

Friedman, Milton. "The Role of Monetary Policy." *American Economic Review* 58
(March 1968): 1–17.

Friedman, Milton, and David Meiselman. "The Relative Stability of Monetary
Velocity and the Investment Multiplier in the United States, 1897–1958." In
Stabilization Policies, ed. E. C. Brown, 165–268. Englewood Cliffs, NJ: Com-
mission on Money and Credit, 1963

———. "Reply to Ando and Modigliani and to DePrano and Mayer." *American
Economic Review* 55 (September 1965): 753–85.

Friedman, Sheldon, and Tom Schlesinger. "Fed Follies: Why Alan Greenspan
Won't Let American Workers Get a Raise." *WorkingUSA* (July–August
1997): 30–36.

Gill, Richard. "The Issue of Monetarism." In *Great Debates in Economics,* ed.
Richard Gill. Pacific Palisades, CA: Goodyear, 1976.

"Gold Mania: Capitalism's Fever Chart." *Monthly Review,* January 1980, 1–8.

Hadley, Jack, Earl Steinberg, and Judith Feder. "Comparison of Uninsured and
Privately Insured Hospital Patients. Condition on Admission, Resource Use,
and Outcome." *Journal of the American Medical Association* 265 (1991):
374–79.

Islam, Shafiqul. "Capitalism in Conflict." *Foreign Affairs* 69 (1990): 172–82.

Kahn, R.F. "The Relation of Home Investment to Unemployment." *Economic
Journal* 41 (1931): 173–93.

Kleiman, Robert T. "'Securities Regulation during the Reagan Administration':
Comment." In *The Economic Legacy of the Reagan Years: Euphoria or Chaos?*
ed. Anandi Sahu and Ronald Tracy. New York: Praeger, 1991.

Kuttner, Robert. "Managed Trade and Economic Sovereignty." In *U.S. Trade
Policy and Global Growth,* ed. Robert Blecker. Armonk, NY: M. E. Sharpe,
1996.

Leimer, Dean, and Selig Lesnoy. "Social Security and Private Saving: New Time-
Series Evidence." *Journal of Political Economy* 90 (1982): 606–29.

Long, William F., and David J. Ravenscraft. "Lessons from LBOs in the 1980s."
In *The Deal Decade: What Takeovers and Leveraged Buyouts Mean for Corporate Governance,* ed. Margaret M. Blair. Washington, DC: Brookings Institution, 1993.

Meeropol, Michael. "A Smoke Screen for Brutal Interest Rates." *The World and I,*
April 1996, 102–3.

"Monetary Report to Congress." *Federal Reserve Bulletin* 66 (March 1980): 177–89.

Munnell, Alicia. "How Does Public Infrastructure Affect Regional Economic Performance?" *New England Economic Review* (September–October 1990): 11–32.

"Oeconomicus." *Xenophon in Seven Volumes.* Vol. 4. Trans. E. C. Marchant. Cambridge: Harvard University Press, 1968.

Peterson, George E. "Federalism and the States: An Experiment in Decentralization." In *The Reagan Record,* ed. John L. Palmer and Isabel V. Sawhill. Cambridge, MA: Ballinger, 1984.

Peterson, Peter. "The Morning After." *Atlantic Monthly,* October 1987, 43–69.

Phillips, A. W. "The Relation between Unemployment and the Rate of Change of Money Wage Rates in the United Kingdom, 1861–1957." *Economica* 25 (1958): 283–99.

Pollin, Robert. "Budget Deficits and the U.S. Economy: Considerations in a Heilbronerian Mode." In *Economics as Worldly Philosophy: Essays in Political and Historical Economics in Honour of Robert L. Heilbroner,* ed. Chatha Blackwell and Nell Blackwell. New York: St. Martin's Press, 1993.

———. "The Growth of US Household Debt: Demand-Side Influences." *Journal of Macroeconomics* 10 (spring 1988): 231–48.

Portney, Paul R. "Natural Resources and the Environment: More Controversy Than Change." In *The Reagan Record,* ed. John L. Palmer and Isabel V. Sawhill. Cambridge, MA: Ballinger Publishing, 1984.

———. "Public Credit Allocation through the Federal Reserve: Why It Is Needed; How It Should Be Done." In *Transforming the U.S. Financial System,* ed. Gary Dymski, Gerald Epstein, and Robert Pollin. Armonk, NY: M. E. Sharpe, 1993.

"The Real Reagan Record." *National Review,* August 31, 1992, 25–62.

"Regents of the University of California v Bakke." *Preview of United States Supreme Court Cases.* October 1977 Term, No. 4 (26 September 1977): 1–3.

Reppy, Judith. "Military R & D and the Civilian Economy." *Bulletin of the Atomic Scientists* 41 (October 1985): 10–13.

Reynolds, Alan. "Clintonomics Doesn't Measure Up." *Wall Street Journal,* June 12, 1996, A16.

———. "Upstarts and Downstarts." *National Review,* August 31, 1992, 25–31.

Roberts, Paul Craig. "Debt, Lies, and Inflation." *National Review,* August 31, 1992, 31–35.

Sawhill, Isabel V., and Mark Condon. "Is U.S. Income Inequality Really Growing? Sorting Out the Fairness Question." *Policy Bites* (Urban Institute), June 1992, pp. 1–4.

Sawhill, Isabel V., and Charles F. Stone. "The Economy: The Key to Success." In *The Reagan Record,* ed. John L. Palmer and Isabel V. Sawhill. Cambridge, MA: Ballinger, 1984.

Shoven, John B., Scott B. Smart, and Joel Waldfogel. "Real Interest Rates and the Savings and Loan Crisis: The Moral Hazard Premium." *Journal of Economic Perspectives* 6 (1992): 155–67.

"Statement by Paul A. Volcker, Chairman, Board of Governors of the Federal Reserve System, before the Joint Economic Committee of the U.S. Congress, October 17, 1979." *Federal Reserve Bulletin* 65 (November 1979): 888–90.

Thompson, Leonard H. "The Social Security Reform Debate." *Journal of Economic Literature* 21 (1983): 1425–67.

Tobin, James. "A Proposal for International Monetary Reform." *Eastern Economic Journal* 4 (1978): 153–59.

———. "A Tax on International Currency Transactions." *Human Development Report* (United Nations), 1994.

Ture, Norman. "To Cut and to Please." *National Review*, August 31, 1992, 35–39.

Turow, Scott. "The High Court's 20-Year-Old Mistake." *New York Times*, October 12, 1997, sec. 4, p. 15.

"United States Steelworkers of America v. Weber"; "Kaiser Aluminum & Chemical Corp. v. Weber"; and "United States v. Weber." *Preview of United States Supreme Court Cases*, October 1978 term, no. 31 (April 5, 1979), 1–3.

Wanniski, Jude. "The Mundell-Laffer Hypothesis." *Public Interest* 39 (spring 1975): 31–52.

Weidenbaum, Murray. "America's New Beginning: A Program for Economic Recovery." In *Two Revolutions in Economic Policy*, ed. James Tobin and Murray Weidenbaum. Cambridge: MIT Press, 1988.

Weisskopf, Thomas. "Use of Hourly Earnings Proposed to Revive Spendable Earnings Series." *Monthly Labor Review*, November 1984, 38–43.

"Will Star Wars Reward or Retard Science?" *Economist*, September 7, 1985, 95–96.

Williamson, Jeffrey G. "Productivity and American Leadership: A Review Article." *Journal of Economic Literature* 29 (March 1991): 51–68.

Books

Aaron, Henry J., ed. *Economic Choices, 1987.* Washington, DC: Brookings Institution, 1986.

———, ed. *The Problem That Won't Go Away: Reforming U.S. Health Care Financing.* Washington, DC: Brookings Institution, 1996.

Bailey, Stephen Kemp. *Congress Makes a Law.* New York: Columbia University Press, 1950.

Baran, Paul, and Paul Sweezy. *Monopoly Capital.* New York: Monthly Review Press, 1966.

Bartley, Robert. *The Seven Fat Years and How to Do It Again.* New York: Free Press, 1992.

Berle, Adolph A., and Gardner C. Means. *The Modern Corporation and Private Property.* New York: Commerce Clearing House, 1932.

Birnbaum, Jeffrey H., and Alan Murray. *Showdown at Gucci Gulch: Lawmakers, Lobbyists, and the Unlikely Triumph of Tax Reform.* New York: Vintage, 1988.

Blair, Margaret M., ed. *The Deal Decade: What Takeovers and Leveraged Buyouts Mean for Corporate Governance.* Washington, DC: Brookings Institution, 1993.

———. *Ownership and Control: Rethinking Corporate Governance for the Twenty-First Century.* Washington, DC: Brookings Institution, 1995.

Blecker, Robert. *Are Americans on a Consumption Binge? The Evidence Reconsidered.* Washington, DC: Economic Policy Institute, 1990.

———. *Beyond the Twin Deficits: A Trade Strategy for the 1990s.* Armonk, NY: M. E. Sharpe, 1992.

————, ed. *U.S. Trade Policy and Global Growth.* Armonk, NY: M. E. Sharpe, 1996.

Blinder, Alan. *Economic Policy and the Great Stagflation.* New York: Academic Press, 1979.

————. *Hard Heads, Soft Hearts: Tough-Minded Economics for a Just Society.* New York: Addison-Wesley, 1987.

Block, Fred, Richard A. Cloward, Barbara Ehrenreich, and Frances Fox Piven. *The Mean Season: The Attack on the Welfare State.* New York: Pantheon, 1987.

Blumenthal, Sidney. *The Rise of the Counter-Establishment: From Conservative Ideology to Political Power.* New York: Times Books, 1986.

Bowles, Samuel, and Richard Edwards. *Understanding Capitalism, Competition, Command, and Change in the U.S. Economy.* 2d ed. New York: Harper Collins, 1993.

Bowles, Samuel, David M. Gordon, and Thomas Weisskopf. *After the Wasteland: A Democratic Economics for the Year 2000.* Armonk, NY: M. E. Sharpe, 1990.

Braverman, Harry. *Labor and Monopoly Capital.* New York: Monthly Review Press, 1974.

Brown, E. C., ed. *Stabilization Policies.* Englewood Cliffs, NJ: Commission on Money and Credit, 1963.

Buchanan, James. *The Demand and Supply of Public Goods.* Chicago: Rand McNally, 1968.

————. *Democracy in Deficit: The Political Legacy of Lord Keynes.* New York: Academic, 1977.

Catholic Church, National Conference of Catholic Bishops. *Economic Justice for All: Pastoral Letter on Catholic Social Teaching on the U.S. Economy.* Washington, DC: U.S. Catholic Conference, 1986.

Cohen, Benjamin. *The Question of Imperialism.* New York: Basic Books, 1973.

Commoner, Barry. *Making Peace with the Planet.* New York: Pantheon, 1990.

Coughlin, Teresa A., Leighton Ku, and John Holahan. *Medicaid since 1980.* Washington, DC: Urban Institute Press, 1994.

Danziger, Sheldon, Gary Sandefur, and Daniel Weinberg, eds. *Confronting Poverty: Prescriptions for Change.* Cambridge: Harvard University Press, 1994.

Davis, Karen. Gerard Anderson, Diane Rowland, and Earl Steinberg. *Health Care Cost Containment.* Baltimore: Johns Hopkins University Press, 1990.

Denison, Edward. *Accounting for Slower Growth.* Washington, DC: The Brookings Institution, 1979.

Dymski, Gary, Gerald Epstein, and Robert Pollin, eds. *Transforming the U.S. Financial System.* Armonk, NY: M. E. Sharpe, 1993.

Edsall, Thomas Byrne, and Mary D. Edsall. *Chain Reaction: The Impact of Race, Rights, and Taxes on American Politics.* New York: Norton, 1992.

Eisner, Robert. *The Misunderstood Economy: What Counts and How to Count It.* Boston: Harvard Business School, 1994.

Fayol, Henri. *Administration industrielle et generale.* 1916. Trans. Constance Storrs as *General and Industrial Management.* London: Isaac Pitman and Sons, 1949.

Ferguson, Thomas. *Golden Rule: The Investment Theory of Party Competition and the Logic of Money-Driven Political Systems.* Chicago: University of Chicago Press, 1995.

Follett, Mary P. *Freedom and Coordination, Lectures in Business Organization.* New York: Garland, 1987.

Foster, John B. *The Theory of Monopoly Capital.* New York: Monthly Review Press, 1989.

Friedman, Benjamin. *Day of Reckoning: The Consequences of American Economic Policy.* New York: Vintage, 1989.

Friedman, Milton. *Capitalism and Freedom.* Chicago: University of Chicago Press, 1962.

Friedman, Milton, and Rose Friedman. *Free to Choose.* New York: Harcourt Brace Jovanovich, 1980.

———. *Inflation: Causes and Consequences.* New York: Asia Publishing House, 1963.

Friedman, Milton, and Anna Schwartz. *A Monetary History of the United States, 1867–1960.* Princeton, NJ: Princeton University Press, 1963.

Galbraith, John K. *Economics and the Public Purpose.* Boston: Houghton Mifflin, 1973.

———. *The New Industrial State.* Boston: Houghton Mifflin, 1966.

Gill, Richard, ed. *Great Debates in Economics.* Pacific Palisades, CA: Goodyear, 1976.

Gillespie, Ed, and Bob Schellhas, eds. *Contract with America.* New York: Times Books, 1994.

Green, Mark, and Norman Waitzman. *Business War on the Law: An Analysis of the Benefits of Federal Health and Safety Enforcement.* Preface by Ralph Nader. 2d ed. Washington, DC: Corporate Accountability Research Group, 1981.

Greenberg, Stanley, and Theda Skocpol, eds. *The New Majority: Toward a Popular Progressiive Politics.* New Haven, CT: Yale University Press, 1997.

Greider, William. *One World, Ready or Not: The Manic Logic of Global Capitalism.* New York: Simon and Schuster, 1997.

———. *The Secrets of the Temple: How the Federal Reserve Runs the Country.* New York: Simon and Schuster, 1987.

Katz, Michael B. *In the Shadow of the Poorhouse: A Social History of Welfare in America.* Rev. ed. New York: Basic Books, 1996.

Kirsch, Clifford, ed. *The Financial Services Revolution.* Chicago: Irwin, 1996.

Klamer, Arjo. *Conversations with Economists.* Totowa, NJ: Rowman and Allanheld, 1984.

Kuttner, Robert. *Everything for Sale: The Virtues and Limits of Markets.* New York: Knopf, 1996.

Lindsey, Lawrence B. *The Growth Experiment: How the New Tax Policy Is Transforming the U.S. Economy.* New York: Basic Books, 1990.

Low, Patrick. *Trading Free.* New York: Twentieth Century Fund, 1993.

Makin, John H., and Norman J. Ornstein. *Debt and Taxes.* New York: Times Books, Random House, 1994.

Mankiw, N. Gregory. *Principles of Economics.* New York: Dryden Press, 1998.

Mayo, Elton. *The Human Problems of an Industrial Civilization.* Introduction by F. J. Roethlisberger. New York: Viking, 1960.

Mills, Nicolaus, ed. *Debating Affirmative Action, Race, Gender, Ethnicity, and the Politics of Inclusion.* New York: Delta, 1994.

Melman, Seymour. *Pentagon Capitalism.* New York: McGraw-Hill, 1970.

————. *The Permanent War Economy: American Capitalism in Decline.* New York: Touchtone, 1974.

Mishel, Lawrence, and Jared Bernstein. *The State of Working America, 1994–1995.* Armonk, NY: M. E. Sharpe, 1994.

————. *The State of Working America, 1996–1997.* Armonk, NY: M. E. Sharpe, 1996.

Moore, Stephen, ed. *Restoring the Dream.* New York: Times Books, 1995.

Murray, Charles. *Losing Ground: American Social Policy, 1950–1980.* New York: Basic Books, 1984.

Niskanen, William. *Reaganomics: An Insider's Account of the Policies and the People.* New York: Oxford University Press, 1988.

Okun, Arthur. *Prices and Quantities: A Macroeconomic Analysis.* Washington, DC: Brookings Institution, 1981.

Palmer, John L., and Isabel V. Sawhill, eds. *The Reagan Record.* Cambridge, MA: Ballinger, 1984.

Pechman, Joseph, ed. *Setting National Priorities: Agenda for the 1980s.* Washington, DC: Brookings Institution, 1980.

Penner, Rudolph G., ed. *The Great Fiscal Experiment.* Washington, DC: Urban Institute Press, 1991.

Perelman, Michael. *The Pathology of the U.S. Economy.* New York: St. Martin's Press, 1996.

Perot, Ross. *Not for Sale at Any Price: How We Can Save America for Our Children.* New York: Hyperion, 1993.

————. *United We Stand: How We Can Take Back Our Country.* New York: Hyperion, 1992.

Phillips, Kevin. *The Politics of Rich and Poor.* New York: Random House, 1990.

Reich, Robert. *The Next American Frontier.* New York: Times Books, 1983.

————. *The Work of Nations.* New York: Knopf, 1991.

Roosevelt, Kermit. *Countercoup: The Struggle for the Control of Iran.* New York: McGraw-Hill, 1979.

Rothbard, Murray. *Power and Market, Government and the Economy.* Kansas City, MO: Sheed Andrews and McMeel, 1970.

Sahu, Anandi, and Ronald Tracy, eds. *The Economic Legacy of the Reagan Years: Euphoria or Chaos?* New York: Praeger, 1991.

Samuelson, Robert. *The Good Life and Its Discontents.* New York: Times Books, 1995.

Schlesinger, Steven, and Steven Kinzer. *Bitter Fruit.* Garden City, NY: Doubleday, 1982.

Schor, Juliet B. *The Overworked American: The Unexpected Decline in Leisure.* New York: Basic Book, 1992.

Shaviro, Daniel. *Do Deficits Matter?* Chicago: University of Chicago Press, 1997.

Shore, Warren. *Social Security, the Fraud in Your Future.* New York: Macmillan, 1975.

Skocpol, Theda. *Boomerang: Clinton's Health Security Effort and the Turn against Government in U.S. Politics.* New York: Norton, 1996.

Smith, Merritt Roe, ed. *Military Enterprise and Technological Change.* Cambridge: MIT Press, 1985.

Steuerle, C. Eugene. *The Tax Decade: How Taxes Came to Dominate the Public Agenda.* Washington, DC: Urban Institute Press, 1992.

————. *Taxes, Loans, and Inflation: How the Nation's Wealth Becomes Misallocated.* Washington, DC: Brookings Institution, 1983.

Steuerle, C. Eugene, and Jon M Bakija. *Reforming Social Security for the 21st Century.* Washington, DC: Urban Institute Press, 1994.

Stiglitz, Joseph E. *Economics.* 2d ed. New York: Norton, 1997.

Stockman, David. *The Triumph of Politics: Why the Reagan Revolution Failed.* New York: Harper and Row, 1986.

Schwarz, John E. *America's Hidden Success: A Reassessment of Public Policy from Kennedy to Reagan.* Rev. ed. New York: Norton, 1993.

Smithin, John N. *Macroeconomics after Thatcher and Reagan: The Conservative Policy Revolution in Retrospect.* Aldershot, UK: Edward Elgar, 1990.

Taylor, Frederick W. *The Principles of Scientific Management.* New York: Harper and Brothers, 1916.

Terkel, Studs *Working* New York: Pantheon Books, 1974.

Tobin, James, and Murray Weidenbaum, eds. *Two Revolutions in Economic Policy.* Cambridge: MIT Press, 1988.

Wanniski, Jude. *How the World Works.* New York: Touchstone/Simon and Schuster, 1978.

Weidenbaum, Murray. *The Future of Government Regulation.* New York: Anacom, 1979.

Woodward, Bob. *The Agenda: Inside the Clinton White House.* New York: Simon and Schuster, 1994.

Index

Civil War, 172, 270, 321n. 5, 347n. 14
class system, 58, 62
Clinton, Bill
  balanced budget agreement of, ix, 1,
    121, 240, 249–53
  early effort against Reagan Revolu-
    tion by, 23, 227–40
  education program of, 232
  health-care reform attempted by, 5,
    121, 245–47, 246n. 6
  NAFTA supported by, 226–27
  1992 election of, 225–27
  regulatory policy of, 115, 246
  on role of government, 18–19
  tax policy of, 23, 112, 226, 228–29,
    231, 233
  Volcker-Reagan program completed
    by, 253–58, 264
  welfare policy of, 247–49 (see also
    welfare reform law)
Clinton, Hillary Rodham, 245, 246
Cold War, 173, 176
Commerce, Department of
  Bureau of Economic Analysis
    investment classification,
    180–81, 253, 326n. 21
  current and investment categories,
    21
  switch from GNP to GDP by, 303n.
    54, 305n. 2
Commoner, Barry, 280n. 6
Community Services block grants, 89,
    90
community work experience programs
  (CWEP), 115
computer revolution, 126, 127
Condon, Mark, 198–99, 331
Congress, historical overspending by,
    19
  See also Republicans in Congress
Congressional Budget Office (CBO),
    104, 178, 250, 337n. 53, 343n. 44
  baseline budget of, 275n. 4
  projections of, 261, 344n. 60
Conrail, 38
conservative economics, 34, 56, 263,
    266
  mainstream critique of, 51–52, 55, 56
  on 1981–82 recession, 102, 103

political takeover by, 271–72
radical economics and, 56–57, 69
role of government in, 35–50
  See also supply-side economics
consumer price index
  in misery index, 286n. 5
  of 1960s compared to 1970s, 29
  tax brackets indexed to, 81
consumer spending, 1980s growth of,
    136
consumption
  GDP and, 161–62
  increased by investment, 126
  private, 22
  subsidized, 94
contracts, government as enforcer of,
    37
Contract with America, 3, 5, 19, 20, 61,
    97, 115, 277n. 14, 278nn. 16, 17, 19,
    289n. 24
  lack of health-care policy in, 121
  limited view of government in, 241
contributory entitlements, 49–50,
    91–96
cooperatives, 279n. 3
corporations
  control of, 346n. 3
  decision makers in, 266, 269
  taxation on, 111
Corrigan, Gerald, 211
cost of job loss, 142, 147–48, 166
Council of Economic Advisers, xv, 13
  under Bush, 125, 128–29, 132, 188,
    190, 191, 212, 214, 334n. 2
  under Carter, 52
  under Clinton, x, 236–41, 244,
    250–53, 262, 343n. 44, 345n. 63
  under Kennedy, 33
  under Reagan, 35, 37, 39, 41, 46, 48,
    78, 79, 92, 125, 169, 346n. 3
Council on Competitiveness, 114, 207
counterfactual, definition of, 163
credit, increased reliance on, 144
crowding-out hypothesis, 19, 43–44,
    131–33, 140, 141, 162–65, 259,
    319nn. 31, 32
Cuban missile crisis, 176
Cuomo, Mario, 221
Cypher, James, 325n. 18

debts
household, business, and private,
321
private, compared to government,
170–72
See also deficits; national debt
defense spending, 3, 43
aggregate-demand effect of, 66, 173,
180, 324n. 14
and allocation of funds, 177–80
call for, in *Contract with America,*
278n. 17, 284n. 20
after fall of Soviet Union, 231
as indirect subsidy to business, 284n.
20
Internet as a result of, 37
as necessary evil, 36
1986–93, 337
1987 as beginning of decline in, 223
as percentage of GDP, 173, 323n. 7
Reagan's increase in, 35, 38, 97–98,
104–5
technological progress and, 178–79,
325n. 18
after World War II, 66, 296n. 17
deficits
antirecession policies and, 54, 295n.
10
under Bush, 209, 222, 344n. 52
business cycle and, 144–45, 174–75,
240
under Carter, 54
Clinton's policy on, 229–31, 235–36
decline of, in 1990s, 5, 278n. 18
effects on economy, 19, 165, 170–76,
272, 282n. 11, 291n. 34
federal plus local, 305n. 4
financing of, 20, 282n. 16
under Ford, 54
future effect of decline of, 259–61
government borrowing and, 44, 174
Gramm-Rudman attack on, 122–24,
132–33, 208, 209
under Reagan, 8, 100–101, 104, 130,
146, 162–65, 169, 315n. 54
structural, definition of, 324n. 9
twin, 129–48
See also national debt
demand curve, 299n. 21

Denison, Edward, 295n. 10
deposit insurance, 190–91
Depository Institutions Deregulation
and Monetary Control Act, 75,
188
depreciation
effect of inflation on, 31, 48
Reagan's policy on, 79, 108
depressions, 21
deregulation. *See* regulatory relief
disintermediation, 77, 78
dividend income
interest income and, 197
rise in, 192–94
dollar
domestic effect of low exchange rate
for, 134–35, 313n. 20
foreign holdings of, 131, 137, 144–46
international-reserve status of, 70–73
rise in value of, during 1980s, 145
slide in value of, during 1970s, 70–
71
after World War II, 65
Dulles, John Foster, 324n. 14
Duncan, Greg, 199–200, 330n. 78,
332n. 79

earned-income tax credit (EITC), 228,
233, 252
economic growth
capability increase in, 16
determination of, 14–19
effects of, on middle class and poor,
3–4
factors of production and, 16
income distribution and, 62–63
since Industrial Revolution, 17, 281n.
6
investment as main cause of, 22
of 1960s compared to 1970s, 25–27,
286n. 1
1996–98, ix, 1
productivity increase in, 16, 18
economic history, need for study of,
6–9
Economic Justice for All, 265–67
Economic Policy Institute, xv, 200,
272, 318n. 26, 348n. 21
Economic Recovery Tax Act of 1981

private property, government as protector of, 37
private sector borrowing (1960–89), 319n. 34, 321
privatization, 289nn. 24, 25
production
  factors of, 14, 16–18
  internationalization of, 139
  means of, 58
productivity growth, 16, 18
  compound rate of growth compared to, 316n. 9
  defense spending and, 179–80, 326n. 18
  investment and, 126–27, 259–61
  job growth and (1960–91), 318
  marginal tax rates and, 244
  1960–90, 155–58
  1960s vs. 1970s, 25–26, 56, 68, 286n. 2
  slowdown in, 68, 166–68, 295n. 10
profit
  in Marxist theory, 59–60
  shares of (1983–96), 250
  rate of
    calculation of, 286n. 3
    definition of, 59
    of 1960s compared to 1970s, 26
    of 1970s compared to 1980s, 315n. 1
  recessions needed to reestablish, 102
Program for Economic Recovery, 35
prosperity after World War II, 28, 63–68, 296n. 17
protectionism, 140, 208, 311n. 76
public choice school, 268, 282n. 11, 284n. 24
public service employment, 89–91

Quayle, Dan, 207

radical economics, 15, 56–57, 263
  conservative economics and, 69
  on 1981–82 recession, 102–3
  power as viewed in, 61–62
  on twin-deficits problem, 141–48
rational expectations school, 291n. 39
raw materials, cheap, 65–66
Reagan, Ronald, 272

entitlement policy of, 86–96, 107, 234–35, 248
judicial appointees of, 84
reasons for popularity of, 55–56
regulatory relief under, 81–86
shrinking of government by, 96–98
summary of policies of, 98–99
tax policy of, 4, 6, 35, 79–81, 101, 105–12, 169, 308n. 36
Volcker's program and, 7–10, 35, 56, 78–79, 98–99, 101–2, 124, 130, 142, 205, 231, 255, 306n. 7
  completed by Clinton, 253–58, 264
  whether success or failure, 149–68, 263–64
Reaganomics, xiii, 34–35, 346n. 4
Reagan Revolution, x, 117, 146, 273
  fruits of, 2–4
  reaffirmation of, in 1995, 25
  role of government in, 4
  stages of, 4–6
  structural changes not produced by, 148
  success of, xi, 2, 5–6, 257–58
real spendable hourly earnings, 147, 314n. 47
recessions
  automatic stabilizers in, 100, 240, 262
  change in policy responses to, 255–58
  deficits in prevention of, 144, 174–75, 240
  future, 261–64, 271
  investment as only way out of, 151
  NBER's identification of, 284n. 21
  1960–61, 34, 285
  1962–94, recoveries after, 243
  1970, 27, 283, 295n. 10
  1974–75, x, 2, 9, 27, 53–54, 151–52, 174, 255–56, 285, 271
  1980, 52, 54–56, 68, 316n. 8
  1981–82, x, 8, 56, 68, 74, 78–79, 91–92, 100–103, 285, 306n. 12
  1990, x, 7, 209–12, 221, 255–57, 262, 281n. 9, 284n. 22, 285, 335n. 15
  peaks and troughs of, 285
  periodicity of, 21–22
  potential causes of, 262

real spendable hourly earnings of, 147, 314n. 47
risk premiums for, 214
See also labor
workfare, 88

Work Incentive (WIN) program, 89, 90, 115
World War II, 269, 270
prosperity after, 28, 63–68, 296n. 17

75 de-reg, Banking 213
85 MORE deReg
105 PRE-EMPTION Full employment
144 Pollin L148
166-7 ?? ! 7
177 11 devs

197 Tables
221 STRUCT. UNEMPLOYMENT
285 UNEMP RATES plus
323 INTEREST PAYMENTS

70 NB - MONETARISM
72
80
81
127 NB VENTURE CAPITAL
128
140 FF
176 13

IMPOVERISL USSR — 324 N14
284 NB 285 Table
267
2 NB 268 NB
303
316 NB
321
324 N14
331

3- INCOME DISTRIB
6- WELL Refo 19 96
38 Contestable MARRIED
44 - NAIRU - by EMD 1970's
74 - MONETARY DE-REG
131 - $ holdings
134 FED IN CONCERT
145 - NB
151 1974-5 RECESSION
166 W. PRODUCTIVITY
176 ST. MKT CRASH 198
264 VOLKER
268. MONEY IN POLITICS